The Work of
Self-Representation

IVY SCHWEITZER

The Work of
Self-Representation

Lyric Poetry in
Colonial New England

The University of North Carolina Press

Chapel Hill and London

Library of Congress Cataloging-in-Publication Data
Schweitzer, Ivy.
The work of self-representation : lyric poetry in colonial New England / by Ivy Schweitzer.
p. cm. — (Gender & American culture)
Includes bibliographical references and index.
ISBN 0-8078-1979-4 (cloth : alk. paper). — ISBN 0-8078-4329-6 (pbk. : alk. paper)
1. American poetry—Colonial period, ca. 1600–1775— History and criticism. 2. American poetry—Puritan authors—History and criticism. 3. American poetry—New England—History and criticism. 4. Christian poetry, American—History and criticism. 5. Poetry—Authorship— Sex differences. 6. New England—Intellectual life. 7. Puritans in literature. 8. Self in literature. I. Title. II. Series.
PS312.S38 1991
811'.109352042—dc20
91-8420
CIP

The lines from *Sphere: The Form of a Motion*, by A. R. Ammons, are reprinted by permission of W. W. Norton & Company, Inc. Copyright © 1974 by A. R. Ammons.

The lines from *H.D. Collected Poems, 1912–1944*, copyright © 1982 by the Estate of Hilda Doolittle, are reprinted by permission of New Directions Publishing Corporation.

The lines from "DeLiza Questioning Perplexities," from the book *Living Room: New Poems* by June Jordan, copyright © 1985 by June Jordan, are used by permission of the publisher, Thunder's Mouth Press.

The paper in this book meets the guidelines for permanence and durability of the Committee on Production Guidelines for Book Longevity of the Council on Library Resources.

Manufactured in the United States of America
95 94 93 92 91 5 4 3 2 1

for Tom and Isaac Jesse

CONTENTS

Acknowledgments   ix

ONE

Introduction. Gendering the Universal:
The Puritan Paradigm of Redeemed Subjectivity   1

TWO

The Paradox of "Practical Conformity":
John Fiske's "Elegy" on John Cotton   41

THREE

The Puritan Cult of the Spouse:
Edward Taylor's Dialectic of Difference   79

FOUR

Anne Bradstreet:
"In the place God had set her"   127

FIVE

Roger Williams's *Key*:
A Gynesis of Race   181

Epilogue   229

Notes   237

Works Cited   281

Index   297

ACKNOWLEDGMENTS

In writing this book, I have benefited from the help of many people; the list of colleagues and friends who have fostered my growth, intellectual and personal, is large. I must first acknowledge the shaping influence, and continued support, of Allen Grossman, who opened for me the rigorous beauties of poetry, and Michael T. Gilmore, who guided me through the beautiful rigors of early American thought. The members of the Department of English at Dartmouth College have challenged, often infuriated, but always encouraged me. In particular, I want to thank Bill Cook, Jim Cox, Alan Gaylord, Blanche Gelfant, Elaine Jahner, Don Pease, Lou Renza, Peter Saccio, Bill Spengemann, and Peter Travis. Barbara Cunningham and Kathy Harp, our administrators, deserve special thanks for their help and humor. I also want to thank the Dartmouth Class of 1962 for acknowledging my teaching efforts and granting me a Junior Faculty Fellowship, which allowed me to devote the spring of 1988 to research.

I consider myself fortunate to have come of age during a period of exciting breakthroughs in feminist literary scholarship. And I was also fortunate in finding at Dartmouth College a thriving, active, and supportive women's community in which I could flourish, intellectually and personally. Teaching in the Women's Studies Program at Dartmouth has allowed me to explore the feminist theory that underlies my reading of seventeenth-century colonial culture. I want to thank, in particular, Anne Brooks, the indefatigable administrator of Women's Studies, for her skillful organizing and, best of all, her friendship. The Feminist Inquiry University Seminar has been a social as well as an intellectual haven for me, providing space to present my own work "in progress" to sympathetic and critically astute ears and to hear the work of my colleagues, which was often on the cutting edge of feminist scholarship. Also, the Feminist Reading Group, which has been active at various times, has served as a more intimate sphere for sharing and learning. It was active at a crucial time in the process of my drafting of Chapter 1. To those sisters who read patiently, urged me on, and believed in me, I owe a large debt of gratitude—they include Lynda Boose, Nancy Frankenberry, Mary Jean Green, Lynn Higgins, Deborah King, Gwen King, Lynn Mather, Marysa Navarro, Priscilla Sears, Sally Sedgwick, Ginnie Swain, Nancy Vickers, Susanne Zantop, and the irrepressible Melissa Zeiger. I owe special debts of thanks to the following women: Mary Childers, for her tireless support, her honesty, and her determination, and for teaching me to play racquetball; Louise Fradenburg, for seeing me through the tenure process, and for demonstrating her faith in me by entrusting me with her three cats a second time; Brenda Silver, for being a courageous, even heroic, senior colleague; Marianne Hirsch, for her generosity in every aspect of life and work, and for the cool hands she offered me during the labor and delivery of my baby and my book; Mary Kelley, fellow Americanist, for her unstinting support from the moment I arrived at Dartmouth, and especially for seeing the manuscript through the publication review; and finally, Carla Freccero, best friend, best comrade, who made important suggestions at crucial moments in the writing process, and some of whose brilliance I hope is reflected in these pages. Other friends who over the years listened to and pulled for me are Robin Caster, Ellen Miller-Mack, and Celeste Phillips. Lissa Weinstein provided information on and insight into the Schreber case. Florence Dore—former student, friend, and fellow rocker—was always there in emergencies and remains a constant source of inspiration.

I also want to thank the Marxist-Psychoanalytic Reading Group, which gathered for a few years on the Hanover plain for many stimulating and provoking hours of companionship and discussion; its members included some of the sisters mentioned above and the following brothers: Dick Corum, David Kastan, Matthew Rowlinson, Peter Stallybrass, and Leo Spitzer. The librarians at Baker Library have been wonderfully helpful—specifically, Sue Marcoulier, Cynthia Pawlek, Lois Krieger, Marianne Hraibi, and the indispensable Patsy Carter of Interlibrary Loan. I also owe thanks to the many students at Dartmouth whom it has been a privilege to learn from and teach. I especially want to acknowledge the students in the Women's Studies Program for their fortitude and friendship, and all the student activists who have renewed my flagging energies and my faith in the power of protest, struggle, and community. Specifically, I want to thank Cirri Nottage, my research assistant for 1989; Elizabeth Cavanagh, my Presidential Scholar and assistant during the summer of 1990; and all the students who did childcare during the period of my research, writing, and revision. Kate Torrey, Editor-in-Chief at The University of North Carolina Press, has been extremely helpful at every stage in the publication process, and the readers for the press, Philip Gura and Linda Kerber, made valuable comments. David Leverenz also read the manuscript and offered many insights.

My parents, Sue and Harold Schweitzer, never lost faith in me and in my dreams; I cannot thank them enough. I also want to thank my family-in-law, the Luxons, for all their support. Special thanks go to Redwing Preschool for providing excellent childcare. The last and best thank-yous go to my spouse, Tom Luxon, and my son, Isaac Jesse. I dedicate this work to you, Isaac, because, as your name (confirmed by my Hebrew name, "Sarah") indicates, you were a surprise, conceived in laughter, and without you, it would have been a very different, less urgent book. And I dedicate this book to you, Tom, because without you, without your reading of every word, your editorial suggestions and generous commentaries, your sacrifices and your love, this book would never have been written.

The Work of
Self-Representation

What would the world be, he said to himself—he was still
thinking of the fat man brandishing his arm—without "I" in it?
—Virginia Woolf, *The Years*

when poetry was a servant in the house of religion,
it was abused from all angles, buggered by the fathers,

ravished by the mothers, called on to furnish the energies
of entertainment (truth) for the guests, and made, at the
same time, a whipping-post for the literal. poetry is not
now a servant in the house of religion. . . .
—A. R. Ammons, "Sphere"

no man will be present in those mysteries,
yet all men will kneel,
no man will be potent,
important,
yet all men will feel
what it is to be a woman,
will yearn,
burn,
turn from easy pleasure
to hardship
of the spirit. . . .
—H.D., "The Master"

"DeLiza Questioning Perplexities":

If Dustin Hoffaman prove
a father be a better mother than a mother

If Dustin Hoffaman prove
a man be a better woman than a woman

When do she get to see
a Betterman than Hoffaman?
—June Jordan

ONE

Introduction.

Gendering the Universal:

The Puritan Paradigm of

Redeemed Subjectivity

The Puritan minister is pale and drawn in the wavering candlelight, his fine features sharpened by overwork and fatigue, and by a burning in the region of his heart that seems to consume him. A large Bible is open before him, and he writes feverishly, now clutching his quill compulsively, now casting beseeching eyes to heaven. All the while he hears, as if in a dream he cannot shake off, that woman, Hester Prynne, demanding of him in a tone that is both stern and tender, "And what hast thou to do with all these iron men, and their opinions? They have kept thy better part in bondage too long already!" (Hawthorne, *Scarlet Letter*, 142). Arthur Dimmesdale, Hawthorne's young Puritan clergyman, replies disconsolately that he is "powerless" to "quit my post, though an unfaithful sentinel." Returning to his room, he pours his remaining passion into composing the "election" sermon he will deliver the following day, shortly before his death. Presumably, after his death he enters heaven (which has before it a large wood-and-iron door to keep out all those not predestined to enter), leaving Hester alone to bear the letter of the iron men—and transform it.

Nathaniel Hawthorne's portrait of the young minister captures and exaggerates the effect of the colonial Puritan patriarchy upon its "sons" and rising stars. As Hester's minister, Dimmesdale is accountable for her soul; as her lover, he is accountable for her heart and the child they produce. Yet in the excruciating irony of the first scene, Dimmesdale, dramatically positioned up above the crowd though more cowardly and hypocritical than anyone, exhorts his "charge" to publicly reveal the name of her partner in sin—a confession he prays she will not make. "Wondrous strength and generosity of a woman's heart! She will not speak!" he discovers with relief (53). Because of her silence, his passion, his paternity, and his sin go unrevealed. In this dramatic moment, what he believes and what he feels are completely at odds.

Students invariably find Hester a stronger, more "masculine" figure than her beleaguered lover, and they wonder what she could have possibly seen in a "wimp" like Dimmesdale. Hawthorne suggests that the blame falls upon grizzled old men like Dimmesdale's senior colleague, the Reverend John Wilson, for whom kindness was, "in truth, rather a matter of shame than self-congratulation," and who, therefore, had no "right" to "meddle with a question of human guilt, passion, and anguish" (50). In "The Custom-House," the apparently autobiographical introduction to the tale, Hawthorne likewise accuses his "grave, bearded, sable-cloaked, and steeple-crowned . . . stern and black-browed" Puritan ancestors of being bitter persecutors, especially of women. Although these progenitors "had all the Puritanic traits, both good and evil," they are remembered mainly for their cruelties, a quirk of history that impels Hawthorne as their representative to "take shame upon myself for their sakes" and remove the curse their sins have brought upon "the race" (11). In order to expiate these sins, Hawthorne loses his head—that is, his sinecure in the patriarchal world of the Custom House, his businesslike, purely mental, and masculine self-image—and becomes, through humiliation, the bearer of his society's passionate and tenderer sentiments, the antithesis of his iron-visaged forebears—"a literary man" (36).

Even with a mother for its hero, *The Scarlet Letter* has been read as the archetypal American story of an individualist, a dissenter, a culturally masculine figure.[1] As an important recent investigation into "manhood and the American Renaissance" contends, implicit in the "Introductory" and in *The Scarlet Letter* itself is Hawthorne's exposure of conventional manliness "as unnatural and potentially persecuting, epitomized in his heartless Puritan ancestors" (Leverenz, *Manhood*, 36). We can question the historical verity of Hawthorne's account of his Puritan precursors and the lurid tale he concocts to mitigate their doleful influence upon his own temperament. My concern, however, is not with "reality" but with representation, for out of representations "realities" are constructed. The characterization of the Puritanism of colonial New England as both pervasively masculine and cruel remains fixed in our national imagination. These were stern, mirthless men pursuing an otherworldly ideal that led them to excoriate all the softness and pleasures of the fallen world.[2]

A belief and practice dominated by men and doomed to failure without the mollifying feminine presence of the Virgin Mary, according to Walter J. Ong and others,[3] colonial Puritanism has also been presented as an intellectual, as opposed to an emotional, phenomenon. Perry Miller's monumental exposition of the New England mind, for all the banked-down fires of Augustinian mysticism he spies within, leaves the impression of coldly rational Ramist logicians who fanatically organized and abstracted their universe through the intricate scheme of technologia; only two women appear to have contributed to that compendious mind, and one of them negatively—the "poor," misguided Mistress Hutchinson (*Mind*, 1:389).[4] Since Miller's ground-breaking work, a considerable amount of scholarship has concentrated on Puritan spirituality. Indeed, a recent trend reemphasizes the affective side of the Puritan experience. Charles Hambrick-Stowe, for example, studies the official ministerial and popular versions of devotional literature that emerged in New England, concluding that "Puritanism was as affective as it was rational. . . . Indeed, the particular forms of public worship and the characteristic private devotional exercises were what made a Puritan a Puritan" (viii). Nevertheless, the sword- and Bible-wielding Judge Hathornes still crowd out the dreamy, angel-voiced Arthur Dimmesdales.

A closer look at Hambrick-Stowe's methodology will help to clarify the problematics. He begins his study with four "vignettes" of spirituality from "representative" Puritans: Captain Roger Clap, a militiaman; the Reverend Thomas Shepard, first pastor of the Cambridge Church; Samuel Sewall, a prominent Boston merchant; and Anne Bradstreet, a poet who was the daughter of one governor of the commonwealth and the wife of another. Confident that this group is "diverse," Hambrick-Stowe offers examples from the private writings of each and finds that "all but Sewall, whom we left in the midst of anxiety and spiritual humiliation, experienced an ecstatic resolution and release of the tension that attended the onset of their devotions. Surprisingly," he continues, "the words all spontaneously used to express outwardly the fire that burned within came from the poetry of the Song of Songs and the associated bridegroom imagery used by Jesus. The feeling of being ravished by Christ, the Great Lover of the mystical tradition, the Bridegroom, was clearly not unique to Edward Taylor, whose poetry seemed so un-Puritan to scholars only a few years ago." Neglecting to pursue the implications of this conventional imagery, Hambrick-Stowe concludes that the experiences of this group "were characteristic of common practice," which was indeed highly "affective" (20).

Hambrick-Stowe's "surprise" at the uniformity of choice among these representative Puritans in their expressions of piety is itself surprising, since orthodox Puritan doctrine disseminated a specific discourse for religious experiences that laypeople and saints from all quarters embraced as their own. The definition of orthodoxy is, after all, drawing a line around experience and interpretation and declaring everything outside of that circle heresy. The metaphor of the soul's betrothal in marriage to Christ was so pervasive, according to Edmund S. Morgan, because "marriage, which the Puritans regarded as the highest relationship between mortals, was generally accepted as the closest comparison to the believer's union with God" (*Puritan Family*, 162). "It is a marriage-covenant that we make with God," declared Peter Bulkeley, and he concluded, "therefore we must doe as the Spouse doth, resigne up our selves to be ruled and governed accordingly to his will" (*Gospel Covenant*, 50; quoted in Morgan, *Puritan Family*, 161). The Puritan clergy applied this basic metaphor to the whole gamut of spiritual relations. Like a lover, Christ wooed the soul, which resisted like a coy woman "full of whorish and adulterous lusts" (John Cotton, *Practical Commentary upon John*, 227; quoted in Morgan, *Puritan Family*, 163). Ministers served as the "friends" of the bridegroom who customarily helped arrange the match between the soul and Christ. Extending the metaphor to the entire Church community, John Cotton compared congregational worship to the sexual love of a married couple: "The publick Worship of God is the bed of loves: where, 1. Christ embraceth the souls of his people, and casteth into their hearts the immortal seed of his Word, and Spirit, *Gal.* 4.19. 2. The Church conceiveth and bringeth forth fruits to Christ" (*A Brief Exposition . . . of Canticles*, 209; quoted in Morgan, *Puritan Family*, 164). Cotton's metaphor spiritualizes female physiology and applies it to the souls and hearts of the congregation, which become spiritual wombs impregnated by God's inseminating Word and bearing the new birth of conversion.

Sermons and learned treatises were not the only places this discourse appeared. It was familiar and common among laypeople as well. No less eminent a personage than John Winthrop readily cast himself in a feminine role in describing his "intercourse" with Christ. Looking over letters that passed between himself and Mary Forth, his first wife,

> and beinge thereby affected wth the remembrance of that entire & sweet love that had been sometymes betweene us, God brought me by that occasion in to suche a heavenly meditation of the love betweene Christ & me, as ravished my heart wth unspeakable ioye; methought my soule had as familiar and sensible society wth him, as my wife could have wth the kindest husbande; I desired no other happinesse but to be embraced of him; I held nothinge so deere that I was not willinge to parte wth for him; I forgatt to looke after my supper, & some vaine things that my heart lingered after before; then came such a calme of comforte over my heart, as revived my spirits, sett my minde & conscience at sweet liberty & peace. (*Life and Letters*, 1:105)

Winthrop evidently took his late wife's experiences with "the kindest husbande" as a model for his own desires toward Christ—desires to be embraced, to make sacrifices, to be the recipient of love. His recollection of "that entire & sweet love" between them, a love in which Winthrop as husband played the traditional role of guardian, teacher, and breadwinner, brings on his rapturous intimacy with God. In the present moment, however, he experiences himself, not in the custodial and dominant role of husband, but in the submissive and obedient role of wife. From his memory of his earthly marriage to his present meditation on God, a radical transformation in his self-conception has occurred. In moving between the supposedly analogous relationships of husband and wife, man and God, Winthrop moves from the dominant to the subordinate position, from masculine to feminine. Even what he forgets to do in his rapturous contemplation is feminized: "look after my supper, and some vaine things. . . ."

So familiar and necessary did this discourse become that Samuel Sewall, who in Hambrick-Stowe's example avoided this metaphor because of his nagging doubts, at another time complained to his journal when an English minister failed to use it: "March 10, 1688/9 would have heard mr. Goldwire, but mr. Beaumont the Minister of Fareham preached from Ps. 45, 15. Doct. Interest and Duty of Christians to rejoice in Christ made good profitable Sermons; but I think might have been more so, if had us'd the Metaphor of Bridegroom and Bride, which heard not of" (Hambrick-Stowe, 108). The pious New Englander knows his Bible well. Psalm 45 is styled "a love song" and strongly resembles the Song of Songs, the Puritans' major scriptural source for the marriage metaphor. The psalm addresses a "King" and a virgin daughter who is to be his bride. Clearly, Sewall was accustomed to hearing this metaphor used to describe an obedient Christian's joy in Christ. Indeed, as Hambrick-Stowe discovers, colonial Puritans in their devotional literature turned frequently to the marriage metaphor to express their deepest spiritual longings. The clergy encouraged this, employing the metaphor as a cru-cial part of orthodox discourse—a discourse intended, as Sacvan Ber-covitch has shown in *The Puritan Origins of the American Self*, to create a homogeneity of belief and behavior, if not the illusion of it.[5] The notion of a cultural consensus painstakingly built by the leaders of New England was promulgated by early literary historians of the period, but it has been challenged by recent scholarship, which finds a healthy diversity of opin-ion among the early settlers. The following examination of the Puritan discourse of spiritual marriage contributes to that trend by considering the implications of gender positioning within the discourse, and suggest-ing how the discourse constructs a rhetoric of the "American self" that, by definition, contains the seeds of its own subversion.

Though often touted as the origin of American individualism, New En-gland Puritanism succeeded precisely to the extent that it quelled the subjectivism implicit in its own doctrines. In their first three decades, the conservative clergy of New England evolved and instituted a form of Puritanism that checked the individualizing tendencies of Reformation thought with what Bercovitch calls "powerful counter-subjectivist" moves. The individual had gained a new prominence through Martin Luther's two central principles: *sola fides*, "which removes the center of authority from ecclesiastical institutions and relocates it in the elect soul" (Ber-covitch, *Puritan Origins*, 10), and *sola scriptura*, whereby "the Bible was made universally available and declared to be sole authority, [and] every man became his own exegete" (28). In order to bolster the bulwarks against the anarchy its doctrines threatened to unleash, the Puritan orthodoxy promulgated a radical interpretation of the *imitatio Christi* and invented and disseminated *exemplum fidei*. Ideally, the elect soul had little to do with the person and body it inhabited. The saint strove beyond a mere imitation of Christ for a "Christic identity" that reconstituted his fallen self as a saved soul; he became an exemplar of faith and was knitted into the church of the redeemed. Likewise, a saint's reading of scripture was to be not personal or idiosyncratic but "Christological": "Like Christ, the Bible could be rightly perceived only by one who had transformed himself in His image. . . . Interpreter and text confirmed one another in their mutual *imitatio*" (28). Not only did these countermoves encourage "a schizophrenic single-mindedness" and express "a sweeping rejection of individuality," but they demonstrate the Puritans' massive attempt to enforce a "regimentation of selfhood" (28).

Every culture provides its members with "organizing fictions" or "ideologies" that define their relations to other people and the world around them, and that teach them the discourses and the social codes upon which cultural meanings and a sense of self are based. This social and historical construction of selfhood is called *subjectivity*, the ongoing ideological process of recruiting individuals and transforming them into subjects who are shaped by, and maintain the set of values held by, the group or class in power.[6] Puritanism, and the particular brand of non-separating Congregationalism practiced by the colonial Puritans, was a religious ideology that, as Darrett B. Rutman so perceptively points out, used language, rituals, and peer pressure to form and maintain the identities of its adherents (114–20). To paraphrase British cultural studies theorist John Fiske, the individual is produced by nature, the subject is constructed by culture, and, according to Puritan divines, the saint is regenerated by grace (258).

Saints were born, like everyone else, as individuals and acquired what they might have called "fallen subjectivity" by being, for example, English and Anglican. To become saints, they had to repudiate, at least in words and actions, those former states so that God might begin to produce in them what I call a state of "redeemed subjectivity," replacing the "old man in Adam" with the "new man in Christ." The apostle Paul identified the various stages of this process in his much-cited letter to the Romans;

emphasizing God as the active principle in the formation of the redeemed subject, he declared authoritatively: "For whom he did foreknow, he also did predestinate to be conformed to the image of his Son, that he might be the firstborn among many brethren. Moreover, whom he did predestinate, them he also called: and whom he called, them he also justified: and whom he justified, them he also glorified" (8:29–30). Theologians expounded upon Paul's statement as a paradigm for the experience of grace, ministers never tired of explicating the stages of salvation for their audiences, and saints anxiously measured their own personal experiences against this timeless and fixed model. As Morgan comments, "It is impossible to say whether the pattern of Puritan spiritual experience was produced by the prescriptions of men like Perkins and Hildersam [prominent English Puritan theologians], or whether the prescription was itself based on experience" (*Visible Saints*, 71). In either case, Puritan conversion experiences replicate Paul's paradigm. Even poets of widely defined Protestant persuasions took it as a major structural and thematic influence (Lewalski, 13–14), though it was the Calvinists who honed it to a fine spiritual art.

The process of turning oneself from self to God regiments selfhood by attempting to obliterate the diversity of fallen selves and replace it with one single, absolute Self. It is a harrowing process, for it involves nothing less than a loathing, a denunciation, and finally an effacement of human and worldly selfhood. Such self-effacement requires a violence vividly communicated in Bercovitch's seemingly endless citations from Puritan texts. From St. Augustine, who would root out "self-love in contempt of God" by sowing in its place "love of God in contempt of one's self," to John Calvin, who demands that we "rid our selves of all selfe-trust," to Thomas Hooker, who urges "Not what Selfe will, but what the Lord will," Puritan divines regaled their audiences with the horrors of Self. Richard Baxter declared: "Man's fall was his turning from God to himself; and his regeneration consisteth in the turning of him from himself to God. . . . The very names of Self and Own, should sound in the watchful Christian's ears as very terrible, wakening words, that are next to the names of sin and satan" (*Puritan Origins* 17–18).

Orthodox New England Puritans made crucial innovations in the content of, and especially in the use to which they put, the paradigm of conversion. Why they needed such a handy form of social control is part of a complex historical account, which I can only touch upon here. In the course of institutionalizing Puritanism's concept of the "true revolution of the saints," between 1633 and 1635 New England clergy began requiring that each candidate for church membership give a public account of his or her conversion experience. This stipulation not only stimulated religious fervor and melded the saints into a group, but it acted as a check upon subjectivism, for individual experience had to conform to the group's—and, by implication, the minister's—notions of saving faith. By 1636, and especially in the wake of the antinomian controversy, however, this test of visible sainthood was being used conservatively to screen out potential troublemakers who held radical sectarian beliefs (Gura, 162–64).

Philip Gura argues persuasively that New England's corporate ideological self-image, stabilized by 1660 and eloquently portrayed by Perry Miller and Sacvan Bercovitch, "was shaped less by any set of ecclesiastical principles than by an unyielding effort to neutralize the influence of those who argued for a much more radical reorganization of the society" (11). In other words, the New England Way, of which visible sainthood was a crucial component, "was nurtured . . . by radical elements" (5), which it appropriated and coopted by subtle adjustments in doctrine and practice. Mary Maples Dunn reinforces and deepens this argument by pointing out that by 1660, in all the church records she examined, "silence had been enjoined on women in the matter of the [conversion] relation" (34). Women, who made up a large part of the voluble dissenters, had, at best, an indirect voice in cases of church discipline, which remained in the hands of men—though increasingly, she finds, "the minister instructed the brethren in their voting." As a result of this conservative wielding of power, "women seem to have been disciplined in numbers out of proportion to their share of congregational populations, and their offenses were increasingly connected with social behavior, not with heresy" (34–35). The genius of the Puritan theocracy was its ability to employ radical ideas in the service of conservative social policy whereby it achieved and maintained social and political stability throughout the seventeenth century. Claiming that historians have minimized the resistance that radical sectarians mounted against the Puritan oligarchy before 1660, Gura asserts provocatively that "New England Puritanism survived as a viable—indeed, a compelling—ideology because of, not in spite of, the nature of these responses to the radicals' challenges" (156).

Though this conclusion can be disputed, it seems clear, as Larzer Ziff has also observed, that "Dominant Puritan culture had in the 1630's defined itself through defining deviancy from it" (*Puritanism*, 77). Ziff merely echoes the formative words of John Winthrop, who, in his lay sermon delivered to the first group of Puritan settlers gathered on the deck of the *Arbella* in 1630, argued that "the Lawe of Grace, or the Gospel . . . teacheth vs to put a difference between Christians and others" (*Winthrop Papers*, 2:284). To bolster its identity, the "tribe" of New England, as Kai T. Erikson points out in his study of the sociology of deviance, sought to measure itself against what it was not, and to discover the ingenious forms that the devil would inevitably take to tempt and try God's chosen people (64). During the period of early settlement, the devil took two forms inextricably associated in the minds of Puritan men: that "*American Jesabel*," Anne Hutchinson (Winthrop, *Short Story*, 310), and the belligerent, satanic Pequot Indians.[7] The persecution of both heretics and Native Americans, or the purging of the body politic and the virgin land of noxious elements that obstructed the furtherance of God's will, offered prime opportunity for New England's corporate identity to coalesce. While I will argue below that for orthodox Puritans gender was constitutive of difference—difference being based on whether one was saved or damned, and salvation being a divinely gendered category—here I want to stress the notion of "otherness."

Identity, signification, and meaning depend upon difference, depend upon declaring that one is *this* and not *that*. Yet the term "identity" suggests a sameness, an identification with someone or something. Psychologists have long acknowledged the play of sameness and difference in the emergence of gender identity, though feminist psychologists have pointed out that masculine identity is primarily defined by difference, by the boy's negative identification with his mother, his first significant Other. The girl does not have to break her initial identity with her mother; thus, masculine identity is considered less stable, harder to achieve, more discontinuous than feminine identity, requiring—at least as our culture defines masculinity—difference against which to define itself.[8] This description fits the way New England Puritanism forged its identity by defining alien doctrines, practices, beliefs, and the persons holding them as different, foreign, unacceptable, and threatening. In this way it declared itself the norm—finding, as John Winthrop propounds, scriptural evidence and support for this claim—and everyone else, the deviation from that standard, the "Other," against which but also through which the Puritans defined themselves.[9]

The paradox of "otherness" is that although the Other is defined as deviant, marginal, the nonself or nonsame, it is absolutely necessary to the existence of the self or same; it is constitutive of Self. Thus, the subjectification of one group depends upon the objectification of another. The philosophical language of Self and Other is familiar to us from the existentialism of Jean-Paul Sartre, who examined the dilemma of the conscious human being condemned to freedom, the Self, pitted in inevitable "intersubjective warfare" with other people, the Other (Jardine, 105). French thought has long rejected Sartre's phenomenology, jettisoning the Cartesian models of rationality and objectivity that locate "certainty" in the ego, for the notion of "alterity," an otherness within the Self that produces "Man's non-coincidence-with-himself," the split, fragmented Self, the "decentered subject" of postmodernism (Jardine, 105–6). Recently, theorists investigating elements common to these two supposedly discontinuous models of subjectivity theorize that they are not as opposed as they first appear.[10] Although postmodernist theories pose themselves against the discourses of Cartesian humanism and phenomenology, the traditions share an androcentric bias that genders both conceptions of otherness as feminine.[11]

Whether the Other is conceived as internal or external to Self, it is necessary for the constitution of Self, but Self and Other are not analogous. Feminist thinkers find in this inequality a description of how androcentric European culture positions "woman" or "the feminine" (the label for an abstract category or set of gendered characteristics different from "women" in their historical specificity[12] and sometimes referring to groups constituted by qualities other than gender) in relation to man. The ground-breaking thinker in this exploration is the philosopher Simone de Beauvoir, who discloses the gendered assumptions in the philosophical ideas of her longtime companion, Sartre. In her classic study, *The Second Sex*, she explains:

In actuality the relation of the two sexes is not quite like that of two electrical poles, for man represents both the positive and the neutral, as is indicated by the common use of *man* to designate human beings in general; whereas woman represents only the negative, defined by limiting criteria, without reciprocity. . . .

Thus humanity is male and man defines woman not in herself but as relative to him; she is not regarded as an autonomous being. . . .

For him she is sex—absolute sex, no less. She is defined and differentiated with reference to man and not he with reference to her; she is the incidental, the inessential as opposed to the essential. He is the Subject, he is the Absolute—she is the Other. (xviii–xix)

Beauvoir's conceptualization is not just relevant to intersubjectivity, but can be applied culturally, for it describes positions of psychic and social relation to which gender has been ascribed, and which then take on the characteristics culturally associated with the particular gender. The Self is central, active, unified, absolute, essential; the occupant of this position is "masculine." The Other is dependent, incidental, different, marginal; the occupant of this position is "feminine." These positions are not exclusive or permanent, and the values and attitudes associated with each are historically specific, varied, and even contradictory. So, for example, Queen Elizabeth, though female, could occupy the masculine position of monarch and simultaneously exploit the associations of virgin; but as a wife or mother, she would occupy a feminine position, and this was a compromise of absolute monarchical power that she refused to make. Culture and history provide a complex array of factors—sex, class, race, employment, marital status, age, to name a few—that place people in the positions of relations they occupy. Some associations have been around so long they come to seem "natural" or divinely ordained; for example, authority, autonomy, and subjectivity are closely associated with masculinity. Another persistent aspect of the Self/Other model of subjectivity is that the place of the Other, the place of "woman," is the place of a nonsubject.

Although it has been easy and convenient for certain cultures to confuse historical women with "woman," women are not the only ones to be cast in the position of Other. Tzvetan Todorov, for example, reads the discovery of America—the Spanish conquest of native populations—as "the discovery *self* makes of the *other* . . . that heralds and establishes our present identity" (*Conquest*, 3, 5; emphasis in original). "Race," like "gender," becomes a figure of otherness, and stands not for Others who "are also 'I's: subjects just as I am," but for "outsiders whose language and customs I do not understand, so foreign that in extreme instances I am reluctant to admit they belong to the same species as my own" (3). The effects of otherness are often dehumanization, objectification, fascination, and the threatening, agentless power that goes along with fetishization and exoticism. Self, the normative category, though in practice white and male, stands, as Beauvoir points out, for the universal, apparently having neither gender nor race—just as it has no ethnicity, or just as a culture's dominant ideology is not "ideological" but "natural." Strangely, the general terms "race" and "gender" become shorthand for "race-other-than-the-dominant-race" and "gender-other-than-masculine," just as "woman" becomes shorthand for "sex—absolute sex" as if men did not have that either.

The Puritan experiment in the New World was not immune to these assumptions that underlay Renaissance European culture. In fact, such assumptions figure prominently in the dynamics of Protestant culture and play a central role in New England's ideological self-identity. Anne Kibbey, for instance, demonstrates the interchangeability of woman and Native American as "similar social categories" against which New England Puritan men exercised a unifying "prejudicial violence" (107). Focusing on the year 1637, Kibbey argues that "the resolution of the antinomian controversy did much to make 'women' a symbolic category of threat to Puritan authority," especially by associating antinomianism and female sexuality, and that "the genocide of the Pequot War was an act of severe prejudice against women, far exceeding the controversy in its hostility, but likewise an event of major symbolic importance to the Puritans" (93). In her close reading of several major texts produced by the orthodoxy to document its version of the events, Kibbey shows how the interchangeability of Hutchinson and "Indians" creates an association between the religiously sanctified violence of war against the "savages" and male attitudes toward women (105–11). It has long been recognized that the events of 1637 were an important turning point for the fledgling commonwealth, but Kibbey and others point out that these crises were "less a breakdown of social order than a struggle to institute a particular kind of social order" that granted legitimacy to the Puritan patriarchy's notion of corporate identity, masculinity, and domination (120).[13]

For most historians of the Puritan experience, the question of whether that experience differed for women, nonwhites, or different classes, let alone *how* it differed, has not been an issue. Hambrick-Stowe, for example, recognizes and even decries the dearth of available material written by Puritan women, but he justifies his generalizing about Puritan modes of devotion from male-authored texts by invoking David D. Hall's notion of "collective mentality" (5 n. 2). Furthermore, "in matters of devotion," he concludes, "lines of class were inconsequential" (4). In a new study of the psychology of the Puritan religious experience, Charles L. Cohen also notices the uniformity in Puritan religious discourse, which, he says, results from "the language in which preachers explicated the *ordo salutis*. . . . Theologians," he continues, "assumed that a single dynamic of regeneration governs all conversions, an asseveration confirmed in the testimonies of the Elect. The experience of grace submerges the peculiarities of gender" (223). This is as it should be, given Paul's exhortation to the Galatians that in the realm of the spirit "there is neither Jew nor Greek, there is neither bond nor free, there is neither male nor female: for ye are all one in Christ Jesus" (3:28). Why, then, one is tempted to ask, when the zealous settlers established their city upon the hill where they were free to covenant churches patterned after the Invisible Church of the elect, could women neither speak nor vote, though they had been judged saints and were thus equal in the spirit to their brethren? Why were Native Americans and African converts treated with suspicion and subjected to more rigorous standards?[14]

Clearly, the universal is not neutral or neuter or race-blind; as those in power have imposed it, the universal is gendered male, and is often conceived as white and middle-class as well. Feminist scholars have described the incongruence between Puritan religious doctrine and social practice as the "subordinate but equal" dilemma introduced by Reformation thought, which Puritan ministers defended by drawing a distinction between the covenant of grace as it would exist in eternity and the social covenant according to which all persons were obliged to remain in the social position to which they had been born (R. Keller, 134, 136).[15] The Pauline doctrine, which granted women a theoretical spiritual equality with their male counterparts, was itself ambiguous and did not erase the inequalities of seventeenth-century bourgeois social and political traditions. The same "natural" inequalities in rank presumably held for indentured servants, Africans, and Native Americans. It would be interesting to pursue the question of how this rift between the spiritual and social realms, between Christ's principles and men's actions, affected women, the lower classes in the colonies, captives, and the native converts, but it is extremely difficult to break through the uniformity of seventeenth-century religious discourse. We are left to read and interpret silences—what people did not, or could not, say. We can, however, study the assumptions upon which the religious discourse was built, and which produce those silences. Such a study reveals contradictions concerning authority and experience in colonial Puritan culture that affect those who speak as well as those who are silent and silenced.[16] Not surprisingly, these effects are still being felt today, and they crop up, almost unchanged, in the critical and historical scholarship that grows out of our Puritan past.

In both colonial Puritan discourse and most current critical discourses, though the audience is mixed, the specific addressee, as well as the consciousness under scrutiny, and the concept of a universal, are construed as male. Take, for example, this passage from Thomas Shepard's sermon series, "The Parable of the Ten Virgins Unfolded," which he preached in weekly lectures beginning in June 1636 and ending in May 1640 to shore up the raggedy edges of doctrine and congregational morale in the aftermath of the antinomian controversy. Shepard asks, "When is the soul in readiness to enjoy Christ?" (70), and he answers in the negative, "Then a man is unprepared for the Lord Jesus his coming, while he wants affections suitable to the majesty, and according to the worth and love of the Lord Jesus" (71). Shepard's usage of "man" here could be simply the masculine signifier used generically, but observe how this universal term gets gendered in the following illustrations he offers:

Suppose a woman knows her husband's love; yet if she have lost her love to him, or if she love him, it is only as she loves another man, not according to the worth of her husband's person, or the greatness of his love. Is she fit now to appear before him, when no heart to receive him? So, although you question not Christ's love to you, and thank God you doubt little of it, yet where is your heart? your love to him? Have you not lost your love, your first love, or second love? If you have love, is it not divided to other things, as wife, child, friends, hopes of provision for them, and too much care hereupon for that? (71–72)

At almost every turn in the six hundred pages of commentary on this biblical parable, Shepard employs generalities concerning "woman" to elucidate the plight of "man," frequently introducing an illustration like the one above with the phrase, "As it is with the woman who. . . ." The visible saints are the "virgins espoused to Christ" (26); Christ, who "appears to his church under several relations and titles . . . appears more fully to her as a husband, or as a bridegroom with whom she is to have her nearest and everlasting fellowship and communion" (111); and the soul regards Christ with "that look as it is with a woman, though she can not do much, nor deserve his love, yet her heart is with him; herself is his, (Cant. vi. 3,) 'I am my beloved's'" (50). "Woman's" social experiences with men form a catalogue of emblems for saints' experiences with God. As obedient wife, she is the emblem of the obedient servant, a figure of righteous passive desire; as adulterer, the figure of apostasy defiling herself by spurning God's love; as harlot, the unsaved pagan turning to other gods; as shrew, the rebel; as childbearer, the evangelist; as nurse and midwife, the preacher. Even her "breasts" are appropriated as emblems of the nurturing Gospels and the ministers who dispense the "milk" of the Word. Woman is also, in herself, a constant threat to a believer's focus on God and the things of God. Thus woman's experience is appropriated as emblematic of man's relations with God, but as a woman she interferes with those relations.

Furthermore, while "woman" illustrates the state of the soul, that soul belongs specifically to men. As the last sentence in Shepard's passage discloses, it is men who are in danger of loving wives more than God, or of forgetting God's love in the day-to-day responsibilities of bread-winning and survival in a fledgling settlement. Concerns about women loving husbands or children too much, though just as real, are not voiced; perhaps they are meant to be inferred by analogy. The specific gender of the addressee surfaces again, unmistakably, as Shepard rhetorically answers objections from his audience on the subject of how to be near to Christ. As he exhorts the saint to "see thou desire nothing but him," the objection arises, "What will become of my wife and children?" "When thou livest, they are thine; but then the Lord's," Shepard responds, in an attempt to quell what are specifically male fears (548). Despite the constant appearance in this text of "woman," the silence and absence of the concerns of women are conspicuous.

Historical accounts of the period replicate a similar set of assumptions about the gender of subjectivity, which Puritan divines like Thomas Shepard reinforce in the founding moments of early North American culture. Consider the following example from Lawrence Stone's comprehensive study, *The Family, Sex, and Marriage in England 1500–1800*. In seeking an explanation for the radical shifts within the microcosm of the family that began in the last third of the seventeenth century and climaxed around 1800, producing a growth in "affective individualism," Stone examines changes in "the macrocosm of the total cultural system, a major reorientation of meaning among those sectors of society which experienced these changes." In doing so, he looks to the "individual," and more specifically, "how the individual regarded himself in relation to society (the growth of individualism) and how he behaved and felt towards other human beings, particularly his wife and children on the one hand, and parents and kin on the other (the growth of affect)" (150). Whatever its intentions, this sentence discloses whose perspective really counts as typical. It is possible to understand the first pronoun in the sentence, "himself," as the generic term for the species; however, in particularizing the subject by mentioning his "wife and children," the universal no longer applies. Clearly, the "individual" in whom macrocosmic changes are recorded, whom Stone studies and theorizes, is not both male and female, but male only, and married with children. Women are not left out of this study or considered only in terms of men; in fact, they are treated in some cases as a separate category of research. Subsequent chapters focus specifically on topics such as "Early Feminist Movements" and "The Education of Women." Nevertheless, women are still a special class, a subset (sub-version and subversion) of the human subject, which is male. The generalizations about subjectivity and individuality drawn from this study can be nothing less than skewed.[17]

Skewed, that is, unless one considers these to be generalizations about males and persons who fit into the category of the "masculine." Mary Maples Dunn does just that when she proposes explaining "the Puritans' loss of a sense of mission and . . . how they handled their guilt," questions that have continued to vex historians, by considering the possibility that "what was seen as a 'declension' was only a loss of *male* piety, that Puritans adopted more stringent gender role differences, and turned their church into a feminine institution" (37). This is precisely how I propose to read Puritan texts, and in the process, to test out Dunn's speculations, which lead us to ask why female church membership in late seventeenth-century New England was invisible—at least in the rhetoric of contemporary jeremiads, and more disturbingly, in the accounts of later historians. Why don't women count? Let me offer one more example to explain my use of the present tense here.

David Leverenz, in his perceptive psychoanalytic study of Puritan rhetoric, *The Language of Puritan Feeling*, confirms what I have already suggested with the examples from Thomas Shepard, that colonial ministers consistently used female imagery to figure the process of salvation. Not satisfied with the stock explanation for this phenomenon—that the mystical marriage of Christ and the Church or soul, derived primarily from the Song of Songs, is the conventional metaphor for the believer's relation with God—Leverenz analyzes the implications of this metaphor using a wide range of psychoanalytic theory. He summarizes one of his major conclusions in this way: "Puritans tried to resolve ambivalences about parental and social authority in a fantasy of dependence. . . . They dreamed of being changed into women and babies and of finding in the Great Father a mothering protector. . . . With the utmost seriousness they reconceived themselves collectively as virgin daughters to prove their heavenly father's virtue" (105–6). Would it not be more accurate to attribute such fantasies to Puritan *men*? Unable to ascertain what role, if any, women played in the articulation of the official collective fantasy, we can nevertheless determine with certainty that some Puritans, probably around half the population, were already women, and some were babies and even virgin daughters. Leverenz speaks as if all Puritans were men and examples of the classic obsessional neurotic son of the Freudian "family romance." Can this be a women's fantasy? Can women dream of becoming what they already are? According to Puritan doctrine, everyone, male and female, young and old, was in desperate need of a radical transformation of his or her very being. Females, however, begin the process of salvation already feminized, in a manner of speaking, as part of their social, cultural, and familial gender role conditioning. Etiquette books and educational manuals of the period indicate that middle-class females were exhorted, trained, and, if that did not work, constrained to be gentle, humble, and submissive to a father or husband in ways that their male counterparts were not.[18] Presuming that women were already "feminine," was the dynamic of conversion different for them? Furthermore, were their spiritual and social roles, or their own self-images, affected by the static virgin-whore conception of "woman" promulgated in this religious theory?[19]

One problem in an otherwise insightful account of the psychology of Puritan men is Leverenz's conflation of biologically determined or philosophically essential sex, and culturally constructed gender. This confusion, which Sigmund Freud himself tried to avoid,[20] derives from some of the psychoanalytic sources on which Leverenz depends, especially Ernest Jones's orthodox Freudian interpretation, "A Psychoanalytic Study of the Holy Ghost." In this essay, Jones argues that Christ

> attains greatness, including final possession of the Mother and reconciliation with the Father, only after undergoing the extremity of humiliation together with a symbolic castration and death. A similar path is laid down for every follower of Jesus, salvation being purchased at the price of gentleness, humility, and submission to the Father's will. . . . Object-love for the Mother is replaced by a regression to the original identification with her, so that incest is avoided and the Father pacified; further the opportunity is given of winning the Father's love by the adoption of a feminine attitude towards him. Peace of mind is purchased by means of a change in heart in the direction of a change in sex. (*Essays*, 423)

If we probe this statement at all, we find its universalism unraveling. The unspoken but unmistakable assumption is that a female does not, and structurally cannot, occupy the position of Christian. Christ is the archetypal son who forgoes his competition with his heavenly father and gives up his murderous instincts in order to reap the benefits of being reconciled with, but not having to be like, such a powerful phallic figure. The superego or the famous Puritan conscience, an internalization of the Father's will and society's morality, is formed in the resolution of the Oedipus complex. But this resolution is gender-specific, as Freud himself pointed out; the girl child does not have to shift the parent with whom she identifies, nor does she properly "resolve" the Oedipus complex because socialized femininity requires that her love object become her father and her desire remain fixated on the male.[21]

Therefore, when Leverenz states that "Jones is right to stress the process of regression, and especially the change in sex" (*Language*, 128), his very language, like Jones's, excludes women—one has to be male or neuter to "change" into a woman. He tries to rectify this when he says, "For the Puritans, the change was really one from whore to virgin, for both men and women" (128)—that is, a change to the stereotyped contradiction of "woman." But even if he means a metaphoric change in sex, what is the status of such a change when not just the logic of one's rhetoric but the redemption of one's soul is at stake? Both men refer to a "feminine attitude," which Jones and, by implication, Leverenz associate with "the extremity of humiliation," "symbolic castration," and "submission." In doing so they perpetuate the historically static view of "woman" as the vulnerable, debased, defeated, and always sexualized opposite of man. That a feminine attitude can be, and for the purposes of salvation must be, adopted by males and females alike indicates that it is not necessarily inherent in or natural to a certain sex, but is a position that a subject can occupy, defined by its relationship to an absolute power— God. For these early as well as for modern thinkers, Christians are assumed to be male like Christ; "woman" is not a person, but a rhetorical position of subordination and subservience to God—which then, all too easily, gets confused with women. Puritan religious discourse instructs and constructs both men and women in these attitudes toward gender and otherness. There is, however, an epistemological and experiential difference between males adopting feminine attitudes, and females adopting them.

I propose, therefore, to read the Protestant paradigm of conversion as a narrative of gendered subjectivity—gendered in the sense that its discourse depends upon figures of gender and also inscribes only the male gender as redeemed subjects. By reading the pronouns literally and refusing to universalize the masculine, in the primary texts from the seventeenth century as well as the critical texts from the late twentieth century, we are forced to read these texts differently—acknowledging the difference implicit in the rhetoric. Texts written by women appear less monologic, and texts written about women and people of color disclose the exclusivity of the Puritan conception of redeemed subjectivity. Reading gender and, thus, difference back into the universal allows us to sketch a more accurate picture of masculine subjectivity and, thus, cultural reality, which we can then apply to various texts to discern their ideological function in the Puritan tradition—a legacy that is with us yet.

By the time the first English settlers landed on the coast of New England, two generations of Puritan divines had assiduously studied Paul's epistles and produced detailed descriptions of the stages of conversion and their accompanying psychological states "so that a man could check his eternal condition by a set of temporal and recognizable signs" (Morgan, *Visible Saints*, 66). It is true that some of the bitterest controversies in New and old England proceeded from differing interpretations of one or more of the stages in conversion, the subtleties of which might have enormous consequences for social practice.[22] But in general, Protestant divines recognized Paul's six stages in the pattern of spiritual regeneration: the *election* of certain people predestined by God before their birth to eternal salvation; the *calling* of the elect saints, which involved their awakening to a sense of their desperate sinfulness, complete helplessness, yet eligibility for all the gospel promises of repentance and saving faith; the saints' *justification* through the forgiveness of their sins and the imputation of Christ's righteousness without which salvation is impossible; their awareness of a new personal relationship to God through *adoption* as his son and heir to heaven with Christ; at the time of justification, the beginning of the process of *sanctification*, whereby the defaced image of God in the soul is gradually repaired and a "new life" begun; and, finally, *glorification*, the complete restoration of the image of God in the soul and the saints' enjoyment of eternal rest, attained only after death (Lewalski, 16–18; Morgan, *Visible Saints*, 67). Since all of this was accomplished not by the volition of the saint himself, but by the will of God, who bestowed upon the saint the gift of irresistible grace, the real anxiety lay in discovering whether one possessed saving faith. Thus, Puritan ministers and theologians set to work analyzing the operation of faith; William Perkins, for example, whom colonial Puritan ministers considered authoritative, discerned no less than ten stages in its acquisition (Morgan, *Visible Saints*, 68). The general pattern that Perkins outlined appears in countless diaries and orally reported conversion narratives. It begins with attendance upon the word of God and a preparatory breaking of the will, which brings the saint to a basic knowledge of good and evil; this awareness leads to the saint's conviction of his sinfulness, the first glimmerings of faith, violent and continual combat with doubts, an "Evangelicall sorrow" or grief over sin, and finally, "true, [that is,] imperfect assurance" (Morgan, *Visible Saints*, 68–69, 72).

The whole process of Puritan conversion affirmed the existence of a new kind of interiority, of a private, unique, inner space—the space of self-consciousness, of subjectivity—only to demand its sacrifice, renunciation, and occupation by Another. For, according to Calvinist belief, the idea of a self apart from God contributed to the Fall, and as a result, interiority and a conception of an autonomous self is innately depraved.[23] God's sacrifice of his only son and Christ's willing submission are the only acts that can redeem humanity from its desolate self by providing it with a model of self thoroughly "converted" and regenerated anew as the soul— the site cleansed of self in which God can appear. Conversion required the willing abdication of will: "not I, but Christ liveth in me," cried the apostle Paul (Gal. 2:20), a paradox that Puritan ministers recommended to their audiences as the epitome of redeemed subjectivity.[24] To be saved is to *allow* oneself to be saved, to allow God to work his predestined will, to be wholly passive yet desirous of God's converting love, to put no faith in self. "The way of the soul," explains Sacvan Bercovitch with the help of Thomas Hooker, "starts 'with a holy despair in ourselves' and proceeds 'with a holy kind of violence' back to Christ; it means acknowledging the primacy of that which is Another's, and *receiving* the ability to respond" (*Puritan Origins*, 17–18; emphasis in original). Only with a wrenching violence can the obdurate will be broken, the sinner be turned back to God, and the self be made to acknowledge its monstrosity, its "extreme folly," and its "most miserable impotence"—so deeply rooted are self-love, self-interest, self-trust (Calvin, 1.1:39).[25] Only by overcoming extreme resistance does the self agree to submit to Another's will. It is not surprising, given this psychology of imposed self-loathing, that the stage in the search for faith that attracted the most attention from Puritan writers was "conviction," or what they called "humiliation," during which the saint experienced complete abjection in realizing his powerlessness and often despairing of salvation altogether (Morgan, *Visible Saints*, 68).

It is difficult, in even a brief description of the conversion process, as it was for Puritan ministers in their longer sermons and treatises, to avoid gendered metaphors. Conversion involves the transformation of all saints, male and female, into feminine vessels, emptied of self and filled with God. Calvin, referring to the figural language of Scripture, describes salvation through the spirit of Christ as "that sacred marriage, by which we become bone of his bone, and flesh of his flesh, and so one with him (Eph. v.30)" (3.1:465).[26] The metaphor of the mystical marriage between Christ and his church, a union that extends to the individual soul, is also common in Catholic literature and is the figure favored by colonial Puritan ministers for expressing not only the resignation to be ruled and governed by God's will, required of saints for salvation, but also the rapturous joys they can expect in their union with Christ. The contemplation of this union, imagining oneself as the "Bride of Christ," prompts the most sensual writing in the Puritan canon—although none of it matches in intensity, violence, or perversity the *locus classicus* of this topos, John Donne's Holy Sonnet, "Batter my heart, three-person'd God," where Christ, the Bridegroom and liberator, becomes the soul's rapist and enslaver (Lewalski, 272).

Puritan ministers use other metaphors to describe the state of the redeemed saint, such as a servant to a master, the body to the soul, a subject to a king, a patient to a physician. Christ himself told his disciples, "Except ye be converted, and become as little children, ye shall not enter into the kingdom of heaven" (Matt. 18:3). Innocence, purity, obedience to authority, and childlike dependency play into the feminization of the saint, since these are also characteristics expected of women in their roles as wives.[27] But, as Margaret W. Masson points out in her examination of the typology of the female as a model for the regenerate in third-generation New England Puritan sermons, none of these relationships combines the voluntary nature of the elect's submission with a sense of status achieved through personal choice or effort (311). Thomas Shepard specifies this crucial aspect of the marriage metaphor for describing the redeemed subject, when he explains: "The soul hence gives itself, like one espoused to her husband, to the Lord Jesus. . . . Servants give work for their wages, and masters give wages for their work, but husbands and wives give themselves one unto another; . . . he that is espoused to Christ gives himself" (31). Shepard implies that mutuality is the quality that makes marriage the most accurate metaphor for the relationship of God and the soul, echoing Calvin's assertion that the point of resemblance between the two forms of connection is "mutual faith" (3.8:18). This, however, betrays a pious anxiety to bind an omnipotent God to the same covenant that binds impotent man. If such mutuality existed between Puritan couples, it fell under a skewed system of domination; for only a wife's willing surrender to her husband's authority captures fully the contradictory position of the saint.

If that saint happens to be male, with the prospects of becoming a husband himself, or a father, the conventional expectations for his social behavior come into sharp conflict with the spiritual requirements of his orthodox belief. The colonial Puritans were guided in their conception of sexual hierarchy and earthly marriage by the apostle Paul, whose recommendations to the early Christians set out a "metaphysics of gender" the "logic" of which structures in a contradiction within the male position.[28] Paul proclaims: "the head of every man is Christ; and the head of the woman is the man; and the head of Christ is God" (1 Cor. 11:3). The same principle characterizes the marriage relation. "Wives," Paul exhorts the Ephesian women, "submit yourselves unto your own husbands, as unto the Lord. For the husband is the head of the wife, even as Christ is the head of the church: and he is the saviour of the body. Therefore as the church is subject unto Christ, so let the wives be to their own husbands in every thing" (Eph. 5:22–24). There is little positional discontinuity from a Puritan woman's social to her spiritual life; she is expected to submit willingly to an earthly husband as well as to a heavenly one. The better she is at her earthly calling—humility, subservience, silence—the more pious she will be at her spiritual calling. This continuity does not exist for men who, as saints, are also expected to submit to Christ—but who, in the hierarchical marital structure, occupy the position of Christ in relation to his church, as the "head" to the body. The effect of this analogy is to equate man with God, and woman not just with flesh, but with the corporate "body" of the mystical Christ, his church. Woman, like the convert, is never adequate as an individual but only as a participant "in a religious collective subject that transcends human limits, uniting Christians to the mystical Christ and to other 'members' of the corporate 'body'" (Kibbey, 53). By contrast, husbands are charged with loving their wives "as their own bodies," as Christ loves the church and gave his body for it (Eph. 5:25, 28), thus putting husbands in a godlike place. Though men are also charged with "submitting yourselves one to another in the fear of God" (Eph. 5:21), their domestic and social superiority and their domination over women remain unchecked.

Redeemed subjectivity is a paradoxical state. Anne Kibbey speaks of "the polarized 'self' of the Puritan convert, who must live both a 'spirituall life' of the soul and an 'outward and temporall life' at the same time" (33). Spiritual rebirth initiates a complete disjunction from one's human birth and life; Puritans were exhorted to "wean" themselves from the things of the world, living in it while not being of it. Both men and women were required to quell the "masculine" aspects of their characters and become, as it were, blank surfaces, cleansed spaces, empty vessels—the "feminine" aspects of character being not the addition of new qualities, but the erasure of human, fallen ones. Thus, men, conceived as "naturally" masculine—that is, willful, active, and assertive—spent their spiritual lives trying to subjugate the qualities society told them they could not help but embody; women had only to go along with "nature." Identification with the characteristics of the mystical bride was, thus, significantly *more* disjunctive for males than for females. As Philip Greven baldly puts it: "for men to be saved they had to cease being masculine" (129) and assume the nonsubjectivity of woman—subjected to a divine husband. This emasculation, the resistance to which is amply recorded in Puritan private literature, was exacerbated by the fact that in their daily life Puritan men were expected to (continue to) be dominant and assertive.[29]

According to several studies, seventeenth-century Puritan child-rearing practices also increased male conflicts. Parents were encouraged to break the will of all children, male and female, and to demand strict obedience to parental authority, thus preparing the younger generation for the resignation of self-will and self-reliance required in the rigorous conversion experience.[30] However, girls, who identified with mothers submissive to husbands, fathers, the state, and Christ, could simply follow that "circumscribed" but "unambiguous" path, while boys were expected to grow up, marry, and act within the family as "earthly analogues for God himself" (Leverenz, *Language*, 101–2). The mixed expectations that resulted from Puritan modes of child-rearing, and that were exacerbated by the contradictory demands of Puritan religious doctrine and social practice, produced a profound ambivalence, especially in sons. David Leverenz's nuanced reading of Puritan sermon rhetoric shows this ambivalence generating and being satisfied by a fantasy of submission and feminization, which veils deep-seated feelings of rage, frustration, vulnerability, and anger at the father/God who demands such humiliation.

The "double language of Puritanism," a discourse that Leverenz traces in ministerial literature, which can imagine a patriarchal God in mothering similes, appears as well in the private writing of Puritan men, who use gendered language to figure their spiritual abjection and the contradictions it posed. Isaac Penington said of his spiritual experience: "The Lord has broken the man's part in me, and I am a worm and no man before him" (Greven, 125). John Rogers captured the conflict he experienced by recommending contradictory behavior to his children: "Gird up therefore the Loyns of your Mind," he told them, and "act with a manly Vigour and Resolution, being sensible of your own utter Impotency, depending only on the Strength of Christ and the effectual Influences of his Spirit" (Greven, 126). One young man, Joseph Bean, became so despondent over his "unchast and immodist thoughts" and "filthy" dreams that while a friend of his got married downstairs, he went "up stars by my Self all alone and thare pleded with God that this Night be the Weden Night betwen Christ and my Soul." Soon after, he dreamed about a boy, "the butifulest that ever I saw any in all my Life," who, while being crushed under Satan, smiled on him with a shining face he took to be the face of Christ. Some months later, Bean finally wrote out a marriage covenant giving himself wholly to God:

> I do here with all my power accept the and do take the for my head husband for biter for worse for richer for poorer for all tims and Conditions to love honour and obay the before all others and this to the deth: I Imbrace the in all thy offices. I Renounce my own worthyness and do here avow the to be the Lord my Righteousness: I Renounce mine own wisdom and do here take the for my only gide: I renounce mine own will and take thy will for my Law. (Greven, 126)

This young Bostonian, himself almost crushed under the weight of the demands of Puritan spirituality, shaped doctrine to fit his needs and thus created an outlet for his homoeroticism. But many men found the contradictory demands of Puritan social life and spirituality profoundly disturbing, sexually disrupting, and even paralyzing.

Women suffered differently, but no less, in this regime. If "woman" served as a figure for the regenerate soul, and if womanly functions such as marrying, giving birth, and mothering were used to describe spiritual processes, why were women and their functions not elevated and ennobled by this use? Clearly, women who fit the Pauline model were applauded, but the effect of approving women for being self-effacing would, presumably, be merely more and better self-effacement. In fact, only a certain scripturally defined and culturally approved notion of "woman" served as the typology of regenerate subjectivity. This notion acted as a particularly insidious form of social control of women, whose devaluation was a valuable resource because, in spiritual terms, it was the vehicle of transcendence. Carol Karlsen points out that "women who failed to serve men failed to serve God. To be numbered among God's elect, women had to acknowledge this service as their calling and *believe* they were created for this purpose" (166; emphasis in original). Women like Anne Hutchinson, who swerved noticeably from the Pauline model of passivity, humility, and obedience, were considered not just heretical but downright demonic. For her doctrinal extravagances and her speaking and prophesying in public the ruling clergy branded Hutchinson as a sexual libertine who threatened the church and state, and a maternal monstrosity who defied the laws of nature. She became, as Amy Lang so thoroughly demonstrates, "the very type of dissent" (69). In the hands of Puritan theologians, the spiritualization of feminine imagery had the effect of erasing the earthly and fleshly femaleness from it. Puritan men appropriated female imagery, but only as a necessary phase on the way to the remasculinization offered by the Puritan conversion narrative in which, ultimately, God adopts the saint as his son and heir and woman/women disappear.

According to the familial logic of Puritan conversion, betrothal to Christ qualifies the spouse for adoption into the divine family and defines the saint's new intimate relationship to his nurturing father (see Rom. 8:15–17). "Sonship," Samuel Willard informs his audience of saints, proceeds from "our Marriage to Christ; so that by becoming his Spouse . . . we are made the Children of God" (*The Child's Portion*, 11; quoted in Morgan, *Puritan Family*, 165). John Cotton explains that "*Adoption* is properly the work of the Father, but Christ being the naturall Son of God, we must be knit unto him, before we can be accounted Sons" (*The Covenant of Grace*, 191; quoted in Morgan, *Puritan Family*, 165). The inconsistency in gender, which no one acknowledged, suggests the spiritual nature of these roles. In the logic of conversion, all saints pass through the feminizing process. Brides become sons and heirs and are thus remasculinized, but they remain on the feminine side of the gender/power divide. Edward Taylor makes as much clear in a rapturous contemplation of his many (subordinate) relationships to Christ, who, in assuming the masculine role, finally subsumes "Ev'ry thing":

> In us Relations all that mutuall are.
> I am thy Patient, Pupill, Servant, and
>   Thy Sister, Mother, Doove, Spouse, Son, and Heire.
> Thou art my Priest, Physician, Prophet, King,
>   Lord, Brother, Bridegroom, Father, Ev'ry thing.
>   (*Poems*, Med. 1.29:20–24)

Does the absence of "daughters" in this vision of heaven indicate that women also become "sons"? Finally, the paternal and patriarchal appropriation of the mother's role seems to be the point here. Calvin, quoting John, emphasizes the logocentric—or, more precisely, the phallologocentric—nature of faith in Christ, which grants "the privilege 'to become the Sons of God, even to them that believe in his name, which were born not of blood, nor of the will of the flesh, nor of the will of man, but of God' (John i. 12)" (3.1:465).[31]

To be born again is to be born of the Word, to be sons of an autogenic Father. The moment in scripture that institutes this elision of the feminine is the conversation between Nicodemus, a pharisee and ruler of the Jews, and Jesus that prefaces one of the Gospels' central statements of doctrine: "For God so loved the world, that he gave his only begotten Son" (John 3:16). Nicodemus comes to question Jesus about his recent performance of miracles and infers his divinity from those spectacles. Growing aware of the Jews' stubborn dependence upon "signs," Jesus answers the pharisee impatiently: "Verily, verily, I say unto thee, Except a man be born again, he cannot see the kingdom of God." Perplexed, Nicodemus asks the practical and self-interested question: "How can a man be born when he is old? can he enter the second time into his mother's womb, and be born?" With a sigh, Jesus explains: "That which is born of the flesh is flesh; and that which is born of the Spirit is spirit." But Nicodemus's incredulity persists. Assuming that rebirth, if it is analogous to natural birth, requires a woman's body, he misses the point altogether. His nagging literalism raises the question of the effect of advancing a theory of (re)birth without mothers.

As the mother's function is subsumed by an all-powerful father who displays maternal qualities, the womb as a metonymy for woman is irrevocably defined as flesh. Thus, man's birth from the womb constitutes a fall from original spirit and God-consciousness into the flesh, the senses, and self-consciousness. This fall from God the Father to Adam occurs through woman but can be redressed only by regeneration through the son, Christ, acting here as a womb-substitute or a willingly castrated phallus, the model of Christian obedience. This initial displacement of the feminine gives rise to the notion that spirit is originary and teleological, man's beginning and end, whereas the flesh, associated with the mother and natural reproduction, is transitory. The maternal, standing for the feminine, stands for that which is temporal, phenomenal rather than substantial, that which must be brought under a higher control and finally transcended. Substance—and, by extension, spirit—is male, which is to say, ungendered. Edmund Calamy, an English sectarian, summed up this line of reasoning with witty concision: "The Soule of Man is the Man of Man" (8). By becoming a "son" the converted saint transcends the flesh and all the sins associated with earthly existence, being reborn with the help of midwifing and nurturing male ministers. Women, doubly displaced, transcend their debased physical natures and become masculine in the sense that the masculine represents the purgation of sexual difference, an asexual universal, the reunion with God in a homogeneous spiritual realm (Thickstun, 8). As sons, the saints draw nearer to the *imitatio Christi* and become eligible, as woman is not, to inherit the Father's patrimony.

What is this patrimony? The colonial Puritans' translation of spirit into religious and social practice reproduced Paul's sexual hierarchy. Men who were judged sufficiently committed to spiritual emasculation were, ironically, rewarded with the perquisites of masculine privilege: social superiority, domination in the home, a voice in the church and community, and a vote in the commonwealth—the usual markers of agency and subjectivity.[32] Women were rewarded with theoretical equality and second-class citizenship. Puritan spirituality offered both men and women the *promise* of full, undifferentiated subjectivity, but it was a subjectivity deferred.

This redeemed subjectivity was also hegemonic, a site where subjects experience the constant contradiction between ideology and their social experience—a site of resistance and struggle.[33] In order to ensure their consent to the system that constrained them, saints became partners in the ideological work of communal self-regimentation: vigilant in policing their own souls and behavior, they also participated in inquiring after and passing judgment upon the souls and behavior of family and neighbors. For, as Max Weber points out, the Protestant legacy is the ethic of work— a vestigial form of the Arminian heresy, which the Puritan fathers preferred to antinomianism because it blunted the feminizing absolute dependence upon the will of God.[34]

There is another kind of work besides that which produces surplus value or industrial and technological progress, and that is the cultural work of reproducing the ideologies by which we recognize ourselves as subjects and the meanings and limits of our individual and social experiences. "Conversion," Rutman said, speaking of John Winthrop as representative of "American Puritanism," was "simply the taking hold of and making personal the religious 'ideology'" by which an individual (and, he argues, an entire generation) resolves his "identity crisis" and then "locates himself with relationship to the value system which the ideology affirms" (117, 119). There is, however, a sense in which specific ideologies and their discourses take hold of the individual and convert him— into a subject. Passing through the defile of femininity, joined in an abjection that was momentously figured as symbolic castration, saints sometimes achieved a strong sense of identity—albeit not their own. The more fully one denied oneself, the more energy was liberated to do the work of God, to be soldiers for Christ.

Condemned to live in the world (Puritans rejected monasticism as the easy way out), the saint must keep steadily at the unending work of redeemed subjectivity, seeking evidences of assurance despite backsliding, doubts, trials, and persistent spiritual combat. It is not surprising that in order to explain how ideology transforms individuals into subjects, and how and why these subjects appear to work freely by themselves without explicit coercion by the state, Louis Althusser invokes Christian authority: "As St. Paul admirably put it," he remarks, "it is in the 'Logos,' meaning in ideology, that we 'live, move and have our being'" (171). Althusser concludes his discussion of "Ideology and the State" with an example of Christian religious ideology that illuminates the ideological workings of Puritan conversion. Like the predestined elect, "individuals are always-already subjects" even before birth (176), and the power of ideology to produce subjects conformable to the dominant interests, like the gift of grace, is "almost irresistible."[35] Like the regeneration of sainthood, the process of constructing and maintaining subjects in place is ongoing and is carried out by institutions such as the Church, "which concentrated within it not only religious functions, but also educational ones, and a large proportion of the functions of communications and 'culture'" (151). As the "dominant Ideological State Apparatus," the Church "recruits" or "transforms" individuals into subjects by a "very precise operation" that Althusser calls "*interpellation* or hailing," and that works like "the most commonplace everyday police (or other) hailing: 'Hey, you there!'" This is the spiritual calling by which God hails the individual by name and demands his obedience. By answering that call and recognizing himself specifically as called, by his "mere one-hundred-and-eighty-degree physical conversion, he becomes a *subject*" (174), because he accepts the place that ideology designates for him.

This process of interpellating individuals as subjects, the conversion of subjects into saints, "presupposes the 'existence' of a Unique and central Other Subject, in whose Name the religious ideology" functions (Althusser, 178). Scripture provides an example in the story of Moses, who liberated the Jews from physical slavery but imposed God's law upon them. Calling to Moses by name, God speaks and defines himself as the unique and absolute Subject, "he who is through himself and for himself ('I am that I am')"; by responding, Moses accepts the hail, and thus recognizes himself as a subject who is subjected to God, "*a subject through the Subject and subjected to the Subject*" (179; emphasis in original). These subjected subjects are God's mirrors, his reflections, as man was made in God's image and must conform to the image of his Son, "a mere subject 'forsaken' by him, . . . subject but Subject," in order to be "recognized" by God as his own on Judgment Day (179–80). This mutual recognition of subjects and Subject, the Puritan notion of covenant, is what Althusser calls "*doubly* specular" (180). It is constitutive of ideology and ensures its functioning because it guarantees the subjects' recognition of each other and the subject's recognition of himself—in the Other (181). Thus, subjects "work by themselves," internalizing ideology's interpellation as conscience.

The "mystery" of this rests, as Althusser points out, in the ambiguous term *subject*, which means both "a free subjectivity, a centre of initiatives, author of and responsible for its actions," and "a subjected being, who submits to a higher authority, and is therefore stripped of all freedom except that of freely accepting his submission" (182). John Winthrop located the same double meaning in Christian doctrine when he addressed the General Court of Massachusetts on the necessity of defeating democratic demands made by certain colonists and advocated instituting a limited civil liberty in an authoritarian state. He explained: "This liberty is maintained and exercised in a way of subjection to authority; it is of the same kind of liberty wherewith Christ hath made us free. The woman's own choice makes such a man her husband; yet being so chosen, he is her lord, and she is to be subject to him, yet in a way of liberty, not of bondage; and a true wife accounts her subjection her honor and freedom, and would not think her condition safe and free, but in her subjection to her husband's authority" (*Winthrop's Journal*, 2:239). Liberty is man's freedom to submit himself to God's higher power—here in the form of elected magistrates, who, being called by the voters, "have our authority from God, in way of an ordinance, such as hath the image of God eminently stamped upon it" (238). True to Puritan form, the most appropriate example Winthrop finds is woman's "freely" chosen subjection to her earthly husband, one that he himself experienced in his willing subjection to Christ, his spiritual husband.

It is important to note that Winthrop's conventional allusion to woman, like all the other uses of "woman," "bride," and "wife" cited in this introduction, is not *about* a real woman or specific women—women, unlike men, were not civilly enfranchised by visible sainthood and were not allowed a vote in churches until 1690, when they far outnumbered men—but constitutes what Alice Jardine designates "discourse *by*, *through*, *as* woman" (36). Jardine calls this "gynesis," the effect produced when "woman" is employed as a figure in discourse, used as the vehicle of man's contemplation, as the Other who makes possible his apprehension of interiority and subjectivity. "Gynesis as process," she finds, "has most certainly always been marginally at work in the West, especially in religious and literary texts" (63), and most recently shows up in postmodernism's dismantling of the "master narratives" of patriarchal culture. Puritanism, like the entire Judeo-Christian tradition, operates by way of dichotomies—time/space, good/evil, light/dark, spirit/flesh, same/other, father/mother—that are clearly gendered. Though these pairs are opposites, they are not equal, but hierarchized. Cultural power and authority, French postmodernist theorists broadly argue, depend upon the suppression, debasement, or appropriation of the female side of these dualities. In their radical rethinking of the Western tradition and its oppressive epistemology at whose center is the conscious, implicitly male subject, postmodernists explore the space outside of the conscious subject, its "nonknowledge," all that has been excluded, silenced, or rendered invisible. This space of otherness is, as I pointed out earlier, conceptualized as feminine. Thus, like Puritan saints who experience themselves in conversion as Brides of Christ and through the disempowerment that accompanies feminization gain a paradoxical sort of power, male deconstructors who speak by, through, as woman also gain a kind of power. For example, in her exploration of Jacques Derrida's relationship to the feminine, Gayatri Spivak argues that the male deconstructive philosopher cannot speak from his place as "Man"; since deconstruction rejects the notion of a unified, fully conscious, "transcendent" subject and demands that the philosopher reject this place as illusory, he must speak as "woman," from a position of *dis*placement (173, 179). Critical positions that reject the Cartesian subject require a similar displacement: reading and speaking *by*, *through*, *as* woman we can disrupt the logic of the official narratives and unsettle the symbolic structures of cultural authority.[36]

Postmodern theory displaces the feminine and revalorizes alterity, while Puritan doctrine appropriates and neutralizes them—the traditions differ in many crucial ways, not the least of which is the logocentrism of Puritanism that postmodern theory is committed to deconstructing. Both, however, come into being in response to historically specific cultural crises in legitimation, and both, rooted in textuality, address the perennial problem of interpretation. But while the gynesis of contemporary French theorists—an unsettling of paternal identity, narrative continuity, and traditional gender arrangements—is self-conscious and undertaken deliberately, the gynesis I have been tracing in Puritan discourse is largely unselfconscious and hardly oppositional.[37] In making the comparison, I only want to suggest, as do the many feminist critiques of postmodernism's "'masculine recuperation' of the feminine," that the patrimony of redeemed subjectivity continues. As Spivak points out, in the Western tradition of literature and philosophy "the discourse of man is in the metaphor of woman" (169).

Part of this legacy is the continuing effect of gynesis on women. "Woman" is staged rhetorically by male writers and thinkers who do not in any way address women (N. Miller, "Arachnologies," 271). Puritan doctrine and postmodern theory have at least this in common: despite their constant allusions to woman and the feminine, neither is very concerned with women, and both dismiss feminism: the first, as heretical and treasonous; the second, as passé or so mired in the liberalism of its origins as to be irrelevant.[38] Puritan women were regaled with exempla from biblically conceived notions of woman, the effect of which was to contain them socially. Have these models changed? If the space of alterity is "feminine," who or what determines what constitutes "feminine"? If "woman" is accepted as the only alternative position for subjectivity in a system that consists of man/woman, does this not keep intact all the binary opposites that debased woman in the first place? Theorizing woman as the male subject's anonymous Other, repressed unconscious, subversive counterpart, or negative space, merely reaffirms the universal nature of maleness, according to de Lauretis (*Alice Doesn't*, 161). Spivak finds real women doubly displaced from the position of speaking subjects because deconstructive discourse must both speak from the place of woman and use woman as an object or figure of its discourse; where "man can problematize but not fully disown his status as subject" (173), women cannot disown what they have never really or fully possessed. What I said earlier about seventeenth-century Puritan women applies as well to the contemporary woman writer and speaker: there is a difference between men speaking from the position of woman, and women speaking from a position that they already, in some sense, occupy.

In recent years feminist theory, working with the insights of Marxism, psychoanalysis, and deconstruction, has been exploring alternatives to this Protestant patrimony, theorizing female subjectiv*ities*—different from the universalized male subject of the liberal, individualist tradition and the decentered subject of postmodernism, but not their Other. In order to articulate a difference that is not an otherness we must deconstruct the binary oppositions on which the Cartesian model of the subject is based. It is more fruitful to talk about subjectivities, identities, and the positions—characterized by sex, class, race, culture, economics, sexual orientation, and a whole plethora of distinguishing marks—that subjects can occupy at various times in their lives. The challenge is to imagine gendered subjectivities that retain the specificity of individual experience, yet to resist the tempting illusions of fixed identity, unity, stability, transcendence, and noncontradiction. Central to this effort is the redefinition of "identity," not as the goal of self-consciousness or self-representation, not as a point, but as part of a process and an explicit strategy for the expression of differences that exist, as de Lauretis says, not only between men and woman, but among women and within women ("Issues," 9, 14)—and, I would add, among men and within men. The Puritan patrimony has exacted a heavy toll on men, a fact borne out by our present "crisis in masculinity."

The purpose of this study is to go back to a characteristically colonial Puritan "imaginative construct"—the paradigm of conversion—in order to trace out the assumptions that governed the conception and articulation of voice and identity in the early culture that has so informed our contemporary world.[39] This has meant framing the notion of subjectivity historically, putting it into the context of seventeenth-century Puritan doctrine and literary discourse. It has also meant reading texts primarily by men, and *re*reading them in the light of gender difference, reading against what Nancy Miller calls "the weave of indifferentiation" that obscures the marks of gendered subjectivity in order "to recover within representation the emblems of its construction" ("Arachnologies," 272). "One of the tasks of feminist criticism in the age of poststructuralism," she goes on to say, "is to read over the familiar texts of the library for the ideological support a culture supplies to its own self-representation" (287). The familiar and not-so-familiar texts of colonial New England have for a long time, it seems to me, needed such an "overreading."[40] If I take liberties with these texts, it is because I respect deconstruction's calling into question the "ideology of 'correct readings'" and so must fabricate "strategic 'misreadings'" (Spivak, 186) that disclose the penetralia of the American self-image.

My overreadings have led to a rereading of the "civil war" within the Puritan heart that supposedly shaped the "American self," our "myth of American exceptionalism," and the rhetorical tradition of our philosophy and literature. This study questions the uniformity of that "self." If the form of subjectivity demanded by Puritan doctrine and practice is, as I claim, hegemonic, then it discloses contradictions between the ideology of doctrine and people's social experiences, male as well as female. I focus primarily on lyric poetry produced in the New England colonies in the century beginning with the Great Migration and ending with the first waves of the Great Awakening, because sermons and treatises detail only the "official" and prescriptive versions of human experience. As Protestant poets in England and New England shaped the lyric into a powerful vehicle for the public dissemination and private exploration of their agonizing pilgrimage toward spiritual identity, they confronted the paradox of the believer: How can I do anything without usurping the authority that belongs only to God, and can only be gained by conceding that it is fully beyond my grasp? The appearance in lyric of a first-person speaker wrestling with all the intricacies of individual consciousness provides fruitful ground for the exploration of the politics of voice, positionality, and the problematics of identity: authority, intertextuality, inscription, prescription. Language, so central in the construction of subjectivities, allows for the exploration of paradoxes that are impossible in our daily, even in our religious, lives.

In my account of Puritan doctrine and colonial history, I have examined the language and imagery of Puritan conversion, especially as it was practiced in New England, as a narrative of masculine subjectivity, as a story by men about men and for men, but told in the metaphors of woman. Colonial Puritan poetry, written predominantly by men and members of the clergy, tells the same story. The following two chapters explore how the poetics of mainstream orthodox Puritan lyric, especially its preeminent public and private forms, accommodate the paradoxical demands of the logic of conversion.

Chapter 2 considers the most popular genre of Puritan poetry, the funeral elegy, which stands at the heart of this tradition. The spiritual pilgrimage of saints bound them inextricably to the communal errand of New England and solicited their conformity to a public model of sainthood epitomized by the powerful patriarchs of the first generation. For more than a century, Puritan writers could barely keep up with the demand for poems that mourned the passing of the founders and enshrined their pietistic examples in a form more easily accessible than the doctrinal language of sermons. Critics are embarrassed by the formulaic awkwardness of these poems, but I read them as important vehicles for the promotion and dissemination of the dominant ideological form of redeemed subjectivity, providing readers with examples of saints' "practical conformity" to God's will. This chapter consists of a close reading of one poem, John Fiske's elegy on John Cotton (1654), a representative example that captures a "son's" self-representation with respect to one of the eminent communal "fathers." Fiske epitomizes the dilemma of the *Puritan* poet: How to author a poem without implicitly insisting on one's authority; how to speak as if Another is speaking through you; how to write as a redeemed speaking subject. Through the use of rhetorical devices, especially anagram and apostrophe, Fiske transforms his own agency and creativity into legitimate, feminine passivity and the discovery of divine will, thus deflecting the authority of "voice" away from himself and onto God.

Edward Taylor, the best-known colonial poet, joins the Puritan experiment rather late, but experiences its wrenching contradictions with an intensity that equals, if it does not surpass, that of the founding fathers. Chapter 3 treats his *Preparatory Meditations* as the flowering of this orthodox tradition—and its culmination. Into the unchanging verse structure of over two hundred meditations he pours all the pent-up energy and violence generated by a lifelong effort to dismantle his fallen self so that God can reconstruct a redeemed subject in the cleared space. Like Fiske, he represents himself as willing his own objectification as he pleads to be "made" into God's instrument to be tuned and played, or a humble vessel containing a drop of God's grace. Although critical discussions have focused on Taylor's reliance upon sacramental theology for his dialectic of Christic identity and difference, I find that his sacramentalism dovetails into an encompassing obsession with the gynetic figure at the heart of Puritan piety—the Spouse of Christ. The extensive project of the *Preparatory Meditations* climaxes in a twelve-year-long celebratory exploration of the Song of Solomon, the biblical book that Puritans read as Christ's love song to his bride. Through this eschatological allegory, Taylor can identify with both the loving Christ and the beloved Spouse, but ultimately he voices his redeemed desire in her words.

Beset by internal contradictions, the Puritan orthodoxy met resistance from two groups within its boundaries that challenged its monolithic version of redeemed subjectivity: women, and radical sectarians. These disenfranchised and often-persecuted groups could not fully recognize themselves in the officially sanctioned paradigms of piety. Their responses suggest the form resistance took, and still takes, within patriarchy.

Anne Bradstreet was hardly a dissenter. We celebrate her today as the first New Englander to publish a volume of poetry, the first "American poet." Yet, because of her culture's proscriptions against the visibility of women, Bradstreet first had to be dragged into the glare of the public light against her will, and then had to be rendered ideologically acceptable. And so she became the "phenomenon" of the woman-as-poet. In keeping with this study's concern, not with the representation of women, but with the discursive deployment of the metaphor of woman, Chapter 4 focuses primarily on the phenomenon of Anne Bradstreet and the various positions that androcentric culture assumed, and continues to assume, by, through, and for her. Like Taylor's use of the persona of the desirous woman and his echoing of the Spouse's words in Canticles, John Berryman in his *Homage to Mistress Bradstreet* (1953) creates her, speaks through her words, and projects his own psychic necessities onto her. She is both his object and his subject: powerful and disarmed. Berryman's postmodern "tribute" acts openly on the attitudes implicit in the forces that first brought Anne Bradstreet to light and put her in her place. This story emerges in my analysis of the pages of male-authored material prefacing her volume, *The Tenth Muse* (1650), through which the woman poet's words must be read. Against this backdrop I place Bradstreet's own self-conscious poetic self-representations.

The orthodox conception of subjectivity, besides being male, is also white. Roger Williams's little-known poetry, which appears in his dictionary of the Narragansett dialect, *A Key to the Language of America* (1643), employs racial otherness to disclose the oppression of a single notion of redeemed subjectivity. Williams was New England's most articulate dissenter, one of the "deviants" against whom the Massachusetts Bay theocracy formed its increasingly conservative self-definition. What was worse, Williams was one of their own, a university-trained and deeply pious nonconformist whose separatist notions took Puritan reasoning to its logical conclusion. The New England clergy considered Williams's renunciation of class privileges and his refusal to accept a settled ministry as a betrayal. His mission to convert the Native Americans showed up their own hypocrisy and greed. In terse and acerbic poetry he exposes the immorality of his own world's religious ideology. The innovative structure of his dictionary sets up a dialogue between the two cultures that offers, through their interaction, the possibility of different forms of subjectivities, different "realities." Even as Williams appropriates and thus reduces the Native Americans to mediating figures in his ironic juxtapositions and clever manipulations of traditional biblical allegory, he cannot help but represent them as subjects in their own right. His rejection of any imposed form of subjectivity, despite his profoundly orthodox Calvinist beliefs, produces an "American" model of intersubjectivity.

By most accounts, the powerfully conservative Puritan ministry and magistracy neutralized and appropriated the radical resistance to which Williams gave refuge in his establishment of Providence Plantation. By ending with the heroic masquerades of Anne Bradstreet and the provocative implications of Roger Williams's little-known poetry, this study seems to point backwards, away from the complications of the Great Awakening and the upheavals of the revolutionary era. I have structured the study this way because I believe the cultural work that Edward Taylor accomplished in his celebrated verse is a cultural dead end. He is the product of fifty years of ideological consolidation. At a time of liberalization in Puritan doctrine and practice, he harks back to the first decades after the Great Migration, resisting the progressive innovations of Stoddardeanism and devising a poetics within the iconophobic discourse of Puritan theology that worked, practically unchanged, for over forty years. Despite critical speculations on his crypto-Catholicism, his sensual language and imagery, and his reluctance to publish his poetry, Taylor is the poet whom the founding Puritan fathers would have most eagerly embraced as one of their own. What we in the present can build upon are the critiques of this cultural consensus, critiques implicit in Bradstreet and explicit in Williams. The opportunity their works offer to explore gender and racial difference provides us with a critical perspective on the androcentrism and disturbing resilience of the Puritan patrimony—the effects of which are still very much with us.

The Paradox of
"Practical Conformity":
John Fiske's "Elegy"
on John Cotton

A severe and determined people like the original colonists embraced an aesthetic equally severe and determined. How appropriate, then, that the most popular genre in Puritan New England was the funeral elegy. Indeed, a large percentage of the rather startling amount of verse produced by the settlers struggling to survive in the new world reflects what Robert Henson identifies as "the Puritans' incessant elegiac activity" (26). The funeral elegy is a specialized form of occasional poem closely associated with lyric.[1] Its popularity stems from its satisfaction of several of the Puritan community's conflicting needs: to look backward in order to move forward; to acknowledge the individual, and individual piety, while reinforcing the sense of a collective mentality; to exploit loss as an admonition and yet reaffirm the communal mission. In a small and tightly controlled society of "visible saints" who believed in predestination, death provided the perfect occasion for a religious employment of poetry and the poeticizing of religious doctrine. As "our first coherent body of verse" (Henson, 26–27), the funeral elegy constituted a central vehicle for the promulgation of the dominant ideological form of redeemed subjectivity.

Elegies have traditionally been a common mode of commemorating the dead, but the specifically Puritan funeral elegy evolved to fulfill particular religious, social, and political needs, making its first "notable appearance," according to Astrid Schmitt–von Mühlenfels, "in England in 1646 at the death of the Earl of Essex, when a whole series of poems and broadsides were printed"; a similar wave of "verse lament" adopting the

English model overtook New England the following year, occasioned by the death of the beloved minister Thomas Hooker (49). The death of important cultural figures—for the English Puritans, leaders and revolutionary heroes; for the colonists, the first generation of founding fathers—brings the English Puritan elegy and its colonial cousin into prominence. The subsequent development of the genre in England and in its colony differs markedly.[2] What the two traditions share is the preservation of heroes and patriarchs for a restless and ambitious, though inherently conservative, middle class. In tracing the political and historical significance of the Puritan funeral elegy in the seventeenth century, John W. Draper concludes, "until Isaac Watts began to liberate nonconformity from the anti-poetic tenets of Calvin, and secured for the dissenter at least the privilege of a hymnology, the funeral elegy was practically the only poetry that his religion allowed him. . . . the sole artistic expression and literary record of the bourgeois mind" (92).

In New England, the "bourgeois mind" of the second generation enshrined the example of their energetic elders in what Henson calls the "thoughtful and deliberate social gesture" of the funeral elegy (11). This description reflects the current critical consensus on the social and public nature of the New England funeral elegy, which, according to critics, was meant "to honor the dead and instruct the living" (Bray, 27), "to lament and exhort in a public way" (Schmitt–von Mühlenfels, 49), "to clarify a society's ideals and make them seem desirable" (Henson, 26). While funeral elegies were written by both clergy and laypeople, as personal expressions of grief as well as didactic lessons for public edification, in general, critics find that for "the Puritan, the elegy was not a personal cry but a communal exercise" (Kenneth Silverman, 127). In a small, isolated, and strictly regimented community where, in contrast to the situation in England, the elegist knew his or her audience by faces and names and addressed a spiritual group as opposed to a political faction, every loss was finally a tribal loss (Silverman, 132).

Even William Scheick, who goes against this current by arguing that the English and colonial funeral elegies were not radically different, concedes that "funeral elegies are indeed principally didactic and communal, though not exclusively or even chiefly in New England" ("Tombless Virtue," 287). Citing the importance of "authorial context" in creating diverse types within the genre, he finds that "efforts to discern intrinsic

patterns within the New England funeral elegy as a literary mode prove
. . . problematic," and he cautions against treating them "collectively"
(287–88). Nevertheless, in discovering one pattern that distinguishes the
New England elegy from the English version, Scheick provides evidence,
not for the integrity of the genre as a literary mode, but for the consistency
of its discourse as a hegemonic cultural practice. Colonial elegists, he
argues, followed the lead of historians and biographers in creating "an
image of society as if it were a collective individual" (291). This pattern,
though "but one thematic strand" in a diverse genre, occurs most frequently in elegies on deceased ministers, where the "consoling communal
frame" implodes and the focus shifts to an image of a collective self
vulnerable to prophetic jeremiads (293). Scheick calls this type the "nonconsoling funeral elegy" (297). As texts, they disqualify themselves as
repositories of knowledge or consolation, exhorting their audiences to
turn their attention to the text within and conform to the model of redeemed subjectivity interiorized in the process of conversion. In merging
the ideology of a collective social self and a configuration of private
interior space, the nonconsoling elegy insists upon a regimentation of
selfhood to a strict social norm in which difference and otherness are
erased and subsumed.

While it is true that not all the subjects of elegies were ministers or
prominent men, the majority of elegies composed in New England in the
seventeenth century were written by men about men, thus reinforcing the
values of a patriarchal theocracy created by men and dominated by fathers.[3] For example, at the end of the century, when elegies still played a
vital social role, Cotton Mather characterized the tradition—of which he
was in some ways the final link—as an unbroken chain of clergymen's
deaths and poetic eulogies beginning with his grandfather, the Reverend
John Cotton: "*Cotton* Embalms great *Hooker*, *Norton* Him: And *Norton's*
Herse do's *Poet-Wilson* trim With Verses. *Mitchel* writes a Poem on The
Death of *Wilson*: and when *Mitchel's* gone, *Shepard* with fun'ral Lamentations gives Honor to Him: and at his Death receives The like from the
(*like-Maro*) Lofty Strain Of admirable *Oakes*" (*Ecclesiastes* [Boston, 1687];
quoted in Kenneth Silverman, 131). According to Mather's obsessive
filiopiety, the entwining of figure and elegiac discourse in the deaths and
lamentations of great ministers insures the very history and continuity of
the Puritan errand in New England.

Despite the diversity of types within the genre of the New England funeral elegy, the nonconsoling type, with its fundamentally social purpose, predominates, and its characteristic form reinforces its ideological function. Influenced by the English model as well as by the funeral sermon and religious biography, New England elegies were often structured with two parts conforming to the topoi of portraiture and exhortation. The portrait of the departed person traces out the course of the saint's salvation by showing how his or her earthly life recapitulates the stages of the Pauline paradigm of conversion outlined in Romans 8.29–30, the ideological implications of which are discussed at length above in Chapter 1: "For whom he did foreknow, he also did predestinate to be conformed to the image of his Son, that he might be the firstborn among many brethren. Moreover, whom he did predestinate, them he also called: and whom he called, them he also justified: and whom he justified, them he also glorified." The first and third of these stages, election and justification, had to be asserted because there were no outward signs of them. The other three stages—vocation, sanctification, and glorification—were thought to be demonstrable and in the elegy were represented by conversion, good works, and blissful dying (Henson, 12). Regaled with such a model, the audience was exhorted "to remember and imitate" (Henson, 26)—that is, to interiorize the model and conform to its paradoxical contours.[4]

The effect of such a procedure was to fit every life worthy of commemoration into the scripturally approved formula for religious experience by sacrificing intimate, realistic, or individualizing details for the ordered, consoling, expected shape of stereotype. Even differences of gender and social position were subsumed by the image of virtuous sainthood, which was basically a male spiritually feminized by redeemed subjectivity. "Convention was of its essence," Henson remarks about the Puritan handling of this form, yet the formula, abstraction, and repetition served crucial social and religious purposes: "indeed, the Pauline pattern seems both comprehensible and imitable in the elegies, where it is free of the technical jargon and exegetical subtleties that hang about it in sermons" (26). The conventions of the Puritan elegy trained and conditioned audiences already anxious about their individual and communal spiritual status. The portraiture sketched out the range of experiences acceptable in the prescribed morphology of conversion, and showed how these experiences could be interpreted within, or fitted to, a scriptural model that, as I have already argued, was especially contradictory for males. The exhortation rallied group guilt to the communal endeavor. In a "textual" life of a Puritan saint, then, the elegy is the lyric denouement of the conversion narrative's prose account.

To examine the representations of redeemed subjectivity as it was constructed by the discourse of the New England Puritan elegy is the purpose of this chapter. In doing so, I will suggest how the paradoxical demands made by the logic of the conversion process—the willing divestment of personal agency—are accommodated by the poetics of the most popular form of Puritan lyric. Colonial Puritan poets, like any visible saint with spiritual aspirations, wrestled with the lifelong paradoxes of the process of conversion, but they required a more immediate and, as it were, practical solution: how to position themselves so that the authority and presence that apparently accrue to the speaking subject in lyric discourse actually appear as God's. It is, perhaps, surprising that issues central to lyric are also central to the process of Puritan conversion, but both are cultural constructions that turn on the elements of voice, identity, subjectivity, and authority.[5] In the following discussion I will emphasize how the lyrical elements of elegy and a specifically Puritan understanding of conversion conspire in the representation of a historically specific notion of redeemed subjectivity, and how that representation is the central feature of a Puritan construction of masculinity. I will examine how, for example, through the figures and tropes of the Puritan elegy, the masculine poetic voice is haunted and finally dominated by other voices, which, in the process of conversion, feminize it. Following deconstructive investigations into the relation of writing and speech, we can see how this Puritan voice is not just invaded by inscription, but is founded upon divine Scripture. Spoken for and written over by God's Word, the male Puritan poet manifests the gynesis at the heart of Puritan conversion by speaking acceptably only when he speaks as woman—when he gives over speaking at all.

Because I want to look closely at the dynamics of New England elegiac discourse, I will focus my analysis primarily on one poem: John Fiske's elegy on John Cotton, composed shortly after Cotton's death in 1652.[6] This elegy is well within the mainstream tradition, illustrating characteristic features of the genre and of the religious doctrines that inform it, and, in fact, establishing some of the colonial elegy's peculiar conventions and tropes. Typically, its author was not primarily a poet, and because the poem served an occasional function it was never published. Nevertheless, Fiske's style and use of biblical metaphors—and, I would add, his orthodoxy—have led readers to regard him as a precursor of Edward Taylor (Bray, 27). I will also note some important connections between these two minister/poets who were both part of the Puritan clerical elite.

"Nothing in John Fiske's career distinguished him from the majority of his clerical contemporaries," comments Robert Pope, the editor of Fiske's *Notebook*, a thirty-year record of church activity and one of the few sources of conversion narratives given before congregations in New England in the seventeenth century (xxxviii). He was born in Suffolk, England, in 1601, and entered the ministry after studying with the eminent Puritan theologians at Cambridge. A nonconformist, he was harassed into giving up his parish and practiced medicine instead, until his emigration to Massachusetts in 1637. There, he was a schoolmaster, farmer, and physician—first in Charlestown, and then in Salem; in 1641 he was called to be the minister to a small new settlement in Wenham. Because of economic hardship, in 1655 he and many of his parishioners moved to Chelmsford, where he continued to serve as minister, though with increasing opposition from some factions in the new church there, until his death in 1677. Married to the same woman for forty-three years, he followed custom and remarried, choosing a widow in his congregation, only a few months after his wife's death. He was remembered for his devotion to his calling; at the end of his life, though weakened by illness and not able to make himself heard in the meetinghouse, he was carried in by the members and preached from his chair.[7]

Fiske was forty-four at the time of Cotton's death, part of the group of clergy that lived to see the demise of the energetic founders and the beginning of the so-called decline in Puritan piety of the 1660s and after. His elegy is a younger minister's commemoration of "A Father in our Israel," one of the "pillars" (ll. 8–9) of the Puritan theocracy, and it has more than a touch of both filiopiety and oedipal tension. Robert Pope gives as one motivation among several for Fiske's decision to emigrate, the recent death of his father (xxxviii)—a loss that patriarchal New England could amply fill. Fiske and his family arrived in Boston in 1637 "during the most hectic months of the Pequot War, an unsettling time in which to establish a new home in a strange land," according to Harrison Meserole (185–86); this was also the troubled time of the controversy that swirled around Anne Hutchinson. In the tumult, John Cotton, clearly the most renowned scholar of the first generation and a charismatic teacher, ran afoul of his fellow orthodox clergy for preaching what the Hutchinsonians and just about everyone else construed as a too-total reliance upon Spirit. This unshakable "Father" of the tribe emerged from the controversy "a marked man," who, as the Reverend Thomas Shepard fulminated in his private journal, "repents not, but is hid only" (Gura, 175).

It is not unlikely that Cotton's duplicitous role in the controversy made a strong impression on the recently arrived young clergyman, who was himself swept up in the tumult. Helping to fill the void left in the leadership of the independently minded Salem church in the wake of Roger Williams's sudden departure, Fiske got firsthand experience in the ideological subduing of a rebellious separatist faction. Cotton instigated Williams's departure and helped install in his place Hugh Peter, a minister comfortable with the nonseparating congregationalism of the reigning clergy in Boston. Fiske served as Peter's assistant. Williams called Cotton a conformist; a historian calls him "a crafty pragmatist" who, within three years of his arrival in Massachusetts, "saw the necessity of permanently altering his own ecclesiastical position to prevent more radical elements of society from gaining power" (Gura, 161). His reversals, especially during the antinomian debate, cast an ironic light on lines from Fiske's elegy that call attention to Cotton's doctrinal tenacity, such as "He who set fast to Truths so clossly knitt / As loosen him could ne're the keenest witt" (ll. 11–12), and to the pride that would not allow him to recant, such as "Woe to that knotty pride hee ne're subdude" (l. 73). Comparing these lines with the "facts" of Cotton's life suppressed by the standard formula of elegy portraiture discloses the airbrushing effect of this standardization.

The many elegies evoked by the death of a powerful figure like Cotton were also occasions for the expression of communal anxiety. As the Puritan experiment ripened, each loss of a minister, leader, or prominent person became a providential warning to the struggling Puritan churches against spiritual laxity. Each death was thought to cause a "gap" in the protective wall that enclosed the garden of the Puritans' New Jerusalem. In an elegy written twenty-five years after Fiske's, for example, Urian Oakes compares Thomas Shepard II to Leonidas at Thermopylae, "The man that stood i'the gap, to keep the pass / To stop the Troops of Judgement[s p]ushing on." Imbuing his fellow minister with heroic powers that make literal what in Fiske's elegy remains figurative (see, for example, line 72, where Cotton's death causes a "Breach"), Oakes declares: "This man the honour had to hold the hand / Of an incensed God against our Land" (Meserole, 212).[8] Only powerful parental figures could intervene so fearlessly and effectively between a wrathful God and his wayward people.

Behind the myth of "declension," historians of the early colonial period have uncovered evidence of a painful conflict between the original generation of Puritan settlers and their second- and third-generation offspring. Not only did "sons" feel inadequate, but apparently "fathers" encouraged those feelings. The whole dynamic is couched in masculinist terms of competitiveness and humiliation. Emory Elliott details how ministers exploited the occasion of loss "by envisioning the covenant as a family contract between God the Father and his New England sons with inheritance of earthly as well as spiritual reward at stake"; this imagery touched "the same fears and sense of inadequacy and shame that the parents had used to impose passivity, obedience, and subjection upon the children" (*Power*, 101). Fiske is not properly a child of the second generation because he was not born in New England, yet he comes of age under the tutelage of the first-generation fathers; his self-representations give evidence of this generational conflict. One of the most acute expressions of the anxiety produced by this conflict is the elegy on Thomas Dudley, lieutenant governor, and for one term governor, of the Massachusetts Bay Colony, and father of Anne Bradstreet:

> A death's head on your hand you neede not weare,
> A dying head you on your shoulders beare.
> You neede not one to mind you, you must dye,
> You in your name may spell mortalitye.
> Younge men may dye, but old men, these dye must,
> 'Twill not be long before you turne to dust.
> Before you turne to dust! ah! must! old! dye!
> What shall younge do, when old in dust do lye?
> When old in dust lye, what N. England doe?
> When old in dust doe lye, it's best dye too.
>
> (Meserole, 505)

Sent to Dudley in 1645 several years before his death, this poem articulates through its agonized redundancy the double fear of the second generation that haunts Puritan elegies: their dread of straying from the pious standard set by their obdurate elders, and the equally horrifying impossibility of escaping such a fate. Harold Jantz speculates that this elegy was composed by John Fiske (34).[9]

The "work of mourning," according to Peter Sacks's psychoanalytic paradigm of the genre, attempts to resolve issues of power, adequacy, authority, and oedipal ambivalence—forces at play in Fiske's elegy on Cotton. The psychoanalytic approach, interesting on its own merits, becomes even more provocative when we recall that the few psychoanalytic investigations of Puritan conversion consider it, at one extreme, as analogous to the resolution of the Oedipus complex; as an oedipal fantasy; or, in a less strictly Freudian view, as a communal fantasy of being reborn to a "better" parent who demands rigid self-control but encourages a childlike dependence. In all these theories conversion, as mourning, is involved with the formation of the superego; and all of them, as I have shown, ignore the specificity of the female.[10] Another way of generalizing the insights of Freudian psychology to Puritan spirituality is to say, as Sacks does of mourning (in his handling, also mainly a masculine tradition), that conversion puts saints through an experience of humiliation and self-effacement that amounts to castration or feminization, in order that they may gain a substitute power, the power of the father, and that the pleasure of submitting to a powerful parental figure is normative in our culture. Feelings of the most intense abjection coexist with momentary flashes of deific empowerment, purity, and love. The text of Fiske's elegy structurally enacts this combination of dismantling and enabling by means of two complementary poetic devices, anagram and apostrophe.

An anagram is formed by transposing the letters of a proper name into a phrase or motto. In ancient Greece Lycophron, one of the seven lyric poets, used anagram to flatter his royal patrons. Since the Middle Ages it has been a textual mode of religious exercise because the phrase or phrases produced by transposing the letters of the name were thought to reveal some hidden aspect or significance about its bearer. Walter Begley, a nineteenth-century English clergyman, compiled a "monumental" work entitled *Biblia Anagrammatica* (London, 1904) which contains almost fifteen thousand anagrams on the *Salutatio Angelica*, the six words spoken by the angel Gabriel to Mary announcing the Incarnation: "Ave Maria, gratia plena; Dominus tecum." Most of the anagrams were composed by Italian monks of the seventeenth century, one of whom alone produced three thousand pentameters and hexameters on the Salutation (Friedman and Friedman, 7). George Puttenham, in *The Arte of English Poesie* (1589), describes anagram scornfully as "a thing if it be done for pastime and exercise of the wit without superstition commendable inough and a meete study for Ladies, neither bringing them any great gayne nor any great losse, unless it be of idle time" (112).[11] Yet he mentions how Queen Elizabeth "took pleasure sometimes in desciphring of names, and hearing how divers Gentlemen of her Court had essayed but with no great felicite to make some delectable transpose of her Maiesties name," and he cannot resist producing two of his own anagrams upon the title of that worthy monarch, the prophetic value of which he does not entirely dismiss in his elaborate explanation (114–15).[12]

Anagram plays a central role in Puritan poetics, although critics disagree about its value and status.[13] R. H. Pearce argues that at least some Puritans regarded anagrams as prophetic (31), and Cotton Mather records, somewhat skeptically, the arguments of those who would "be willing to plead a *prescription* of a much higher and elder antiquity for them."[14] Respected ministers and scholars like John Wilson enthusiastically practiced this form of "discovering" divine messages in ordinary life, often reading several anagrams in the name of an eminent Puritan saint.[15] Robert Daly cites Cotton Mather's dismissive remarks on Wilson's well-known propensity for "*anagrammatizing*," calling it nothing more than "a *little sport of wit*"; if not prophecy, then at least moral edification, he concludes, drove the Puritan penchant for anagrams (150). The elegy to Thomas Dudley quoted above probably came into being because the writer "found" in the patriarch's name the monitory phrase of the poem's anagram, "ah! old, must dye," and could not resist playing out its providential message about his own keenly felt fears.[16] Still, Jonathan Edwards, writing in the afterglow of the Puritan heyday, took the divine signification of names as a *given* upon which he argued a typological view of the natural world, reasoning that "if God had so much regard to the names of persons, that they might signify things chiefly remarkable concerning them, why should we think he would not in His ordering the nature of things have respect to spiritual things so as to signify and represent them?" (49). For the Puritan, the insight derived from the anagram was part of God's "ordering" of the human realm, a means of communication fitted to the fallen human senses and available to human reason.

Elegies in which the motto discovered in the name of the deceased dictated the major theme or imagery of the poem were popular in New England for the first hundred years. Fiske, then, is in excellent company when he opens his elegy with this notation following the title:

$$
John \begin{cases} Cotton \\ Kotton \end{cases} \textit{after the old English writi'g}
$$

Anagr:

O, Honie knott

He fudges the spelling, substituting a "k" for a "c" and reading the "j" as an "i"; Puttenham fudges in a similar way and justifies it (see note 12 to this chapter). I have no explanation for the presence of the "e."[17] Fiske's manipulations bear out Meserole's point that "this sort of poetry was obviously facilitated by uninhibited seventeenth-century orthography" (xxx).[18] It seems clear, however, that Fiske "wanted" to read this particular phrase in Cotton's name, and cast about for an unobjectionable way to do so. If we peer behind the veil of naiveté often cast over theological explanations for Puritan poetics, we can find practical motivations behind their anagrammatic activity.

Orthodox Puritans of the mid-seventeenth century who composed poetry found themselves in a dilemma. They were forbidden by their strict reading of the Second Commandment to "create" images, and therefore they had to find, first, theologically legitimate means of generating poetic discourse rather than "creating" it, and, second, a position from which to speak not as willful subjects, but as willing objects.[19] Being restricted in so many other ways, Puritan poets evidently took great delight in the "proof" of divine inspiration they spied in their own ingenuity. More importantly, however, the anagram, operating at the level of the signifier and systematically antirepresentational, served as a strategy for circumventing the heresy they saw in any implicit claim to independent human creation.[20] Viewed in this way, the use of "anagrams as a method of discovering the Divine Will" does not "trivialize the concept of Revelation," as Hyatt Waggoner prissily fears (13–14), but ties this inscrutable force to a particular psycholinguistic mode that makes it available to inspired "reading." The Puritans' fascination with anagrams was part of an involvement in the materiality of textuality that encompassed their use of acrostics and shape poems and their incessant fondness for punning. Finding or producing fortuitous significances was their way of calling attention to God's presence on the very material level of names and words. Such a poetics enabled practitioners to write, not on the basis of their empowerment as writers, but as astute readers of God's Word and words; it allowed poets to exercise authority and ingenuity and yet deflect these dangerous acts of willfulness away from themselves and onto God. Far from being a provincial or anachronistic or unsophisticated mode, anagram has survived the gaucheries of colonial New England to become the figure *par excellence* of the materiality of words celebrated by the French "New (and 'New New') Novelists" (L. Higgins, 473).[21]

While anagram calls attention to the materiality of signifiers and, in elegy, the crucial "signifiers" of election, apostrophe is the figure in lyric that calls attention to voice. Recent attempts to resituate the genre of lyric in the light of postmodern theory have highlighted apostrophe as "the figure of all that is most radical, embarrassing, pretentious, and mystificatory in the lyric, even seeking to identify apostrophe with lyric itself" (Culler, *Pursuit*, 137). The heightened speech of apostrophe, where the poet literally "turns away" (its meaning in Greek) from the audience to address an absent or dead person or inanimate object, is a stock convention of elegy. By virtue of the initiating anagram, "O Honie knott," Fiske's elegy is cast entirely in the form of an apostrophe to the anagrammatized Cotton and reiterates invocation at crucial moments in the poem (ll. 2, 29, 69, 95). The function of apostrophe in elegy as well as in the ode (the form of lyric where apostrophe predominates), according to Jonathan Culler, is to establish the identity of the speaker as a poetical and prophetic voice (*Pursuit*, 142). The speaker calls upon a natural object or a dead person in possession of desirable powers as if they were subjects. Not only does this dramatize the speaker's ability to call—an assertion of voicing, acting, and willing—but it establishes a discursive relationship with an object-called-upon-as-subject, which helps constitute the poetic speaker's identity. "Thus," Culler remarks, "invocation is a figure of vocation" (142). He refers to poetic vocation, but we can read apostrophic discourse theologically as well, to imply spiritual vocation. The *Oxford English Dictionary* (*OED*) indicates that sixteenth- and seventeenth-century writers used the word "conversion" in a rhetorical sense as an equivalent for the figure of apostrophe, both involving a "turning" of attention. Walter Schindler, examining Milton's invocations, argues that during the Reformation, with its revival of the Psalter, invocation becomes synonymous with prayer, and is a preparation for divine response, the most dramatic being God's call to spiritual vocation (10). The Puritans make a similar association when they regard poetic inspiration as an index of divine grace.

But the conversion that spiritual vocation initiates, I have argued, requires the rejection of fallen subjectivity and an ambivalent attitude toward individual autonomy. Sanctification, the second conventional stroke in elegy's portraiture, according to Samuel Willard, gives men "Power or Ability" only to "Glorify God by practical conformity to his Revealed Will" (Sermon 131, "A Compleat Body of Divinity," 495; quoted in Henson, 14). The saint is made powerful in order to conform to God's will, not to exercise his or her own. Apostrophe as a (fictive) procedure that confers voice, power, and subjectivity would appear to counteract the deflection of autonomy and willfulness located in anagram. But Fiske, through his anagram, calls upon what is and is not Cotton's proper name; in apostrophizing the anagrammatized name, the poet invokes not the dead person but a divinely transposed phrase that stands for Cotton in his literally and spiritually converted state. Fiske's constitution of his voice and power through the invocation of "honie knott" identifies him with a powerful speaker whose power derives from the thoroughness of his willing submission to God's will. Cotton as "honie knott" is (represented as) the paradox of spiritual conversion.

To establish his own identity as spiritually adequate—that is, as elect—Fiske must identify with Cotton; not, however, as the living or recently deceased subject of the elegy, but as a figure of speech: the converted, anagrammatized object. Paul de Man explains this rhetorical strategy when he points out that the "latent threat" inhabiting figures like prosopopoeia, which make the dead or inanimate speak, is that, according to the symmetrical structure of the trope, "the living are struck dumb, frozen in their own death" ("Autobiography as De-facement," 928). This muteness and solicitation of death—the death of agency—are precisely what, in the logic of redeemed subjectivity, Fiske must strive to achieve: saints were exhorted to be "dead" to the world, weaned from its values, silent the better to hear God's voice, passive the better to do his work. Similarly, Anne Bradstreet recognized that in the face of the inexplicable death of her infant grandson, the only acceptable—but emotionally unsatisfactory, not to mention aesthetically paralyzing—posture, was silence: "With dreadful awe before Him let's be mute," she declares, quickly qualifying her verbal abdication of power with the ambiguous conclusion of the couplet: "Such was His will, but why, let's not dispute" (*Works*, 237, ll. 9–10).

In Fiske's elegy, this abdication of inventive power takes the form of willing self-objectification, a process that begins at the very start of the elegy, where the poet's employment of the conventional topos of modesty amounts to a simultaneous acknowledgment and undermining of the constitutive nature of apostrophe:

> With Joy erst while, (when knotty doubts arose)
> To Thee we calld, o Sir, the knott disclose:
> But now o and alasse to thee to call
> In vayne tis thou no Answer give or shall.
> Could loud Shrickes, could crys recall thee back
> From deaths estate we wold our eye ne're slack
> O, this our greife it is, lament shall we
> A Father in our Israel's ceas't to be
>
> (ll. 1–8)

Calling was effectual only in the past, when Cotton lived and was called upon directly and respectfully as "Sir" to dispel "knotty doubts" and "disclose" the "knott" of dissension and uncertainty. It is vain, Fiske asserts, to apostrophize him now because he cannot answer; nor can the "shrickes" and "crys" of the bereft church members "recall" their dead leader. As if enacting the failure of apostrophe, these lines turn the "O" of their address into the conventional "o and alasse" of grief that has no apparent object. But, as de Man concludes, "Death is a displaced name for a linguistic predicament" (930). The formal lament for Cotton demonstrates that it is not apostrophe that is ineffectual, but the apostrophizing of Cotton's proper name.

I implied earlier that Fiske strained the conventions of the anagram to produce his felicitous motto; his use of it suggests why. The *OED* lists at least twenty literal and figurative meanings for the word "knott" that were current in the seventeenth century, several of which Fiske exploits. As far as I have been able to tell, however, the conjunction of the two words was the poet's/God's invention. Both words have extensive networks of connotations. Used separately and together, "honie" and "knott" provide the controlling imagery in the portraiture section that evokes Cotton and an entire atmosphere associated with him.[22] The use of "knott" in the first two lines quoted above gives an example of Fiske's poetic technique. The theological doubts that Cotton quelled were "knotty" like their untangler. The punning aspect of this technique is related to anagram: puns retain the outward order of the word, while making use of shifts at the level of meaning. They are a common feature of Puritan style. In the exhortation section of the elegy, Fiske's punning on Cotton's name takes the place of anagram.[23] By the way in which "knott" can act as noun, verb, and modifier, we know we have entered a linguistic realm where signifier and signified, while not quite set free, seem more loosely tied (sorry!) to strict—modern critics would say, tasteful—rules of figurative elaboration. "Poetic demand," Meserole explains, "was for the greatest number of meanings to be discerned from the word and yet made applicable to the person who was subject of the poem"; the poet constructed "a fugue of meanings from a single word," and so, "since it pushed words to the very limits of usage, the anagram can be called Baroque" (187). But what is the point of Fiske's baroque elaboration? Upon closer examination, we will see that it serves to unveil the figure behind the figure (really, the disfigurement) of the anagram, the face behind the defacement of autobiography, which deprives as it restores (de Man, "Autobiography as Defacement," 930), providing the ultimate model of redeemed subjectivity.

The imagery related to "honie knott" touches every aspect of Cotton's physical, spiritual, and figurative existence and shows them all to be interconnected, pointing to a single frame of reference—Christ. For example, in the opening section of the portrait, Cotton is described as "Hee who his Flesh together bound ful-fast / No knott more sure whilest his life did last" (ll. 13–14), a crabbed passage that suggests Cotton's sturdy hold on life or his ability to subdue his "Flesh"—his fallen desires. The capitalization of "Flesh" and the referential indeterminacy of "Hee" and "his" suggest Christ's similar knot of flesh, the miracle of his incarnation, which will redeem the fallen body. A few lines later occurs the requisite "blissful death" that the Puritans took as a sign of salvation: "'Twixt whose life, death, the most sweete harmony" (l. 18). The development of Cotton as exemplar culminates in the conventional glimpse of the dead body that ends the portrait, filtered, of course, through the controlling imagery: "This knott so we have seen lien broknly / By knotts so breathlesse, so crookt, crackt" (ll. 63–64). There is a suggestion here of an almost Christlike martyrdom at the hands of Cotton's faithless community. In other elegies, Fiske makes this more explicit, as in his lament for Nathaniel Rogers, where he states bluntly, "Our sins they are that then Him hastned hence" (Jantz, 129). As the century advances, this topos becomes conventional and more dramatic. For example, Oakes cries "Our sins have slain our *Shepard!*" (Meserole, 219). In order to get the full impact of the layers of meaning woven into this moment of communal visualization and communal guilt, we need to look at the associations built up through the images of honey and knot.

Jantz points out that Fiske's anagram contains the two salient features of Cotton's character that the poet will develop in his portrait: his personal charm, and his subtle intelligence (32). Cotton is figured as a cluster of grapes, a knot or clot of honey in a hive, a garden plot—all of which suggest fruitfulness, fertility, and a regenerative spiritual power intensified by the concentration of the delicious substance, as in this metaphor for the precious man: "we as in a honi-comb a knott / Of Hony sweete, here had such sweetenes Gott" (ll. 21–22). Puns abound as the poet plays on the meanings of "comb" and "knot" in the hair, and on the Germanic word "Gott" for God, reinforced by the capitalization. The implication is that Cotton, like naturally arising honey, types out the sweetness of God, a kind of communal source of grace and delight.

Sweetness indicates divine and saving grace, while the knot stands for strength, as in this classical allusion for Cotton's spiritual worth : "A gurdeon knot of sweetest graces as / He who set fast to Truths so clossly knitt / As loosen him could ne're the keenest witt" (ll. 10–12). A "guerdon," according to the *OED*, was a poetical term for a reward, recompense, or requital, and thus it associates Cotton with the great redemptive gift of Christ.[24] The way Fiske uses the term suggests simultaneously the strength of the "Gordian knot," which according to myth could be untied only by the next king of Asia and was cut by the sword of Alexander the Great. Thus, the figure expresses both the "sweetest graces" intricately bound up in Cotton's Christlike character, and the tenacity with which he

clings to the truths of revelation despite the attempts of the "keenest witt"
to loosen his hold.

Presenting Cotton's extensive learning brought forth some of Fiske's
best puns and betrayed his worst fears. Cotton is the one "who the knotts
of Truth, of Mysteries / Sacred, most cleerely did ope 'fore our eyes" (ll.
15–16). His was an intellectual ability "sweetened" with the honey of
saving grace: "Knotts now adayes affrayd of are most men / Of Hony if
expose'd feare none would then / I guesse why knotty Learning downe
does goe / 'Twould not, if as in him 'twere sweetned soe" (ll. 43–46). I
speculated earlier that these references to Cotton's triumph over heretical
forces were an indirect gloss on his duplicitous role in the antinomian
controversy, for which the picture of his unassailable righteousness and
zeal had to compensate. Toward the end of the portrait, Cotton is remembered primarily for his ability to stifle discontent through brilliant argument: "Hee tho invincible thrô softnes did / The knottiest peeces calme
and cleave amid / Such was hee of such use in these last dayes / Whose
want bewayle, o, and alas alwaies" (ll. 59–62). These hints of dissent
within the Puritan ranks prepare the reader for the exhortation in the
second part of the elegy.

The terms Fiske chooses (or pretends to discover) also make an implicit case for Cotton's orthodoxy, a case designed to put to rest whatever
doubts may linger among those who recalled Cotton's nearly disastrous
association with the antinomian Mistress Hutchinson. "Honey" is associated with the biblical description of Canaan as the "land of milk and
honey." More specifically, both honey and knot are related to trees and
form part of the "Tree of Life" imagery developed at length in the poetry
of Edward Taylor. Fiske extolls Cotton as

> A vine tree seene, a plant of Gods owne hand
> In it this knott of sweetest parts did stand.
> The knott in place sublime: most eminent
> As, his, no Branch could challeng like extent
>
> (ll. 33–36)

In this compressed passage, Cotton is figured as the fruit of a grapevine
planted by God and as a knot in the wood of a tree from which a branch
grows. James Bray discovers in the first two lines an allusion to Cotton's
own work, *A Brief Exposition of Canticles* (London, 1649), where he used

the metaphor of "clusters of vine-grapes" to describe New England's ministers, including himself (227; quoted in Bray, 29). Typologically, this connects the New England ministry with the spiritual fertility symbolized by the giant grape cluster carried out of Canaan by the scouts and brought to Moses. It also alludes to the breasts of the beloved in Canticles, which "shall be as clusters of the vine" (7:8), a popular image of the spiritual "nourishment" dispensed by God's ministers of the Word. The lines also point to Cotton's connection with Christ, who styles himself "the true vine" (John 15:1). In comforting his disciples, Jesus continues the metaphor, saying, "my Father is the husbandman" and "ye are the branches. He that abideth in me, and I in him, the same bringeth forth much fruit" (John 15:1–5). In the elaboration of the knot image Cotton is compared to Christ, the "most eminent . . . Branch" to grow from the knot or graft upon God's tree of life, which, according to Bray, represents the Church (29). This tree takes us from the Garden of Eden through the Crucifixion to the Last Judgment (see also Revelation 14:18 for apocalyptic images of grape clusters). Just as on earth no one could match the "extent" of Cotton's privileged access to God, so in heaven Christ occupies the "place sublime" to which (in glorification, the last step in the process of salvation) Samuel Willard claimed the souls of believers on their death immediately pass (Henson, 22).[25]

The meanings and values associated with the words of the anagram are not static; Fiske develops Cotton's portrait following Ramist logic, which insists upon the systematic treatment of a subject through dichotomy. According to this mode of discourse, writers observed and then divided their subjects into "arguments," which were then analyzed and arrayed in antithetical pairs. It was a didactic method aimed at discovering and applying the "truth" God had already placed in the world for humans to discover; whatever its merits or demerits, it provided Puritan writers with a practical method, consistent with their theology, for the apparent production, rather than the creation, of discourse.[26]

In Fiske's elegy, the antithetical presentation sets up an alternating rhythm. For example, when the account of the marks of salvation concludes with the stock lament, "Even hee who such a one, is ceas'd to bee" (l. 17), the focus shifts to the negative connotations of the key word: "Knotts we doe meet with many a cue daily / Which crabbed anggry tough unpleasing bee" (ll. 19–20). "But," the poet counters, Cotton is extraordinary, a "knott / Of Hony sweete" like a "honi-comb" (ll. 21–22). Still bringing up disturbing associations of knots in nature and allowing the sounds in the key word to transmute, the poet continues, "The knotts and knobbs that on the Trees doe grow / The bitterest excressences we know" (ll. 23–24). In subsequent lines this obscure reference turns from natural trees into the typological "vine tree" planted by God carrying the branch that is both Cotton and Christ, as discussed above. The next passage brings out the most negative associations and provides a corrective spiritual interpretation:

> The knott sometimes seems a deformity
> It's a mistake, tho such be light set by
> The knott it is the Joynt, the strength of parts
> The bodies-beauty, so this knott out-starts
> What others in that place, they ought to bee
> Even such a knott exemplar'ly was hee
>
> (ll. 37–42)

That which stands so far above the common run, Fiske suggests, may seem deformed, out of place, but as a "joynt" the knot is a point of connection that permits articulation: movement, cohesion, and "the bodies-beauty." Cotton functioned in the church as a well-designed joint. He stood out as an example for others and filled a high, important place, the joint between the human and divine, like the mediator Christ.

Harold Jantz recognizes in this justification of knots "an illuminating epigram on Baroque aesthetics" (32), which are knotty, tangled, and apparently deformed, but which reflect a view of the world in which every disparate thing can be encompassed by and related to the focal point—in this case, Christ. To elaborate the central images as widely and complexly as possible, and then to bring all the dispersed material under one organizing head, displayed not only the skill of the poet, but the existence of a "transcendent signified" behind all words. Michael Clark lights upon Fiske's image of the "honeyed knott" to stand for the transcendent materiality of Puritan aesthetics, which forms "a dialectic" between visible and invisible worlds, "not a contradiction" ("Honeyed Knot," 76). Ramist dichotomizing was extended by Fiske's baroque technique, producing what Northrop Frye identifies as a structure of "apocalyptic" metaphor "in which everything is potentially identical with everything else, as though all things were inside a single infinite body," and "the conception of 'Christ' unites . . . all categories in identity" (*Anatomy of Criticism*, 136, 141). For example, the individual words of the anagram create an antithesis of sweetness and strength, which has a biblical parallel in the figure of Samson (Judg. 14). When applied to the saint, these opposites represent the conventional complementary qualities of love and zeal thought to characterize the "practical conformity" of humans to God's will (Henson, 15), the two major strokes of the second half of the portrait. "Meeknes Humility forbearance too / This lovely knott to love the most did woe" (ll. 47–48), the poet declares, further emphasizing Cotton's "charity his wisdom meeknes eke" (l. 57). Patience, submission, even passivity are the necessary complements of knotty strength, incisive intellect, and apparent deformity. According to Kenneth Silverman, the "duplicity" expressed by the anagram is manifested in all aspects of Puritan elegiac discourse: in "a deliberate awkwardness" of tone and syntax, "a fervently glad distress," and the combination of gentleness and ferocity in "the idealized great man"; this pervading sense of the knottiness of fallen human existence, sweetened by the honied presence of divine grace, imbues not only Fiske's elegy but "nearly everything the Puritans wrote" (127).

This principle of dichotomy extends to include the opposite meanings of the words of the anagram themselves. Knots, from the opening of the elegy, have signified difficulty and darkness. As Fiske muses on the nature of the sin in the Puritan community that "caused" Cotton's death, he speaks in the metaphoric language of his theme: "This knott thereof so surfetted we see / By hony surfetted we know som bee" (ll. 65–66), a sentiment echoed by Anne Bradstreet in her "Meditations Divine and Moral": "Sweet words are like honey: a little may refresh, but too much gluts the stomach" (Hensley, 273). Silverman suggests that the image of the "knott" provides Fiske with an epistemological "theory" of God's inscrutability: "The course of human events, as man looks upon it to determine its causes, is labyrinthine and perplexing, a knot. . . . What is given to man as a dense tangle is in God's mind, His Hidden Will, a beautiful plan that man cannot understand" (126). Knots, like cryptograms, signify sites of spiritual darkness, which, when illumined, are beautiful revelations of the divine will. Those who can bring light to this darkness—mediators, explicators, and examples like Cotton—disclose the sweetness or spiritual grace hidden in knots. Cotton's words, therefore, contained not merely the sweetness of flattery but the nectar of grace. To be surfeited with such honey boded ill indeed.

Finally, through this method of opposition, Fiske arrives at the paradox that is the emblem of the ideology of "practical conformity": "Hee tho invincible thrô softnes did / The knottiest peeces calme and cleave amid" (ll. 59–60). Cotton himself is the knot or paradox. Represented as invincible in his faith, his perseverance, his zeal—in contemporary parlance, a soldier for Christ—he nevertheless conquered, reconciled, and converted the "knottiest" or most difficult elements threatening the Puritan errand with patience, gentleness, and love. In a similar, but less effective, way, Benjamin Woodbridge's elegy on Cotton opens by developing the paradoxical qualities of this saint:

> Here lies magnanimous Humility,
> Majesty, Meekness; Christian Apathy
> On soft Affections: Liberty in thrall;
> A Noble Spirit, Servant unto all.
> Learnings great Master-piece; who yet would sit
> As a Disciple at his Schollars feet.
> A simple Serpent, or Serpentine Dove,
> Made up of Wisdome, Innocence, and Love.
>   (ll. 1–8; in Meserole, 410)

Never mind the impossibility, or at the least difficulty, of achieving such a state of contradiction. In other venues, Puritan divines acknowledged the "warfare" between sin and grace that characterizes the continuous process of sanctification in the believer's life. In the Puritan elegy, however, even the "difficult cases" like John Norton were made to fit the ideal of zeal tendered with love.[27]

The conversion of stubborn, hardened, or knotted hearts was the business of Puritan ministers, and their medium was language. Woodbridge points out that Cotton's paradoxical nature produced extraordinary oratorical effects: "Spake many Tongues in one: one Voice and Sense / Wrought Joy and Sorrow, Fear and Confidence" (ll. 43–44; in Meserole, 411). Likewise, an extrapolation of the anagram produces a metaphor for Cotton's style as well as for his pastoral abilities:

When knotty theames and paynes some meet with then
As knotty and uncouth their tongue and pen
So 'twas not heere, he caus'd us understand
And tast the sweetnes of the knott in hand.
When knotty querks and quiddities broacht were
By witt of man he sweetely Breathed there.

(ll. 51–56)

These lines imply that Cotton's style of writing and oratory are the opposite of "knotty and uncouth." Later in the elegy, denouncing the increasingly worldly tastes of Puritan Boston, where Cotton can no longer
exercise a mitigating influence, Fiske asks, "shall playne preaching be
accounted bad"? (l. 86). "Plain," the label critics customarily give to colonial Puritan writing, describes an epistemology as well as a literary style,
for Fiske's lines also imply that style is a reflection of content as well as the
state of the speaker's soul. What is "knotty" here are "theames and
paynes," which produce a dense, mystifying, confusing style. Cotton's
style allows his audience to "tast the sweetnes" of knotty religious doctrine
by facilitating their understanding. So committed was he to his ministerial
mission that he "Left none that loved light, in knotts to seeke" (l. 58). But
the imagery of taste specifically alludes to the spiritual efficacy of Cotton's
style. To say that his sermons tasted sweet implies that, like the sacrament,
they liberally dispensed the saving Word of God and helped the soul in
the work of regeneration. These rhetorical skills were considered a reflection of his sanctified soul, and of the harmony between his internal state
and its external manifestations. Thus, the passage leaves us with a God-
like image of Cotton breathing a language sweetened with divine grace
over contentious doubters. By contrast, Fiske's own self-consciously knotty style suggests that he has not yet attained such a balance, that he is still
in the process of regeneration, merely a "lisping child" in relation to this
"Father in our Israel."[28]

By the end of the portrait section, some seventy lines long, Cotton's
imitation of Christ in terms of the traditional *imitatio Christi*, and his
identification with Christ as the mediator, have been established in countless ways. Thus, when the elegist calls upon his audience to view one last
time "This knott . . . lien broknly" (l. 63), the suggestion of Christ's
ultimate sacrifice is inevitable and readily understood. This moment of

group consciousness climaxes in the only invocation of the full anagram in the poem (the other one is the announcement of the anagram in the title):

> O knott of Hony most delightfull when
> Thou livd'st, thi death a sad presage hath ben
> Have Ben? yea is, and is, and is alas
> For woe to us, so greate a Breach when was
>
> (ll. 69–72)

These lines are the emotional heart of the elegy. The poet calls upon the lost saint as an anagram, a figure of speech, giving him the status of an object rather than a subject. Unlike the opening of the elegy, where calling to the dead fails, here apostrophe achieves a moment of success. Lines 69 and 70, though they describe the delight experienced by the community in the past when Cotton lived, exist in what Culler calls a "timeless present," which he finds "is better seen as a temporality of writing . . . a special temporality which is the set of all moments at which writing can say 'now'" (*Pursuit*, 149). To apostrophize the hony knott is different from calling upon the living minister with the childlike cry "o Sir," for that was truly in the past. This apostrophe, mediated by anagram and by the figurative activity that precedes it, lifts its speaker out of the paradigmatic story of conversion it has just told in the portrait section and the apocalyptic denouement it fears and expresses in the exhortation. This moment of fictive discourse with a potential presence also constitutes the only consolation offered in this elegy.

A return to the present and to the implications of this loss is inevitable. As if in a dream, only half-listening to his own words, the poet catches the meaning of "hath ben," asks incredulously, "Have Ben?" and then hammers home the immediacy of the narrative present (as opposed to the fictive apostrophic present) with the triple repetition of the present-tense verb, like strokes nailing down the coffin lid.[29] Thus begins the conventional exhortation. Cotton's death is like the loss of a vital stone in the wall that Puritan New England built to protect itself from God's wrath and from the threats of infidels and apostates, both within and without. This language describes a vulnerable collective self obsessed with integrity, purity, conformity, and the insulation of the "body politic" of the theocratic commonwealth. Into this breach or gap must step a successor or heir; one of the traditional functions of elegy is to indicate the successor, but this text betrays its traditional function by presenting the issue of continuity as problematic.[30] So, for the remainder of the elegy, the audience confronts a wound (an old meaning of "breach") from which its spiritual life blood flows unchecked. Interpreting this loss as a "sad presage," Fiske bewails the internal threats he senses in a series of lines beginning with the word "Woe": the truths of scripture dispensed by Cotton will be ignored, factions will develop, unrighteous ways will dominate, and warnings will not be heeded (ll. 74–77). These exhortations are addressed to others ("Woe to them . . . Woe they . . ."), but in summing up Fiske includes himself and his entire audience: "Woe to us all if mercy us forsake" (l. 78)—that is, if God withdraws his merciful and tolerant attitude toward New England, now that one of its powerful intermediaries is gone.

As if to mark the shift from portraiture to exhortation, the metaphor of the hony knott drops away and Fiske introduces another figure for the dead saint, an extended pun on the name "Cotton":

A Mercy once New England thou hast had
(You Boston cheifly) in thi Cotton clad
Some 'gan to count't too meane a dresse and sought
Silk Velvetts Taffeties best could be bought
These last will soyle, if first doe soyle also
How can we think but Naked we shall goe

(ll. 79–84)

Fiske's punning is admirable; he even finds in the name evidence of Cotton's "plain" preaching, which he fears is going out of "fashion," and so he asks, "Must silken witts, must velvet tongues be had" (l. 85). But the point of his punning is its constancy and seriousness. To be "clad in Cotton" is to be dressed with mercy, clothed with Christ. Line 84 cautions all Puritans to heed the words of the Preacher, remembering that fine clothes cannot hide their original spiritual nakedness, that consolation is not to be found in material comforts: "As he came forth of his mother's womb, naked shall he return to go as he came, and shall take nothing of his labour" (Eccles. 5:15).[31]

"I feare a famine," the poet continues, speaking of the spiritual famine bound to follow the loss of those nurturing breasts, the great ministers of the first generation. It is a loss that New England Puritans felt to be

analogous to the loss of the early church fathers—of Paul, Simon, Stephen, the "nursemaids" of the church the Puritans claimed they had
recovered and reestablished. In a rare use of "I," Fiske expresses his own
fears for New England, and in the remaining lines of the elegy he turns
his attention to himself, or so it seems. I quote the passage at length in
order to be able to examine it closely:

I feare a famine, pinching times t'ensue
Time Such may have, slighted mercy to Rue
My wakened muse to rest, my moystned pen
Mye eye, my hearte which powred out this have ben
Cease try no more, for Hee hath gayn'd his prize
His heavenly mansion 'bove the starry skie
Returne thee home and wayle the evills there
Repent breake off thi sins Jehovah feare

   O Jehovah feare: this will thi wisdom bee
   And thou his waies of mercy yet maust see
   Returne thou mee;   And turned bie
   Lord unto thee;   even so shall I.
               Jo: Fiske

                 (ll. 87–99)

The elegy concludes on the word "I." By emphasizing the first-person
pronoun and the individual voice and view, Fiske invites an examination
into the elegy's dynamics of positionality.

Putting aside for a moment the poet's strategies of identification with
his subject, the location of his voice with regard to his audience, while
varied throughout the poem, is fairly clear until the end. Throughout
most of the portraiture, he includes himself in the "we" of eager solicitors
of Cotton's vast learning and bereft mourners. This is standard; Kenneth
Silverman remarks that Fiske's elegy on Samuel Sharpe "opens with the
New England elegy's quint-essential phrase: 'Us saies,'" (127)—the solitary poet speaking in the voice of the community, or the communal voice
speaking through a self-designated representative. Shifts in the equation
occur when, for example, the poet holds up Cotton for the group's inspec-
tion and addresses his audience as "yee," or "You Boston," clearly separating himself from his auditors for didactic purposes. In the ritual wail,

the poetic speaker shifts back and forth between lamenting the loss to "us" and fearing the existence of "them"—an unspecified though contentious faction hostile to Cotton, and thus to the "New England Way," who must be suppressed. The most radical shift is not one of perspective but of address, the apostrophes, which turn away from the audience and speak directly to the deceased, but are still spoken by the communal voice ("O knott of Hony / . . . thi death a sad presage . . . is alas / For woe to *us*" [ll. 69–72]).[32] Only twice does the poet say "I" in the body of the poem, both times to articulate his own fear and lend emphasis to it. The unique self-presentation of the elegy's finale, however, brings us to a consideration of the effect of the poet's identification with his "subject."

The only reference to the poet's muse occurs in this last section. The muse as a figure of poetic inspiration was commonplace even in the theologically grounded poetry of the colonial Puritans, and calling upon muses or rejecting their help became popular in elegies as the century waned. Its appearance here seems incongruous because it calls attention to the individuality of the poet's endeavor and his instruments of writing: "My . . . muse, my moystned pen / mye eye, my hearte" (ll. 89–90). The emphasis falls upon "my," where before the speaker was scrupulously part of the tribe. In apostrophizing his exhausted muse, putting it to rest and begging, "Cease try no more," the poet signals the conventional end of mourning, which here signals the completion of the Pauline paradigm. His mourning muse can cease "for Hee hath gayn'd his prize / His heavenly mansion 'bove the starry skie" (ll. 91–92); Cotton has been glorified, the third and final step in the elegy's representation of the process of salvation.

In the saint's glorification lies his reward, the metaphor for which is latent in the theme-word "knott." Knots commonly stood for ties that bind and join—especially the marriage knot, which was a popular Puritan metaphor for the spiritual marriage between the soul and Christ. The final stage of salvation promises this union, which even the soberest Puritans depicted in highly erotic and sensual terms as an ecstatic consummation. According to the imagery of this metaphor, all saints, and the Church as a whole, become the "Bride of Christ," an apotheosis of the feminization process that characterizes the discourse of conversion and a redemption of the castration that that process represents for males. Edward Taylor, Fiske's successor in this orthodox tradition, employs the image of the knot as a key word to produce an elaborate set of related meanings in much the same way as Fiske, but he makes explicit the sexual/spiritual nuances implicit in the metaphor:

> A curious Knot God made in Paradise,
>   And drew it out inamled neatly Fresh.
> It was the True-Love Knot, more sweet than spice
>   And set with all the flowres of Graces dress.
> Its Weddens Knot, that ne're can be unti'de.
> No Alexanders Sword can it divide.
>   ("Upon Wedlock, and Death of Children"
>   (1682/83), ll. 1–6; in *Poems*, 468)

This "curious Knot" is at once an Edenic garden planted by God's own hand with "all the flowres of Graces," and especially "the True-Love Knot." It is also the "Weddens Knot" between man and woman that, unlike the Gordian knot severed by a human hand, "ne're can be unti'de," and is thus a figure for the "True-Love Knot"—the spiritual marriage between Christ and the soul. This meaning is not explicit in Fiske's elegy, but it is suggested by the sensuality and eroticism of the image of the "hony knott" and the "delight" it affords.

Cotton has found his "home" in God's mansion, but he leaves the Church and New England vulnerable and his elegist without a rhetorical figure, without an intermediary to God, and apparently cut off from the spiritual community by virtue of the position he must occupy in order to exhort his fellow Puritans—as a solitary prophet crying in the wilderness. The last lines of the elegy shift from apostrophe to imperative: "Returne . . . Repent . . . feare . . ."—the language of jeremiad. The speaker, now addressing his audience as "thee" and "thou," advises them to return "home," and instead of bewailing Cotton's death, "wayle the evills there" (l. 93). Since they do not heed Cotton's teachings and warnings—that God is merciful to those who believe—and obviously do not have his strength of faith (it is hinted that their faithlessness is a cause of Cotton's death), the only "wisdom" left to them is "feare" of Jehovah. To remain unredeemed is to be simultaneously willful yet weak in faith; it is to be unlike Cotton. To be saved is to submit to the will of God and become invincible in one's faith like Cotton: the divine paradox.

In recommending Cotton to his readers as a model saint, the poet recommends their immersion in paradox. An emblem for this in his text is his interdependent use of anagram and apostrophe. In one sense, for the poet as representative of the community to call upon Cotton is to solicit his aid and his power, and to identify with him—who, in turn, is identified with the sacrificial Christ. But to call upon Cotton as an anagram is to reduce him from a powerful human speaker to an object without a human voice whose rich significances must be teased out by the poet; the poet, the reader of names and maker of puns, becomes necessary. As anagrammatized object, however, Cotton exemplifies the conversion of the willful fallen subject into the passive object of God's will. Mere personhood becomes emblematic sainthood as the person is absorbed into the pattern of conversion. In his capacity as a minister, Cotton himself advanced a symbolic reading of scriptural imagery; he instrumentalized it. As anagrammatic image he becomes a text written by the divine hand waiting to be discovered and interpreted; he is instrumentalized.[33] Like the passage from Scripture that organized the Puritan funeral sermon, a source for the Puritan elegy, the anagram is a text to be opened, analyzed, and applied. Thus, Cotton is the signifying object, a kind of divine text, an occasion for and vessel of divinely sanctioned poetic discourse. When deployed by the poet, the anagram-cum-apostrophe gives him a voice that is not his own, and which is scribal, not verbal. The only subjectivity that can be constituted by invoking Cotton as the powerfully textual, unvoiced image, is paradoxical: to be saved is to be soft and invincible, hyperfeminized and hypermasculinized, not oneself but an imitation, the *imitatio Christi*. To be saved is to be defaced, disfigured, made Other.

In elegizing his subject, the elegist seeks evidence of his own state of grace by courting his own defacement. One means of self-defacement is the silencing of one's voice, sacrificing literary creativity for the discovery and display of texts already written by God. A modern theory of anagram explains how the idea of literary activity as production rather than creation undercuts the autonomy and freedom of individual speakers. Between 1906 and 1909 the Swiss linguist Ferdinand de Saussure filled ninety-nine notebooks with exercises in decoding mostly Latin and ancient Indo-European verse for the anagrams, or "hypograms" as he later called them, they contained. Saussure's anagram consists of a proper name, often the name of a deity, whose letters, syllables or phonemes are recognizably dispersed over a passage of verse. Though never transposed into a motto

or message, Saussure's phonetic anagram operates as "a kind of privileged subtext" (L. Higgins, 484) that not only emphasizes a name but
insures its presence, however broken, scattered, and embedded, throughout the text. Saussure speculates that poets were simultaneously constrained and inspired by this requirement of composition, which he compares to the rigors of rhyme (Starobinski, 96).

Unlike rhyme, however, the presence of the theme-word of the anagram, especially if it were the name of a god whose efficacy was to be
believed, had its own disseminating power.[34] Jean Starobinski, who edits
and comments upon Saussure's notebooks, concludes, "To the question
What lies directly beneath the line? the answer is not the creative *subject*
but the inductive *word*. Not that Ferdinand de Saussure goes so far as to
erase the role of artistic subjectivity, but it does seem to him that this
subjectivity can produce its text only by passage through a *pre-text*" (121).
In posing "intertextuality" as the precondition for text production, Saussure's theory of "les mots sous les mots" (Starobinski, xi) describes what
typological studies of Puritan literature have already demonstrated: that
embedded in the words of the Puritan text stand the words of Scripture,
and embedded in Scripture (for the Spirit-led hermeneut) is the Word of
God. Clearly, these two versions of anagram operate in systems with
opposing intents. To the question, What speaks behind the subject? Puritans would promptly answer: God. Saussure declined to speculate, but
the poststructuralists spawned by his linguistic theories would also answer
that question promptly, though with a variety of technical terms for their
anchoring principle: language.[35] Despite the different bases of each sort
of anagram (Saussure's has a phonetic base, and Fiske's a semantic),
Saussure's researches shed some light on seventeenth-century colonial
aesthetics.[36]

"Perhaps this theory demonstrates a deliberate desire to evade all problems arising from a creative *consciousness*," Starobinski continues (121). (I
have argued that for the Puritan poet, the emphasis falls on "creative," not
"consciousness." In order to evade the heresy of independent creativity,
the Puritan poet needs at least the illusion of throwing himself upon the
mercy of divine creativity.) "Behind the many words produced by the
poetic discourse lies a unique word. . . . The poem is only the *developed
potential* of a single vocable—a vocable which, to be sure, is chosen by the
poet, but chosen as an ensemble of united capacities and obligations"

(Starobinski, 121). Not surprisingly, Starobinski echoes Meserole's earlier use of the metaphor of a "fugue" to explain the anagrammatic development through a theme-word (Starobinski, 28). In the Puritan system of anagram, the elegy is the developed potential of a single signifier. Christ is that unique, inductive word, "the subject of all signs as both their maker and meaning," to which, Cotton himself tells us, all signs ultimately return (Clark, "'Crucified Phrase,'" 291). Though never mentioned in the poem, Christ is the unspoken word mediated by and lost in the loss of Cotton. Of course the poet "chooses" to speak. He also consciously develops the thematic potential in the words of the anagram, but his "choice" and his will/ability to develop a theme or trope skillfully reflect his status as a redeemed subject. The ultimate effect of Puritan poetics is to transform the poet into (or allow him to think of, and represent himself as) a transcriber of heavenly words. As the divine whisper tells George Herbert in "Jordan II," "*There is in love a sweetnesse readie penn'd: / Copie out onely that, and save expense*" (ll. 17–18; in *Works*, 103). And Edward Taylor sues his God to be made a "scribener" of the divine original. As his pleas for self-objectification suggest, to be a scribe implies for Taylor an even more radical illusion: that of giving up writing altogether, to become the reader of divine grace.[37]

As if this were the discovery he has made in the process of producing the elegy, Fiske ends the poem with a remarkable turning of its focus onto himself, the speaking voice, and a returning of the poetic system upon itself. The formal function of the elegy has been accomplished. Mourning for Cotton has ceased; the muse has been dismissed. In the final lines the poet mourns for his community and for himself as if they and he are the dead, the spiritually lost.[38] Yet, they cannot "return" without the intervention of Cotton: "And thou his waies of mercy *yet maust* see" (l. 96; emphasis added). In the final short prayer that concludes the elegy, the positions of speaker and audience, and even their identities, come unhinged. The lines are almost cryptic; their position on the page and the absence of punctuation multiply the possibilities of readings. The imperative "Returne" suggests that it is entreaty or prayer, but its object is ambiguous. If we read the positions here as those of the previous lines, where the poet addresses the community as "thou," then we can gloss the passage as follows: Turn to the Lord and you will be returned to his favor, as I will also be. There is, however, too much thematic pressure on the word "Returne" to read it so simply. For example, this passage echoes the opening of the elegy, where the mourners called upon Cotton by name but failed to "recall thee back." The turning away of God from his chosen community was foreshadowed in the failure of this initial invocation/vocation. "Returne" is, in a sense, the essence of the central apostrophe to the hony knott: return from that place which you have striven your whole spiritual life to attain; return to us for we are bereft without you. "Returne" is also an epitome of the process of conversion. The Hebrew for "return" is *shûbh*, which also means "to go back again." This was a word from common speech that the Old Testament prophets borrowed and endowed with theological significance to emphasize the conscious turning away from sin involved in repentance. The sincere penitent had to reverse entirely the direction of his or her life. "Turn us, O God of our salvation," the psalmist cries, speaking for his people (Ps. 85:4); "Return ye children of men," God replies (Ps. 90:3). Insistently, the Hebrew prophets called for the return to God and the preparation of the heart (Pettit, vii). New Testament writers affirmed the necessity of total self-transformation by adapting the significance of *shûbh* for their own purposes. In both traditions, "turning is imperative, for on it depends eternal life" (Cohen, 5–6).

The plea to "Returne," then, opens the elegist's prayer for the power, will, and desire to be turned back to God. One reading of the highly ambiguous first line of the final prayer, "Returne thou mee," casts the solo elegist as a petitioner of God. Return yourself to me, return me to you: the reversibility of these requests hardly seems to matter, but it is resolved by a phrase that clarifies the direction of the movement: back, "Lord unto thee."[39] The last line is in the conditional, the mood that prayer takes at the conclusion of over two hundred of Taylor's *Preparatory Meditations*, which remembers the contractual nature of Puritan faith: if you return me to you, then even I, willful, lost, but truly penitent I, will be turned. No longer the admonishing minister, the speaker asks humbly to be reoriented, turned toward God, his back to sin. His salvation depends upon his being turned and returned like the elegy he writes, and also like the trope he expounds. In the sense that to "turn" also means to "trope," and was employed in the seventeenth century to refer particularly to anagrammatizing, the poet requests that he be transformed from the turner of tropes into a trope himself.[40] One suspects he wishes to become like the anagram he has discovered in John Cotton's name, which he has turned skillfully and obsessively in his elegy to display the evidences of vocation, sanctification, and glorification he also wishes to contain and display.

Through the poet's signature at the end, "Jo: Fiske," his authorizing mark, he becomes part of the text he has produced, and like that text he is, finally, a production of divine intent. But as Clark explains, one specific feature of Puritan semiology is "the irremediable difference between sign and spirit" ("'Crucified Phrase,'" 290). However humbled, self-effacing, and passive, the producer of signs can never, in this life, make the leap over to spirit. Representation allows him to come quite close; it allows him to imagine bridging the gap, and it allows him to articulate paradoxical requirements that no one can fulfill. He can represent himself as an object of God's will and mercy, but he is left with the contaminating residue of his own desire to be that object. In the closing prayer, an apostrophe in which the poet actively calls for and wills that which would subordinate his will, he desires to constitute himself with respect to God. He calls in the hopes of being called upon by God, not by his proper earthly name, but by the new name into which his fallen self will be transposed.

By calling in this way, and by enacting his spiritual calling, his vocation, through the gesture of apostrophe, the poet highlights a tension in Puritan aesthetics between the two poetic forces of narrative, the progressive temporal location of events, and lyric, "characteristically the triumph of the apostrophic" (Culler, *Pursuit*, 149). The regimentation and formula in Puritan spirituality and Puritan culture derive from a dependence upon narrative. Scripture provides the paradigmatic story both for the conversion process of the individual saint and for the typological constitution of the elect nation. The nonseparating congregationalists who made the perilous journey to settle in the New World adopted both of these stories. They applied this idea so rigorously that, according to Sacvan Bercovitch, they imbued the state they established and the land they invaded with the personhood of one of God's elect. Puritan piety demonstrates an obsession with living out this story in the prescribed ways, with engaging in constant and painful introspection in order to find "evidences" of the outlines of this story in one's experiences. The burden of imitating this model narrative was oppressive, not only because it shaped and limited human experience, but because its conclusion had been determined without reference to one's desires or actions; the outcome of the story of salvation had been predestined by God before a person's birth. Furthermore, humans had no access to the already decided conclusion of the story of their spiritual lives, nor could they, strictly speaking, effect the predetermined outcome. Consequently, they worked, lived, prayed, and communed with each other and their God in the desperate hope that the conclusion of the story they had been conditioned by countless sermons and spiritual handbooks to tell about their inner experiences would match the one God had always already chosen for them.

The lyric mode presents an alternative to the relentless horizontality of the Puritan narrative. Lyric has traditionally been regarded as a vertical mode, which fixes or captures a moment of intensity and is capable of an immediacy unavailable to narrative. As Northrop Frye points out, the lyrical embraces a sense of the discontinuous, for there "we turn away from our ordinary continuous experience in space or time, or rather from a verbal mimesis of it" ("Approaching the Lyric," 31). This discontinuity, which is not simply identifiable with the subjective, is "often linked to a specific, usually ritual occasion" marked by "an identity of subject and object" (32). Frye goes on, borrowing from the thought of Gerard Manley Hopkins, to further define the lyrical impulse against narrative as "a more meditative kind, which turns away from sequential experience and super-imposes a different kind of experience on it" (33).

The similarities between the apostrophic moment of lyric and the moment in Puritan conversion of the *shûbh*, "return," should be obvious. Ideally, for the Puritan saint, the moment of divine grace initiated a whole new life story by superimposing the Christic story upon the old, fallen, Adamic tale. As regeneration takes place, the outlines of the old story grow fainter as the broad strokes of the new story become more visible, become the saint's own story. The soteriological narrative keeps the mystical moments of direct communion with God in check; in fact, the history of New England Puritanism can be understood as the theocracy's attempt to contain the lyrical, antinomian, feminine elements, which threatened the masculine order and continuity embodied in reason, ministers, and magistrates, but which continuously cropped up as the logical conclusion of the Puritans' unquenchable thirst after an unmediated relation with God.[41] This tension plays itself out in the verse of Fiske's elegy, where the ideological task is the reaffirmation of the paradigmatic story, but the fervent desire of both poet and audience is for those atemporal moments of lyric in which God appears.

> *Upon the much-to-be-lamented desease*
> *of the Reverend Mr. John Cotton*
> *late Teacher to the Church at Boston N. E.*
> *who departed this Life 23 of 10. [16]52.*
>
> *John* {*Cotton*
>   {*Kotton* *after the old English writi'g*
>   *Anagr:*
>   *O, Honie knott*

With Joy erst while, (when knotty doubts arose)
To Thee we calld, o Sir, the knott disclose:
But now o and alasse to thee to call
In vayne tis thou no Answer give or shall.
Could loud Shrickes, could crys recall thee back   5
From deaths estate we wold our eye ne're slack
O, this our greife it is, lament shall we
A Father in our Israel's cea'st to be
Even hee that in the Church a pillar was
A gurdeon knot of sweetest graces as   10
He who set fast to Truths so clossly knitt
As loosen him could ne're the keenest witt
Hee who his Flesh together bound ful-fast
No knott more sure whilest his life did last
Hee who the knotts of Truth, of Mysteries   15
Sacred, most cleerely did ope 'fore our eyes
Even hee who such a one, is ceas'd to bee
'Twixt whose life, death, the most sweete harmony
Knotts we doe meet with many a cue daily
Which crabbed anggry tough unpleasing bee   20
But we as in a honi-comb a knott
Of Hony sweete, here had such sweetenes Gott
The knotts and knobbs that on the Trees doe grow
The bitterest excressences we know.

his soule Embalmd with grace 25
    was fit to soare on high
and to receive its place
    above the starry skie.
now grant O G[od that we]
    may follow afte[r him] 30
surviving worlds ocean unto thee
    our passage safe may swim.

A vine tree seene, a plant of Gods owne hand
In it this knott of sweetest parts did stand.
The knott in place sublime: most eminent 35
As, his, no Branch could challeng like extent
The knott sometimes seems a deformity
It's a mistake, tho such be light set by
The knott it is the Joynt, the strength of parts
The bodies-beauty, so this knott out-starts 40
What others in that place, they ought to bee
Even such a knott exemplar'ly was hee
Knotts now adayes affrayd of are most men
Of Hony if expose'd feare none would then
I guesse why knotty Learning downe does goe 45
'Twould not, if as in him 'twere sweetned soe
Meeknes Humility forbearance too
This lovely knott to love the most did woe
In knotts what greate adoe to gayne the hearte
Yee had it heere, he did it free impart 50
When knotty theames and paynes some meet with then
As knotty and uncouth their tongue and pen
So 'twas not heere, he caus'd us understand
And tast the sweetnes of the knott in hand.
When knotty querks and quiddities broacht were 55
By witt of man he sweetely Breathed there.
His charity his wisdom meeknes eke
Left none that loved light, in knotts to seeke
Hee tho invincible thrô softnes did

The knottiest peeces calme and cleave amid   60
Such was hee of such use in these last dayes
Whose want bewayle, o, and alas alwaies
This knott so we have seen lien broknly
By knotts so breathlesse, so crookt, crackt, or fly
This knott thereof so surfetted we see   65
By hony surfetted we know som bee
The cause nor in the knott nor hony say
Thro Temper bad, unskilfulnes this may
O knott of Hony most delightfull when
Thou livd'st, thi death a sad presage hath ben   70
Have Ben? yea is, and is, and is alas
For woe to us, so greate a Breach when was
Woe to that knotty pride hee ne're subdude
Woe they who doe his Truthes dispenct exclude
And woe to them that factions there contrive   75
Woe them whose wayes unrighteous survive
Woe they that by him warning did not take
Woe to us all if mercy us forsake
A Mercy once New England thou hast had
(You Boston cheifly) in thi Cotton clad   80
Some 'gan to count't too meane a dresse and sought
Silk Velvetts Taffeties best could be bought
These last will soyle, if first doe soyle also
How can we think but Naked we shall goe
Must silken witts, must velvet tongues be had   85
And shall playne preaching be accounted bad
I feare a famine, pinching times t'ensue
Time Such may have, slighted mercy to Rue
My wakened muse to rest, my moystned pen
Mye eye, my hearte which powred out this have ben   90
Cease try no more, for Hee hath gayn'd his prize
His heavenly mansion 'bove the starry skie
Returne thee home and wayle the evills there
Repent breake off thi sins Jehovah feare

O Jehovah feare: this will thi wisdom bee   95
And thou his waies of mercy yet maust see
Returne thou mee;   And turned bie
Lord unto thee: even so shall I.
                           Jo: Fiske

THREE

The Puritan Cult
of the Spouse:
Edward Taylor's
Dialectic of Difference

Edward Taylor also longed to be transformed from a turner of tropes into
a trope turned by and returned to God. Beginning his career as a Congregational minister to a tiny, isolated frontier town only a few years
before John Fiske's death in 1677, he confronted much the same dilemma
in his roles as an orthodox Puritan minister and a poet: How can I write as
the instrument of God? How can I speak divine praise uncontaminated by
fallen, selfish desire? Taylor approached these issues, as did his colleague
Fiske, by strategic and doctrinally sanctioned representations of the sinning and saintly speaking subject. In the prefatory poem that introduces
Taylor's lifelong opus—two series of lyrics entitled *Preparatory Meditations
before my Approach to the Lord's Supper. Chiefly upon the Doctrin preached
upon the Day of administration*, comprising 216 poems composed over a
forty-three-year period—he casts himself as a trope turned by a much-
esteemed and much-emulated English minister/poet, George Herbert.
In the "Prologue," Taylor muses:

> Lord, Can a Crumb of Dust the Earth outweigh,
>   Outmatch all mountains, nay the Chrystall Sky?
> Imbosom in't designs that shall Display
>   And trace into the Boundless Deity?
>   Yea hand a Pen whose moysture doth guild ore
>   Eternall Glory with a glorious glore.

>   (ll. 1–6)[1]

His eternal life, it seemed to Taylor, depended upon the answer to these literary/spiritual questions.

This is probably the most self-consciously "literary" moment in the *Preparatory Meditations*. Because of its position at the head of the two series, and the form its spiritual queries take, the "Prologue" constitutes Taylor's *ars poetica*, and it is thus appropriately intertextual. Taylor borrows its stanza structure, a form he will use without variation in every Meditation, from Herbert's "The Church-porch," a prefatory poem that stands at the opening (literally and figuratively) of *The Temple*, his book of religious verse. As Taylor's statement of poetic purpose, the "Prologue" has no explicit scriptural text; it meditates, rather, on another poem by Herbert entitled "The Temper" (I), from which Taylor rifles almost every image and some of the phraseology for his own Meditations. "The Temper" (I) proved such a gold mine for Taylor because it begins with the complaint that haunts his entire poetic/spiritual endeavor:

> How should I praise thee, Lord! how should my rymes
>   Gladly engrave thy love in steel,
> If what my soul doth feel sometimes
>   My soul might ever feel!
>
> (ll. 1–4)[2]

This is the problematics of the lyric moment, and also the problematics of spiritual conversion: it is ecstatic but discontinuous and evanescent; it interrupts the orderly procedure of the saintly life's narrative development. God comes with a bang and then withdraws, leaving humans limp, stunned, and obliged to begin again the painful climb up the winding stair of self-denial and spiritual exercise, toward the landing of self-effacement and acceptable praise.

In ways this chapter will outline, Edward Taylor's *Preparatory Meditations* confront the related issues of lyric and spiritual conversion with which Fiske grappled in his elegy, and which Herbert so artfully expressed. Yet, the strategies of self-representation that Taylor deploys to resolve his poetic/spiritual dilemma resemble the self-positionings of John Donne more than those of either Fiske or Herbert. Fiske, as we saw in the previous chapter, speaks in the privatized public realm of the Puritan collective self. The politics of his self-effacement imply gendered positions, which are never made explicit. Taylor, like Donne, explicitly genders the positions of his desire and sexualizes his relation to God. Rather than the persona of the prattling child, which some readers have attributed to him, Taylor adopts more pervasively the position, voice, and tactics of a desirous woman, a petulant betrothed, or an anxious lover.[3] As we will see, the resistance and violence accompanying the process of self-abandonment that Taylor deemed requisite for sacramental preparation more closely echo the feminine voice eroticized by the paradoxes of Donne's "Holy Sonnet XIV" than the childish and fruitless protests of the troubled speaker of Herbert's "The Collar."

Nevertheless, from Herbert, Taylor learns that saintly desire and poetic inspiration are inexplicably bound. For example, in the course of "The Temper" (I), Herbert suggests to God that signs assuring him of his salvation would assuage his anxieties. These he never receives. What he learns is that the only solution to his desire for adequate praise and soteriological assurance is a renunciation of the desire for certainty and confirming signs altogether, and letting God do all:

> Yet take thy way; for sure thy way is best:
>   Stretch or contract me, thy poore debter:
> This is but tuning of my breast,
>   To make the musick better.
>
>   (ll. 21–24)

Being poor and in debt to God, who has given his son to ransom the sinner's eternal life, the poet has no choice but to submit to the extremes of emotion, his breast stretched and contracted like the strings of an instrument. All this is but fine-tuning of his heart, he wittily quips, which improves the quality of the music that God, the musician, plays upon him.

Taylor captures these extremes of emotion in the opening, breathless question of the "Prologue," which echoes Herbert's query to God in "The Temper" (I), "Wilt thou meet arms with man, that thou dost stretch / A crumme of dust from heav'n to hell?" (ll. 13–14). In both cases, the human writers diminish themselves by representing themselves as not only mortal and trivial (dust), but tiny and insignificant (crumb). And yet, curiously, they are to "spell" the stature of God ("The Temper" [II], l. 16), and handle a pen that will "Display / And trace into the Boundless Deity" ("Prologue," ll. 3–4). Herbert's solution to his spiritual and psychological problems, as Stanley Fish demonstrates, also provides the resolution to his poetic problems (161); in his realization that God has made both the angels that fly and the dust that falls, he understands that no matter which place he occupies at any given moment, "Thy hands made both, and I am there: / Thy power and love, my love and trust / Make one place ev'ry where" ("The Temper" [I], ll. 26–28). The difference in position between flying angels and falling dust is only an illusion of fallen consciousness, which God's power, and man's trust in that power, can overcome. In the ingenious bestowal of understanding that comes in "The Temper" (I), the wonder of God's mercy is making the poet part of the action; as Fish points out, "make" in the final prayer has a multiple subject (162).

Taylor's solution to the dilemma of faith and praise in the "Prologue" is less metaphysical and more concerned, as Taylor always is, with emblematic and signifying objects—here, the instruments of the writing process—and how he can include himself in God's process as one of those objects. This is the literary version of the self-representational strategy pervasive in the *Meditations*. Taylor, like Herbert, recognizes that he is God's creature and incapable of soteriologically effective action without divine agency. Even with the most exalted of writing equipment—a pen made from "an Angels Quill," "Sharpend on a Pretious Stone," "And dipt in Liquid Gold," writing "In Christall leaves"—even with these thoroughly spiritualized implements, "It would but blot and blur yea jag and jar / Unless thou mak'st the Pen, *and* Scribener" ("Prologue," ll. 7–12; emphasis added). The act of writing merges here with the act of worship, a highly ritualized and symbolic performance carried out with objects that themselves resonate with significance. The result is a perfect conflation of the love of God and the love of language to which this poem obliquely alludes: an illuminated manuscript. Taylor's desire is focused not on producing his own work, but on copying over the work that God has already written. He is a "Scribener" "design'd / To make my Pen unto thy Praise alone . . . / And Write in Liquid Gold upon thy Name / My Letters till thy glory forth doth flame" (ll. 13–18). Tracing over and illuminating the name of God, he cultivates for himself the illusion of writing "My Letters" over God's name and fusing the two signatures. This, therefore, defines what it is for Taylor to "write aright" (l. 26), to write punningly and redundantly, as a redeemed subject: tracing one's letters—the letters of one's fallen name, or of love letters or poems—onto God's name over and over, until the flame of desire is kindled in a chilly and resistant heart.

Taylor's act of faith is highly aesthetic and highly literate: a "display" for God, and a display of God's glory refracted through a humbled—that is, a formerly arrogant or self-reliant—instrument. There is less genuine resignation in Taylor's poem than in Herbert's, and consequently more explicit self-abasement. Whereas Herbert blurs the spatial, temporal, and epistemological distinctions that differentiate his specificity from God's omnipresence, Taylor identifies himself in more explicit terms as a metaphoric sign: "I am this Crumb of Dust" (l. 13), he declares, who is nothing—but who can, with God's grace, "Imbosom in't designs" (l. 3) to portray the deity in human language. In the peaceful and resigned conclusion of Herbert's poem, both God and poet "make" the center and the circumference that is God indistinguishable. In the course of Taylor's cruder and less tranquil resolution, he and God do not act together; rather, as happens at the end or in the course of almost every Meditation, he asks God to "make" him something other than he is, into an instrument of divine truth—here, a "Scribener" instead of a writer. In his human capacity he does not work with God, but, like Donne, he demands: "make me new" ("Holy Sonnet" XIV, l. 4).[4]

Taylor's concern with semiology, with representation through signs, comes from the sacramental framework of the *Preparatory Meditations*. As their long title quoted above indicates, the *Meditations* were intended to help Taylor prepare for the administration and reception of the sacrament of the Lord's Supper, "the nearest harbor of divine access" (*Treatise*, 184), by readying his mind and heart for the "strict examination, wherein we are to prove ourselves that we be approved of God for this ordinance in the judgment of our own consciences" (*Treatise*, 201). It is not surprising, then, that Taylor echoes and amplifies Herbert's opening complaint and tone of resignation from "The Temper" (I) in the final stanza of an unnumbered Meditation entitled "The Experience," which recounts a moment of intimacy with Christ experienced at the sacrament:

Oh! that my Heart, thy Golden Harp might bee
  Well tun'd by Glorious Grace, that e'ry string
Screw'd to the highest pitch, might unto thee
  All Praises wrapt in sweetest Musick bring.
  I praise thee, Lord, and better praise thee would
  If what I had, my heart might ever hold.
                    (ll. 25–30; p. 9)

What is metaphor in Herbert becomes outright self-objectification here. Taylor prays to be Christ's "Golden Harp," deflecting any identification with David, the harpist of the Psalms, away from himself and onto Christ. Rather than making the best of his emotional extremities by describing them as "tuning," he asks to be "Screw'd to the highest pitch," pushed to the limits of his capacity in order to produce adequate praise.

The quatrain of this stanza exemplifies the final prayer of the majority of the Meditations, over two-thirds of which make a similar allusion to musical instruments. Through this and other imagistically paired systems, Taylor can position himself in intimate relation to Christ without actually identifying or merging with him. Nevertheless, he captures the wished-for mutuality that drives covenant theology. By figuring himself as Christ's instrument, he expresses his desire to be the object of Christ's activity, to be passive and receptive and, like an anagrammatized John Cotton, instrumental—a medium purified by the touch of a master musician and created for the sole purpose of serving his purposes. By figuring Christ as the musician, Taylor lays all agency upon divine will. A kind of bargaining goes on here, as if he recognizes that the double bind of the covenant of grace—you must worship me, but I make all independent human agency impossible—gives him some small leverage. What is true of the relationship of instrument and musician is broadly true for the other reciprocal images Taylor develops, such as the container and contained (purse and money, cabinet and pearl, cage and bird), vessel and liquid, plant and garden, garden and gardener, singer and song: they define each other and complete each other, like author and scribe (at least, in a preprint world), or illuminator and manuscript. The "Prologue" provides two more examples in its final prayer, in which Taylor desires to "shew [Christ's] Properties to shine most bright" (l. 28) in the same way that stems display flowers or that jewelry shops exhibit gems. God's works are his subject matter and exhibit beauty and value; the poet/saint, with God's approval, provides merely the means of exhibition.

By sufficiently diminishing and deauthorizing himself, Taylor can be included in the spiritual expression of God's glory. I am not the first reader to point out that this rhetorical strategy replicates the operation of grace in the morphology of spiritual conversion where, "with a holy kind of violence," the sinful self is purged and the soul gropes its painful way back to Christ (Hooker, *Heautonaparnumenos* 26; in Bercovitch, *Puritan*

Origins, 17). The sacramental framework of Taylor's poetics confirms the connection. Taylor followed the policy of his New England predecessors and conservative brethren who maintained that the sacrament of the Lord's Supper was not a converting ordinance, but one reserved to full church members who had proved themselves, at least to the satisfaction of the congregation, elect souls: communicants attending the Supper required the presence of grace to help them in "discerning the Lord's body" and thus make a worthy, truly spiritual reception of the nourishment in the creatures of bread and wine (*Treatise*, 203). Preparation for the sacrament consisted of examining the soul and coming to a reasonable assurance that it possessed saving grace—or the "wedden garment," as Taylor described this impalpable essence to his Westfield congregation—necessary to provide "the knowledge of the spiritual mystery of the feast" that celebrated the marriage of Christ and the soul (*Treatise*, 203).

Critical discussion has focused on the semiology of the sacrament and its influence on Taylor's poetics as a way of approaching the dilemma of faith and praise and the poet's position in that dilemma, as summarized above. Michael Clark recently reviewed the major arguments concerning the crucial question of representation in Puritan aesthetics: the relation of worldly signs and their spiritual significance—an aesthetic version of the theological/metaphysical question of the relation of the visible and invisible orders. To illustrate his finding that "the Puritans insisted on having it both ways, defining their faith in an invisible world through a precise and systematic delineation of the limits of the visible" ("Honeyed Knot," 70), he cites their sacramental theology: Puritans like Taylor and the eminent second-generation minister and theologian Samuel Willard argued that the materiality of the sacramental signs (the bread and wine) had to be recognized, thus stipulating a mediated apprehension of divine truth, but that the sacramental meaning or signified (body and blood) does not inhere in the signs (74). In other words, and to summarize a complex theological point, in order for saints to experience communion with Christ in the sacrament, they had to discern the difference between the signs (the bread and wine) and what they signified (the body and blood), as well as the mysterious "Sacramental union" that joined them momentarily and joined the soul momentarily to Christ.

Clark explains these seemingly contradictory attitudes—the belief in the necessity, as Taylor put it, to illustrate "supernatural things by natural," and the equally strong belief that fallen language (or gesture of any kind) is inadequate to express divine truth—as a dialectic rather than a contradiction ("Honeyed Knot," 76). Though Puritans believed that ultimately the visible and invisible realms would be unified, their grounding in Calvinism led them also to believe that there was an "irreducible difference" between the two ("Honeyed Knot," 69). It is this sense of difference that interests me; for, in a dialectical fashion, difference not only enables saints to experience the identity with Christ that is the basis of communion—eating his body and taking on his righteousness—but it also governs Taylor's strategies of self-representation.[5]

Kathleen Blake also turns to Taylor's sacramental theology to explain the deferral at the heart of Puritan poetics. The illustration she cleverly lifts from his poetry will help situate my exploration of difference in Taylor. Blake pairs the action and intent of the sacrament with the miracle of the Incarnation: in the former, flesh signifies spirit; while in the latter, spirit is incarnated in flesh. The "union" that occurs in each is not symmetrical, but the perfect interpenetration of spirit and flesh exemplified by the Incarnation sanctions the expedient, temporary, and metaphorical union that effectuates sacramental worship in which, as Protestant theology resolutely maintained, "Two realities touch, but they do not transubstantiate" (Blake, 8).

In this way, Puritans believed that an embodied soul can experience a momentary fusion with the divine essence while maintaining the distinctness of spirit and flesh. Taylor, like other Puritan divines, illustrated this dialectical movement by distinguishing between the "espousal" of the soul to Christ celebrated in the "wedden feast" of his parabolic interpretation of the Lord's Supper (see Matt. 22:1–14; *Treatise*, 8–9), and the consummation of the marriage, which will only occur in heaven after death. "They only touch and part, as in a kiss," Blake reiterates (19), alluding to Taylor's "intriguing" plea to Christ: "Oh! let him kiss mee with his orall kisses" (2.97:16). So central is this gesture to Taylor's poetics, Blake concludes, that Taylor's "orall kiss" stands "as a very fair description for metaphor as it is conceived in the Protestant poetic of seventeenth-century England and America" (24). Unfortunately, Blake ends her examination just where the role of difference in the form of *gender* difference becomes apparent. She does not mention that the scriptural text for the Meditation in which this plea appears is Canticles 1:2: "Let him kiss me

with the kisses of his mouth"—"Canticles" being Taylor's name for the
Song of Solomon, the biblical book that Puritans read allegorically as an
expression of spiritual love-longing couched in erotic terms—or that the
Meditation itself explores the problematics of discerning grace in the
language of the "Holy Spouse," which stands as a figure for the
poet/saint. If, as Blake argues, Taylor's practice represents the function of
metaphor in Protestant poetics, then he speaks this language of difference
in a feminized voice and from the position of woman, the paradigmatic
redeemed subject.

The purpose of this reexamination of Taylor's *Preparatory Meditations* is
to illustrate the contentions I laid out in some detail in Chapter 1: that
Puritan doctrine was geared toward male saints, who were compelled by
the logic of spiritual conversion—figured as a rape or ravishment, or, at
the very least, an irresistible intrusion—to position themselves in relation
to God and Christ as feminized, deauthorized, self-denying souls; and
that Puritan doctrine provided gynetic figures, especially the figure of the
Spouse of Christ, to negotiate the sexually figured relation between man
(gender specific) and God. What becomes clear in Taylor's personal and
idiosyncratic lifelong wrestling match with the images, constraints, and
power plays of Puritan doctrine is that gender, and more specifically sex,
allows him to represent and maintain the requisite difference that the
Augustinian strain in Puritanism, with its mystical tug toward unmediated
vision, always threatens to dissolve. In the eyes of the orthodox, patriarchal elite, heretical women like Anne Hutchinson wanted to impel the
commonwealth of saints headlong in this dangerous direction of immediate revelation (and, thus, amorality and libertinism) in which human—
that is, male—authority could be thoroughly discounted and nullified by
a greater divine authority. And yet, this is clearly the specter that beck-
oned as the logical conclusion of the Puritan doctrine of justification,
especially in the hermeneutically slippery hands of John Cotton. But
rather than empowering women, Puritanism empowered (in the paradoxical way in which subjects are both empowered and subjected) feminine
positions and abstract female figures that could—with some conditioning,
and considerable effort, and with mixed results—be occupied by men.

From this paradoxical conception of power, as I have already pointed
out, men won social and secular privileges and the religious prerogative of
filling God's place on earth with respect to everyone and everything else in

creation. Sacramental worship awarded saints a similar prerogative in the form of a paradoxical notion of agency. Just as Spousehood led to adoption as a son and heir of God, the radical passivity that defined the state of conversion conferred upon elect souls the right of communing with Christ in the most august ritual at the heart of Protestant piety. "Come up to this, you come up to all," Taylor told his Westfield congregation of the Lord's Supper: "For this is of the highest ascent, and attained to in the last place, as the perfecting and crowning ordinance. Hence come up to this, and you come into an universal conformity unto Christ in all divine ordinances of an ecclesiastical nature" (*Treatise*, 183–84).

There are many reasons why Taylor valued the sacrament so highly, and why, toward the end of the seventeenth century, New England was in the midst of what E. Brooks Holifield has dubbed "a sacramental renaissance" (196–97).[6] One of the least-mentioned reasons is that the Supper was the only Christian rite that, after preparation, called for the active participation of the saint; in Taylor's words, sacramental work requires both the passive and active obedience of the saint in emulation of Christ (see Med. 2.81:28–29). Clarifying this point for his congregation, he explained that "the work of conversion knocks at the door of the ear, and so enters into the soul"—an operation in which the saint is completely passive; but the Supper "calls for the exercise of the faith of communion, saying 'take eat, take drink,' which is a call to exercise such a faith upon Christ signified by the elements as can communicate spiritual sweetness, deliciousness, comfort, and nourishment unto the New Man" (*Treatise*, 96, 82--83). The "formative" activity required for communion, a point of doctrine that Taylor explored poetically in Meditation 2.106, which also bears upon his deployment of language, is wholly dependent upon the prior and absolute passivity of conversion, and so it is a legitimate—that is, a paradoxical or disempowered—form of agency, originating with the divine Spirit housed in human bodies, not the fallen self.

The figure most appropriately positioned and officially sanctioned by Puritan doctrine as the paradox of conformity and legitimate agency is the Spouse of Christ. The Spouse, as we shall see, desires as a woman; to identify and participate in that desire allows the saint actively to bring about his own passivity and receptivity, his own defacement and deauthorization. In addition, through the recurring metaphor of the spiritual marriage in which the Spouse is a central element, Taylor splices together the sometimes inconsistent representational systems of the sacrament with its image of the "wedden robe" and prominent Christology, and the spiritual marriage allegorized in the Song of Solomon, in which Christ's beloved speaks her praises and desires. By melding these two systems, Taylor creates a complex strategy for splicing himself as sacramental object into Christ's redeeming and eternal love. He also manages strategically to preserve the difference inherent in his fallen, earthly state, yet to bind himself to the promises of a healing union.

It is important to note that Taylor is not unusual in his promulgation of what looks like a Puritan cult of the Spouse. Like his colonial predecessors, he viewed difference and otherness as femininely gendered; the issue was whether difference was positively or negatively valued. For example, he was fixated on the issue of church membership, which he based on the exclusion of all except those who could give a credible account of their experience of conversion. For him, the glory of the Puritan plantation rested upon its commitment to establishing and upholding a church composed of "visible saints," a membership as close as it was humanly possible to come to God's "Invisible Church"—the roster of predestined elect chosen by God before time. Taylor envisioned this church as "Christ's Curious Garden fenced in / With Solid Walls of Discipline / Well wed, and watered, and made full trim" ("The Soule Seeking Church-Fellowship," ll. 26–28 [*God's Determinations*, in *Poems*, 454]). Exclusion defined and protected the sanctity of this garden, modeled after the luxuriant enclosed gardens that King Solomon created for the pleasure of his beloved Spouse. This allegory also provided both ministers and magistrates with an analogical language of marital exclusivity by which they figured the spiritual and moral purity of the political state and the individual soul. This analogy explains Taylor's use of the seemingly inconsistent phrase "Well wed" to describe his vision of "Christ's Curious Garden"; he, like his Puritan brethren, understood the "Guarded, Engarden'd" Church (Med. 1.3:2), as well as the individual souls that composed it, to be signified by the Spouse of Christ. Taylor echoed mainstream thought when he asserted that the orthodox discourse of Christ's spiritual marriage to the soul and Church was "the language of the faithful ministry of the gospel, as 2 Cor. II:2: 'I have espoused you to one husband, that I may present you a chaste virgin to Christ,' when it hath effected a work of grace upon the soul" (*Treatise*, 19).[7]

Given the language that orthodox Puritans used for the covenant of grace, it is not difficult to understand why the liberalizing practices of Solomon Stoddard, a neighboring minister in Northampton, filled Taylor with a holy fury. Stoddard led the way to more inclusive church membership by rejecting the Half-Way Covenant and baptizing all adults who consented to the church's articles of faith—but it was his policy of admitting communicants to the sacrament of the Lord's Supper without evidence of conversion that, for Taylor, invalidated the concept of "visible sainthood" and caused a dangerous breach in the protective wall surrounding New England's garden. Taylor labored mightily to shore up the crack, but in 1728, a year before his death, his successor guided the Westfield congregation into an adoption of Stoddard's practices (Rowe, *Saint and Singer*, 293). According to the logic of Taylor's discourse and dogma, such practices threatened the purity of the corporate church and the souls who comprised its body as the enclosed garden and chaste bride. "Not to prepare" for the sacrament, Taylor argued, "is to abide in a sordid and filthy, naked and sinful state" (*Treatise*, 23). To worship unworthily was tantamount to defiling one's own body and soul and those of one's fellow communicants—a kind of spiritual fornication or adultery.[8] Taylor himself endured persecution and left his native country "to avoid such mixt administrations of the Lord's Supper, and to enjoy an holy administrating of it to the visibly worthy" in the new churches established in the New World (*Treatise*, 126). His response to Stoddard's innovations was to adhere more rigidly than ever to the elder generation's strict doctrines and exclusionary practices—an inflexibility registered in the history of his ministry, which reveals him to have been a stubborn and severely pious leader (Stanford, xvi–xvii; K. Keller, 35–42).[9]

Taylor's severity and loyalty to the old order are not surprising. He was, like the "American" poetic tradition whose origin he is often said to represent, beset by belatedness, a son who wanted to be a patriarch. Born in Leicestershire, England, around 1642, he was too young to participate in the victories of the Saints during the civil war, though growing up in a "hotbed of non-conformity" shaped his "puritan character and convictions" (Stanford, xii–xiii). After the Restoration in 1660, Taylor was barred from university training and other means of livelihood for refusing to subscribe to the Act of Uniformity of 1662. Arriving in Boston in 1668, he was welcomed by important men of the community and spent the next three years as an upperclassman at Harvard College with the responsible position of butler. But he had missed the heady glory-days of God's chosen people establishing their city upon the hill: the vigilant orthodoxy of the Cambridge Platform of 1648 had given way to the liberalizing accommodations of the Half-Way Synod of 1662; the founders' energy and sense of mission had been diminished by death, sectarian struggle, and the sheer expansion of the colony. Elegizing the minister John Allen, who, like several other influential patriarchs, died during his stint at Harvard, Taylor captures the survivors' sense of abandonment and imminent collapse: "And hearing something Crash, there's cause to doubt / Another Stud is broke, or Stake pluckt out / Out of its place" in the "Temples for Christ" built by the original builders (*Minor Poetry*, 30–31, ll. 25–27, 42). Recounting all those who are "gone hence," Taylor cries at this elegy's conclusion, "Shall none / Be left behinde to tell's the Quondam Glory / Of this Plantation?" (ll. 58–60).

Recapturing a bit of the Puritan errand's "Quondam Glory" may have been what motivated Taylor to accept the call as minister to the small community of Westfield on the colony's westernmost frontier. This move, according to Thomas Davis, gave Taylor "an opportunity of reenacting the saga of the first generation, of being himself a founding father" and rekindling their vision (xiii). Taylor lived in Westfield for almost sixty years, ministering to its congregation. During that time he strove to shape a visible church according to the orthodox and increasingly outmoded Puritan vision, despite challenges from his progressive neighbors. His public life, however, does not reveal—as his poetry does, in excruciating detail—the psychic contortions involved in living out the paradoxes of a practical conformity to God's will. At varying intervals, he closeted himself away from his responsibilities as minister, physician, frontier farmer, and family man, to contemplate his role in the ritual heart of Puritanism around which he organized a vigorous devotional piety. The role he played in this private world could not have diverged more sharply from his everyday life, where he was expected to lead the small Westfield community as its teacher and spiritual guide, direct the church, speak out in sermons, write treatises, explicate scripture, advise the town, dispense necessary medical treatment, and rule in his own home. The demands of Puritan doctrine required, however, that in the spiritual realm he throw off the worldliness of the world, "wean" himself from its temptations and false securities, and be meek as a lamb, trusting as a little child, subordinate as a woman, dependent and obedient as a wife. Only a powerful form of meditation, and a driving motivation, could produce such a psychological transformation.

Under the enormous pressure of the conflicts built into his beliefs, Edward Taylor produced the most extensive canon of lyric poetry to come out of Puritan New England. The *Preparatory Meditations* were never published and were not intended for publication. Nor was this poetry circulated among friends, as Anne Bradstreet's manuscript was, although Taylor's long drama of the soul's salvation, *God's Determinations*, may have been read by members of the Westfield congregation. In the hermetically sealed world of his private meditations, there is no audience other than himself and God. All the poses he strikes are free from the considerations that usually constrain writers and shape their rhetoric—considerations that affect all the other poets in this study, who are profoundly conscious of the public nature of their work, self-consciously address readers, imply certain types of readers, and worry whether their audience is hostile or sympathetic, converted or skeptical. By contrast, Taylor can write in a space free from such distractions. His overriding concern is the acceptability, not only of his efforts, but of his very self, to an audience—God—before whom he can only fail with a failure necessary for his success. His meditations, then, constitute raw acts of self-didacticism and self-witnessing, the verbal exercises and discursive lessons of a masculine consciousness learning the ropes of the Puritan ideology of redeemed subjectivity.

By identifying himself rhetorically and ontologically with Herbert's trope of the "crumb of dust" in the prefatory Meditation, the "Prologue," with which I began this discussion, Taylor sets in motion the dialectic of difference characteristic of his self-representations. As in this trope, he figures himself as an object, not a subject, silent and passive, tiny and insignificant, earthy and anonymous—as different from the God whose praises he desires to sing, as night from day. It is an example of what Charles Mignon called Taylor's "decorum of imperfection," and of the meiosis whereby the poet diminishes himself only to amplify, though always unsuccessfully, his God (1426–27). But similarities lurk in this seemingly trivial self-image that spell the poet's incomplete identification with the incarnated Christ of the sacrament. Taylor emphasizes Christ as the "Theanthropy," a God-man, the perfect reconciliation of flesh and spirit. What he receives in the sacramental elements are "Theandrick

Blood, and Body" (2.111:25), both the divine and human natures of
Christ. "Dust" is the mortal condition of the human flesh Christ takes on,
its origin and its end, a signifier that links the flesh of the "old man" in
Adam, made from dust, with the resurrected flesh of the "new man" in
Christ that endures eternally. The second term of the figure links Taylor
to the signifier of this flesh, which at the Lord's Supper is bread. For
Taylor, Christ is "The Purest Wheate in Heaven," ground up and
kneaded into "this Bread of Life . . . / Disht on thy Table up . . . / Gods
White Loafe . . . / Food too fine for Angells . . . / Heavens Sugar Cake"
(1.8:21–30). As a "crumb," Taylor signifies his earthly flesh and its participation as a tiny morsel of Christ's abundant and life-giving "Soule
Bread," of which God himself invites the lowly crumb to "Eate thy fill"
and live (1.8:27–28).

The difference that this self-image promotes serves Taylor's purposes
admirably. By casting himself as a worthless and inconsequential speck,
he avoids pride and confidence, which smack of hypocrisy, and augments
the godsend of a mite's ability to handle the pen of divine praise. Yet, in
his abjection, he participates in the sacramental signifiers of the incarnated Christ, the smidgen of Christic identity that betokens grace. Another poem plays on the pun of "mite/mote" and "might/Almighty,"
creating a similar effect (see Med. 2.95, which also repeats the
crumb/dust pair). It is more than a part/whole relationship, something
between metaphor and metonymy. Central to this strategy of self-
representation is the play of difference and identity, and the promise of
union held out in both qualities.

Explicit gendering of these positions occurs in the first Meditation of
the first series, one of the few numbered Meditations without a scriptural
text, and a poem that complements the "Prologue," being an introduction
to the major theme of the series. Taylor begins by extolling what for him is
God's most significant act:

What Love is this of thine, that Cannot bee
  In thine Infinity, O Lord, Confinde,
Unless it in thy very Person see,
    Infinity, and Finity Conjoyn'd?
    What hath thy Godhead, as not satisfide
    Marri'de our Manhood, making it its Bride?
                      (1.1:1–6)

Christ, in his "very person," effects the marriage of infinite spirit and finite flesh, of God and man, of "Bread of Life" and "crumb of dust." Here, at the very threshold of forty-three years of poetic meditative activity, Taylor invokes the divine act that defines the terms of his meditational life: a divine love so abundant that it overwhelms the gap separating the finite and infinite realms and joins them. But this flooding does not begin to express the fulness of God's love for man. In the hyperbolic second stanza, Christ's love fills up this world and overflows "Hell; wherein / For thine Elect, there rose a mighty Tide!" (1.1:9–10). This tide of love turns, in Taylor's characteristic and sometimes gruesome visual imagination, into a river of redemptive blood, bleeding through Christ's veins "To quench those flames, that else would on us feed" (1.1:12). Christ's love is measured by his sacrifice and suffering. Taylor never tires of exclaiming in wonder over the marriage that is Christ, and the spiritual marriage that he holds out as eschatological promise to redeemed souls.

The problem, and the point of the meditational exercise, is the poet who asks, in the final stanza, to be a personal recipient of Christ's overflowing love, "for Love I would. / But oh! my streight'ned Breast! my Lifeless Sparke! / My Fireless Flame! What Chilly Love, and Cold? / In measure small! In Manner Chilly! See" (1.1:14–18), he mourns. Even in the face of God's "Matchless Love," a love incomparable and also auto-igniting, and with the knowledge of the marriage promised by Christ, the poet's heart is cold, resistant, dead. His unresponsiveness shames and confounds him. By milking the conceit of the marriage, Donne explained his lack of affect by admitting that his soul was betrothed to Satan, and challenging the power of God to annul that prior commitment. In this early Meditation Taylor does not bother to analyze his malaise; rather, he sets up the conditions of its amelioration, and his imagery is almost as sexual, though not (yet) as masochistic as Donne's: "Lord blow the Coal: Thy Love Enflame in mee" (1.1:18), he prays at the end, depicting himself as an inert lump of potential energy that God's animating breath must fan into flames. This solicitation of desire is risky business, however, for both the punishments of Hell and the longing for Heaven stoke fires in the human heart.

Noting Taylor's allusion to the spiritual marriage at the very opening of the *Meditations*, and acknowledging the influence of sacramental theology in his poetics, Albert Gelpi argues that "Taylor describes the incarnation-al mystery in sexual terms" (35). But Gelpi also recognizes another crucial factor: that Taylor borrows his imagery and sexual terms from Canticles, the biblical book that served as the chief source for his poetry. Sixty-six Meditations, almost one-third of Taylor's total output, take scriptural texts from Canticles. Moreover, an extended celebration of the Bride and Bridegroom forms the climax of Taylor's poetic activity: all but four of the final fifty Meditations, written in the last twelve years of his life, take their texts from Canticles, forming the longest continuous sequence in the two series. Some scholars view Taylor's immersion in the discourse of Canticles as incipient mysticism.[10] Charles Hambrick-Stowe, however, demonstrates just how common Taylor's enraptured rhetoric was in a wide range of Puritan devotional styles (20). Other scholars explain his focus as a function of his advancing age and eschatological hopes (Hammond, 191), or as a withdrawal from the increasingly hostile theological progressivism of eighteenth-century New England into a "celebration of the embosomed soul in the womblike bower of Solomon's *hortus conclusus*" (Davis, xix)—but Taylor also *begins* his *Preparatory Meditations* by contemplating scriptural texts from Canticles in which the Spouse praises the beauty and excellence of her Bridegroom. Meditation 1.1, discussed above, introduces the theme of the spiritual marriage. Meditations 1.2, 1.3, 1.4, 1.5, and 1.6 draw their imagery and, more importantly, their lyric impulse from the Spouse's highly sensual praising of her beloved, and Meditation 1.7 takes as its text Psalms 45, the other major source in Puritan theology for the metaphor of the spiritual marriage. As Barbara Lewalski states, the Song of Solomon "may fairly be said to encompass and dominate Taylor's poems" (417).[11]

Most commentators shy away from the sexual implications of the allusions to Canticles in the *Meditations*, or try to dispell them with disclaimers about the allegorical exegetical tradition in which this biblical book was read by Puritans. Gelpi, along with Karl Keller, is one of the few commentators who do not; his insights are revealing, especially when we understand that they pertain specifically (though not intentionally) to Puritan men. He places Taylor in a line of "[male] Christian poets who saw their manhood broken by God's holy lust," who are linked by "the incarnational conviction that in the human fusion eros and agape are inseparable and that man is woman before God" (36–37). Although "restrained by the Calvinist distrust of the unregenerate body" (37), Taylor nevertheless translates the heavily erotic dimension of his imaginative world through the strategy of his first Meditation, which, according to Gelpi, "is to establish the sexual basis for the subsequent figures of speech depicting his experience of grace" (37). In Gelpi's analysis, this strategy is the development of the paradox of the spiritual marriage "through the antithetical but primary elements of fire and water, telling the same mystery in terms of interdependent opposites" (34). Emphasizing that man and God are "not just joined but *con*joined reciprocally and mutually" (33), Gelpi errs on the side of mystical wish fulfillment.[12] A predominant feature of the fantasy of heterosexuality that governs the Puritan rhetoric of conversion, as well as the conventional image of poetic inspiration through a muse, is the radical passivity of the feminine participant: she can desire, but even that desire must be for the blinding and all-powerful penetration by a superior force. Rape, as anyone who has been its victim can testify, is not a sexual act but an act of violence and domination. By soliciting divine attention in the form of ravishment—even if, as in Donne's scenario, that ravishment is the paradoxical condition of your soul's chastity—the Puritan saint puts himself at the mercy of divine power, the power of the Other. Such a relinquishment implies that violence and domination are necessary to wrench the eternal soul from the fallen and corrupt self. Taylor's position, as figured in the final prayer of Meditation 1.1, exemplifies this radical disempowerment, because even a passive, reactive desire eludes the poet: He begs that "Thy Love"— God's love and desire for man, as if man's love and desire would not be sufficient—be kindled in the cold hearth of his heart.

Where Gelpi sees symmetry, Taylor is always careful to preserve the dialectic of difference. Furthermore, his position in what Gelpi calls "a Calvinist version of the *conjunctio oppositorum*," the *hieros gamos*, or holy marriage, of alchemy (41), is nowhere as straightforward as the dance of coupling pairs of static opposites. We can follow some of the logical and positional shifts that Taylor makes as he restages the founding moment in the Judeo-Christian tradition of the installation of difference as gendered, and implicates himself directly in that moment.

The moment occurs in the unnumbered Meditation, "The Experience," which ends, as discussed above, by troping on Herbert's figures for his resolution of the dilemma of faith and praise. Unlike most of the other

Meditations, which are staged as if they precede the sacrament, this poem retells the poet's experience at the Supper. An uncanny "shine" overtakes his soul at his fleeting vision of

> My Nature with thy Nature all Divine
> > Together joyn'd in Him thats Thou, and I.
> > Flesh of my Flesh, Bone of my Bone. There's run
> > Thy Godhead, and my Manhood in thy Son.
> >
> > (ll. 9–12; pp. 8–9)

Taylor, who usually addresses Christ, seems to be addressing God the Father here with a description of his revelation of the incarnate Christ, the "Him thats Thou, and I"—a completion of the primal triangle of the Puritan psyche. The words he uses, "Flesh of my Flesh, Bone of my Bone," will be familiar to God as the phrases of the originary marriage "ceremony" in Eden that Adam speaks to Eve, as told in the second version of the creation story. God brings the woman to Adam to be named generically and positioned according to her origin: "And Adam said, This *is* now bone of my bones, and flesh of my flesh: she shall be called Woman, because she was taken out of Man" (Gen. 2:23). Like the "I do" of our modern ceremony, Adam's phrases are performative. With his words he acknowledges that a part of his body has been taken out of him and made "other"; this part comes from him, but is clearly now different from him and subordinate to him—God insures that. "Man-like, but different sex" is Milton's apt description of Eve in *Paradise Lost* (8.471), a Puritan text that has been described by Marshall Grossman as "the epic of the origin of generic Man," which necessarily contains an account of "the origin of sexual difference" (155). Grossman's Lacanian treatment of the "question of Woman" in Milton argues that Eve stands for the production of difference (sex) within the same (self), and that it is at her expense but also with her complicity that Adam more fully knows and defines himself as an autonomous and self-conscious subject. "The price of the subjectification of Adam," Grossman concludes, "is to be the subjection of Eve" (150).[13]

It should be no surprise that Taylor addresses God in the voice of the first man; in subsequent Meditations, he personally takes on Adam's sin in the fall (see, for example, 1.31 and 2.33). Nor is it surprising that in a description of marriage Taylor would almost automatically reproduce

Adam's words. If, as I speculated earlier, he addresses God in his role as Father, as one of the partners in the marriage, who then occupies the position of Eve, the figure of difference? The only logical choice is Christ. The incarnated Christ is flesh and bone, the divine spirit embodied in order that the old man in Adam can more fully know and define himself as a *redeemed* subject, as a new man in Christ. In a Protestant pantheon emptied of female figures, difference has to be mapped out by gendering positions of relation. The difference that is flesh and the body is traditionally feminine. Christ in his role as mediator, as the fleshly, albeit perfect, and perfectly obedient son, is feminized and provides saints with the best model of conformity to God's will. The *imitatio Christi* is, in this sense, a verbal gesture, the willingness and ability to say to God, with Christ, "Thy will be done." Christ's position in this scheme, however, is not fixed. In his position as Redeemer, God's general and right-hand man, and as the Bridegroom, Christ is clearly masculinized, a stand-in for God the Father. Taylor captures the oscillation in the positions accorded to Christ, the figure who overcomes the unbridgeable abyss between flesh and spirit, the visible and the invisible: "Once at thy Feast, I saw thee Pearle-like stand / 'Tween Heaven, and Earth" ("The Reflexion," ll. 25–26; p. 14), he recalls, envisioning Christ in the gap that separates earth and heaven, mediating between man and God across the defile of difference. As Bernard of Clairvaux explained in one of his celebrated sermons on Canticles, Christ is himself the "kiss" of God's mouth, the metaphor for the reconciliation of same and Other that occurs within him (10).[14] In a sense, the spiritual marriage takes place within Christ so that it can take place between Christ and the human soul.

Taylor's positions in this triangle imitate the cross-gendered positions of Christ. Part of his sinfulness is his resistance to God's will, a masculinized force that places him, sometimes unwillingly, in the feminine and receptive position. In the marriage of "Thy Godhead, and my Manhood in thy Son" that he celebrates in "The Experience" (l. 12; p. 9), he is clearly the fleshly nature and, therefore, feminine—just as in the spiritual marriage promised to the elect in heaven, he occupies the place of the Spouse, a sexually female figure. But he speaks the marriage words of Adam concerning Eve, inverting the doctrinally assigned roles of bridegroom and bride. This experimentation is in keeping with the *dialectic* of difference that Taylor keeps in play. As Cecelia Halbert discovers in her assessment of Taylor's use of the "Tree of Life" metaphor, he attempts a fully reciprocal, mirroring imagery that ultimately fails (34). There is, indeed, an arrogance in Taylor's boasting that Christ is "Flesh of *my* Flesh, Bone of *my* Bone." He makes the relationship seem so personal. This self-assertion flames out dangerously in the abrupt shift in tone in stanza five where he insists upon his "Right"—that is, his rightful place in the hierarchical cosmic scheme guaranteed by his relation to God through Christ, his patrimony. He demands imperiously that the very "Angels Bright" be unseated to make room for him in the place next to God's throne, justifying his claim with the argument that he has a body like Christ, while the angels are bodiless. In this case, the difference of flesh is positively valued, because totally spiritualized. So, the words of Adam that Taylor speaks also highlight his fallen nature. Identifying with Christ in the sacrament and in Christ's role as son and child of God gives Taylor the illusion of divinity. But finally, he is, like Christ, as Eve is to Adam, a part and apart.

A similar, and perhaps analogous, slippage in terms and positions occurs in Taylor's explanation of the Lord's Supper through Christ's parable of the chosen and unchosen (Matt. 22:1–14). In the series of sermons bound together under the title *Treatise Concerning the Lord's Supper*, Taylor tells his congregation that the "wedden" celebrated by the "feast" of the Supper constitutes Christ's "marriage unto the soul; He espouseth it, and promiseth it marriage, and God declares it that He is married unto His people. Hence the usual title He gives her is 'spouse' in the Canticles. Now He will have this His marriage celebrated. It is a matter of the greatest concern. It is the result of all His gospel wooings; it is the efflux of the greatest love" (*Treatise*, 17). By alluding to the title of the elect from Canticles—"spouse"—Taylor draws a connection between the two weddings, which complicates the saint's positions at these feasts. Sacramental worship interpellates him as a "guest" at the wedding celebration who must be in possession of the "wedden garment" of grace, which only God can weave within his soul, and which it is his religious obligation to discern before attending. This robe is the cloak of "justification," the stage in the saint's progress in which God accepts Christ's satisfaction for his sins and imputes Christ's righteousness to him to cover his true state of unworthiness. Although only imputed to a saint, Christ's righteousness nevertheless really belongs to him to the extent that he belongs to Christ.

The justified saint, therefore, "apprehended his spiritual condition in terms of a radical paradox, whereby he is perfectly holy in Christ in heaven even while he remains radically sinful in his earthly state" (Lewalski, 17). This paradox was heightened by the saint's position in the spiritual marriage of Canticles, where he takes up a more intimate relation with Christ in a clearly feminine position. This metaphor interpellates Taylor as the Spouse of Christ, a redeemed soul and Church member, participating in Christ as his mystical body, chosen and beloved though different from, and subordinate to, Godhead. In this position, Taylor can radically displace himself from his present, earthly state and imagine himself replaced in the future in woman's place.

The overlapping of these discourses produces an expanded view of the spiritual marriage, which Jeffrey Hammond outlines in his study of the eschatology of Taylor's *Meditations* on Canticles. Many orthodox Puritans held that all of earthly life is a preparation for the ultimate consummation of heavenly bliss, promised in the sacrament but very nearly bestowed upon the faithful soul in the act of meditating on the Song of Solomon (194). According to the orthodox exegetical tradition, this biblical book played a special role in revealing the Gospel because it anticipated the historical Jesus and his Incarnation as Christ at the same time as it celebrated a mystical Christ, timeless and free of historical specificity, as he was before his Incarnation, and as he would be when saints finally encountered him in heaven (194). "To meditate upon the Bridegroom," Hammond explains, "was to attempt a more direct view of the eschatological and essential Christ than could be generated by means of any other scriptural figure" (194–95); "no text," he concludes, "was considered a more sublime revelation of the celestial future of the elect soul" (196). The liturgical parallel to Canticles' "foretaste" of heaven was the sacrament of the Supper (203).[15]

A more direct conflation of the feminine position of Canticles and the sacramental ritual occurs as Taylor meditates on the text, "My spouse" (Cant. 4:8), the title through which Christ as the Bridegroom interpellates his Bride. Taylor has yet to recognize himself in this call, so stunned is he by the discrepancy between the parties to the betrothal. The vast difference between them saps most of his verbal energy. In a veritable orgy of incongruously mated but related images, such as God and mud, the King of Glory and a worm, Monarchs and mites, Glory and shame, Angels and ants, Taylor marvels for several stanzas at the truth of Isaiah's prophecy: "Thy Maker is thy Husband" (1.23:24). Part of the wonder of this marriage, he confesses mournfully, is not only his baseness, but his backwardness "When Christ doth Wooe: and till his Spirit bee / His Spokes man to Compell me I deny" (ll. 39–40)—a clear statement of the soul's radical dependence upon the Spirit for the gift of grace. And so, he prays:

> Seing, Dear Lord, its thus, thy Spirit take
> And send thy Spokes man, to my Soul, I pray.
> Thy Saving Grace my Wedden Garment make:
> Thy Spouses Frame into my Soul Convay.
> I then shall be thy Bride Espousd by thee
> And thou my Bridesgroom Deare Espousde shalt bee.
> (1.23:43–48)

Since he cannot be interpellated as a spiritual subject under his own name, he prays for Christ to infuse "Thy Spouses Frame" into his soul. He can answer Christ's call as the Spouse because that is to answer in the name of an Other. Line 45 invokes the metaphor of the "Wedden Garment," which Taylor considered necessary for attendance at the "Wedden," and which positions the speaker as a guest at the feast. Yet in line 46 he asks to be "framed"—that is, to have his desires disposed like the compliant desires of God's Spouse, no longer simply a guest and observer but an eager partner in the marriage being celebrated.[16] The colon at the end of line 45 suggests that these ideas are more than parallel, that line 46 is an elaboration, clarification, and intensification of the line preceding it. To be a bidden guest is to be called. To be the beloved woman is to be chosen and enabled by your lover to answer that call.

Meditation 1.23 gives us the opportunity to consider how the figure of the Spouse functions as spiritual persona for Taylor. Karl Keller reads this Meditation as a recapitulation of the story of atonement in "erotic terms" with Taylor "playing the role of a desirous woman, as he does in most of his Meditations" (213). Like Gelpi, Keller discovers in Taylor's work the operation of an "erotic scheme of salvation . . . : God as Lover, mankind as the Beloved One, the seduction, and the loving reaction in man that amounts to regeneration. Through such erotic terms," he concludes, "the doctrine of atonement is turned into poetic metaphor" (213).[17] Representing himself in the guise of a "desirous woman," Taylor

satisfies some of the paradoxical requirements of Puritan theology's redeemed subjectivity, since woman was thought to be inherently passive,
submissive, and "feeble," in Keller's words, and her desire was construed
as the desire to be obedient, dominated, possessed, even ravished. But
this formulation does not account for the problematic nature of desire in
Puritan thought. If man is nothing and God is all, is any desire legitimate?
Is passive desire something humans can understand?[18] Taylor constantly
laments that "Though I desire so much, I can't o're doe" (2.4:31). Evident in this complaint is the split between the "I" that desires and the "I"
paralyzed by self-consciousness. William Scheick defines the saint's
"consent" to God's will as requiring "the full consent of one's will and the
free, deliberate willing of God's will" (*Will*, 70–71). Taylor himself describes the kinds of desires appropriate for the state of grace when he
exclaims: "Thy Service is my Freedom, Pleasure, Joy, / Delight, Bliss,
Glory, Heaven on Earth" ("The Return," ll. 31–32; p. 10). "See, waile,
and Will thy Will, I must, or must / From Heavens sweet Shine to Hells
hot flame be thrust" (1.16:11–12), he continually admonishes himself.
This "seemingly paradoxical view of man's freedom" is analogous, in
Scheick's mind, to John Winthrop's "willing subjection" of Christians to
Christ and the theocratic state, though he omits Winthrop's explanatory
comparison to the "willing" subjection of wives (69 n. 36).

This attitude of submission, epitomized by Christ's perfect acquies-
cence as the willing castrate, is precisely what the majority of Taylor's
prayers imply that he does not yet possess. "Lord, make my Soule Obedient: and when so, / Thou saist Believe, make it reply, I do" (1.25:29–
30), he prays, requesting the total erasure of his own will in order to
accomplish the self-denial that God requires. If his soul were tractable, if
he found himself framed as the Spouse, then God could speak through
him the words of the marriage vow, "I do," affirming an obedience divinely constructed. Is it still obedience, when one has no choice in the
matter? David Leverenz has described Taylor's poetic voice as "imperious
yet abject, as if he had to make himself into a battered wife to be Christ's,"
capturing the violence, coercion, and masochism latent in the theology
governing the construction of Taylor's poetic voice.[19]

For example, taking his cues from the Spouse who says of her beloved,
"thy name is as an ointment poured forth" (Cant. 1:3), Taylor lauds
Christ as "A Box of Ointments, broke; sweetness most sweet. / A surge of

spices: Odours Common Wealth, / A Pillar of Perfume: a steaming Reech / Of Aromatick Clouds: All Saving Health. / Sweetness itselfe thou art" (1.3:7–11). Addressing Christ in a paraphrase of the Spouse's words, Taylor is adoring and expansive. He amplifies her images, but at this point in his spiritual development he cannot measure up to her model of perfected desires, and he wonders absurdly, but with a logic perfectly consistent with the images of fragrant stimulants that he borrows from her praise, "Am I denos'de?" (1.3:19) that I cannot smell such richness myself. His concern is with applying the doctrines he draws from the model of the Spouse to his own spiritual life. Thus, he prays near the end of this Meditation, "Lord, breake thy Box of Ointment on my Head" (l. 37), a request that to us seems inelegant and inappropriate; but this violence, invited and welcomed, is an integral part of the Puritan soul's preparation. Helpless to aid in his own purgation, Taylor needs God's sweetly perfumed and healing ointment to rain down on him with enough force to clear out the noxious odor of "stincking Carrion" (l. 24) and "Dunghill Damps" (l. 34), the reek of his own sinfulness and mortality, which blocks his olfactory sense. Only then will he truly be able to smell Christ's sweets as his Spouse does—that is, to experience Christ as the confirmed saint will be able to. The consequence of this metaphorical sensory access is a transcendent flight toward union with the Beloved: "My Soule shall in thy sweets then soar to thee" (l. 41).

Taylor's *Meditations* abound with the violence necessary to wean fallen men from the sin of self-reliance. Meditating on God's omnipotence, he cries, "Oh! that this, Thine Authority was made / A Golden Anvill: and my Contemplation / A smiting Hammer: and my heart was laid / Thereon, and hammerd up for emendation. / And anvilld stoutly to a better frame" (2.53:13–17)—to "Thy Spouses frame." The image of a heart at white heat on a smith's forge, reminiscent of the sacred emblems popular in the sixteenth and seventeenth centuries,[20] involves the participation of the poet himself, whose "acts" of contemplation are the metaphorical hammer smiting his own heart. This Meditation ends in an ecstasy of solicited violence whose erotics are fueled less by seduction and more by an imitation of Christ's martyrdom:

Lord let thy Doctrine melt my Soule anew:
　And let thy Scepter drill my heart in mee:

And let thy Spirits Cotters pierce it through
　　Like golden rivits, Clencht, mee hold to thee.
　　Then thou and I shall ne'er be separate.
　　Thy Praise shall be my Glory sung in state.
　　　　　　　　　　(2.53:43–48)

This is the dark side of the spiritual marriage, displayed in metaphors unsettling to visualize. Though the "rivits" are "golden" and therefore holy, Taylor's heart still must be bolted to God through a spiritualizing process that requires his internalization of doctrine and recognition of God's kingly, phallic power (and conversely, his own absolute helplessness). The image of drilling a hole through the heart and piercing it with spiritual "Cotters," pins split at the end so that when put through a hole they can be spread and bent backward for a firm grip, has sexual and sadomasochistic overtones. Taylor welcomes such metaphoric operations upon his heart, for they are like the "good pleas" Christ as his advocate will "anvill . . . / Out of his Flesh and Blood" to redeem the sinner's soul (1.39:26–27). He further justifies this torturous process with the argument that "Nails made of heavenly Steel, more Choice than gold / Drove home, Well Clencht, eternally will hold" (ll. 29–30). The text delights in the way the nails of the crucifixion "secure" the speaker's own position for eternity. The clenching or gripping of nails into the wood of the cross, and of rivets into the substance of the soul, suggests also hands and teeth clenched in pain. Human consent to God's will is not easily or painlessly won.[21] When Taylor processes these "womanly" desires to be made and remade, riveted and crucified, through the figure of the Spouse in Canticles, both the violence of his imagery and his debilitating spiritual anxiety markedly decrease.

The Spouse is not properly a literary persona for Taylor because his burning needs are not for achieving solely literary effects, except insofar as they are also meditational and spiritual ones that he can chart by the response of his own affections, not readers' reactions. From a doctrinal point of view, the Spouse's attributes, and especially her desires, stand as the ultimate model for male saints of the feminizing dependence upon, obedience and practical conformity to, God's will required of them for salvation. In Taylor's iconography, the position of the Spouse is the highest and most encompassing of the relations open to him with respect to

Christ. In a Meditation on the promise recorded in 1 Corinthians 3:23, "You are Christ's," which follows the longest, and most anxiety-ridden, of all of Taylor's Meditations, he takes on the querulous tones of a slighted and insecure lover or first wife who demands: "Am I thy Child, Son, Heir, thy Spouse, yet gain / Not of the Rights that these Relations claim?" (1.37:29–30). Expanding this inquiry in the terms of physical intimacy, the poet laments that now he is willing, but God, perversely, hangs back: "Am I hop't on thy knees, yet not at ease? / Sunke in thy bosom . . . / Lodgd in thine Arms?" (ll. 31–33), he pursues relentlessly. The final two instances offered by the speaker are the most serious ones and cover the rituals of the sacrament and the marriage: "Set at thy Table, yet scarce tast a Dish / Delicious? Hugd, yet seldom gain a Kiss?" (ll. 35–36). Despite the hectoring tone, there is something playful in the poet's ability to call God on the carpet as an inattentive husband.

The solution to the saint's anxiety over the lack of evidence of his divine relation takes the form of a spiritual impregnation that will, as usual, remake the poet, here as a fruitful graft onto the Tree of Life specifically modeled on the figure of the Spouse of Canticles. Taylor prays at the end of the section:

> Make me thy Branch to bare thy Grapes, Lord, feed
>   Mee with thy bunch of Raisins of the Sun.
> Mee stay with apples; let me eate indeed
>   Fruits of the tree of Life: its richly hung.
>   (1.37:25–28)

Bearing Christ's grapes is tantamount to receiving the sacramental benefits of his fruit, the holy wine of his blood. But this sacramental emblem is considerably intensified by the intertextual resonance in line 27, where the grapes are merged with the apples requested by the Spouse in Canticles 2:5 as she enters Christ's banqueting house: "Stay me with flagons, comfort me with apples: for I am sick with love." Line 27 conflates the first two phrases of Canticles 2:5 to cover the sacramental gestures of eating and drinking and parallels them directly with the Spouse's impassioned requests. From her position, the appeal for "apples" transforms this already resonant fruit into a complex allegorical figure. The apples represent Christ in his sacramental guise, the ordinances he instituted to sustain believers, and the spiritual influences conveyed in those rites.

They also stand for the promised fruits of the Tree of Life onto which Taylor desires to be grafted, growing in a garden that restores, yet supersedes, the garden of Eden—where eating apples from another tree, the Tree of Knowledge, caused the Fall from grace. In a later Meditation, the apple tree of Canticles is associated with the Tree of Life promised in Revelation (see Med. 2.161A:35–40). In Taylor's Puritan allegory, the figure of the Spouse in Canticles redresses Eve as the victim of Satan and corrupter of Adam, and overturns her original transgression against God and the "natural" hierarchy of the sexes. The Spouse, as Taylor represents this figure, puts woman back in the place God had originally set for her.

Further evidence that the figure of the Spouse assuages Taylor's anxiety comes in Meditations 2.96 and 2.97, whose texts invoke the celebrated and much-theorized kiss that the Bride, confirmed in her betrothal, boldly begs from her suddenly subdued Bridegroom. The poems actually meditate on the continuation of the verse alluded to in Meditation 1.37, discussed above, which follows the Spouse's request to be stayed and comforted, "for I am sick of love" (Cant. 2:5). The Spouse needs this comfort because the Bridegroom has turned his face away—has withdrawn his spiritual influences. In this context, Taylor projects his own fears of spiritual abandonment and backsliding upon this figure and finds in the qualities he attributes to her sudden solace and an uncharacteristic relief. For Taylor, the Spouse personifies "that ardent Flame of Love" (2.97:2) for which he petitioned Christ in the very first Meditation of the first series. When Christ, the sun of her world, "doth weare a Cloude" (2.97:23) and appears to "stop such acts of love and grace" (2.97:17) that before sustained her, she does not despair, but "In passionate affection seemed to move" (2.97:4). Taking comfort in the Spouse's sustained affections, Taylor desperately wants to be able to say that, if he were tried, "such ardent flames would rise / Of true Loves passion, in its Blinks or Blisses, / As in the Holy Spouse's heart that cries / Oh! let him kiss mee with his orall kisses" (2.97:13–16). In other words, she manages to maintain her faith whether she experiences "Blinks or Blisses"—moments of doubt in the absence of God's face, or the ecstasy of belief in God's presence—while he cannot.

The Spouse solves the dilemma of faith and praise that Herbert articulated for Taylor in "The Temper" (I) by giving the lie to the perennial stereotype of inconstant woman, governed by the moon, lunacy, pagan goddesses, and the like. This spiritual model of idealized womanhood has a quietly transforming effect on Taylor, who can accept that "Such as enjoy [Christ's] Love, may lack the Sense / May have thy love and not loves evidence" (2.96:29–30). Instead of complaining of the incongruence between his overwhelming desires and his limited capacity, and thus requiring a rape of his will, he can opt for a less invasive and less intense form of intimacy with God:

> But listen, Soule, here seest thou not a Cheate.
>   Earth is not heaven: Faith not Vision. No.
> To see the Love of Christ on thee Compleate
>   Would make heavens Rivers of joy, earth overflow.
>   This is the Vale of tears, not mount of joyes.
>   Some Crystal drops while here may well suffice.
>   (2.96:43–48)

"Because thou hast not all, say not, thoust none" (l. 36), he chides himself. The imagery of this Meditation rewrites Meditation 1.1, in which the poet called on God's love to overrun his heart with its "mighty Tide" of redemptive sacramental liquid (1.1:10). Now, a few "Crystal" drops from Christ will suffice. In fact, so sure is Taylor that "Though I be dark: want Spectacles to prove / Thou lovest mee: I shall at last see Clear" (2.96:51–52), he can for once invert the positions of the musical allusion that ends the majority of Meditations and imagine a time when "My little mite of Love shall musick sweet / Tune forth on thee, its harp, that heaven shall greet" (2.97:53–4). This prayer is cast in the future tense, but it is no longer conditional. For with the model of the Spouse's constancy before him as a guide and goal, Taylor seems confident enough to represent himself in an active role as a musician who, though diminutive, tunes Christ as his responsive instrument to produce praise.[22]

The Puritans read Canticles as an allegory of eschatological promises: the joy and delight of the Bride and Bridegroom would be fulfilled by the elect soul and its savior. More than the pledge of 1 Corinthians 3:23, "You are Christ's," explored in Meditation 1.37 (discussed above), Canticles affirmed the mutual relations of the soul and Christ, the heart of the covenant of grace, and the central paradox of the spiritual marriage. Taylor's formulation of this paradox comes in the concluding declaration of Meditation 2.69, the last in a short series of meditations on Canticles: "Propriety is mutuall" (l. 39). He explores this paradox in more depth in an ecstatic poem, Meditation 2.79, as he contemplates its amorous version in Canticles 2:16: "My Beloved is mine and I am his." Taking these words of the Spouse as authoritative, he uses them to defend Calvinism's notion of "the union (that blesst thing) / To Christs Blesst Person, Happy Enkentrism" (2.79:63–64) against the heresy of "sherlosism," the doctrines of Dr. William Sherlock, Dean of St. Paul's (see Taylor, *Poems*, 228n). Yet, as incensed as Taylor became in defense of the reality of the mystical union, he preserved the difference on which it was based. In giving his own life to purchase the soul of his Spouse, Christ blurs the boundaries between man and God, so that the poet senses an interpenetration in which "I am no more mine own, but thine, probate, / Thou not so thine, as not mine too thereby" (2.79:15–16). Yet, what is proper and mutual is not equal or logical; it is also probationary. Within his discovery of "Mutuall propriety" (l. 19) arise "strang appropriations" (l. 29), including the paradox that though Christ and the saint both give themselves, they finally retain their integrity and do not merge. Furthermore, the price each pays is unequal; ironically, man strikes the better bargain. And finally, miraculously, Christ gives all he has, yet remains rich. Meditating on this mystery, Taylor realizes the necessity of the complete selflessness epitomized by Christ: "my down laying of myselfe I see / For thee, 's the way for mee to blessed wealth" (ll. 51–52). In the Meditation's final twist, purchases and gifts become indistinguishable as the pun on "deare" suggests, and the reciprocity of the mystical union imports celestial bliss of a distinctly poetic kind, as man and Christ "by each / For each, make each to one anothers deare, / And each delight t'heare one anothers Speech" (ll. 56–58). Taylor's "Mutuall propriety" is the paradisical interchange of holy conversation.

When, at about seventy years of age, Taylor turned his gaze almost exclusively to explicating passages from Canticles, it is fair to say that he had arrived at a "plateau of assurance" in his spiritual pilgrimage (Lewalski, 423–24). I have already described the ways in which he embedded his sacramental theme in the framework and imagery of the spiritual marriage. More importantly, however, the Song of Solomon reiterated the hermeneutic experience of sacramental worship and provided Taylor with ample opportunity to thematize that experience in order to make it his own. The Puritans construed Canticles as a text with a secret that is revealed exclusively: a text that excludes those who do not possess the key, who are not themselves possessed. Readers must decode it, yet possessing the code requires membership in God's Invisible Church and indicates an elect soul. Thus, reading Canticles correctly is like an effective reception of the Lord's Supper; it requires interpretation that depends upon the saint's active spiritual participation—"the exercise of the faith of communion" (*Treatise*, 82)—because Taylor understands Canticles as an allegory.

In her study of the orthodoxy of the late Meditations, "Sacred or Profane?: Edward Taylor's Meditations on Canticles," Karen Rowe demonstrates that Taylor basically agreed with "traditional Puritan exegetical principles" as expounded by James Durham, whose study, *Clavis Cantici: or, an Exposition of the Song of Solomon* (1668), he owned. Durham, says Rowe, argued that the Song was allegorical by nature, because its meaning was impossible to ascertain without a spiritual interpretation (129–30). Orthodox exegetes of Canticles made a reader's ability to comprehend the eschatological message of the erotic love song, while avoiding a carnal understanding of its language, proof of spiritual commitment and of a desire to transcend the purely earthly self (Hammond, 198). Reading spiritually was part of Taylor's self-imposed test of his conformity to God's will, which is why he represents himself not as a willful writer but as a willing and will-less reader of Christ, God's "rich Love Letter" (Med. 2.8:21) sent down from heaven and inscribed upon the cleansed and purified blank sheet of his heart.[23] The hermeneutic experience of "right reading" becomes a kind of sacrament, not only for Taylor, but for other orthodox Puritans.[24] Like John Fiske, reading and troping upon images divinely anagrammatized in proper names, Taylor meditated on the sensual and sometimes patently absurd images in Canticles of the Bride and Bridegroom in order to prove himself an apt reader of God's text. Reading beyond a literal level that fairly insisted on sensuality was like projecting oneself out of one's body and fallen mind. Furthermore, for the poet to "write aright" ("Prologue," l. 26), he had first to "see . . . aright" (1.35:38). Taylor acknowledges that for his heart to open, God has to "Open mine Eyes . . . / Take off their film, my Sins . . . / Cleare my Sight" (1.35:38–39, 43). To open the "eye of the heart" he has to read from the right place.

The right place is, of course, the position of the Spouse. Just as saints are bound to read the signifiers of the sacrament with the aid of grace from the human side of the "kiss," so they are obligated to interpret the allegorical song of the Bride from her place and also in her place—what amounts to a Puritan gynesis. The Spouse's femininity institutes the difference requisite for union. She takes the place of Christ's "Body mystick" while he, praised as the "Head" (2.151:8–9) and representative of the Father, occupies the masculine position of power. In several of the Meditations in these series, Taylor occupies the position of petitioner and probationer, seeking identity with the Spouse as the model of Christ's beloved, and membership in the Spouse who represents "an agrigate" (2.133:27) "that doth consist of all / Gods blesst Elect regenerate within / The tract of time from first to last" (2.136:31–33). His insistence on the collective meaning of the Spouse reinforces spousehood as a feminine position prescribed to all the elect with respect to Christ, a position of *achieved* redeemed collective subjectivity. At the same time, his relation to this feminine signifier is extremely personal. He no longer needs to objectify himself in ritual objects. Through her he speaks as other than his earthly self, as the redeemed subject, uttering his desire for union with the divine in a role traditionally designated as feminine and scripturally sanctioned.

The fitness of this figure for Taylor's purposes rests in the way the Spouse simultaneously accommodates and disarms difference. On the one hand, she has all of Christ's perfected qualities: "His Person, offices, his Grace and Shine"; "He and his All yea all of him, is mine" (2.133:6, 5), Taylor says, speaking directly in her voice, rehearsing the moment when he can truly embrace Christ in "Mutuall propriety." This is precisely what differentiates the Spouse as persona from the "desirous woman" or "lisping child" whose voices Taylor uses at other moments in the *Preparatory Meditations*. She is a version, as we will see in a moment, a reflection, an exact copy, of Christ—and thus wonderfully articulate in the rich metaphors favored by God for the presentation of his otherwise impalpable mysteries to human comprehension. On the other hand, though the Spouse is a powerful and attractive figure who speaks and utters her desire, nothing she says is her own. Her gaze is fixed on the perfect object—Christ—and is therefore eminently acceptable. Styled by

Taylor, in a paraphrase of Canticles, as "thou fairest of all Women kinde" (2.129:8), she subsumes Eve, the Virgin Mary, ancient queens, mythic beauties, and all the Lauras and Beatrices of sacred and secular poetry. She is the cosmic principle of femininity, existing solely as the desire of the Other, and at his desire—never for or by herself, not having what could be called a self or subjectivity. She is the absence of fallen self, the model of redeemed subjectivity, a projection of divine narcissism. She is the alterity of spiritual conversion, the Other who constitutes Christ as Self, a "body" without flesh, soul engendered, but controlled. Although she is feminine, her presence does not contaminate heaven with female-ness because the Spouse is woman divorced from women.

And yet, the Spouse's very existence as a theologico-cultural entity reinforces patriarchal domination of women, because her empowerment derives from her complicity with androcentrism. She maintains her place to the extent that she is willing—really, incapable of doing otherwise, as the totally effaced creature of Christ—to stay put in that place. The structure of the spiritual marriage fixes her as essentially subordinate and eternally subservient, the "mystical body" supporting Christ who is the head and crown. Nonetheless, she is necessary for Christ's completion, the Other who completes him in the mystical and ecclesiastical sense. Taylor addressed this paradox in Meditation 2.51, and on the same topic there is also a rather bizarre sermon extant. "How can the Church be said to fill him, who indeed fills all things in all?" he asks at the outset of his homiletic exposition. For almost the entire sermon, his explanations trip over their own rhetoric and come to rest, finally, in tautology. Here is just a brief, illustrative sample:

> She fills Christ top full, because She is his Fulness, and indeed he fills her out of his all filling Fulness, that she might be his Fulness filling him again. He makes her Compleate that she might Comple-ate him. She is Compleate in him, who is the head of all Prin-cipalities, and Powers: and he is Compleated in her Who is his Body and Fulness of him that fills all in all. Hence there is in Some Sense a mutuall Inbeing One in the Other and a mutuall Compleating one of the other. For as the Head being a relative term hath no Comli-ness without its body: So the Body being a relative term, hath no

Compleatness without the head, nay, they are both either monstrous,
or Mangled if either be without other: or Severed a Sunder.
(*Christographia*, 300)

The Spouse's strange power of completing the divine fulness, Taylor
hastens to remind his congregation, "is not of Christ as to his Person: but
as to his Polity. Not as the Son of God: for so it would be blasphemie: But
as to His Mysticall Body" (*Christographia*, 307). Saints, therefore, should
aspire, not to be like women, but to read, speak, and complete God as the
Spouse does. Spiritual conversion should endow saints with a gynetic
principle, a metaphor for reading and speaking, "a woman-as-effect," as
Alice Jardine defines gynesis (25). For the figure of the Spouse brings
together the necessary subjection of being a redeemable object easily
written upon and easily read, and the necessary redeemed subjectification
of reading perfectly.

The texts Taylor chooses from Canticles highlight the Spouse's role as
object and reader, and they seem to position Christ in precisely the same
role. The first and longest continuous sequence of poems on Canticles
texts, Meditations 2.115 to 2.153, is divided roughly in half: the first
section, Meditations 2.115 through 2.133, focuses on Canticles 5:10–6:2,
passages containing the Spouse's extravagant praise of her beloved. The
second unit, Meditations 2.134 through 2.153, focuses on Canticles 6:4–
7:6, verses in which the Bridegroom praises the attributes of his Spouse.
The next short sequence, Meditations 2.156 through 2.157B, meditates
on the banquet in Canticles, linking it explicitly with the sacrament of the
Lord's Supper. In the final short sequence, Meditations 2.160 through
2.165 (all of which were written when he was over eighty), Taylor returns
to the texts he used for his first Meditations, Canticles 2:1, and works
through the verses in which the Spouse describes her entrance into her
lover's banqueting house and her intense love-sickness. Speech by the
Spouse clearly frames the entire extended celebration and is the place in
which Taylor wanted to fall silent, but his section on Christ's praising of
the Spouse indicates that he was not ready to give up his masculine
identification. It is in this section, in fact, that the appropriation of the
Spouse for Christ's narcissistic purposes is most clearly revealed.

Taylor selects Canticles passages that are the least doctrinal and the
most ornamental in the text. They only obliquely tell the "story" that

Protestant exegetes, in sharp contrast to Catholics, discovered in the book, the narrative of the paradigmatic spiritual life: how the Spouse as soul and Church finds, loses, and regains her beloved Christ again (Lewalski, 60–61). The texts Taylor explicates are extended descriptions of the outward appearance of the Bride and Bridegroom, so that he can comprehend and display the spiritual beauty of the lovers by reading their elaborately metaphorical bodies. Canticles 5:10–16, for example, focuses on the Beloved's ruddy complexion, his golden head, eyes like doves, cheeks like beds of spices and lips like lilies dropping myrrh, hands set with gold rings, belly of ivory overlaid with sapphires, legs like pillars of marble, and sweet mouth. Christ's praises of the Spouse in the second part of this sequence are, if anything, more elaborate. The texts call attention to her beauty "terrible as an army with banners," her eyes that overcome, hair like a flock of goats, teeth like a flock of sheep, temples like pomegranates, the shoes on her feet, the joints of her thighs like jewels, her navel like a round goblet and belly like a heap of wheat set about with lilies, her two breasts like young roes and her neck like a tower of ivory.

Taken as a whole, this approach looks dangerously like the "blazon" of Petrarchan love lyrics, in which the poet praises his beloved by anatomizing her, by separately extolling parts of her face and body—a rhetorical fragmentation aimed at displaying the power of the beloved's features over the lover's gaze, which, nevertheless, leaves her grotesquely cut up, powerless, and silent. Taylor spiritualizes these body parts and physical attributes by drawing forth the divine meaning of their signifiers—the essence of the sacramental operation. He first establishes the metaphorical nature of the biblical text upon which he will exercise a sacramental vision. In one of his sermons, Taylor cites Canticles 5 to his congregation, "wherein the Severall parts of [Christ's] Body are Set out by rich, and weighty Metaphors, that cannot bee well understood of anything so fittly, as to emblemize" what Taylor calls "the Glory of his outside. For his Works are his rich Ornaments"—that is, his glorious qualities and spiritual accomplishments (*Christographia*, 443–44). He goes on, in the prose as well as the poetry, to analyze each image for its spiritual import, so that, for example, Christ's golden head is "as a note of the Surpassing excellency of Counsills, and Determinations"; "his Cheeks as a bed of Spices with Sweet flowers v. 13, to import the admirable Sweet inravishment of his Countenance to the Spiritualized Eye. His Lips as Lillies dropping

Sweet smelling Myrrhe, to sett out the exceeding Excellency and Saving efficacy of his Word"; and so on (*Christographia*, 444). The saint is obliged to meditate upon these glorious visual signifiers of Christ until his heart opens to their influences: "And that the glory of these ornaments may affect our hearts we are calld to behold him with the Crown wherewith he is Crowned in the Day of his Espousalls, and in the day of the gladness of his heart" (443). In these rich metaphors, Taylor says, addressing Christ, the "Spirits Pensill hath thy Glory told" and "Rapts thee up in Glorys fold" (2.123B:13, 17). Although he fears that in "commenting on the Same . . . My Muse will thy bright glory smoot" (ll. 12–14), he also knows that a commentary on Christ's artistry, even though imitative, is the closest he can come to the source of heavenly discourse, and he prays that "some bright flashes of [Christ's] glory" will touch his eyes, and be reflected in his glasses (ll. 15–16), thus blinding his natural eye so that he may see with his spiritual eye, Christ's eye.

Christ is both the object of the hermeneutics of right reading and its enabler. In the characteristic way that spiritual meaning inverts fleshly understanding, both the Spouse and the poet are converted from active readers into passive and reflecting mirrors in which they are to read the image of Christ. In a Meditation based on one of the Spouse's summary blazons, the text "His countenance is like Lebanon, Excellent as Cedars" (Cant. 5:15), Taylor asks Christ to lead him up to the mount of Lebanon and show him "an Aspect bright of thee" which will open "the Valving Doors" of his heart—"the Casements of thy Faith in mee"—"And give my Souls Cleare Eye of thee a Sight / As thou shinst its bright looking Glasses bright" (2.125:1–6). Metaphors of visual access slide into one another: Christ's countenance is a mountain view; the saint's heart is a window of faith opening onto this view, which is also the holy land; the soul's eye catches a glimpse of Christ as he shines into the window, which acts as a mirror to reflect his image back to him. Clearing up Taylor's spiritual sight enables him to "read" Christ in the scriptural name, Lebanon, and its "metaphors" (ll. 7–8), because once his ear and eye "Having their Spirituall Casements opening," then all the spiritual meaning displayed by Christ in his self-representations, "Thy Shine and Smell of Lebanon Crowd in" (ll. 38–40). This request recalls an earlier Meditation on the typological figure of Moses, called into God's service and God's presence at the top of a mountain. Taylor dubbed the Old Testament leader a "Looking Glass" reflecting Christ's "Dazzling Shine" to human eyes (2.9:1–2).

Moses is a type of Christ, but Christ himself appears in the "Gospell Glass" of Canticles, reflected in the words of his Spouse's praises. His "pert percing fiery Eye" (2.119:2) is an organ of spiritual power and irresistible attraction; just a "glance" of its "amourous beams," the poet confesses to Christ, can "fetch as upon golden Ladders fine / My Heart and Love to thee in Hottest Steams" (ll. 26–28). In another Meditation, Taylor, speaking as the Spouse to her twelve handmaids who question her about her lover's absence, urges them to visualize Christ, "ev'ry minim of thy Humane Frame. / Deckt up with Nature's brave perfections right, / And Decorated with rich Grace, Whose Flame / In Sparkling Shines do ravish with delight" (2.128:7–10). The emphasis falls on Christ's "Person," Christ as an object accessible to the fallen human senses, especially the visual sense. The Meditation goes on to summarize the spiritual significance of Christ's body parts enumerated in previous poems. This is a God accommodated to the fallen senses. The poet, who positions himself watching the scenario from the sidelines, and who is neither as ignorant as the handmaids nor as confident as the Spouse, prays that Christ's flame will "Fall through thy Gospells Looking Glass with might, / Upon my frozen heart, and thaw the Same" (ll. 56–57).

Christ's words are like mirrors magnifying and reflecting back to the saint the fiery, glorified divine image he hopes to find burned into his heart. In another Meditation in this series, the poet prays for a heart like a "Chrystall looking Glass" (2.132:32). The figure is witty and redemptive: crystal, a pun on Christ's name, is clear—that is, purified of self-image—and transparent so that Christ's countenance can shine through it. In an earlier version of this same image, the poet prayed for his "person" to become Christ's looking glass, and then invited him to "cast thou thine Eye. / Thy Image view that standeth shining there" (2.92:38–40). With a heart like a cleared, shiny surface, the poet promises Christ to "yield thee the Object right / Of both thy Spirituall Sight and Smell most clear" (2.132:37–38)—himself hidden behind Christ's own blinding reflection. Actually, Taylor hopes none of himself will be seen in that spectacular blaze. With this prayer echoing in our minds, Taylor ends the Spouse's praising of Christ by meditating on the verbal mirror glinting at the heart of Canticles: "I am my beloved and my beloved is mine" (Med. 2.133).

In the second half of the long sequence, Taylor emulates Christ by praising the "spirituall beauty" of his Spouse. By reversing the positions of speaker and object, woman is explicitly put into the place she has always occupied. It may seem inappropriate to talk of the traditional male bonding over the body of woman that feminist readers have discovered in a wide historical range of masculine relations, yet Taylor indulges rather conspicuously in this power play. For example, after an extensive and particularly challenging bit of exegesis in which he explicates Canticles 7:4: "Thy Neck is like a Tower of Ivory: thine Eyes are like the Fishpools of Heshbon, at the Gate of Bath Rabbim: thy Nose is like the tower of Lebanon that Looketh towards Damascus," he concludes, "And hence these Metaphors we spirituallized / Speake out the Spouses spirituall Beauty cleare" (2.151:49–50). The strong sense of hermeneutic accomplishment here derives, as the opening address to Christ indicates, from Taylor's triumph at having subdued the tempting, evanescent "world" by contemplating the Spouse instead. "My Glorious Lord, how doth the Worlds bright Glory / Grow great?" he begins; "Yet loe, thy Spouse doth ware a Shine / That far ore shines the Worlds bright Shining Story" (ll. 1–3). Though the "we" can refer to the tradition of orthodox commentators with whom Taylor is in dialogue in this series on Canticles,[25] or the members of the Invisible Church in which he hopes to be included, the Meditation addresses Christ directly. Thus, man and God, rubbing shoulders clubbily in that "we" of line 49, share the position of active spiritual hermeneuts, battling worldly influences through a feminine figure of transcendence.

The lush metaphors of Canticles, which in the previous section spoke out Christ's "brightest beauty cleare" (2.119:29), also apply to the Spouse. And while these metaphors elevate her above the run of ordinary women, they also serve to make her the subservient creature of Christ's primary narcissism. For example, while Christ's "brisk" eye pursues saints' hearts with "amorous beams" and "fetches" them up, panting and aroused, to heaven, the Spouse is looked upon—an object of contemplation, the object of male gazes. Taylor even deliberately misreads biblical passages to "spiritualize" this Christ-centered reading from them. Even as he explicates Canticles 6:10: "Who is she that looks forth as the morning, fair as the moon, clear as the sun, terrible as an army with banners," a passage as much about the Spouse looking out as about how she appears to others, he casts her in the now-classical terms of the male gaze that robs its object of her subjectivity. One's ability to look out at the world and how one looks and is perceived are intimately related. The "as" of the Canticles text is ambiguous; it is unclear whether the Spouse gazes out at the moment the sun beams down on the world, or whether her bright appearance resembles the shining sun to an observer. Taylor loses no time in exploiting the ambiguity. He exults in his marriage to Christ, which will make him both "looke like / The glorious morning" (2.143:7–8), and "Looke forth like as the Morning" (l. 4). This same doubling applies to the Spouse, who both looks forth regally with "sharp lookes" (l. 31) and is "adorned like the morning Cleare" (l. 43).

Despite the duplicity of readings, the controlling perspective of this Meditation was set out much earlier in stanza three, where angels are invited to join man in admiring Christ's handiwork:

When we behold a piece of China Clay
  Formd up into a China Dish compleat
All spiced ore as with gold Sparks display
  Their beauty all under a glass robe neate,
  We gaze thereat and wonder rise up will
  Wondring to see the Chinees art and Skill.

  How then should we and Angells but admire
  Thy Skill and Vessell thou hast made bright thus
Out for to look like to the Morning tire
  That shineth out in all bright Heavenly plush?
                    (2.143:13–22)

To compare the Spouse to a fancy dish of white porcelain flecked with gold is to treat her as a treasured and precious object. The comparison reveals not only that the Taylor family might have displayed exotic Chinese ware in their breakfront, but also how Taylor regards feminine beauty. Unlike Adam, also formed from clay by God's hand and enlivened with his breath, the Spouse-as-dish is fragile, foreign, and aesthetically pleasing, glazed and hardened, kept protectively "under a glass robe neate." This hardly squares with the exalted claims of the Canticles passage, which grandly compares the Spouse to the sun, the moon, and a fierce army equipped for war, defiantly flying its colors. No doubt Taylor intended this comparison as high compliment; his evident admiration for the skill that shaped the china dish is analogous to his amazement over Christ's skill in forming the soul as a holy "Vessell" for his drops of grace. At this moment, however, the poet's memories of his own frequent prayers to be made into vessels less polished and valued, are dim. Though the Spouse may be the epitome of vesseldom, the comparison constitutes both Spouse and saint as objects through which Christ can view and admire his own skill; she is a screen on which the artist who has created her projects his talents. Even royalty, "Kings, Queens and Ladies," are "Enravisht at her Sight, how she out sends / Her looks like to the morning filld with Bliss" (2.143:50–52). The Spouse's appearance is ravishing because her looks "send out" the light of the sun/Son.[26]

Taylor's own gaze in these poems is uncomfortably split. He wants to maintain his attention fixed upon Christ as a dutiful spouse, and at the same time to look with Christ at his Spouse. In Meditation 2.147 he excuses his split focus by arguing that because he loves Christ "for thy sake thy all fair spouse should wear't / Some glances of the same I to her beare" (ll. 11–12). This Meditation, whose biblical text is Canticles 6:13 ("That wee may look upon thee"), positively revels in the pleasure Christ takes in looking at this beloved, and the pain her absence causes: "Oh Shulamite Our eye much bleeds. / Turn turn that it may look on thee right out. / That we may looke upon thee, and behold / Thy ravishing beauty that thy sweet face unfolds" (ll. 15–18). So overwhelming is this face-to-face encounter with the divine, that Taylor has to remind himself that it is not the bodily eye but "the internall Eye Sight takes this thing," and not unaided, but "with Christ's Eye Salve annointed / Is on this beauteous face alone well pointed" (ll. 33, 35–36). Taylor's verbal sign of the highest of spiritual activities is fixing his sights on God's face and reading the messages there. In the final prayer he begs Christ to apply holy salve to his eyes "That they may view thy Spouses Beauty pure, / Whose sight passt on thyselfe do thence Resolve / To lodge and with the Shulamite Endure / That grace shed from this fulness make her shine / Brightst in mine Eyes to sing her praise and thine" (ll. 38–42). Returning to the words of the scriptural text, Taylor implies that the Spouse picks up the grace "shed" from Christ's "fulness," which makes her the "Brightst" luminary in Taylor's interior sky, so that for him to look upon her is to bathe in the reflected light of God that shines in her face.

In an orientation that pits him against his identification with the Spouse, Taylor consistently praises her in terms of a spiritual beauty that is not her own. In the final prayer cited above, for example, she glistens brightly because the fulness of Christ's grace falls upon her. In Meditation 2.135, Taylor addresses her and says, "[your] spirituall beauty doth arise with Shine / Of th'Beams of the blesst Son of Righteousness, / Glazing thy face with glory all Divine" (ll. 2–4) This beauty is a reflection of Christ, the Son/sun, who radiates his own light upon the smooth, empty, and crystalline surface of the Spouse's countenance, which mirrors it back exactly. "All Sparkling Glory," Taylor continues, "like as Moses Face / Shining was dreadfull so is thine with grace" (ll. 5–6). The Meditation goes on to develop a picture of the Spouse as the Church Militant, "Terrible as an Army with Banners," a kind of Spenserian Britomart. The reference to Moses as a servant of God whose face glowed from gazing on the divine countenance, recalls him as the typic "Looking glass" and highlights the allusion to mirroring surfaces implied in the opening description.

In other Meditations, the Spouse's "rich Sunshining Grace" shimmers, not because she is her own source of light, but because she captures the sun's beams. She is Christ's receptacle; the "golden liquour" of his grace runs "Into thy Spouse's heart" (2.126:23–24). Any flaw or imperfection, any "wrinckle" or "freckle on the beautious face" is covered by the "Silk and Satin Robes, than milk more white / Oh Christ's own Righteousness o're all hath place" (2.134:37–40). As is customary in a man's world, woman's beauty, here represented allegorically, is measured in physical, and even specifically facial, terms. Beauty construed in physical terms usually leads to woman's sexual objectification. The Spouse reflects Christ's spiritual good looks; "Hence," the poet informs her with what we would today label machismo, "all thy Beauty fits thee for Christ's Bed" (2.134:41).

Taylor clearly enjoys his position as Christ's second and sidekick. Nevertheless, participation in the Spouse's attributes is his surest strategy for soteriological inclusion in the holy dyad. Identification with the Spouse produces some of Taylor's best poetic efforts and some of his most absurd requests. For example, he composed two tightly structured and allusively complex poems interpreting the scriptural comparison of the Spouse's temples to pieces of pomegranates. The fruit's ruby-red color suggests blushes—spiritualized as "spirituall flushes" (2.139:12)—the signifiers of modesty, a trait requisite in the seventeenth century for properly feminine behavior. These ingenious Meditations also provide a physiological explanation of "blushes" as the facial signifiers of an effective arousal of feminine spiritual desire. Taylor explains that the "purest blood . . . / Impregnate with the working Spirits ripe" comes up "through th'Arteriall Gate / Into the Head" and "Warm and work the Brains . . . / And sharpen do thine Eyes with Spirituall Strains" (2.139:13–24). The Spouse's "Countenance hence is the Looking Glass" into her heart (2.140:19–20), wherein Taylor views the emblem of feminine obedience and humility, which is the authentic coin of the spiritual realm for purchasing grace. Not surprisingly, Taylor's final prayer requests Christ to make his own temples like pomegranate "That I may ware this Holy Modesty / Upon my Face maskt with thy Graces blush, / That never goes without Humility" (2.140:32–34). In order to mask his own identity with Christ's, he has to emulate the Spouse who is the divine love object of Christ and has no identity apart from him.

The spiritualizing of already unimaginable metaphors drives the poet to the brink of the absurd. For example, meditating upon the Spouse's hair as like a flock of goats grazing on mount Gilliad (Cant. 6:5), he prays to be one of "thy Spouses Curled hairs," a saint sitting in assembly, prepared "with thy Spirits Crisping pins" (2.137:25, 33). In a moment of particular abjection, he cries: "May I a member be, my Lord, once made / Here of thy Spouse in truest Sence, though it bee / The meanest of all, a Toe, or Finger 'rayde / Ist have enough of bliss, espousd to thee" (2.143:61–64). Unconcerned with the strict logic or consistency of his interpretations, Taylor explicates Canticles' most sexually charged description of the Spouse's navel and belly in spiritually charged terms: he imagines her pregnant with "The Spirits babes conceived in thy Soule" (2.149:21) and nourished on the creatures of the Lord's Supper. The depiction of pregnancy and parturition includes obstetrical details like the mother's "Grone" (l. 24), the "Races of Saints [that] do from her belly flow" (l. 47), and the "Spirituall Babes hang sucking of her breasts" (l. 49). Only his overscrupulous use of the adjective "Spirituall" prevents this particular explication from slipping back into the carnal and physical realm. In a subsequent Meditation, Taylor represents himself as one of the spiritual-maternal Spouse's "spirituall babes," and considering Canticles 7:3

("Thy two breasts are like two young Roes that are twins"), he asks Christ to "put these nibbles then my mouth into / And suckle me therewith I humbly pray" (2.150:13–14). This appropriation of female functions to signify the operations of grace, the fruitfulness of the church, the nourishment of the Gospels, and the maternal qualities of God and Christ, is fully consistent with orthodox exegesis and with the gynesis of Puritan theology.[27]

Taylor evinces the oscillation in position characteristic of his particular gynesis. Repeatedly, he sues Christ to make him "a member of thy Beautious Bride," for "I then shall wear thy lovely Spouses Shine / And shall envest her with my Love beside / Which with thy graces shall a dorn her fine" (2.151:55–58). Participating in the Spouse, he wears her "Shine," the reflected glory of Christ's justification with which she is clothed. Then, switching positions, he, like Christ, bestows upon the Spouse a love that, like Christ's divine graces, will enhance her. She covers him with her reflected shine; he embellishes her with a love primarily directed at Christ. This mutual "deck[ing] up" enables Taylor to "sing the Bridall Melodies" of his own epithalamium (2.151:59–60), celebrating the consummation of his approaching marriage to Christ after death, yet also emulating the aged Solomon, "of all fallen men / The perfect'st piece that Nature ever bred" (2.13:19–20), and Christ, in his position as the eternal Word, the ultimate author of Canticles.

These are opposing but not exclusive strategies of identification. Meditation 2.152 celebrates the Christ who "gildest ore with sparking Metaphors / The Object thy Eternall Love fell on" so that "The inward Tacles and the outward Traces / Shine with the Varnish of the Holy Ghost" (ll. 6–7, 13–14). This reflected "shine" originates in Christ's "Rhetorick displaid," in the "Speech" vented like perfume in Canticles' sumptuous and sensual images (2.145:13, 19). Understanding that these shining robes of words that dress the Spouse in "sparkling shine most bright" can also apply to him, Taylor sums up all his prayers of this section, asking to be any mere part of the Spouse's body, an object of rhetoric, the referent of Christ's signifiers. Set against this is Taylor's desire to emulate the master poet himself. Complaining that Christ's "work" has grown "Too larg to be by my Souls limits spand" (2.153:3), he asks to enter Christ's "Angell Palace" to borrow "Angelick Organs" with which to imitate the "Silver Metaphors and Tropes" that Christ lavishes upon his Spouse (ll.

4, 5, 11). It is the power of this rhetoric—or, as Taylor describes it in another Meditation, "The glory of thy powerfull words" (2.158:49)—that carries "Such influences from thy Spouses face / That do upon me run and raise thy Joy / Above my narrow Fancy to uncase" (2.153:14–16). Hermeneutic activity, because it is working with, on, and in the language of God, provides the poet with the greatest inspiration, far greater than his limited, fallen imagination can encompass. "Hence," he tells Christ, "I come to your doors bright Starrs on high" begging that you "imply your pipes herein" so that Taylor may play upon them (ll. 19–20). This is a further variation on the closural musical allusion and it suggests that Taylor has reached another "plateau of assurance." Neither poet nor God takes the role of instrument; rather, the poet asks to borrow a heavenly pipe from "Angelick Organs" to play specifically "Winde musick," an instrumentation closely associated with the presence of the Holy Spirit. Significantly, the poet makes a promise that implies his own, redeemed, agency, and also his physical death, saying that "for this I borrow, / I'le pay thee more when rise on heavens morrow" (ll. 23–24).

In his close reading of the language of Canticles, Taylor finds confirmation of his interpellation, personally and individually, as a redeemed subject in both of the positions he has used repeatedly to figure his participation in the spiritual marriage signified in the sacrament of the Lord's Supper: guest, and Spouse. "Callst thou me Friend?" he asks incredulously; "What Rhetorick is this?" he wonders, as he meditates on Canticles 5:1: "Eat oh Friendes and drink yea drink abundantly oh Beloved." Using hyperbole, to which the marriage of kings and worms always rouses him, he claims he cannot imagine himself reciprocating the assertion: "The Poles may kiss and Paralells meet . . . / And Sun the Full moon buss . . . / "'Twould be too much for Speeches Minted Stamp. / Sure it would set sweet Grace nigh on the Wrack / To assert I could befriend thee" (2.156:5–9). Yet, God's grace certifies the incredible words that in any other case "would be counted sauced blasphemy": "Friend, and Beloved calld to and welcom'd thus / At thy rich Garden feast with spiced joy" (ll. 16, 13–14). These "Gospell Hony Dews" (l. 21) are Christ's scriptural words, his rhetoric of friendship and betrothal by which he calls his saints personally, his eloquent metaphors of praise, the sacramental fruits ripe with grace. Like friends drinking to each other's health and lovers plighting their troth, Christ drinks a cup of honied wine and bids Taylor "pledge thee and I pledge will" (l. 28). The spiritual exchange of vows seems almost at hand.

The last Meditations in the sequence on Canticles are almost all fragmentary. Taylor was old and frail. A severe illness in 1720, from which he only partly recovered, forced him to cease his ministerial and poetic activities five years later. As he draws closer to the long-awaited union with God, Taylor's representations of the intimacy between Christ and his Spouse resonate with an intensity accumulated over a lifetime of poetic and spiritual engagement. For some readers, these last poems evince a poignant impatience to die (Hammond, 207–8). They share another salient feature. In Meditations 2.160 to 2.165 Taylor returns to Canticles 2:1–5, verses that opened his Meditations over forty years earlier, in which the Spouse utters her most passionate declarations of self-bestowal:

> I am the rose of Sharon, and the lily of the valleys. As the lily among thorns, so is my love among the daughters. As the apple tree among the trees of the wood, so is my beloved among the sons. I sat down under his shadow with great delight, and his fruit was sweet to my taste. He brought me to the banqueting house, and his banner over me was love. Stay me with flagons, comfort me with apples; for I am sick of love.

The final Meditations do not, however, mention the Spouse, or speak of her in the second person, as Meditations in the earlier sequence do; rather, they address Christ in the very voice of the Spouse, in paraphrases and elaborations of the words of the texts in which Taylor's protestations of his "shrimpy" Love, and his childlike supplications to be fed and filled, merge with the Spouse's ardent love longings. "Oh! Shake the tree and make these apples fall / Into my Wicker Basket oh how free / Art thou my Apple tree, surpassing all" (2.161B, 31–33), she/he exclaims, taking up Eve's place beneath the apple tree of Christ, poised to catch the precious windfalls, which are now delightful and redemptive to eat. She/he calls her/his beloved "My Lilly, my Rose and Crown," "My Shade for comfort," and "a bright Love knot" (2.163:19–24)— addressing Christ in the words of the Canticles texts. "Thou has brought me into thy house of Wine" (2.164:19), she/he relates, where moderation and mere sufficiency are no longer relevant. Christ is not just sweet, but "the best of sweeting" (2.163:4), and the conclusion of Meditation 2.163 demonstrates the saint/Spouse's uninhibited response to that superlative in a discourse fully integrating images of the sacrament and the Canticles banquet:

> Then glut me Lord, ev'n on this dainty fare,
>   Here is not Surfeit; look upon this dish:
> All is too little to suffice, this fare
>   Can surfeit none that eatest; none eate amiss,
>   Unless they eat too little. So disgrace
>   The preparation of the banquit place.
>   (ll. 55–60)

Then the scene of this poem dissolves, and it shifts from an abstract time and space to the specificity of the pretext's locale. The "I" speaks from under Christ's shade tree in the midst of the garden, the paradise of the momentary apocalypse afforded her/him by the sacrament, remembering a desire satisfied in the past, suffused with a desire being satisfied in the present. This simple declaration near the end of the Meditations could stand as a recapitulation of Taylor's lifelong preparatory process:

> While I sat longing in this Shadow here
>   To tast the fruite this Apple tree all ripe
> How sweet these Sweetings bee. Oh! sweet good Cheere
>   How am I filled with sweet most sweet delight.
>   The fruite, while I was in its shady place
>   Was, and to mee is now sweet to my tast.
>   (2.163:61–66)

There is no conditional tense here, there are no bargains or anticipations—just a direct statement confirming the joy of present experience. Shielded from the fiery radiance of divine presence by Christ in his "Mediatoriall" guise (l. 38), the speaker finds a peace figured, appropriately, in gustatory terms. Embowered in the pleasant "shade" of Christ's spiritual influences, her/his taste—the sensory medium of divine access—is almost completely renovated, thereby making available the full benefits of the apples of eternal life.

Taylor's ability to sustain heartfelt praises in the Spouse's voice suggests his achievement—at least for the brief, discursive space of the later

Meditations—of the spiritual subjectivity she represents: beautiful in obedience, modesty, submission, passivity. The fusion of the speaking subject of the poems and the literary/scriptural persona enacts the fusion of the two positions Taylor has continually marked out for himself, as a visible saint, in the Puritan symbolic economy: guest at the Supper, and Bride of Christ. The "I" in these final poems slips imperceptibly back and forth between observer and participant, between the constraints of earthly existence momentarily transcended in the sacramental kiss, and the spiritual "freedom" willingly to consent to God's will. "I am sick of Love" (Cant. 2:5) is the theme of the final Meditation. In this cry it is impossible to separate the old, ailing man in the sick body impatient to experience Christ's embrace, from the beautiful, lovesick Spouse he will become in that caress. Within this slippage, Taylor inscribes difference by taking on feminine gender and transcends it by locating that difference in the spiritual realm, which is a realm without difference, without woman. As we will see in the next chapter, women—historically specific, flesh-and-blood Puritan women like Anne Bradstreet—suffer almost insurmountable difficulties on account of this appropriation. In her own era and well into ours, Bradstreet confronts an androcentric tradition that finds woman such a hospitable locus for the exploration of its own anxieties, that it can hardly allow women to engage in their own work of self-representation.

Anne Bradstreet:
"In the place
God had set her"

On the first of July, 1650, a volume of poems by Anne Bradstreet was entered in *The Stationer's Register* for Master Stephen Bowtell, a publisher and bookseller in London. This was the first volume of poetry by a single author to come out of the New World. Almost from that moment, Bradstreet ceased to be merely a cultivated, astute, and intelligent private woman in a ranking New England family, and became a cultural phenomenon—the spectacle of a woman-as-poet, a marvel deserving of wonder, but also a threat requiring serious attention.[1]

Bradstreet's intellectual achievement was not the problem. Puritan women, especially middle-class and aristocratic women educated in the Elizabethan tradition, were not barred from literacy or a functional education. In fact, the rigorous and introspective piety of Puritanism required that women as well as men read, comprehend, and pass on the basic doctrines of scripture. Perhaps more importantly, it ensured that women had some private space in which to meditate upon their spiritual state. Bradstreet herself makes this clear in the thoroughly conventional portrait she draws of her mother, Dorothy Dudley, whose piety is illustrated by the fact that "in her closet constant hours she spent" in private religious devotion ("An Epitaph on my Dear and Ever-Honoured Mother," l. 16).[2]

What mainstream Puritan culture could not abide was women's independence or visibility in the public sphere. For women to trespass on what was a male preserve was tantamount to bringing (the female) sex into heaven—an act not just presumptuous, but sacrilegious because it upset the divinely ordained hierarchy of social relations in the fallen world. Governor Winthrop expressed the prevailing attitude in his frequently cited comment on the tragedy of Anne Yale Hopkins, wife of the governor of Hartford, Connecticut, and aunt of the founder of Yale University: she was "a godly young woman, and of special parts . . . who was fallen into a sad infirmity, the loss of her understanding and reason, which had been growing upon her divers years, by occasion of her giving herself wholly to reading and writing, and had written many books" (unfortunately, none of these books survives). Winthrop goes on to chastise Hopkins's husband, who, "being very loving and tender of her, was loath to grieve her" by curbing her activities, and thus realized too late the error of his indulgence. "For," Winthrop concludes, "if she had attended her household affairs, and such things as belong to women, and not gone out of her way and calling to meddle in such things as are proper for men, whose minds are stronger, etc., she had kept her wits, and might have improved them usefully and honorably in the place God had set her" (*Winthrop's Journal*, 2:225).

God had set woman in her place, a place subordinate to man—and as far as Winthrop was concerned, displacement spelled tragedy for women, chaos for men. Women who strayed into prominence in the public eye were not regarded as speakers with opinions, but as gaping mouths and unchecked tongues that betokened unregulated bodies and promiscuous minds. Giving themselves wholly, in the governor's sexualized language, to intellectual pursuits was dangerous for women, who could not handle such unfeminine activities and threatened the stability of the social order.[3] Bradstreet knew this, and thus she began her poetical efforts by composing poems modeled after the popular male-authored poetry of her time. Though she might have harbored secret ambitions about their publication and her own fame, she did not presume to bring her poems out in print. Ironically, it was her family who, in her name, violated the canons of female behavior and pushed her into the glare of the public eye.

Her family's indulgence of Bradstreet's unfeminine occupation, and, compounding that error, their publication of her productions, completely ignored Governor Winthrop's authoritative counsel on the tragic fate of Anne Hopkins. Far from silencing Bradstreet, her family encouraged her poetry and worked actively to publicize and disseminate it. Their motivation for flouting class and cultural mores is complicated, as we shall soon see, as are Bradstreet's responses to their manipulations and her unlooked-for notoriety. Most important for this study is that her family's activities on Bradstreet's behalf constitute an appropriation, not merely of her voice, but of her subjectivity and agency, for their own strategic purposes—another facet of the Puritan gynesis. Bradstreet, I contend, is treated in the public and social sphere like the figure of the Spouse of Christ in Edward Taylor's orthodox fantasy: a figure that is at once subject and object, but that is always the male subject's means to a "higher" end.

Gynesis, as discussed earlier, operates not through the representation of historical women, but as the discursive deployment of a historically specific metaphor of woman. Because of the way in which gynesis abstracts real women into discursive figures of woman, the following examination is not about Bradstreet's struggle for voice, authority, and subjectivity; rather, it concerns her constitution as a figure of gynesis at the hands of the New England Puritan patriarchy. Thus, I focus primarily on how Bradstreet as a cultural figure was (and continues to be) constructed and used by masculinist Puritan culture, and I touch only briefly upon her self-representations. By placing in the foreground the male readers and writers through whose eyes and words Bradstreet must continue to be read, I am trying to suggest the difficulties women have confronted and continue to confront in the work of self-representation.[4]

Even before her poetizing came to light in London, Bradstreet recorded the disapproval and censure of her literary activities that she experienced in Puritan New England. In "The Prologue," an *ars poetica* that introduces her most ambitious work, a metrical history of four ancient monarchies, she apologizes for and justifies her unfeminine subject matter and occupation, while complaining bitterly:

> I am obnoxious to each carping tongue
> Who says my hand a needle better fits,
> A poet's pen all scorn I should thus wrong,
> For such despite they cast on female wits:
> If what I do prove well, it won't advance,
> They'll say it's stol'n, or else it was by chance.
>
> (ll. 27–32)[5]

Supported by her family and a circle of literate friends who believed that women could handle both a darning needle and a poet's quill, Bradstreet produced thousands of lines of historical and didactic verse—a distinctly unfeminine endeavor during an age in which, if women did compose poetry, they were confined (or confined themselves) to religious verse, epitaphs, and "the silent art of translation" (Lamb, 116, 134).[6] Unlike her less-fortunate nineteenth-century fictional counterpart, Hester Prynne, who falls prey to promiscuous thoughts because her sole means of expression *is* the embroidery needle,[7] Bradstreet did not, so far as the historical record and her autobiographical meditations indicate, stray from the path set out for her. Other than her privately transgressive poetical activity, she was a model of educated middle-class Puritan womanhood.

Yet, when Bradstreet's brother-in-law, John Woodbridge, took a manuscript of her poems to Master Bowtell in London and had them published without her knowledge or consent, he could not bring himself to name her a poet. The title of the volume, bestowed presumably by Woodbridge or one of his English confreres, styles the unknowing and unknown Bradstreet as *The Tenth Muse, lately Sprung up in America*. Without explanation, this presumptuous designation disappears from the second edition of Bradstreet's poems, published posthumously in Boston in 1678, which retains only its descriptive subtitle: *Several Poems, compiled with great Variety of Wit and Learning, full of delight*. John Rogers, a near relation of the Bradstreets, most probably was the editor of this second edition. Although the title page announces that revisions were made by Bradstreet herself, and the prefatory poem, "The Author to Her Book," indicates that Bradstreet made changes on *The Tenth Muse* with the intention of republishing it, we cannot be sure what changes she made and what changes she authorized, if any.[8] It is telling, however, that the revised title shifts the reader's focus away from the author to her works, away from the phenomenon to her accomplishments. For it was probably not lost on Bradstreet, whose relationship with the nine sisters was uneasy at best, that Muses are not poets.[9] Undoubtedly, her brother-in-law imagined that he was conferring a great honor upon the first "American" poet, who just happened to be female, by adding her to the bevy of goddesses presiding over the ancient arts and sciences, thereby casting her as the very essence of poetry. Would he have dared lavish such an honor on Edward Taylor, if a manuscript of *The Preparatory Meditations* had, improbably, fallen into his hands? And can we trust the naming abilities of someone who presents the author as a latter-day Antaeus sprung from the soil of the New World—which was not even her native soil—when it is obvious that Bradstreet is thoroughly a product of late Renaissance English culture, and that her poetic pastime serves as an escape from the harshness and loneliness of wilderness conditions?

Elevating Bradstreet to the status of a Muse is the quintessentially double-edged gesture that characterizes Woodbridge's attitude toward his would-be poet, and it influences the rest of the prefatory material, a good deal of which picks up on his references to the mythological origin of poetic inspiration. The significance of the Muse in Puritan aesthetics was in flux at that moment. The nine sisters of classical mythology harked back to pagan tropes for authorship, which the tradition of sacred writing had largely rejected. Interestingly enough, it was Guillaume Du Bartas who in the sixteenth century reimagined a single and thoroughly Christian muse, "L'Uranie"—the name Milton took up later in the seventeenth century for his celestial muse, Urania, who presides over Book 7 of *Paradise Lost*. Milton makes it very clear that Urania is not one of "the Muses nine," and comparing her to Calliope, mother of Orpheus and leader of the nine sisters, he explains "thou art heavenly, she an empty dream" (7.6, 39). Both Du Bartas and Milton, as good Puritan poets, shift the authority of speech onto their heavenly Muses and away from themselves as mere mortal mouthpieces. "Sing heavenly Muse" (1.6), Milton charges the figure of God's Logos; "Say goddess, what ensued . . ." (7.40), he requests, echoing epic invocations.

The Muse-poet relationship is a particularly vexed site of power relations.[10] One factor remains constant: it is rigorously heterosexual. Muses are female, poets are male: in the seventeenth century these gender ascriptions were commonplace to the point of seeming natural and divinely ordained. Thus, when brother John names his worthy sister Anne the "tenth Muse," he is deliberately attempting to "manage" the threat of a woman quietly defying her culture's double messages about women's capabilities and women's roles, by putting her back into a feminine place. He does this by attributing to her a status higher than that of mere poet— a mythic, even goddesslike, and controlling status. But every woman who has been put on a pedestal knows that this kind of deification is disarming, a back-handed compliment, for it has the desired effect of denying her the status of subject, speaker, agent, or author. Advancing Bradstreet to the status of Muse stamps her as irreducibly, even archetypically, female, and has the effect of sensationalizing her poetic production while at the same time devaluing it. Her achievement can be recognized, but it cannot be taken seriously as a threat to male dominance or real definitions of power, position, and authority.

The contradictory logic of this strategy for the containment of women poets is not specific to the seventeenth century but continues in strikingly similar forms in the twentieth century, if Anne Bradstreet is a representative case. In 1953, the poet John Berryman published his critically acclaimed *Homage to Mistress Bradstreet*, a purportedly "historical," but more accurately confessional, poem that features an erotic interaction between the two poets, but which is written primarily in Bradstreet's voice.[11] Carol Johnson, reviewing Berryman's poem in 1964, begins by corroborating the patriarchy's opinion of "Anne," as she is often, condescendingly, called by modern critics: "The muse is not, strictly, a poet and Mistress Bradstreet, the 'Tenth Muse Lately Sprung Up In America' in all strictness perhaps never was one except through the accommodation of the metonymy"; all is put to rights, however, because "some 300 years after her death she has become literally the muse of a poem among the few distinguished efforts of substantial length in its period" (388). Thus, a woman mistaken for a poet is rescued from misprision by a male poet who accurately repositioned her as his source of inspiration. Johnson does notice that Berryman "receives his voice from her" (393), yet she claims that Bradstreet serves in this capacity so effectively because of "the endearing incompetence of her verse" (388).[12]

Among the many power trips taken by Berryman in his poem, not the least ironic is his sending of critics and readers scurrying back to Bradstreet's poetry to try to determine why, in his own words, "I chose to write about this boring high-minded Puritan woman who may have been our first American poet but is not a good one" ("Changes," 100). In an essay written in 1965, Berryman gives three reasons that sum up his complicated and overdetermined relationship to Bradstreet: he claims that, in fact, he "did not choose her—somehow she chose me"; that "one point of connection, at any rate, [was] the almost insuperable difficulty of writing high verse at all in a land that cared and cares so little for it"; and despite this link, he admits that he "was concerned with her, though, almost from the beginning, as a woman, not much as a poetess" ("Changes," 100). The connotations of that last word are devastating; not even women writing poetry at the time wanted to be associated with a "poetess."[13] Still, agreeing "naturally," that her poetry is inferior, he does not hesitate to borrow liberally from it to achieve some of his best effects. The threat of the woman-as-poet is revealed when even Berryman, with nothing to fear from the long-dead poetess, grants her a power over his imagination, but at the same time has to put her back into her "rightful" place. Ambivalently, he makes her both his object and his persona. I want to linger for a moment over this contemporary example of gynesis wrought upon the seventeenth-century poet who is the focus of this chapter, to tease out some of the subtle power plays that were and remain features of masculine "recuperation" of woman.

First, Berryman's allegation that Bradstreet "chose" him suggests, in the spiritual/erotic language in which male poets traditionally address their earthly muses, that the power to choose was all on her side. But this courtly discourse is an ancient mode of equivocation. By calling his poem an "Homage," he implies that he puts himself under obligation to a figure whom he reveres and also wants to flatter. The term derives from the Old French *homme*, man or vassal, and the Latin *humus*, earth, and denotes a solemn feudal ceremony by which in return for a fief, as a tenancy of land, the recipient acknowledges himself the man or vassal of a lord and recognizes the rights and duties inherent in this relationship. Bradstreet uses the term in her dedicatory poem to her father to describe how her Quaternions (four long poems on the four elements, humors, ages of man, and seasons) "wait upon"—that is, are beholden to—his four poems, which preceded and influenced her creations: "I bring my four times four, now meanly clad / To do their homage unto yours, full glad" (ll. 14–15). Her use of the term stresses literary obligation almost more than filial respect. A similar emphasis would hold for Berryman's title, except that he publicly denies his interest in Bradstreet's poetry and, instead, asserts his interest in her "as a woman." This "interest" becomes palpably sexual in the middle section of the poem, when the male poet's voice enters into dialogue with the voice of Bradstreet who has been narrating the events of her life. In oblique, suggestive, and sensual phrases they parry and thrust, looking for an opening as lovers do. Finally, the male poet announces, "I have earned the right to be alone with you," to which the Bradstreet voice responds, "What right can that be? / Convulsing, if you love, enough, like a sweet lie" (27.6–8). It seems clear from her response, that the

Bradstreet voice recognizes the "sweet lie" in her wooer's rhetoric. The tropes of courtly praise and the equivocal self-abnegation of an homage have always been a polite mask for sometimes illicit sexual desire, and a pretext to sexual domination.

Berryman's equivocal "homage" to Bradstreet has much the same effect as her brother-in-law's elevation of her to the status of Muse: it recognizes and deauthorizes at the same time. The modern appropriation is the more insidious, however, because Berryman dismisses Bradstreet's poetic productions altogether, and then is free to raid and deploy them as he wishes. And Berryman's appropriation of Bradstreet has been just as successful as Woodbridge's, because readers have only recently begun to question seriously the status of the character he calls "Bradstreet." Hyatt Waggoner, for example, recommends a reading of Berryman's poem as an introduction to Bradstreet's work and to themes and images particularly "American" (8). Elizabeth Wade White, Bradstreet's biographer, endorses Waggoner's recommendation because, she argues, the strangely wrenched syntax, the psychological method, and the historical setting of the poem seem to bring the woman and her environment eloquently to life. Neither Waggoner nor White seems disturbed by the ventriloquistic nature of her voice, the appropriation of her life, or the unsavory central action of the poem. They do not question the male poet's assumption that he can claim the right to be alone with "Bradstreet" because, like all the other Beatrices and Lauras of the male tradition, she is his creation, a figure who has sprung from his imagination and his desire, over whom—in the poetic sphere—he has total control. Berryman clearly exercised this control by distorting the historical facts of Bradstreet's life to suit his own purposes.[14] But if we view the "homage" in terms of sexual politics, even the colonial honorific "Mistress" takes on sinister connotations. Berryman's Bradstreet is "mistress neither of fiery nor velvet verse" (12.8), but it is she, the poet cries, "who mistress me from air" (33.4). The power connoted by this term is an ambiguous one. For, by imagining himself her "man," especially in sexual terms, he can "lord" it over her. By implication, her femininity, her difference, constitute him masculine, powerful, controlling. And by comparison her "bald / abstract didactic rime" and "proportioned, spiritless poems" (12.5–6; 42.6) can only make his impassioned poetic ventriloquism look good. Making men look good is part of the traditional role of woman. In a witty and strategic retort to contemporary critics who would silence her, Bradstreet commented about her own poetry, "This mean and unrefined ore of mine / Will make your glist'ring gold but more to shine" ("The Prologue," ll. 49–50).

This is not to dismiss Berryman's claims that he was chosen, compelled, and in the thrall of his Muse's power, but rather to deconstruct those claims. The sexual politics obliquely implied in the title he gave his poem are supported by the biographical context of the poem's composition. Sarah Provost points out that the technical and creative breakthrough represented by *Homage* was, in fact, preceded by another major work, *Berryman's Sonnets*, which was only published in 1967. Drawing upon an obsessive and humiliating adulterous affair Berryman had in 1947, the sonnets depict the poet at the mercy of a willful, wild, and flamboyant woman he calls "Lise." Finally released from his compulsion to compose poetry directly to and about Lise, he cast around for a subject that would allow him to fathom the tumultuous experience—in publishable form. As Provost recounts, he first began a verse play about Katharine Nairn, an eighteenth-century adulterer and murderer, but abandoned it (69–70). In the middle of 1948 he wrote the first eleven lines of *Homage*, but could go no further. For the next five years, he read and researched, finishing the poem in an anguished burst of creativity. Comparing the two works, Provost argues that the figure of Bradstreet is a tempered, toned-down, and pliant version of Lise (71). Whereas, in his poetic rendition of the "real" affair, Berryman construes himself as the victim and fool, in the later, "idealized" affair with his compliant creation it is not even clear that he is married, and he maintains rigorous control of events as well as of his writing. In short, he uses the fictional ghost of real Anne to exorcise the real ghost of a fictional Lise.

It is a compelling thesis because it answers the nagging question of why Berryman did not, for example, choose to pay homage to a woman like Emily Dickinson, who actually was an important influence for his poetry. An imaginary seduction of the virginal "woman in white" might have been as potentially rewarding as tempting a "boring, high-minded Puritan woman," and in the process he would have been able to meditate on poetry clearly not inferior to anything yet written in this country.[15] But if, as Provost contends, domination of woman coupled with the exorcism of his personal guilt over his own disastrous affair are his motives, then Dickinson would have proved too independent, recalcitrant, unassimilable, and unfeminine. Besides, her poetry cannot be dismissed, though it can be read, as it has been for many years, as somehow "beyond" gender. Finally, Dickinson's religious faith is altogether too modern and existential for Berryman's purposes. He needs a simpler, and morally starker faith, one that can produce vivid and picturesque soul-writhing and tranquil sweet peace—and Bradstreet's evident struggles with Puritanism eminently qualify, as does the poetess herself. The Bradstreet that comes through in her poems and autobiographical prose is womanly to the core, patient, modest, and mild, with a maternal and hard-earned faith. Not only is she the colonial foremother of "American" poetry, but she is also a woman deeply committed to motherhood, as revealed by her laments over her inability to conceive. It is precisely the difference of gender that entices and challenges Berryman, a difference he wants to maintain, exploit, and transcend all at the same time. For, as Provost discovers much to her surprise, Bradstreet is both Berryman's idealized, quintessentially feminine mistress, and the persona through which he projects his own struggles with guilt, creativity, and God.[16]

Berryman conjures up a woman who serves both as a figure of otherness and as a figure of self, docile and accommodating, yet intelligent and discriminating.[17] In order to present these conflicting qualities, he structures the poem around a pattern of rebellions and submissions based upon the same dynamic he and other readers discern in Bradstreet's own writings. The poem opens as the male poet presents Bradstreet thoroughly defined by and through the men and masculine presences around her. Describing her as "a patient woman," he imagines her waiting in heaven for her husband who outlived her by thirty years, and he seems "to see you pause here still," waiting for the poet to "summon" her from the past (1.3–4; 3.2). He pictures her "in moments odd" poring over the work of her poetic mentors, "Sylvester, Quarles," who, he assumes, supervised her poetry. Her poetic reading was not critical, but just another way of keeping "bright eyes on the Lord" (1.5–6), he implies. Projecting himself upon the deck of the *Arbella* that windy day in 1630 as it landed in Boston harbor, the poet modulates his voice into the Bradstreet voice in stanza 4 line 8 by imposing himself upon her as yet another dominating, restraining male presence in her life: "I come to check, / I come to stay with you, / and the Governor, & Father, & Simon, & the huddled men" (4.6–8).

Evoking the hardships and suffering of those years, Berryman's

Bradstreet figure recounts how, in the famous words from a letter to her children, "my heart rose, but I did submit" (7.8). She bows to the conventional notion that women must be governed, protected from the external temptations of heresy as well as from the lure of their own impulses: "I must be disciplined, / in arms, against that one, and our dissidents, and myself" (11.7–8). Her spiritual life is another arena in which she struggles in vain against masculine forces. Trying to understand her childlessness, she recounts how at fourteen God punished her with smallpox for "sitting loose from" him. When God returned, "That year for my sorry face / so-much-older Simon burned, / so Father smiled, with love. Their will be done" (14.3–5). God punishes her body for her carnal mind. Men decide her fate without consulting her, yet she resigns herself to husband, father, and God with Christlike obedience and barely sublimated erotic energy: "I kissed his Mystery" (14.8). Later, after she has consented to the "affair" with the twentieth-century poet and is consumed with guilt and shame, she imagines her damnation and recalls the devil's promise to spare woman if she agrees to be his tool. But with a painful insight she realizes the uniformly oppressive nature of male power, and she cries: "Father of lies, / a male great pestle smashes / small women swarming towards the mortar's rim in vain" (37.6–8). Here she appears to recognize and condemn her oppressors while at the same time acknowledging her vulnerability; God, father, and devil coalesce into a looming phallic pestle that grinds helpless, antlike women into a powder.[18] Her God is not paternally benevolent but sadistic, continually sending her physical chastisements to amend her errant soul. As she ages, and is beset with poor health, the death of children, and the burning of her house, she says, "I look. I bear to look. Strokes once more his rod" (50.8), as God satisfies himself in a barely concealed display of phallic power. Yet she begs, "torture me, Father, lest not I be thine!" (39.1).

Although hailed as a "historical" poem, Berryman's account only half-heartedly historicizes his character's seemingly masochistic spirituality and the psychological oppression of an intelligent and ambitious woman hedged about by the Puritan patriarchal order in which, as she says, "they starch their minds" (24.1).[19] And what of the male poet's participation in that phallic power to which he subjects his female protagonist, but which he shrinks from condemning? With a relative freedom to create her in his own image, as it were, Berryman underplays any of her unfeminine qualities and conjures her specifically as a body: "Out of maize & air / your body's made, and moves. I summon, see, / from the centuries it" (3.1–3). He has her dwell upon her diseases and bodily infirmities and vividly describe her bout with smallpox, "what my Friend / brought me for my revolt when I moved smooth & thin" (28.7–8). In what seems like taking revenge on the "fair sex," he flagrantly disregards the biography and imagines her disfigured by pockmarks (4.5; 28.1–2). Although he is the one to initiate contact, breaking in on her thoughts unceremoniously and dragging her into his no-man's-land of adulterous desire, in the exordium of the poem he implies a mutuality in their attraction: "We are on each other's hands / who care. Both of our worlds unhanded us" (2.7–8). Later, he attributes the physical initiation of their affair to her, as she is the one who asks to be touched and kissed. In doing so, he insinuates that women are more sensual and dependent on physical contact than men.

Berryman creates Bradstreet vulnerable and then takes advantage of it. Softening her up with his rhetoric of sympathy and caring, he proceeds with deliberate calculation to woo and tempt her to an adulterous passion that overwhelmed him with shame and brings her to a terrible crisis of faith. The way he enters her world is a perfect case in point. Appalled by the "riddling," haggling, and logic chopping of the Boston Puritan clergy (22.6; 23.4), Bradstreet's voice deplores John Cotton's abandonment of Anne Hutchinson during the antinomian controversy. Hutchinson is a woman, unlike her supposed friend, who "rings forth a call," blasting a hole in the wall protecting Puritan New England (24.6–7). She is outspoken and dares to be visible, and Bradstreet's conservative (and realistic) response is "should she?" (24.7). Inevitably, she is quashed. Berryman portrays Hutchinson as Bradstreet's closest friend, though there is little historical basis for this. As the Bradstreet figure mourns Hutchinson's exile, crying, "Bitter sister, victim, I miss you," the voice of the male poet interrupts her and the first dialogue of the opening gambit in the seduction ensues, their voices alternating, beginning with the male poet's:

—I miss you, Anne,
day or night weak as a child,
tender & empty, doomed, quick to no tryst.
—I hear you. Be kind, you who leaguer
my image in the mist.
—Be kind you, to one unchained eager far & wild

and if, O my love, my heart is breaking, please
neglect my cries and I will spare you. Deep
in Time's grave, Love's, you lie still.
Lie still.

$$(25.3-26.4)$$

Echoing her words of empathy, implying a previous acquaintance, and
playing upon her "motherly" instincts by comparing himself in his weakness to a child, he imposes his own weird need between the two women.
Berryman's note to this passage is illuminating. Speaking of the male
poetic voice, he says: "He is enabled to speak, at last, in the fortune of an
echo of her—and when she is loneliest (her former spiritual adviser
having deserted Anne Hutchinson, and this her closest friend banished),
as if she had summoned him; and only thus, perhaps, is she enabled to
hear him" (*Homage*: "Notes"). His last speech quoted above, in which he
throws her the line about how, though his heart is breaking, he will stop if
she wants him to, does make the continuation of his attentions dependent
on her desires. He has her respond coyly, "You must not love me, but I do
not bid you cease" (26.8). It is, however, unmitigated heterosexist nerve
for him to think that in her despondency over the loss of her best woman
friend, she necessarily wants a man, and thus summons him!

Berryman's aggression toward women is barely concealed. The above
passage contains a pattern of words the male poet uses repeatedly to put
woman back in her place. Describing his vision of Bradstreet at rest in
"Time's grave," he notes her peacefulness—"you lie still"—and advises
her (against his own urgings) to dismiss his suit and "Lie still"—that is,
remain peacefully at rest in the past. The word "still" also occurs three
times in stanza 1 and twice in the final stanza. It suggests remaining in
place, motionless, even stagnant, like a still pool, or fixed, like a "still"
photograph; it also suggests being silent, subdued, or hushed, quiet and
tranquil. As an adverb, "still" describes a condition that existed previously
and will exist in the future, despite other factors—a condition that is
steady, constant, or eternal. The conflation of adjectival and adverbial
meanings calls up Keats's strangely applicable and subliminally sinister
invocation of his Grecian urn, "Thou still unravished bride of quietness."
At the same time that the male poet imagines Bradstreet peaceful and
silent in the past and wants her to remain that way as a source of constancy for him, he is maneuvering to drag her into the tumult of adulterous

passion, unquiet speech, and breach of faith. When "still" is applied to the verb "lie," the gentle imperative "Lie still" takes on threatening implications of enforced silence or immobility and continuing deception; recall the Bradstreet figure's earlier invocation of the "sweet lie" of "convulsing" love.

The threat surfaces more openly when Bradstreet's character fulfills the poet's ambivalent desires and asks to be touched, kissed, talked to. Then, in what Berryman describes as "an only half-subdued aria-stanza" ("Changes," 101), his love song takes on aggressive forms:

> —It is Spring's New England. Pussy willows wedge
> up in the wet. Milky crestings, fringed
> yellow, in heaven, eyed
> by the melting hand-in-hand or mere
> desirers single, heavy-footed, rapt,
> make surge poor human hearts. Venus is trapt—
> the hefty pike shifts, sheer—
> in Orion blazing. Warblings, odours, nudge to an edge—
>
> (31.1–8)

The erotically charged, wet, and burgeoning world of New England spring, with its college students innocently "hand-in-hand" and less-sanguine loners nursing private raptures, fills the poet's heart at the moment he achieves his conquest. But this fades rapidly into a threatening night-sky world with intimations of conflict between the goddess of love, formerly a menacing carnivorous plant, and a mythic giant and hunter who terrorized the sisters known as the Pleiades and was eventually slain by Artemis. Venus, who once trapped men in her "engines" (see Bradstreet's "Elegy upon . . . Philip Sidney," l. 27), is now herself trapped by Orion's sharp pikes, and the stars have become weapons. By the end of this stanza, love is a prisoner, and the sounds and smells of nature that "rapt" Bradstreet and brought her a glimpse of heaven (see "Contemplations," ll. 8–15) bring the lovers to a dangerous precipice.

In the course of their bizarre intimacy, the male poet confesses to murderous feelings and an unrestrained "western lust" that fills his mind with images of Nazi atrocities: "I trundle the bodies, on the iron bars, / over that fire backward & forth; they burn; / bits fall. I wonder if/ *I* killed them. Women serve my turn" (33.2; 34.1–4).[20] "Dreams!" responds his generous mistress, fulfilling her role; "You are good," she tells him, despite all evidence to the contrary, and she prays to her God for "mercy for him and me" (34.5; 39.3). Still, he is torn by unbelief. While she can affirm that "God awaits us," he is despondent. "I cannot feel myself God waits" (34.8–35.1), he admits, expressing the dark heart of his fears, which leads to an unexpected ritual mutilation of the woman's body:

> . . . Man is entirely alone
> may be. I am a man of griefs & fits
> trying to be my friend. And the brown smock splits,
> down the pale flesh a gash
> broadens and Time holds up your heart against my eyes.
>
> (35.4–8)

While he does not quite believe that the world is devoid of God ("may be"), he implies that he is far from any source of meaning. The next image, a kind of caesarian birth performed on the Bradstreet figure's brown-smocked body by "Time," images forth the effects of his wrenching doubt. Perhaps her faith is unbelievable; perhaps she, his creation, is unbelievable, and he requires visual evidence, her heart—seat of her emotions and faith—delivered up to him. There is also a sense in which time measures her heart (faith) against his eyes (skepticism), and finds him wanting. The excision of her heart, a violation of her body and a metaphorical theft of her soul, can be read as an emblem of how in his doubt he has forced her open in an "unnatural" birth where her sex becomes a Christlike gash, a wound, yet still the only way to her heart, her faith—to that which he does not and cannot possess except through violence. To be loved and known, woman must be sacrificed.

By contrast, Berryman has the Bradstreet figure narrate her bodily decline and impending death in sexual terms that contradict the forced, adulterous opening: "Light notes leap, a beckon, swaying / the tilted, sickening ear within. I'll—I'll— / I am closed & coming. Somewhere! I defile / wide as a cloud, in a cloud, / unfit, desirous, glad—" (53.4–8). In an ecstasy of eschatological desire, her body seems to evaporate into the air. But the male poet retains his relentless preoccupation with her body, and reserves for himself the details of her burial. He wants to make sure that, this time, she is dead and gone, and he sends her off with imagery alternately tender and grotesque:

—You are not ready? You are ready. Pass,
as shadow gathers shadow in the welling night.
Fireflies of childhood torch
you down. We commit our sister down.
One candle mourn by, which a lover gave,
the use's edge and order of her grave.
Quiet? Moisture shoots.
Hungry throngs collect. They sword into the carcass.

                                                    (54.1–8)

First, he positions her as Christ's spouse, declaring her "ready"—a judgment that, as Bradstreet's own final poem "As Weary Pilgrim" asserts,
only Christ is fit to decide ("Lord make me ready for that day, / Then
come, dear Bridegroom, come away" [ll. 43–44]). But the movement is
resolutely downward, and the emphasis falls on her deceased "carcass,"
not on transcendence or her released soul. The contradictory image of
fireflies "torching" her to her final rest captures the poet's need to return
her to a childlike status, diminutive and fanciful—a small body that glows
intermittently. It would take thousands of fireflies to flame like a torch. As
he distances himself from her, his voice takes on the detached tones of a
preacher, addressing mourners and referring vaguely to "a lover." Then,
with a kind of Marvellian glee, he watches as the "hungry throngs" of
worms pierce her body. Marvell's mistress was more "coy," but her corpse
was just as indispensable to satisfy the poet's lust for power, immortality,
and song.

   Ironically, just as Bradstreet's imaginary body is the locus for the male
poet's aggression, it provides her with an identity and power that he
envies. According to Berryman's own account, "the moment of the poem's
supreme triumph" is the birth of Bradstreet's first child ("Changes," 101),
a passage that must be set against the forced birth cited above. The
tension, rhythm, and emotions accelerate in an extended, hallucinatory
description of labor:

    . . . everything down
    hardens I press with horrible joy down
    my back cracks like a wrist . . .

... I work thrust I must free
now I all muscles & bones concentrate
what is living from dying?

$$(19.5-20.3)$$

Then, just as she can no longer endure,

it passes the wretched trap whelming and I am me

drencht & powerful, I did it with my body!
One proud tug greens Heaven. Marvellous,
unforbidding Majesty.
Swell, imperious bells. I fly.
Mountainous, woman not breaks and will bend:
sways God nearby: anguish comes to an end.
Blossomed Sarah, and I
blossom . . .

$$(20.8-21.8)$$

In this irreducibly female and quintessentially feminine experience, the Bradstreet figure finds herself competent, powerful, and blessed by God. Unlike Venus, who in the poem allows herself to be caught, the Bradstreet figure eludes the trap of love. Her only refuge from her harsh and oppressive world is her "Beloved household" (22.1), where her delight in her children reinforces her sense of identity: "When by me in the dusk my child sits down / I am myself," she declares peacefully; "How they loft, how their sizes delight and grate" (42.1–2, 5). By comparison, "The proportioned, spiritless poems accumulate. / And they publish them / away in brutish London, for a hollow crown" (42.6–8). Literary notoriety is barbarous, worldly. Finally, when "Evil dissolves, & love, like foam; / that love. Prattle of children powers me home" (39.6–7). "That love" is the adulterous, evil love with which she is tempted; her mother-love allows her to resist her "demon-lover's" blandishments and return to domestic fidelity and religious hope.[21]

The triumph of body, will, and faith here is woman's. Despite the male poet's relentless imposition of control, he can only experience these triumphs by appropriating them. In fact, Bradstreet had the children *and* the poems; after much suffering and doubt, she achieved a hard-won faith.

Furthermore, "Lise" left Berryman to return to her husband and child (Provost, 77). Berryman recreates Bradstreet not simply as the object of his love or lust, but as a wishful recreation of himself: empowered by the physical exertion of birth, which he can experience only vicariously as the "couvade" of poetic creation,[22] cleansed of his sins of doubt and wandering lusts. By inhabiting her body, he can imagine the "proud tug" that "greens Heaven," and the unqualified love that overcomes devious lust. By speaking through her voice he can try on the beliefs he cannot sustain in his own world, quieting his own doubts with a faith that would elude him for many years. In a note he typed up for the ending of *Homage* he explained: "Upon her turn away from evil, with her help, *he* finally turns" (Haffenden, 28; Berryman's emphasis). And by projecting his shameful desires onto her, and watching her agony and redemption, he can exorcise his guilt publicly and be cleansed and freed. In veiled ways, Berryman even acknowledges the poet in his mistress. At one point she asks him to "Sing a concord of our thought" (32.8), seemingly giving tacit permission for his appropriation of her voice. But the imperative "Sing," as Berryman would have known, is what poets traditionally request of their muses.[23] Bradstreet had already sung of the concord of thought between herself and Simon in the love lyric, "To My Dear and Loving Husband." Again, the poet speaks his vain wish through one who has known such harmony and has sung it.

In the coda, the male poet acknowledges his hidden darkness: "I am a closet of secrets dying," he admits ruefully (55.6), associating his own moral corruption with the decline of modern, postwar society. In the final stanza, remembering the candle he placed at his creation's graveside, he calls himself a "lost candle" (57.8) and asks that her "benevolent phantom" (56.2) might "Hover, utter, still, / a sourcing" for his flickering, firefly-like flame (57.7–8). These verbs connote confined, circumscribed activity, which is countermanded by the accumulated resonances of "still": can one hover and be unmoving, or utter and be silent?

By his comments on this poem, Berryman encouraged a reading of *Homage* as an experiment in the fluidity of identities, opening himself to the presence and power of an upright, uptight Puritan goodwife. Males have, for centuries, taken on female or feminine personae to summon the unconscious and irrational forces necessary for philosophy and poetry. At the same time that Berryman was writing *Homage* in the United States, theorists in France were boldly exploding and rearranging the notions of identity, narrativity, history, representation, phallocentrism, and gender in a movement that we now call "postmodernism." But Berryman's multiple positions in the poem, and his gynesis, finally do not problematize the central, unified consciousness of man or put his own discourse into question in any significant way.[24] The male poet's voice begins and ends the poem, framing and containing the speech of the woman he imagines. He resurrects Bradstreet, confines her to her body and the traditional feminine role of reproduction, narrows and distorts her, dismisses her poetry, and buries her. He speaks his own self-loathing through her: their dialogue repeats exchanges Berryman had with Lise and is the verbal representation of their sinning. Yes, he allows her to speak a subjectivity through him. What does she/he say? He has her speak her desire for him—what every man wants his woman to say—while he maintains his place in the phallic order that appropriates her voice.

Historically, Bradstreet's was a poetic voice reluctantly brought into public view. One of the ironies of her path-breaking volume is that she did not want it to happen—that way. *The Tenth Muse* came into being through the machinations of the men around her, who brought it out because the spectacle of a woman speaking served their interests. They could communicate certain clan and tribal truths most effectively through her voice. This story is told in the pages of prefatory material that introduce Bradstreet and accompany her into the public world where she dared not stray alone, a role Berryman happily took up three hundred years later. Some readers, however, including Helen Campbell, the major source for most of Berryman's information on Bradstreet, argue that she was persuaded to allow a trusted family member to seek publication of her manuscript of poems because they deserved a wider audience and she, as a woman, could not seek publication herself. Campbell asserts that there is no evidence to conclude otherwise, and that "the elaborate dedication [to her father] and the many friendly tributes included, indicate the fullest knowledge and preparation. All those whose opinion she most valued are represented in the opening pages of the volume" (225). But these testimonials are only partly for Bradstreet's benefit, and they are friendly only up to a point; they speak to a larger, predominantly male audience and disclose the anxieties of that audience concerning the phenomenon they purport to justify. In order to understand how a woman can be made to speak for her clan, her tribe, and a whole social order imposed upon her from without, we need to look closely at the context in which Bradstreet, for very good reasons, did not want to speak.

Even Campbell admits that Bradstreet's champions "felt it necessary to justify this extraordinary departure from the proper sphere of woman, a sphere as sharply defined and limited by every father, husband and brother, as their own was left uncriticised and unrestrained" (225). It is doubtful that anyone, including men, in Puritan New England felt they had such license; the success of the ideological conditioning of spiritual conversion ensured that no one ever felt free or unconstrained. Nevertheless, women's behavior was particularly circumscribed—which is what makes the appearance of Bradstreet's volume all the more curious. Why would the New England family second in rank only to the Winthrops, and tied to them by marriage, want to advertise the fact that a distaff member routinely drank from what Cotton Mather called the "Circean cup" of poetic intoxication, which, if it was to be indulged in by mature males only sparingly, could not have been considered tonic for a young mother who had a large household and was the wife of an important colonial administrator?[25] Bradstreet's poetry, however, was the height of propriety: it was studious and didactic, comprising a résumé of the famous French Huguenot poet Du Bartas and Sir Walter Raleigh, and elegies to worthy Elizabethan figures like Sir Philip Sidney and Queen Elizabeth, and ending with a pious declaration "Of the vanity of all worldly creatures." And though her heart burned for some "small acknowledgment" of her poetic worth, Bradstreet herself was an honorable, unpretentious Puritan woman who, left to herself—so the logic goes—would have not pursued notoriety beyond the bounds of her small world of intimates.

The number, as well as the kind, of testimonials that adorn the entrance to *The Tenth Muse*—or, alternatively, obscure it from view—belie an anxiety about what it is these testimonies think they are recommending to the reader. Introductory letters and endorsements were commonplace sixteenth- and seventeenth-century publishing protocol. "Epistles to the reader," such as the letter that prefaces Roger Williams's *Key to the Language of America* (1643; see Chapter 5, below), were necessary to excuse the author's inadequacy and explain just why he had brought his half-formed brainchild into the public eye; and poetic appreciations, like Jonathan Mitchell's verse introduction to Michael Wigglesworth's best-seller, *The Day of Doom* (1662; in Meserole, 412–13), whetted readers' appetites. But the use of more than one or two testimonials was unusual, being reserved either for important occasions, such as Ben Jonson's publication of his collected works in 1616, which was meant to make a big splash, or for posthumous works, such as the publication in 1623 of Shakespeare's First Folio, which has five prefatory poems and a prose dedication.

By these standards, the prefatory material of *The Tenth Muse* is excessive. It includes an epistle to the reader, not from the author but from her substitute, John Woodbridge, who also contributed a seventy-six-line poem; a "humorous" short poem by Nathaniel Ward, close friend and neighbor of the Bradstreet family; a third short poem by Woodbridge's brother Benjamin, who accompanied him to London; five other short poems, all initialed and thought to be by English friends and acquaintances of the Woodbridges who had been shown the manuscript in London; and finally, two anagrams and a couplet thought to be by John Wilson, the notorious anagrammatizer of Boston (see Chapter 2, above). Bradstreet's second edition, *Several Poems*, removes one of the initialed poems and adds a stilted and allusive verse appreciation by John Rogers, the probable editor, and John Norton's pompous funeral elegy on Bradstreet.

Furthermore, Bradstreet's admirers endorse more than they appreciate. Woodbridge's letter addresses several of the fears he anticipates a reader may have about this volume, not the least of which is "unbelief, which will make him question whether it be a woman's work, and ask, is it possible?" (*Works*, 3). He answers in the affirmative, but hastens to add the infamous disclaimer: "it is the work of a woman, honoured, and esteemed where she lives, for her gracious demeanour, her eminent parts, her pious conversation, her courteous disposition, her exact diligence in her place, and discrete managing of her family occasions, and more than so, these poems are the fruit but of some few hours, curtailed from her sleep and other refreshments" (3). Contrary to expectations, Bradstreet has not stepped out of her place, defined by God and Governor Winthrop as domestic angel; the phrase "exact diligence in her place" only begins to suggest the care Bradstreet must have taken *not* to seem out of the ordinary or dissatisfied with her lot, and it speaks worlds of anguish. She managed to accomplish poetically what few men of the age accomplished, while fulfilling the demanding role of wife and mother as well.

The disbelief of male readers that Woodbridge foresees suggests the general attitude of the age toward the intellectual capabilities of women, and it anticipates the later insidious use of male authentication of female voices. For example, in 1757 Martha Brewster of Lebanon, Connecticut, published a volume entitled *Poems on Divers Subjects*, containing seventeen poems and two acrostics. Her authorship, however, was contested by a number of people who forced her, before witnesses, "to paraphrase a Psalm extemporaneously" to prove her ability (Watts, *Poetry*, 26). Fifteen years later, the first volume of poetry by Phillis Wheatley, an African slave living in Boston, was introduced by a letter from her master explaining just how a slave and a female came to write poetry, buttressed by an attestation of authenticity signed by eighteen prominent Bostonian men, including the governor, the lieutenant-governor, John Hancock, and the Reverends Charles Chauncy and Mather Byles. The advertisement assures readers that Wheatley "has been examined by some of the best Judges, and is thought qualified to write" her poems; the still-skeptical reader is advised that the original of this document "may be seen by applying to *Archibald Bell*, Bookseller, No. 8, Aldgate-Street" (2).

The impressive array of "metrical seals of approval" (White, 260) by prominent men from England and New England that graces the first pages of *The Tenth Muse* implies that Bradstreet's family anticipated disbelief and, at the least, disapproval for what Bradstreet had been doing, and for what they had compounded by bringing it out in print. Woodbridge gives several weak reasons for acting against the poet's resolve that her manuscript "should (in such a manner) never see the sun" (*Works*, 3). He explains, as much to her as to his audience, that he "found that divers had gotten some scattered papers, affected them well, were likely to have sent forth broken pieces, to the author's prejudice, which I thought to prevent, as well as to pleasure those that earnestly desired the view of the whole" (3). There is a slight sense here of playing upon the novelty of a book of poetry by a woman. And Woodbridge's fears were justified; in 1664 a pirated edition of Katherine Philips's poems appeared after her circulating manuscript aroused considerable interest (White, 288). But under these circumstances, might not Bradstreet have agreed to publication and assisted in it? Why the family conspiracy? In his poetic tribute, Woodbridge vindicates his actions on aesthetic grounds but couches them in the same metaphor of the book as baby that Bradstreet will later use to record her angry reaction to the usurpation of her creative efforts: "If you shall think it will be to your shame / To be in print, then I must bear the blame; / If't be a fault, 'tis mine, 'tis shame that might / Deny so fair an infant of its right / To look abroad" (ll. 55–59), he rationalizes. But even if infants were granted some rights in the seventeenth century (which is doubtful), the opportunity to leave their parents was not one of them. In addition, poems do not have rights, but the handlers of women poets and the reproducers of children do. Elizabeth Wade White comes closest to implying that Bradstreet's family exercised those rights when she speculates, "It is also quite possible that they felt that the publication of *The Tenth Muse* would prove, to those in England who watched the progress of the colony with critical appraisal, that opportunities for cultural development and expression, even for women, were not lacking there" (256–57).

It is quite possible that the Bradstreet and Dudley families had even more at stake than making a contribution to the propagandizing of the Puritan experiment in the New World. The context that explains Bradstreet's own reluctance to publish as a result of her acute awareness of the prevailing attitudes toward intellectually achieving and visible women, also reveals a series of tribal and familial pressures that made the publication of *The Tenth Muse* almost a necessity for the Puritan theocracy and one of its leading families. First of all, "woman" had been a heated topic of debate among the literate classes ever since the first volleys of what is known as the "querelle des femmes" were loosed in the tenth and eleventh centuries. During the Renaissance in England, popular controversies raged over the "question of woman," fueled by the wide dissemination that could be achieved with printed material. A number of treatises both castigating and defending women appeared at the turn of the seventeenth century; a fresh pamphlet war broke out in 1615, and in 1620 the question took on renewed intensity couched in terms of fashion and styles of dress, only to resurface again in 1639–40 in another round of pamphlets and "lectures."[26] Not only the essential nature of woman, but practical questions concerning education, occupations, behavior, and treatment were aired in these printed debates.

The Massachusetts Bay Colony did not have a good record insofar as the treatment of women was concerned. From 1636 to 1638 Governor John Winthrop and the Boston clergy reacted with barely concealed hysteria to the threat they perceived that Anne Hutchinson and her followers presented to their authority, the integrity of the "New England Way," and the future of the fledgling theocracy. Hutchinson was so dangerous, according to the Puritan divines, because she was a woman unchecked, out of her place, and therefore out of their control. Although Bradstreet was no longer living in Newtown (Cambridge), having moved to Agawam (Ipswich) in 1635, it is impossible that she did not know of the tumult her countrywoman was causing, and of the clergy's reactions. Both her father and her husband were among the magistrates who examined Hutchinson at her trial in 1638.[27] Around this time, several other cases involving women's defiance of male hegemony cropped up. In 1637 an unnamed woman of the Boston congregation was so desperate over her spiritual state, and so unable to find consolation in the rigors of covenant theology, that she threw her baby down a well to insure her damnation. The baby was saved by a passerby (*Winthrop's Journal*, 1:230). Dorothy Talbye of Salem, known as a godly woman, began hearing revelations urging her to kill herself, her husband, and her children; the church cast her out. After punishments and reforms, she gave in to the blandishments of her inner voices and broke the neck of her three-year-old daughter "that she might free it from future misery." Winthrop records that the magistracy hanged her in 1638 (*Winthrop's Journal*, 1:282–83). Another Salemite, a Mistress Oliver, began preaching Hutchinsonian views and demanded to "be admitted to the Lord's Supper without giving public satisfaction to the church of her faith, etc., and covenanting or professing to walk with them according to the rule of the gospel"—that is, she refused to speak when required to do so. She stood up to the severe magistrate John Endecott, and persisted in her views despite threats, imprisonment, and whipping (*Winthrop's Journal*, 1:285–86). Then there was the tragedy of Anne Hopkins in 1645, mentioned earlier, whose uncontrolled activities led her to a different kind of "madness."

In 1647, the scourge struck the Dudley family directly. Sarah, Bradstreet's second-youngest sister, returned alone that year from London, where she had journeyed to meet her husband Benjamin Keayne, the son of a prominent Boston merchant. Letters home reported that she had taken up preaching in public. On her return to Boston, she regaled the First Church of Boston with her views, and she was "in open Assembly Admonished of hir Irregular Prophesying in mixt Assemblies and for Refusing ordinarily to heare in ye Churches of Christ" (transcript of MS records of First Church of Boston, 1630–87, 24; in White, 174). When her husband accused her of immorality as well as religious enthusiasm and refused to live with her, Thomas Dudley persuaded the colonial court to grant a divorce on the grounds that "his daughter was mentally irresponsible rather than deliberately profligate" (White, 176). The fate of her only child, Hannah, is not clear from the records.[28]

Sarah Keayne did not reform. Shortly after her divorce, the First Church excommunicated her for her "Irregular Prophecying" and also for "odious, lewd, & scandalous uncleane behavior with . . . an Excommunicate person" (MS record, 25; in White, 176). She was permitted to remarry, as a consequence of Dudley's argument to the court that she needed the supervision of a man. He selected for her a man of lower social status named Thomas Pacey. After this second marriage, she disappeared from the limelight. She died in 1659 at age forty in poverty, disinherited by her father and dependent on his other heirs for a yearly maintenance. Although Bradstreet named her second daughter after Sarah, she, like the rest of the family, remained silent on the painful topic of this family scandal.

In the journal where he recorded most of these cases, Winthrop associates these women with Anne Hutchinson, whom he describes as "of a haughty and fierce carriage, of a nimble wit and active spirit, and a very voluble tongue, more bold then a man" (Winthrop, *Short Story*, 263). The element common to all is their speaking or acting in defiance of male rule, and thereby overstepping the bounds of their gender—speaking, especially in public, makes women masculine and, therefore, unnatural and dangerous. Winthrop associates Talbye with Hutchinson for her assertions of direct communion with God, her proud bearing, and her "despising of the ordinance of excommunication" (*Winthrop's Journal*, 1:283); the law of the saints was not hers. Mistress Oliver, who confronted men of power in their own arena—in church—"was (for ability of speech, and appearance of zeal and devotion) far before Mrs. Hutchinson, and so the fitter instrument to have done hurt, but that she was poor and had little acquaintance." Winthrop recounts how, when she was whipped for reproaching the magistrates, "she stood without tying, and bare her punishment with a masculine spirit, glorying in her suffering." She also "had a cleft stick put on her tongue half an hour" for her criticisms of the magistrates, the colony's equivalent to the scold's bridles used in England on shrews (1:286).

These women, however, were not the stereotypic shrews and scolds of the pamphlet wars or of English stage comedy. As indicated by the violence they committed against their families, they were considered "unnatural," and their influence threatened the entire social and religious order established in New England. Winthrop reported ominously that "in the assemblies which were held by the followers of Mrs. Hutchinson, there was nourished and trained a keen, contentious spirit, and an unbridled licence of tongue, of which the influence was speedily felt in the serious disturbance, first of domestic happiness, and then of public peace. The matrons of Boston were transformed into a synod of slanderous praters, whose inquisitional deliberations and audacious decrees, instilled their venom into the innermost recesses of society; . . . the whole Colony was inflamed and distracted by the incontinence of female spleen and presumption" (*Short Story*, 83; quoted in Martin, 63). Images of infection, uncontrollable speech, and "incontinent" female bodies slide imperceptibly into one another, as in the case of Sarah Keayne. The overturning of the domestic hierarchy leads inevitably to the overturning of the church and state, as the Bostonian matrons become a competing "synod" of spiritual leaders denouncing a male clergy that would not even grant them a vote in church matters. Women in Boston were taking their spiritual lives into their own hands, and all on account of one woman's powerful and independent tongue.[29]

It is just possible that after the antinomian controversy had wracked the commonwealth, and after the family scandal that suggested the spirit of Hutchinson had not been completely eradicated and was liable to take root in unexpected places, the Dudley clan was eager to bring into public view the good daughter, the pious, humble, diligent, exemplary wife and mother who on her own would never have dared speak in public, yet whose speech was eminently acceptable, being a rather modest imitation of men's speech. Just at the time that Sarah Keayne returned home, John Woodbridge left for London with Bradstreet's manuscript. Thomas Dudley, the patriarch of the clan, would be deputy governor until 1649; after the disturbance over his younger daughter's behavior, he needed something to recoup his clan's lost esteem, some public event that would dissipate the pall created by Sarah Keayne's public displays, something we now call "spin control." It is just possible he found it in his oldest daughter's unexceptionable speech. Bradstreet's self-representations were representations that the family could control, objects of cultural exchange that they could manipulate.[30]

There are hints in Woodbridge's prefatory epistle that the "unmentionable" sister and her dishonorable actions may have been on his mind as he wrote. In his very first sentence, he bemoans his own lack of wit and confesses, "I fear 'twill be a shame for a man that can speak so little, to be seen in the title-page of this woman's book, lest by comparing the one with the other, the reader should pass his sentence that it is the gift of women not only to speak most but to speak best" (*Works*, 3). Woodbridge *is* being witty, however, by implying that the case of his glorious sister reverses the usual stereotype of shrewish women whose "curse" it is to "speak most." Joseph Swetnam's notorious treatise, *The Arraignment of Lewd, idle, froward, and unconstant women . . .* , published in London in 1615 and answered boldly by "Esther Sowernam" and "Constantia Munda," put the issue this way: "As a sharp bit curbs a froward horse, even so a curst woman must be roughly used, but if women could hold their tongues, then many times men would their hands" (Henderson and McManus, 209).[31] Bradstreet, as Woodbridge would have it, gives the lie to this image of woman. Hers is the "gift," not the curse, of speech, and though it is "natural" for her sex to speak more than man, the marvel of this paragon is that she also speaks better than he. The glowing description that follows (cited above) of Bradstreet's "exact diligence in her place" neatly lays to rest the ghost of Anne Hopkins, who neglected her family affairs; the mention of "her pious conversation" and "discrete managing of her family occasions" slays the specter of Anne Hutchinson and all of her ilk, including sister Sarah the divorcée, who disrupt families and, thereby, the state.

Finally, Woodbridge caps off the implicit contrast of one sister with another by comparing their "progeny." In his poetic tribute to Bradstreet, which deferentially follows Ward's poetic appreciation, he points out that the product of her poetic labors is "so fair an infant" ("To my dear Sister," l. 58). Winthrop and his cronies lost no time in broadcasting their smug allegations that Hutchinson and her supporter Mary Dyer, who was

later hanged on the Boston common for being a Quaker, both miscarried
what interested observers called "monstrous births." These were taken as
a divine sign of their spiritual "miscarriages" of thought and behavior. In
his "Preface" to Winthrop's account of the Hutchinson affair, Thomas
Weld gloated: "And see how the wisdom of God fitted this judgement to
her sinne every way, for look as she had vented misshapen opinions, so she
must bring forth deformed monsters" (*Short Story*, 214). Women's speech
that defies the party line—that usurps male authority and, thus, is not
inseminated by legitimating masculine influence—is monstrous and deformed. Bradstreet's speech, nurtured by her father and her legitimating
male poetic precursors, validates the dominant Puritan ideology and is
"fair" and whole and healthy, fit for public display. It is not accidental that
when Bradstreet wrote about seeing the "kidnapped" fruits of her poetic
labor in print, she called it "Thou ill-formed offspring of my feeble brain"
("The Author to her Book," l. 1). The metaphor of childbirth for
creativity was a common one, and Bradstreet's hobbling child is a far cry
from Winthrop's claims of the dissenting women's "monstrous births."
But Bradstreet's figure makes the same connection between women's
minds and their bodies that seems to have obsessed many in Puritan New
England. In an angry and rebellious gesture, Bradstreet counsels her
"brat" to answer questions about its father by saying "thou hadst none" (l.
23). Her illegitimate child, "ill-formed" perhaps because of male interference, suggests a subtle connection between the goodwife, hedged in by
convention, and the loose-tongued female rebels who spoke their minds.

Women are the "inferior sex," Woodbridge casually asserts, as he admonishes male readers not to "turn more peevish then women, to envy
the excellency of the inferior sex" (*Works*, 3). As the "superior sex," he
implies, men can afford to be generous with their praise and recognition.
His advice echoes, but with more sinister overtones, Bradstreet's own
ambiguous lines from "The Prologue":

Let Greeks be Greeks, and women what they are
Men have precedency and still excel,
It is but vain unjustly to wage war;
Men can do best, and women know it well.
Preeminence in all and each is yours;
Yet grant some small acknowledgement of ours.

(ll. 39–44)

And indeed, the attitude that Woodbridge, as representative of the family, held concerning women and work was enlightened, sophisticated, and, for the times, progressive; it was far from the "beetle-head" Puritan censors and "men of morose minds" and "severer eyes" whom Bradstreet condemns in her elegy on Sidney for wanting to limit her reading (ll. 28–30). Her freedom to read was crucial, since reading provided her access to the masculine world she could not otherwise enter. Yet beneath Woodbridge's liberality is the lurking fear, not that women, given relatively equal access and opportunity, will demand equal status, but that they will surpass the efforts of men; and that men, thereby, will indeed become more "peevish then women" and even turn into women.

Woodbridge's opening, unfavorable comparison of himself to the witty author he introduces is conventional and rhetorical; but as in the case of Berryman's title, when the two players are structurally and radically unequal, these literary conventions have a double effect: on the one hand, they include women in the exclusive fraternity by treating them no differently from men, and thus ignoring or erasing their irreducible differences; or they acknowledge women's differences, in which case the conventions place women in positions of inferiority and virtual exclusion. Woodbridge implies that his comparison of himself to Bradstreet will benefit her, echoing a passage from "The Prologue" cited above where she implies that the inferiority of her verse will enhance the work of male critics to which it is compared; this advantage, however, is severely limited by Bradstreet's being always and already "the inferior sex." Woodbridge creates an ambience of humorous, yet serious, competition between the genders, which colors all the prefatory material. The implication is that women who trespass will be judged—and they will be judged as women. We are never allowed to forget about sex: it is "a shame for a man . . . to be seen in the title-page of this woman's book"; "the gift of women"; "men turn more peevish then women"; "woman's work"; "work of a woman"; "the worth of these things (in their kind)" (*Works*, 3). A woman's intellectual production is gendered; it is a thing of a "kind," a discourse marked by the body and by its inferiority—even if readers are liable to mistake it for the work of a man.

In the eighteen-line offering by Nathaniel Ward that follows Woodbridge's letter, the "competition" between male and female becomes thematically explicit. In tight, Elizabethan couplets, and without ado, the contest gets under way:

Mercury showed Apollo Bartas' book,
Minerva this, and wished him well to look,
And tell uprightly, which did which excell,
He viewed and viewed, and vowed he could not tell.

(ll. 1–4)

Drawing upon Bradstreet's admission in "The Prologue" that her reading of the renowned (now obscure) French poet Du Bartas inspired her own poetic ambitions, and drawing upon the obvious similarity in their subject matter and conception, Ward pits the young female poet against the dead male master. Each book has its same-sex champion, a Roman god, who in turn sues Apollo to decide "Sex weighed, which best, the woman, or the man?" (l. 8). Apollo appears here, and especially in the poems by Bradstreet's English admirers, as the masculine spirit of the classical arts, a rather non-Puritan type who conquered and ruled over the nine female Muses. The "humor" of Ward's poem is said to derive from his rendition of this god of light as resembling "the simple cobler of Aggawam," Ward's persona in his popular satire on contemporary issues—an aged, opinion-ated, and misogynist windbag. Unable to decide which book is better, the hapless pedant gives up, while the younger gods laugh and say, "it was no mar'[ve]l / The Auth'ress was a right Du Bartas girl" (ll. 11–12). The voice of age and experience has the last word:

Good sooth quoth the old Don, tell ye me so,
I muse whither at length these girls will go;
It half revives my chill frost-bitten blood,
To see a woman once do ought that's good;
And shod by Chaucer's boots, and Homer's
    furs,
Let men look to't, lest women wear the spurs.

(ll. 13–18)

A close friend of Bradstreet's from their days in the wilderness settlement of Ipswich, and not a man given to sentimental displays of affection, Ward paints her as the exception that proves the rule. Women are "girls," extravagant and inexplicable, who never, it goes without saying, achieve anything of merit; the rustic cobbler says they have "but a few Squirrils brains to help them frisk from one ill-favour'd fashion to another" (Ward,

26).[32] As a result of being "a right Du Bartas girl"—that is, influenced, defined, and named by a male precursor—Bradstreet has for once "done good," but it is barely enough to revive the "old Don" from his wintry lethargy.

The compliment to Bradstreet's achievement here is interestingly back-handed. Ward's Apollo is unable to tell the woman's book from the man's, not because Bradstreet has achieved as much as Du Bartas, but because she has imitated him so well as to be indistinguishable from him. This is meant to be serious praise, but like other conventional usages, it has a peculiar sting when applied to a woman imitating a man. For instance, Sidney attempted a verse translation of Du Bartas, and Milton borrowed heavily from his monumental tome, *The Divine Weekes and Works*, in composing *Paradise Lost*; it is within the realm of possibility that Milton would have borne being called "the English Du Bartas," but never (to his face, no less) "a right Du Bartas boy"! In her own poetry, Bradstreet tries to lay comparisons with Du Bartas to rest. For example, in her homage to him, she implies that his influence gave her writer's block ("In Honour of Du Bartas, 1641," ll. 2–6, 14–19); in the dedication she defends herself from daring to "wear his wealth" ("To Her Most Honoured Father," l. 38)—that is, to imitate his style—and critics who have compared the two poetic styles agree with her.[33] She realizes it is best not to compete with him on his terms, and, despite her self-deprecation, she recognizes her own, very different abilities: "A Bartas can do what a Bartas will / But simple I according to my skill" ("The Prologue," ll. 13–14). Yet her "friends" harass her with comparison to an early influence that, in essence, infantilizes her and robs her of her own voice and poetic identity. And that, precisely, is the point: deny the difference when woman is willing to wear a masculine mask and serves your purpose—and invoke it when the mask slips, or she speaks for herself, in order to put her back in her place.

But if young girls have become like old men, then old men, so the logic goes, have become like young, indecisive, silly girls. Ward's depiction of Apollo as a laughable, decrepit, and witless pedant who cannot make a critical discrimination suggests the level to which he thinks the masculine practitioners of the arts have sunk. With his "mouldy nose," "cracked leering glasses," and "chill frost-bitten blood" (ll. 5, 6, 15), he is hardly in shape to marshal a defense against trivial, but energetic, girls. Ward concludes his condescending appreciation of the woman poet by warning men that they are in danger of losing their taken-for-granted dominant position: unless they don the rather aristocratic emblems of the classic poets, "Chaucer's boots, and Homer's furs," women will usurp the masculine privilege of speaking and humiliate them by taking over the pointed phallic "spurs" with which to goad them.

Comparison prevails as the mode of John Woodbridge's verse dedication to his sister-in-law, the next poem in the sequence. Having compared her, in his letter, to men, he now measures her against women—a divide-and-conquer tactic. The London literary scene at mid-century contained surprises for the New England pastor who had left his homeland in 1634, not the least of which was the spectacle of women authors: "Some books of women I have heard of late," he explains, "Perused some, so witless, intricate, / So void of sense, and truth, as if to err / Were only wished (acting above their sphere)" (ll. 19–22). Do these female authors err because they "act above their sphere" (not necessarily their capabilities), or because they perversely desire to appear to err? Woodbridge, though of a younger generation than Ward, echoes the older man's misogynist opinion that women's vanity, even when it takes the form of desiring intellectual "esteem," forces him to wonder "If women are with wit and sense inspired" at all (l. 28). None of this, of course, applies to Bradstreet, who will "affirm" and "confirm" her sex's intellectual capacity. Meditating on this quandary, Woodbridge resolves it only superficially: "Theirs was the person's, not the sex's failing, / And therefore did bespeak a modest veiling" (ll. 33–34). In other words, the witless women authors he read in England failed, not because they were female, but because they were ungifted, and thus should have modestly veiled or hidden their ambitions. Sex, it seems, is no longer the deciding factor in literary success; but Woodbridge cannot abide such gender-blindness for long. In holding Bradstreet up as a paragon and pretending to redeem the female sex through her, he parodies her passionate vindication of women through the heroic figure of Queen Elizabeth: "You have acutely in Eliza's ditty, / Acquitted women, else I might with pity, / Have wished them all to women's works to look, / And never more to meddle with their book" (ll. 35–38).

Despite the achievements of queens and middle-class housewives, Woodbridge continues to believe that work is restricted to and by gender—that because what Bradstreet has done is "rare," other women

cannot also aspire to it. As recompense for her tokenism, he offers her a
pedestal and explains the origin of the title of the volume: "And if the
nine, vouchsafe the tenth a place, / I think they rightly may yield you that
grace" (ll. 41–42). Apparently, he has forgotten about Bradstreet's unfortunate collision with "the nine," recounted at the end of her elegy on
Philip Sidney (ll. 76–85): refusing her guidance, inspiration, and solace,
they grab her pen and drive her out of Parnassus as a trespasser. Acting as
the guardians of the august literary tradition that Bradstreet wishes to
enter, the Muses could be rejecting her on the grounds of talent; but
Bradstreet makes it clear that her sex is the issue (*Complete Works*, 152, l.
124). This is *her* trope for her relation to the classical tradition. Brother
and sister seem to have different ideas on where the anomalous woman
poet belongs, if at all.

Woodbridge's discussion of women's capacities suggests he was familiar
with the current terms of the "querelle des femmes" in England. Ostensibly (and half-heartedly), he denies that sex has anything to do with poetic
achievement, yet his text is obsessed with describing Bradstreet in terms
that do not allow the reader to forget her gender. For example, after
making the usual disclaimers of humility in the opening, Woodbridge
continues with this bit of gallantry:

> There needs no painting to that comely face,
> That in its native beauty hath such grace;
> What I (poor silly I) prefix therefore,
> Can but do this, make yours admired the more;
> And if but only this I do attain,
> Content, that my disgrace may be your gain.
>
> (ll. 11–16)

He is still trying to justify his own speaking, when it is her speech he is
supposed to facilitate and showcase. The difference between this comparison and the one that began his prefatory letter is that here he extols
the beauty of Bradstreet's face as a figure for her poetry, and compares his
"prefixes" to the cosmetic trickery she does not need because of her
"native . . . grace." She does not need it, and yet he affixes it. Worse, he
turns her intellectual achievements into the physical qualities for which
women have always been admired and pedestaled. Painted faces, as Roger
Williams insists in the next chapter, are associated with whores—and

especially, for Puritans, the whore of Babylon (standing in Puritan typology for the Church of Rome), the archetypal seducer of men. Using the same terms, John Winthrop harangued Anne Hutchinson as the *"American Jesabel,"* infecting the minds of the women of Boston who would, in turn, catch their husbands with their seductive tongues, tongues busy talking instead of kissing (Barker-Benfield, 79). Woodbridge uses a word to describe the arguments of the witless London authoresses that connects them to the first *"American Jesabel"* and her followers: the word is "intricate" (l. 20), and its position in the line isolates and emphasizes it. One possible meaning is "complex" and "involved," but that valence is too positive for an adjective that must complement "witless." The *OED* suggests, "perplexingly involved and complex," "embarrassing," "obscure," "entangling and ensnaring through trickery." Intricate arguments, even with the negative connotations of the latter definitions, are far from "witless"; rather, they are dangerous, like the seductive trickery of "voluble" women. Bradstreet is "comely," graceful, and without the need for paints; she is "artless"—another double-edged, back-handed compliment—the very antithesis of the London literary tarts. But Woodbridge's discourse of contrast begins to double back on him. His rhetoric implies that Bradstreet's achievement is intelligent, clear, unseductive, and worthy of admiration—in other words, it is masculine but not threatening, because in all other respects Bradstreet is the exemplary woman. What the "other" women have done is witless yet dangerous, immodest yet trivial, the height of feminine seduction, yet masculine because "above their sphere," and threatening because out of place. Two conflicting notions of women's potential masculinity are at work here. In the end, however, Woodbridge returns Bradstreet to her gender with a vengeance when he asks readers to admire her poems as if we were admiring her face.

The emphasis on Bradstreet as woman continues to the end of the poem. As he plays out the figure of her book as a fair infant that deserves "to look abroad," to know and be known to the world, Woodbridge comes logically to an image of unnatural birth, an image that Berryman also employs to suggest his violent appropriation of woman's voice. Pretending to put himself "in her place," Woodbridge anticipates Bradstreet's reactions to his audacious act by spinning out a sequence of emotions meant to get him off the hook. He begins soothingly,

. . . I know your modest mind,
How you will blush, complain, 'tis too unkind:
To force a woman's birth, provoke her pain,
Expose her labours to the world's disdain.
I know you'll say, you do defy that mint,
That stamped you thus, to be a fool in print.
'Tis true, it doth not now so neatly stand,
As if 'twere polished with your own sweet hand;
'Tis not so richly decked, so trimly tired,
Yet it is such as justly is admired.

(ll. 59–68)

The untimely publication of a work that its creator feels has not yet come to term is, even in Woodbridge's eyes, a forced birth, a theft, a humiliation. While he admits that the volume would have benefited aesthetically from Bradstreet's editorship, he implies that her "neatening" and "decking" and "trimming" and "polishing" (actions that all fall into the category of "women's" work) would not change the poetry's substance, which is still admirable. Besides, as a woman's attempt at art, it need not be particularly "finished"; it is remarkable enough as it is.

The several registers of images at play in this passage clash, however. First, there is the modesty topos, with Bradstreet's blushes, protests, and complaints. This slips into the image of her caesarean or premature birth, with its provocation of pain and humiliating exposure in the throes of labor—in seventeenth-century New England, labor and delivery were events attended exclusively by females (Ulrich, 126–29). Then he allows her some real anger and defiance and accusations of being made the fool, which he quickly modulates into harmless images of feminine primping, cleaning, and fussing, practically defusing Bradstreet's justifiable fury. He implies that the symbolic value of the volume's publication is, in fact, more important than the mere author's desire for authorial control or poetic standards. Is it going too far to say that she, also, is a creation, a creature of her family and its codes, of her culture and its images, of her religion and its doctrines, all of which control and script her? It is chivalrous for Woodbridge to "dare outface the world's disdain for both, / If you alone profess you are not wroth" (ll. 73–74), except that he has created the dragon against which he vows to defend her. In the final couplet he admits that not even her anger counts: "Yet if you are [wroth], a woman's wrath is little, / When thousands else admire you in each tittle" (ll. 75–76). Bradstreet's womanly anger and artistic integrity are trivial in the face of fame and her family's greater need to refurbish their image.

The next six poems form a group connected by their brevity and their noticeably different, uncomplicated tone of admiration. The first is by Benjamin Woodbridge, John's younger brother, who knew Bradstreet in New England. The rest were solicited by Woodbridge from friends and acquaintances living in England among whom he circulated Bradstreet's manuscript. They wrote without knowing the author, and their verses serve both as courteous complements to an accomplished lady and as endorsements of their friend's project. All the poems are initialed; Elizabeth Wade White, Bradstreet's biographer, proposes identities for four of the five English admirers from among several literary men whom Woodbridge knew in his years at Oxford, 1628–34. She speculates that on his return to England, he might have sought them out as "the sort of scholars who would have been inclined to look with a fair amount of sympathy at this manifestation of female virtuosity" (260–66). Perhaps living in London protected them from the provincialism of the colonies. They might have been familiar with the various pamphlet wars on the "woman question" currently taking place, and they certainly would have had much greater exposure to publicly active women—the interregnum being a period when female religious activists and sectarians were tolerated and highly visible.[34]

In general, these poems are classical in orientation, with references to Apollo's wit at having used "female laurel [to crown] his brow" ("C. B.," l. 2), and assurances that Bradstreet encompasses the qualities of all the traditional female personifications, "The Muses, Virtues, Graces" ("B. W.," l. 2). One poet calls her a "golden splendent star" rising in the west and outshining "swift-winged Phoebus, and the rest / Of all Jove's fiery flames" ("N. H.," ll. 11–15). What is immediately apparent in this hyperbole is the unequivocal nature of the admiration. "H. S." simply avows:

I've read your poem, Lady, and admire,
Your sex to such a pitch should e'er aspire;
Go on to write, continue to relate,
New histories, of monarchy and state:

And what the Romans to their poets gave,
Be sure such honour, and esteem you'll have.

His confidence in Bradstreet's continued achievement and in society's
recognition of it are admirable, especially since Rome did not have any
poets of her sex to lavish with honor and esteem.

For these men, the "contest" between men and women for poetic
superiority seems to have been decided—and in woman's favor. With
good-humored amusement, Benjamin Woodbridge concedes for his sex:
"Mankind take up some blushes on the score; / Monopolize perfection
no more; / In your own arts, confess yourselves outdone, / The moon
hath totally eclipsed the sun" (ll. 5–8). Taking up Nathaniel Ward's connection of Bradstreet with Minerva, the virgin goddess devoted to the
moon, he transforms woman's futile attempts to achieve parity into a long-
deserved and belated accession to equality. In the 1650 edition, his punning spelling of "Menopolize" drove the point home nicely. In "Upon the
Author," the poet ("C. B."), instead of comparing Bradstreet with Du
Bartas, uses a paraphrase of Bradstreet's own praise of her mentor to
praise her: in "In Honour of Du Bartas," she extols him as "the quintes-
sence of an heroic brain," "pregnant" with ideas and commanding a
"comprehension vast" (ll. 63, 75); "C. B." commends Bradstreet's "sublime brain [which is] the synopsis of arts" (l. 4) and concludes: "False
fame, belie their sex no more, it can / Surpass, or parallel, the best of
man" (ll. 7–8). The rhythm calls for the inversion of "surpass" and
"parallel"; the "or" makes no sense otherwise, unless the poet means to
indicate a retreat from his claim that woman can surpass man to the more
moderate assertion that they "parallel" the paragons of the male sex. Only
the facetious offering by "R. Q." takes a mocking tone toward the "war"
between the sexes. Beginning with a rousing call to "Arm, arm, soldados
arm; horse, Horse, speed to your horses" (l. 1), the poet warns his fellows
against "Gentle-women [who] vent their plots in verses" and on subjects
like monarchies (ll. 2–3)—an allusion to Bradstreet's extensive poem
"The Four Monarchies" (the monarchy being an especially sensitive topic
in England after 1642). The conclusion of this verse, however, has its fun
by dragging up the tired stereotype of vain, lazy, sensual women: "March
amain to London, they'll rise, for there they flock, / But stay a while, they
seldom rise till ten o'clock" (ll. 5–6). It is not surprising that this poem
disappeared from the second edition.

The stilted and urbane poetic sponsorship of an unknown woman living in a colonial outpost is completed by two anagrams and a couplet most probably by John Wilson, another New England minister and a good friend of Nathaniel Ward. Wilson came over from England with Winthrop and the Bradstreets in 1630 and became teacher at the first church established in Charlestown, a man known for his piety, learning, and propensity for making anagrams. He was also one of the ministers Anne Hutchinson accused of preaching a covenant of works, the Arminian heresy that dulled the soteriological requirement of absolute passivity and allowed humans to have some active part in the reception of saving grace. Wilson's light in the Boston church had been eclipsed by the advent of the charismatic preacher John Cotton, who arrived in 1633, followed shortly by the Hutchinsons. As her views became more popular, Hutchinson's "infectious contempt," according to E. S. Morgan, "reduced his influence in the congregation to the vanishing point" (*Puritan Dilemma*, 142). The arrival of the Reverend John Wheelwright, a fiery nonconformist preacher and brother-in-law of Anne Hutchinson, who with Cotton was silenced by the bishops in England, aggravated Wilson's weakened position. The congregation of the First Church moved to have Wheelwright made a teacher in an attempt to bolster the Hutchinsonian faction, whose views he heartily endorsed. Winthrop, a member of the church, understood the threat represented by Wheelwright, and, always a staunch ally of Wilson, he blocked the election. In the ensuing melee, Wilson became one of Hutchinson's most determined enemies (Morgan, *Puritan Dilemma*, 150).

If, indeed, Wilson composed the closing anagrams for Bradstreet's volume, his interest in its success and his attitudes toward women's visibility would be roughly parallel to those of his old friend and fellow wordsmith Ward, and his peer Thomas Dudley. His applications of the popular Puritan form are brisk and upbeat:

Anna Bradestreate   Dear neat An Bartas.
So Bartas like thy fine spun poems been,
That Bartas' name will prove an epicene.

Anne Bradstreate.   Artes bred neat An.
(*Works*, 9)

Like Ward, with whom he shared the same late-Renaissance education that would have included large amounts of the French poet in Joshua

Sylvester's English translation, Wilson associates the young woman poet with Du Bartas. And like Ward, his compliments take the form of asserting how wonderfully "Bartas like" Bradstreet's poems are. But Wilson's anagrammatizing makes a deeper and more insidious claim. It is wit and a bit of prophecy that his second anagram discovers in Bradstreet's name a temperamental propensity to the "artes," but he also discovers in Bradstreet's name another name superimposed over her married name, which replaced her maiden patronymic: "An Bartas," as if she is married or related to Du Bartas, or so indistinguishable from her precursor as to be named by him. To take this to its furthest extent, she is reborn ("bred" in the second anagram also suggests this) and thus renamed as a female version of the male master. The extent of her achievement of likeness to Du Bartas, Wilson quips, will demonstrate that the name "Bartas" is "an epicene," a term from Latin grammar applied to nouns that, without changing their grammatical gender, may denote either sex; the great poet remains masculine but can encompass the female imitator, who remains feminine but is subsumed by the masculine name. Besides the appropriate allusion to classical languages, Wilson may also have had in mind Ben Jonson's comedy, "Epicene, or The Silent Woman," which was produced in London in 1609 when Wilson was a young man. The plot involves a greedy nephew who tricks his wealthy uncle into marrying a woman he believes to be his perfect mate because she utters "but six words a day." After the wedding, Epicene transforms into a merciless shrew who constantly harasses her husband. In the end, Epicene is revealed to be a boy whom the shrewd nephew has trained and employed to drive his uncle to give him a large inheritance. The ideally silent woman turns into a shrew and a "he" if she is not properly named and managed, Wilson's anagram implies. While delving into Bradstreet's name, the ingenious old anagrammatizer finds an author whose name is flexible enough to incorporate her different gender and under whose shadow she can safely and successfully speak while, in effect, remaining silent. These linguistic divinations are a fitting conclusion to the context in which the Puritan patriarchy delivered Anne Bradstreet's poetry to the world.

Having worked our way through what I believe is an ideological construction of Anne Bradstreet and *The Tenth Muse*, we (and I speak here for a late-twentieth-century female and feminist reader) arrive at the work itself. What we find is, at least to my mind, disconcerting. First, the long poems of the Quaternions and "The Four Monarchies" are in a state of incompleteness that no poet, however untutored, over-eager, or amateurish, would have permitted for publication. Poems break off in mid-thought and short, personal apologies are inserted. The elaborate dedication to Thomas Dudley is extremely personal, especially in light of the sometimes highly impersonal tone of much of the poetry that follows, and excruciatingly, embarrassingly self-abasing. Perhaps that is just what the family wanted, and just what was needed to justify a daughter's poetry—poetry that was historical, philosophical, and epic in scope, matching her father's own "four sisters," four poems "on the four parts of the world" now lost. Even Bradstreet senses the challenge implicit in her "four sisters," "Who for their age, their worth and quality / Might seem of yours to claim precedency; / But by my humble hand thus rudely penned, / They are your bounden handmaids to attend" (ll. 16–19). Paternal authority demands that the daughter disclaim all thoughts or hints of over-reaching, and feminine humility obediently produces rude, harsh, and "ragged lines" (l. 43).

As we read through the poems it also becomes clear that the sponsors who recommend Bradstreet to the world have read her poetry either carelessly or very selectively. They pounce on her fawning homage to Du Bartas, but ignore her opening call in "The Prologue" to end the "war" of comparison between the sexes. Echoing her own disclaimer of competition, made to her father, she concedes, somewhat in the tone of an experienced mother placating a spoiled child, that "Men have precedency and still excel, . . . / Men can do best, and women know it well" ("The Prologue," ll. 40, 42), and she then asks to be recognized for what *she* is— a she, not an epicene or a protégé of Du Bartas, whose achievement deserves recognition for what it is, not what others want or need it to be. "Give thyme or parsley wreath, I ask no bays" (l. 48), she demands firmly, requesting homey, domesticated herbs; yet she is figured by one of her sponsors ("C. B.") as the very laurels with which Apollo wittily crowned himself—another inflationary objectification, where woman's achievement is appropriated as a sign of male dominance of the field.

In stark contrast to the competitive tone of much of the prefatory material, several of Bradstreet's "Quaternions" are structured as "contests," which are resolved, not through the conventional hierarchy of winners and losers, but by defusing competition altogether. For example, the four elements begin their Quaternion by arguing "Which was the strongest, noblest, and the best, / Who was of greatest use and might'est force" (ll. 2–3)—and yet Bradstreet's avowed purpose is to show "How divers natures make one unity" ("To Her Most Honored Father," l. 35). The four humors eventually agree to unite in "perfect amity" and form "a compact body, whole entire" (ll. 607, 609). Working harmony, not competition or upsmanship, is part of what critics call Bradstreet's "gynocentric vision."[35] Perhaps a practiced, interested, and modern eye is needed to read Bradstreet's feminist leanings, as well as her bitter irony, her revealing ambiguities, her frustration; to perceive, in short, what Adrienne Rich calls "the stress-marks of anger, the strains of self-division, in her work" (22). But it should not have been hard for her male contemporaries, if they were really looking, to see the admiration for the powerful though disgraced queens and empresses of antiquity that she records in "The Four Monarchies"; the antagonism that she imagined the classical Muses felt for her poetic attempts in the elegy on Sidney; the delight she took, in the same elegy, in cataloguing examples of female transvestism and subversive female power presented by Ovid and mythology; and her apotheosis of Queen Elizabeth, who does not merely "acquit" the female sex of the aspersion cast upon them, as John Woodbridge allowed ("To My Dear Sister," ll. 35–36), but acts as a Christlike figure whose return to earth will inaugurate a millennium of female dignity.

Also painfully apparent in *The Tenth Muse* are moments when Bradstreet takes on the patriarchal voice and denigrates her own sex. For example, all the personifications in the Quaternions are feminine—except, of course, in "Of the Four Ages of Man." Cheryl Walker points out two prominent examples, one in the biblical paraphrase, "David's Lamentation for Saul and Jonathan," and the other in the "Choler" section of "Of the Four Humours." Biblical paraphrasing was a common poetic exercise; it is perfectly appropriate that an apprentice Puritan poet chose to speak in the voice of David, the model poet of the Psalms. But in choosing such a model, and such a situation—the eulogizing of David's comrades, one of whom happens to be a deposed king—Bradstreet puts herself in the position of Judith Fetterley's as-yet-unresisting female reader, forced to identify against her sex in order to participate in the emotional and political dynamic of the poem and the masculine dynamic of writing. When she renders David's tribute to Jonathan's affection as a love "Exceeding all the love that's feminine" (l. 40), she validates the Platonic ideal that the truest love exists between friends who are equals and applies only to men. In her capacity as poet, Bradstreet elevates an affectional model that defines itself specifically against the female sex, and thus excludes her. She can enter into such a relationship only by writing about it and can only write about it in a masculine voice.

Choler also voices the patriarchal view of woman in her account of how she and her mother, Fire, have undergone a gender transformation. Formerly "masculines," they have become "feminines awhile; for love we owe" to the sisterhood of the humors, "which makes us render / Our noble selves in a less noble gender" ("Of the Four Humours," ll. 36–39). Choler is arrogant, obnoxious, and condescending, and she is silenced and forced to unite with her three sisters by the gentler Phlegm, who argues that too much Choler in the brain produces madmen and tyrants (ll. 578–79). Although the put-down of woman is spoken by a persona whose superiority is discredited, the lines indicate, as Walker says, Bradstreet's "willingness to represent the views of the patriarchy" (9). Timothy Sweet argues that Bradstreet was fully conversant with the elegiac and epic conventions of the public genres dominating *The Tenth Muse*, which structurally demand masculine speakers and feminine objects, and that she self-consciously exposes the discursive power plays produced by androcentric assumptions (157–58). In an earlier essay on the three elegies in *The Tenth Muse*, I demonstrated how Bradstreet attempts to position herself as a "son" of the Renaissance tradition, rather than the daughter of a powerful Puritan patriarch, in order to inherit the poetic privilege to speak publicly.

When Bradstreet professes the "preeminence" of men at the conclusion of "The Prologue," however, she accepts the gendered role of a daughter as one of the few means she has of speaking at all. She accepts the position scripted for her by her family, her culture, and her religion, even though that acceptance is not complete or dogmatic. The poems of *The Tenth Muse* give ample evidence of her ambitions, resistances, and frustrations, consciously and unconsciously expressed; yet they could be and were read by her male sponsors as perfectly acceptable to their values. The volume received general praise and was mentioned approvingly by the likes of Cotton Mather, in his *Magnalia Christi Americana*, and

Bathsua Makin, an educated English woman, in her treatise *An Essay to Revive the Ancient Education of Gentlewomen in Religion, Manners, Arts and Tongues* (London, 1673; in White, 283–84). It was listed (twice!) in "A Catalogue of the most Vendible Books in England" for 1657 along with works by Cowley, Crashaw, Donne, Drayton, "Dubartas," Herbert, Herrick, Milton, Lady Margaret of Newcastle, Quarles, Shakespeare, Waller, and Wither (White, 272). It was the one book of poetry in Edward Taylor's library. Amazingly, Bradstreet manages to appear suitably modest as a woman, conventionally humble as a poet, and doctrinally sound as a Puritan. It is unfortunate that the one poetic appreciation written by a woman—Bradstreet's sister Mercy, wife of John Woodbridge, last mentioned in 1829—is now lost and was not included in the sheaf of prefatory material, even anonymously (Watts, *Poetry*, 21).[36]

By her own account, Bradstreet responded strongly to the publication of *The Tenth Muse*. The fact that no more of her poetry appeared in print during her lifetime suggests that, despite her family's having broken the taboo, she never overcame her aversion to self-publication. The only record we have of her reactions is "The Author to Her Book," a finely wrought, pointed poem that became the preface to the second edition, *Several Poems*. Taking up her brother-in-law's reference to her volume as an "infant," Bradstreet expands the metaphor over the whole poem. To Woodbridge's eyes, this infant is "fair" and worthy of display. To Bradstreet, it is "ill-formed" as a result of her "feeble brain" (l. 2); it is blemished (contains errors), lame (metrically uneven), and ragged (unrevised). Her emotions are jangled upon seeing again the child so cruelly snatched away: "At thy return my blushing was not small, / My rambling brat (in print) should mother call, / I cast thee by as one unfit for light, / Thy visage was so irksome in my sight" (ll. 8–11), and she abandons it for a time. But recognizing the book as "mine own," she embraces her brainchild and tries, in vain, to amend its flaws.

Also a response to the complicated appearance that her family and culture fashioned for her, this poem operates on several levels at once, managing to be thoroughly conventional and subtly subversive at the same time. It is an important poem because it suggests Bradstreet's heightened awareness of the gender politics of women's visibility. With the surprising appearance of *The Tenth Muse*, Bradstreet better understood how it was she could appear and speak in public with impunity while her sister Sarah could not. Precariously positioned, she mouths the attitudes about herself and her writing ("feeble brain," "ill-formed offspring") that she now knows are required in order to justify her appearance in print. She might even half-believe them. But it is crucial to remember that Bradstreet addresses her book after having read and absorbed the messages of the prefatory material marshaled by her brother-in-law. She, too, reads and writes her self-representations through the eyes of the Puritan patriarchy.

The analogy of childbirth and creativity was commonly used by both male and female writers; seventeenth-century men also gave unflattering descriptions of their book-children when excusing their efforts to critics and readers.[37] But in this instance, Bradstreet gives the trope an unusual twist by representing her child as having no father, though it had several poetic fathers (the dedication casts Thomas Dudley as her model and muse) and more than enough paternal and avuncular sponsors. She insists that it has been "exposed to public view" without her consent and so appears illegitimately, even though a whole patriarchal culture is willing, even over-eager, to "own" it. Bradstreet may have in mind Spenser's admonition "To His Booke" from *The Shepheards Calendar*, which begins: "Goe, little book! thy selfe present, / As child whose parent is unkent," and goes on to instruct his offspring, "if that any aske thy name, / Say, thou wert base begot with blame." There is a difference, however, between a male poet claiming that his book has a father who is an unknown "shepheards swaine," and a female poet disclaiming a father for her book at all. Perhaps it is the altogether too willing "ownership" of her child by the Puritan fathers that Bradstreet wants to repudiate here.

As seems always to be the case, Bradstreet's figure can be read in mutually exclusive ways, a technique common to women's poetry that Alicia Ostriker calls "duplicity." As a poetic strategy, duplicity was honed to a fine art by nineteenth-century women poets who were "driven by something forbidden to express but impossible to repress," who had ideas that "must be simultaneously denied and affirmed" (41). Different from irony, where the unstated meaning cancels out what is stated, duplicity allows contrary meanings to coexist with equal force because, Ostriker argues, "they have equal force within the poet" (40–41). By directing her child, "If for thy father asked, say thou hadst none," Bradstreet suggests both that she and her offspring have been abandoned by a father who could not claim them, and that she is eager to disavow male participation altogether. She veils her potentially threatening rejection of male involvement and her embrace of female separatism by echoing Spenser's self-effacing instructions to his poetic child, thus locating her poem safely within the literary topos of authorial humility. Her book's inadequacies seem finally to amuse more than anger her, and she sends it out into the world dressed in homespun to roam "'mongst vulgars" (l. 20).

Using the conventional trope of the book as baby within a New England Puritan discourse that associates women's speaking with the products of their bodies, Bradstreet makes subversive claims that determine the directions her poetic self-representations will take in her later work. Though ashamed at first, she acknowledges the deformed and ragged child that she has produced *by herself*, and acknowledges it not once, but twice, since she implies that she is revising the text in order to send it out once again in a second edition. Furthermore, as Susan Stanford Friedman argues in her fascinating study of gender-specific uses of the childbirth metaphor, Bradstreet's "analogy defies the cultural prescription to procreativity. Like the male metaphor, her comparison of motherhood and authorship reminds the reader of their historical separation. But unlike the male metaphor, her analogy subverts that contextual resonance instead of reinforcing it" (81). It is important to note that Friedman emphasizes that "the distinction between female and male discourse lies not in the metaphor itself but rather in the way its final meaning is constituted in the process of reading" (82). A reader-response approach to Bradstreet's poetry helps explain why her male contemporaries were able to "read" her poetry selectively: they heard a woman making a learned allusion to Spenser's perfectly acceptable work, not one subversively bringing together the creativity and procreativity her culture has rendered mutually exclusive. Bradstreet quietly asserts that she is both poet (not muse) and mother, speaker and woman. In doing so, she revalorizes a proscribed union of roles that her culture deemed, at the least, unnatural—and at the worst, satanic.

This revalorization represents a significant advance over Bradstreet's conspicuously self-deprecating use of the analogy in *The Tenth Muse*. In her homage to Du Bartas she apostrophizes him as a "pregnant brain" inseminated by God's love and delivering "sacred works" (ll. 75, 78), while she is "barren" and able to bring forth only a "homely" poetic "flower" (ll. 14–15). The fact that Bradstreet experienced difficulty conceiving a child reinforces the connection between her creativity and pro-creativity, both of which she portrays as dependent upon a masculine presence, the will of God. Du Bartas's superior literary fertility reveals the insidious religious resonances of this trope. Not only is the male poet superior in masculine executive capacity, but he is superior as a feminine vessel of divine insemination—his brain is superior to both her brain *and* her womb. As Friedman points out, the Christian tradition appropriated the images of generative power in ancient Near Eastern Mother God-desses and transformed it into the power of the Word wielded by a masculine deity and his son: "mind became the symbolic womb of the universe" (76). Bradstreet's resistance to this appropriation is her por-trayal of Queen Elizabeth, through references to her emblem the mytho-logical phoenix, as giving birth to herself. In "The Author to Her Book," Bradstreet represents her poetic creativity with similar implications of defiant virginity and self-fertilization. By asserting that her book has no father, she gestures toward reappropriating for herself the generative power of the word reserved for male speakers, and the regenerative power of the Word reserved in Christianity to God the Father.

"The Author to Her Book" marks a crucial moment in the history of Bradstreet's self-representation. Ironically, she was not impelled by her book's success to continue trespassing upon male precincts—perhaps she no longer needed to. In her remaining twenty years, she composed pri-marily lyric poems and spiritual meditations in a voice more private, less controversial and ambitious, yet irreducibly gendered: the voice of wife, mother, and grandmother. Subjects garnered from her personal experi-ences with children, marriage, the burning of her home in Andover, and especially her spiritual struggles replace the more ostensibly "historical" and "metaphysical" subject matter of the Quaternions, "The Four Mon-archies," and the early elegies. Critics as traditional as Elizabeth White and as radical as Adrienne Rich compare this voice to the formal, imper-sonal, and public voice of the early work, and find it authentic and origi-nal; Bradstreet leaves the role of dutiful daughter and finds strength and inspiration in her roles as mother and wife.[38] Cheryl Walker explains the shift by arguing that in Puritan New England "the mother remained the archetype of female power," and she contends that Bradstreet "makes writing poetry contiguous with motherhood" (11), not competitive with it. Opposing this view, Timothy Sweet considers the later poems and

Bradstreet's lyric persona to be a retreat from her challenges to classical discourses of gendered power relations, and an acceptance of a limited, domesticated discourse and the "comfortable" culturally prescribed "woman's place" (168–169): "Where the early elegies demonstrate that subjectivity could in some cases be detached from the gender assigned to the poet," he concludes, "the domestic poems merely reproduced the ideology of social discourse which reifies gender" (169).

The radical shift in Bradstreet's voice is not easily explained, nor is it noncontradictory. To my mind, it hinges on her desire, unambiguously expressed in "The Author to *Her* Book," to speak poetically as a female subject. Whether inadequate or powerful, she represents her poetic subjectivity in the image and reality of motherhood. Adrienne Rich, who in her foreword to Jeannine Hensley's 1967 edition celebrated Bradstreet's widely anthologized domestic poems, confessed in a "Postscript" published in 1979 that her essay "shows the limitations of a point of view which took masculine history and literature as its center"; as a result, she ignored the "tension between creative work and motherhood" that beset Bradstreet as well as Rich herself (21). Reading from a feminist perspective, Rich insists that we must ask new questions that probe the seemingly unperturbed surface of Bradstreet's domestic poetry. Using the double-edged metaphor of motherhood, Bradstreet subversively reconnects what patriarchal culture severs: woman's body and her brain. In doing so, however, she seems to allow herself to be put back into the place that, according to Governor Winthrop, God had set her. Is Bradstreet's self-representation as a satisfied child-bearer and rearer different from, or less problematic than, Berryman's poetic imposition of that role upon her?

The crucial difference lies in a woman's sense of having a choice—and, after her initial presumption and poetic success, Bradstreet did have some limited choice. Yes, she accepts the roles set out for women in Puritan culture, but she carries with her some consciousness of the ideological interests they serve. For example, the elegies composed on the deaths of her infant grandchildren and young daughter-in-law express a maternal sadness laced with barely concealed anger at a deity who wields his awful, life-destroying power so arbitrarily and in seeming contradiction to women's life-bearing capacity. Maternity conferred upon her a double responsibility with respect to her children. In the letter that Bradstreet left them as part of their maternal inheritance, she conflates her physical giving of birth to her children with her responsibility to aid their rebirth spiritually: "as I have brought you into the world, and with great pains, weakness, cares, and fears brought you to this, I now travail in birth again of you till Christ be formed in you" (*Works*, 241). Puritan mothers were expected to share in the religious instruction and moral training of children, but Bradstreet goes further. Echoing here the words spoken by the apostle Paul to his wayward flock in Galatia (Gal. 4:19), she voices her fears for her children's souls while subtly reappropriating the (re)generative function "natural" for women but reserved for male ministers, who appropriated to themselves the role of spiritual midwife to the Puritan soul. If she had insisted upon fulfilling this role publicly "in mixed assemblies," she would have become like Anne Hutchinson, a poisonous seducer. Within the domestic sphere, she can be another apostle, both literally and figuratively.

During the 1650s, a period of intense spiritual struggle, Bradstreet explores the Puritan construction of redeemed subjectivity and its figuration of woman. It is an indication of the power and resilience of Puritan religious ideology that its requirements finally take precedence in Bradstreet's life. In one of her many prose meditations of this period when, in her words, "my soul hath been refreshed with the consolations which the world knows not" (*Works*, 250), she articulates the same hierarchical ladder of relations between herself and God that we saw in Edward Taylor's poetry:

> Lord, why should I doubt any more when Thou hast given me such assured pledges of Thy love? First, Thou art my Creator, I Thy creature, Thou my master, I Thy servant. But hence arises not my comfort, Thou art my Father, I Thy child; "Ye shall be My sons and daughters," saith the Lord Almighty. Christ is my brother, I ascend unto my Father, and your Father, unto my God and your God; but lest this should not be enough, thy maker is thy husband. Nay more, I am a member of His body, He my head. Such privileges had not the Word of Truth made them known, who or where is the man that durst in his heart have presumed to have thought it? (*Works*, 250)

Like Taylor, Bradstreet progresses through an ascending spiral of opposing roles for "Thou" and "I," which culminates in the marriage relation in its individual and collective forms. Both poets quote the same passage from Isaiah 54:5, in which the Old Testament prophet addresses a degenerate Israel and assures the people that "thy Maker is thy husband": Taylor's Meditation 1.23 uses this exact phrase (l. 24). The context of this biblical passage reiterates characteristics of redeemed subjectivity crucial to both Bradstreet and Taylor and emblematic of their different relations to the figure of the Holy Spouse. Isaiah follows up his oracular declaration by stating, "For the Lord hath called thee as a woman forsaken and grieved in spirit, and a wife of youth, when thou wast refused" (54:6). The prophet employs the figure of woman abandoned and rejected to describe the frame of mind most receptive to God's call and the position of the soul when it is most likely to heed that call—a forsaken woman presumably being more abject and receptive than a forsaken man. Bradstreet as woman and wife can hear herself interpellated directly in this image; her personal identification was no doubt intensified by the opening of chapter 54 of the book of Isaiah: "Sing, O barren, thou that didst not bear; break forth into singing, and cry aloud, thou that didst not travail with child: for more are the children of the desolate than the children of the married wife, saith the Lord." The great prophet reinforces Bradstreet's belief that affliction, and her particular affliction of childlessness, tempers the soul. Taylor, as man, Puritan, and husband, has to go through several metaphorical operations to hear himself called in this passage by God.

Bradstreet's dealings with her God are, as a result of her gender, very different from Taylor's lifelong intimacies. If anything, her relationship to God is less direct, and it illustrates the Puritan patriarchy's success in barring women from what a historian of the period calls "covenant activism"—what Anne Hutchinson boldly condemned as "works"— reserved for men (Barker-Benfield, 86). Bradstreet's God is paternal in the extreme, and she acts toward him, she tells her own children, "like an untoward child, that no longer than the rod has been on my back (or at least in sight) but I have been apt to forget Him and myself, too" (*Works*, 242). This fatherly God demonstrates his concern for her spiritual state by sending physical afflictions as "corrections," "to humble and try me and do me good" (241). The manuscript found after her death abounds with poems and meditations written in thanksgiving for both the suffering and the relief God sends to her body in order to amend her soul.

The most important and doctrinally orthodox mediation between Bradstreet's soul and God was her earthly husband, Simon. In her amatory verses, probably written in the late 1640s, she celebrates her marital union with the passionate language Taylor reserved for his paeans on his sacramental union with Christ: "If ever two were one, then surely we," she begins the poem "To My Dear and Loving Husband," referring to the human union that for a woman directly anticipates the spiritual union with Christ. The position of woman, constant in the human and spiritual marriage, highlights the fundamental ambivalence built into Puritan social and religious doctrine. On the one hand, all saints supposedly participated in the Reformation's "priesthood of all believers" and strove for an intimacy with God, the aptest metaphor for which was the earthly marriage of husband and wife. But within that temporal contract, wives were subject to husbands as all saints were subject to God. Women were supposed to defer to men in all things, and wives were supposed to look to husbands for the spiritual access vouchsafed to everyone in the Gospels. Milton expressed this hierarchy with his usual authoritative concision when he characterized the divinely ordained relationship between Adam and Eve: "He for God only, she for God in him" (*Paradise Lost*, 4.299). Readers have called Bradstreet's love poem un-Puritan because her earthly love takes precedence over her heavenly one. But the final couplet indicates that the couple's reward for such earthly love is heavenly love, and that their loving earthly lives may help gain them a blissful afterlife: "Then while we live, in love let's so persevere / That when we live no more, we may live ever" (ll. 12–13).

The lovers in this poem may be equal in affection, but they are not equal in position. Her love, though unquenchable, can be satisfied by his returning love; yet she cannot repay his love, which can only be matched in heaven. This reflects Bradstreet's understanding of the structural inferiority of woman's social and religious roles. Bradstreet expands the metaphor of her marital situation and explores it in a series of poetic "letters" written to her husband in his absence "upon public employment." In these poems she works up a complex series of linked analogies that express the natural, human, and spiritual justifications for her subordinate position, a subordination counteracted by the eloquence of her voice. In "A Letter to Her Husband," she rehearses a paradox that fascinated contemporary male poets of impeccable caliber: "If two be one, as surely thou and I, / How stayest thou there, whilst I at Ipswich lie?" she demands (ll. 3–4).[39] Exploring the paradox, she develops an extended

conceit in which she is the earth made wintry by the absence of her
husband, the sun; his masculine heat wards off frosts and produces "those
fruits," her children, who console her momentarily by reflecting back to
her their absent father's face. Bradstreet draws upon conventional Renaissance notions of sexual anatomy, which held the womb to be inactive,
providing the inert material that was activated by the male's vitalizing
sperm.

   But there is more at work here than just witty conceits. When, after her
husband's return, Bradstreet wishes that "my Sun may never set, but burn
/ Within the Cancer of my glowing breast" ("A Letter to Her Husband,"
ll. 20–21), she combines her erotic longings with an astrological knowledge of the heavens, and with her spiritual aspirations to have the "Son of
Righteousness," Christ, enshrined within her heart (the emblematic correlation of sun and Son is made explicit in her Meditation 71 [*Works*,
289]). In the final couplet she speaks the same phrase from Genesis that
Taylor used in "The Experience" to describe his marital union with God
through Christ: "Flesh of thy flesh, bone of thy bone, / I here, thou there,
yet both but one" (ll. 25–26). Adam's words accepting Eve as his flesh,
and as his wife who will signify flesh, intensify the emotional union between Bradstreet and her husband, which transcends their physical separation. In speaking these words to her husband she anticipates Milton's
Eve, who addresses her husband in similar terms: "O thou for whom /
And from whom I was formed flesh of they flesh, / And without whom
am to no end, my guide / And head!" (*Paradise Lost*, 4.440–43); both
wives declare their submission to their husbands. Bradstreet takes comfort in a union that operates over time and space and foreshadows the
eternal union she hopes to achieve with her heavenly husband, whom she
describes in a later poem as "a more beloved one / Whose comforts far
excel" even the comforts of her dear Simon ("In My Solitary Hours," ll.
17–18).

   With its complex resonances, Bradstreet's conceit links together the
three spheres of her existence, creating an "organic" and apparently
unassailable justification for woman's subordinate position. In the natural
realm, woman is like the earth lacking its own source of heat, which it
receives gratefully from the life-giving sun/man, the star around which
the earth revolves. In the human realm, woman is a wife, fixed in her place
at home. About this separation, Bradstreet laments that "worst of all, to

him can't steer my course, / I here, he there, alas, both kept by force" ("Another," ll. 23–24; p. 229)—the husband held in place by the force of public obligation, the wife by the sheer force of cultural prescription. Finally, in the spiritual realm, the Son is her spiritual husband and her only source of spiritual life and warmth. The three masculine figures center and stabilize the three interlocking levels of woman's world. As the sun is the center of her natural world, her husband is the center of her human world, and Christ is the center of her spiritual world. How Bradstreet feels about such fixed and constraining positions, these witty and polished poems do not say.

Later in life, however, Bradstreet did receive solace by meditating on Christ in his role as the Bridegroom, and on the personal eschatological assurances she derived from her hopes that she would be his Bride. But, unlike Taylor, Bradstreet takes on the role of Bride explicitly only at the very end of her writing career. Her self-representations, exemplified by her "letters" to her absent husband, imply her Spousehood indirectly through the poetic figures and scriptural paraphrases she employs. She does not glory in fulfilling the role of the Spouse set forth in Canticles, but presents it as the doctrinal and emotional conclusion of her lifelong struggle to accept the place that God has set her. Resignation to this place permeates her final compositions. As early as the mid-1650s, Bradstreet's meditations and poems begin to show the world-weariness of a much older person (she was then in her early forties). The short verses in hymn meter composed in this period become plaintive and simplistic; the meditations become increasingly doctrinal and sprinkled with scriptural paraphrases. As illustrated by her journal entry for 8 July 1656, sixteen years before her death, her repeated exclamation is "Come, Lord Jesus, come quickly" (*Works*, 251)—an allusion to the last chapter of Revelation, which is also the last chapter of the Bible, in which Jesus promises to "come quickly" to those who await him (22:7, 12, 20).

Only in Bradstreet's last poem, "As Weary Pilgrim," does she speak in the role of the Bride of Christ, and then only through a combination of intertextual allusions that resist an easy or complete identification with New England Puritanism's official gynetic figure, the Spouse of Canticles. "As Weary Pilgrim" is a valediction to the world, and especially to the frailty of the body—a condition with which Bradstreet, physically disabled in one way or another for most of her life, was painfully familiar.

The doctrine of the poem is conventional, casting human life as a trying pilgrimage through dangers and discomforts, and salvation as a longed-for release from strife and spiritual struggle. The conclusion, however, develops a muted erotic tone, as Bradstreet envisions her physical death and describes her decaying flesh as "the bed Christ did perfume" (l. 32) with his own supreme sacrifice. Spiritualizing the flesh so that it is worthy of union with bodiless soul, Christ is Bradstreet's spiritual guide and model, simultaneously her means of access and her goal. In the final image of the poem, the bed Christ provides, where the stench of rotting flesh is transformed into the fragrance of divine love, becomes the eternal bower of a heavenly consummation:

> Then soul and body shall unite
>   And of their Maker have the sight.
> Such lasting joys shall there behold
>   As ear ne'er heard nor tongue e'er told.
> Lord make me ready for that day,
>   Then come, dear Bridegroom, come away.
>   (ll. 39–44)

In the final prayer, the union of soul and body parallels the marriage of Christ, as the Bridegroom, and the pilgrim, Bradstreet, as the Bride; the woman saint remains, even in the final glory of salvation, the signifier of the body, a speaking subject only insofar as she acknowledges that she can only be thoroughly "made ready" by Christ's position as Bridegroom and his agency as Redeemer.

Bradstreet's calling as the Bride in the final line of the poem is dependent upon a readiness that is not yet fully ripened. Charles Hambrick-Stowe has an ingenious reading of this last line that confirms my sense of its resistance to the appropriating discourse of Canticles. He proposes that the line is a conflation of two distinct scriptural sources: the first half of the line echoes the midnight cry of an unidentified voice awakening the virgins with the news of the Christ's advent, "Behold, the bridegroom cometh; go ye out to meet him" (Matt. 25:6); the second half of the line echoes the Bridegroom's call to his beloved in Canticles 2:10: "Rise up, my love, my fair one, and come away." In the first phrase, Hambrick-Stowe argues, Bradstreet speaks longingly to her beloved Christ, and in the second phrase Christ responds with his urgent desire for her to leave this world and join him in eternity, a reading supported by Bradstreet's capitalization of the second "Come" in the manuscript version of this poem, as if to begin a new sentence (Hambrick-Stowe, 19). Thus, Bradstreet speaks the feminine saint's plea, "Come, dear Bridegroom," as well as the masculine deity's invitation, "Come away," combining them provocatively in the same line. The association of Matthew 25 with the espousals of the Song of Solomon may have been commonplace for the eschatologically minded Puritans, since Edward Taylor also associates them, and thus it may have been a conveniently oblique means for Bradstreet to represent herself as the Spouse.

It remains only to notice one last twist in the complex dance of echoing voices that is Bradstreet's farewell to earthly life and poetry. The Bride-groom's urgent invitation from Canticles 2:10 with which the poem con-cludes is indirect speech, part of the Spouse's passionate avowal to her beloved, from which Taylor takes the epigraph to his final Meditation spoken completely in the Spouse's voice: "I am sick of love" (Cant. 2:5). Bradstreet's speaking, like Taylor's, is a form of unspeaking—we would expect no less from a Puritan poet. Yet, within that speaking, if we listen carefully, we can attune ourselves to the subtle displacements that Bradstreet sets up in order to both be and not be the figure of Puritan gynesis.

FIVE

Roger Williams's *Key*:
A Gynesis of Race

Roger Williams is not known as a poet. He emerges from colonial history as the "Apostle of Soul Liberty,"[1] a champion of religious toleration, freedom of conscience, and the separation of church and state. Just as the theocracy of the Massachusetts Bay Colony was struggling into existence, Williams arrived and interrogated its ideology of redeemed subjectivity, challenging the right of the church to demand religious conformity and the right of the state to enforce it. For acting on his beliefs, he was exiled from the commonwealth for life. His major ideas are contained in a series of polemical tracts for which he is duly famous. However, his most acerbic critique and detailed representation of an alternative vision of subjectivity can be found in the short poems that conclude each chapter of his first published work, *A Key into the Language of America*.[2] Printed in London in 1643, this little-known and highly censored book embellishes an account of the language of the Narragansett Indians with observations on their culture and with poetic meditations, such as the following from chapter 18, "Of *the Sea*":

> *They see Gods wonders that are call'd*
> *Through dreadfull Seas to passe,*
> *In tearing winds and roaring seas,*
> *And calmes as smooth as glasse.*
>
> *I have in* Europes *ships, oft been*
> *In King of terrours hand;*
> *When all have cri'd,* Now, now we sinck,
> *Yet God brought safe to land.*
>
> *Alone 'mongst* Indians *in Canoes,*
> *Sometime o're-turn'd, I have been*

Halfe inch from death, in Ocean deepe,
Gods wonders I have seene.

(179)[3]

The poem develops a theme central in the *Key*, that of God's merciful interventions on a day-to-day basis in the life of the truly righteous—namely, Roger Williams. Suddenly, a sound Puritan lesson has a more political spin: why would the God of John Winthrop appear regularly to a person on whom the Massachusetts General Court never wanted its populace to lay eyes again? Read as an assertion of divine providence in two complementary examples of miraculous rescues at sea that are told from a first-person perspective, the poem makes the point that the same divine wonders appear to the receptive eye on a European-built ship full of pilgrims, or in an overturned canoe in the wilderness surrounded by natives. The provocative paralleling of these two circumstances discloses the speaker's attitude toward his company, and throws into sharp relief Williams's work of self-representation.

The short poem does not derive its effect from the customary "opening" of events to reveal the providential hand of God, which appears on cue and without much fanfare in the second stanza. Rather, the emphasis falls on the framing lines of the poem, a device unique in Williams's small poetic canon, where "I" and "they" are juxtaposed: both share an experience common to all Puritan emigrants to the New World—the ocean crossing—which came to represent in Puritan discourse the trial or test, not only of endurance, but of zeal in one's spiritual calling.[4] But the change in perspective from the first to the last lines stresses a vital difference between Williams's conception of his faith and his representation of the Europeans' faith: his is solitary, theirs is social. Furthermore, he implies that an inevitable concomitant of communal perception, of being part of a "they," is coercion and conformity.

The flat tone of voice that recounts the test of faith in stanza 2 detaches the teller from the incident and makes us wonder if the frightened passengers have "seen" anything at all. Huddled together on the deck of a ship, bewailing their imminent demise as the seas sweep over the rails, these figures lack any dignity. The anticlimactic conclusion of the incident, "*Yet God brought safe to land,*" makes their fear seem melodramatic. Their only utterance, "Now, now we sinck," bespeaks self-interest and weak faith. The third stanza evokes in a few deft strokes the narrator's parallel experience in the wilderness. Though "*'mongst* Indians," he is "*Alone*" confronting his God and his fate. The evidence of his faith comes in the understated fact that what his sea-borne brethren feared has indeed happened to him—he has been in an overturned canoe "*Halfe inch from death, in Ocean deepe.*" Yet, neither he nor his native companions cry out in fear. In both cases, in a group of civilized Christians or alone among the unconverted, the speaker singles himself out as the faithful one, the true perceiver of God's power and mercy.

Nevertheless, the second stanza remains ambiguous. The speaker places himself at the mercy of God in the first two lines, but it is unclear whether he is one of the "*all*" who cry out. Constraints of meter and the awkward, compressed diction of this form make nuances hard to determine and inhibit a wide range of tones. Williams, as I will explain shortly, has conscious and unconscious reasons to cultivate ambiguity and provide his audience with competing interpretations of his position in the *Key*. In this text, irony most often derives from a juxtaposition of perceptions, which may be the case here. For example, the arresting phrase "*Alone 'mongst* Indians" implies that the Native Americans do not constitute company for the speaker. He differentiates himself from them, seeming to lump them together as foils for his own individualized self-representation. By analogy, then, he also differentiates himself from his own kind in his ambiguous representation of his experience on the ship—a distinction that, for reasons of racial and cultural identity and common persecution, he might want to blur or disguise. At the end of the poem, however, the speaker's surprising rejection of identity with his fellow Christians is clinched by the final line's inverted repetition of the first line, where the *I*'s individual perception of God's wonders takes precedence over what *they* have seen.

When we consider this poem in the context of the chapter it concludes, the very meaning of the "wonders" perceived alters drastically. The following vocabulary and observation precede the poem:

Wauaúpunish.	*Hoyse up.*
Wuttáutnish.	*Pull to you.*
Nókanish.	*Take it downe.*
Pakétenish.	*Let goe* or *let flie.*

Nikkoshkowwaúmen.	*We shall be drown'd.*
Nquawupshâwmen.	*We overset.*
Wussaûme pechepaûsha.	*The Sea comes in too fast upon us.*
Maumaneeteántass.	*Be of good courage.*

Obs. It is wonderfull to see how they will venture in those Canoes, and how (being oft overset as I have my selfe been with them) they will swim a mile, yea two or more safe to Land: I having been necessitated to passe waters diverse times with them, it hath pleased God to make them many times the instruments of my preservation; and when sometimes in great danger I have questioned safety, they have said to me: Feare not, if we be overset I will carry you safe to Land. (177–78)

From the above observation, we learn that the "wonder" is not the mere fact of survival, but the courage of the narrator's Narragansett companions. Unlike the cowering, supposedly faithful, Europeans, they venture out to sea in flimsy canoes, swim to safety, and promise to rescue the fearful white man. This display of bravura might not impress most colonial Puritans, who regarded the native inhabitants of "their" land as savages. Unable to conceive of or tolerate the subjectivity of native peoples who were racially different, English colonists systematically destroyed the tribes, a genocide rationalized by Puritan ministers as "a sacred act of violence" (Kibbey, 102).[5] For Williams, however, the courage, competence, and consolation of the Narragansett are an important part of "*Gods wonders*," since God has made them "the instruments" of the narrator's providential preservation.

A reading of the self-representation in this poem becomes even more complex when we consider its allegorical significance, a level of meaning never far from Roger Williams's mind. Orthodox Puritans regarded their ocean crossing as typological—that is, as an event linking their personal and corporate spiritual venture to the Old and New Testaments. Typologically, the ocean crossing recapitulated baptism, on the personal level, and the crossing of the elect nation of Israel over the river Jordan out of bondage and into the freedom of the promised land, on the corporate or national level. Williams rejected the notions of national election and of New England as the antitype of Israel. His reading of Scripture revealed to him the timeless and allegorical nature of his own experiences. An astute reader of the New Testament would recognize in Williams's description of his sea voyage an identification first with Christ, who, traveling on a ship with his disciples, slept through a great tempest until they woke him, crying, "Lord, save us: we perish"; Christ rebuked them, saying, "Why are ye fearful, O ye of little faith?" (Matt. 8:25–26). This context provides the example of one passenger unconcerned with the sea's violence, and clears up the ambiguity of the speaker's role in the poem's second stanza. Such a reading, however, sets up a parallel between the author and Jesus that orthodox Puritans of the Massachusetts Bay might have found troubling.

Next, Williams's audience might notice echoes of the experiences of the apostle Paul, who also set out on evangelical voyages at the beginning of Christianity. The general observation that precedes this poem, an exclamation on "the depth of the Wisedome and Power of God" who created the seas, paraphrases Romans 11:33, the letter in which Paul declares his role as Apostle to the Gentiles. The implications of this allusion are startling, but not because of the identity it establishes between Paul and Williams through their missionizing work. In Paul's narrative of his shipwreck recounted in Acts 27:24, an "Angel of God" comes to him in a dream saying, "Fear not."[6] What force possessed Williams to put these words of divine consolation into the mouth of his Narragansett companion? Does it license the reader to draw certain conclusions about the role of Native Americans in Williams's critique of the Puritan conception of redeemed subjectivity? After all, Williams declares himself the apostle to the Native Americans, as Paul became the Apostle to the Gentiles, but in his world it is a Narragansett rather than an angel who consoles him and confirms his faith.

Read on multiple levels, the poem from chapter 18 that we have been discussing illustrates Williams's complex strategies of self-representation. The "I" of the poem is set up against a "they," European Christians with whom we—and they—would expect Williams to identify. We will see how he exploits that expectation all through the *Key*. This "they" is juxtaposed with another group, the Native Americans, with whom Williams resides, and whom he humanizes, through the representation of their language and culture; ennobles, and even divinizes, through allegorical association; and yet objectifies, as divine instruments. The parallel that Williams draws between these two groups, in contrast to himself, heightens the speaker's isolation and understated superiority. By the end of the poem, he is the one who truly sees wonders and who truly knows what those wonders are.

Williams's claim to see and know more accurately than either the English or the Native Americans derives its rhetorical force from a concept of difference that is distinctly Puritan, but that diverges in important ways from the concepts of difference we have already examined. In previous chapters, I demonstrated that John Fiske and Edward Taylor, representatives of mainstream Puritanism's public and private lyric strains, labor under the spiritual necessity of self-displacement. Both strive for the spiritual feminization required by their religious beliefs—Fiske as a passive, receptive object, Taylor as the Spouse of Christ; their poetry outlines the parameters of redeemed subjectivity, recording a discursive and psychological drama of their resistance, failure, and momentary success. By contrast, Anne Bradstreet can only manage, but cannot escape, her cultural, social, and religious figuration as "woman." Her displacement does not serve her own spiritual ends, but the political interests of her tribe. Though she is a family member of the powerful New England elite and thus an insider, her subject status, to anticipate Williams's colonialist discourse, is analogous to the subject status of the colonized; she is part of the dominant culture but is marginalized with respect to it—an outsider hedged in.

Roger Williams was himself a victim of the Puritan intolerance of difference, having been permanently ejected from the body politic. His role is the inverse of Bradstreet's position in Puritan culture; he is the insider cast out. As such, he was figured in official Puritan accounts in derogatory feminine terms, as an enthusiast, a hysteric, and a poisonous viper.[7] But whereas Bradstreet's critique of her culture was easily coopted and misread, Williams's critique is augmented by the force of self-critique. Well-versed in the conventional Puritan discourse, still commonplace in our time, in which difference, and therefore oppression, is gendered, Williams nevertheless avoids these figures through which his displacement was rendered. Instead, he uses the same discourse of racial categorization employed by the New England Puritans to subdue what they thought of as an uninhabited wilderness, but uses it subversively to mark the place of the literal outsider as a spiritually empowered position from which to speak.[8] I call this strategy a gynesis of race. The application of the term "gynesis" to Williams's displacements strains its meaning, yet I am trying to identify a rhetorical feature that persists in Puritan discourse and epistemology—a constitutive relation to difference and otherness, which is figured through various identifying categories, all subsumed under the metaphors of gender. As we will see in the following discussion, in both his poetry and the complicated structure in which he sets it, Williams maps difference onto the racially othered figure of the Native American, which he uses to mount a subtle and sustained critique of the Puritan ideology of redeemed subjectivity.

Significantly, the poetry in the *Key* has historically been its most expendable component. Judged apart from its original context, as is usually the case in modern anthologies of colonial literature, the poetry sounds facile and preachy, distinguished only by its arresting imagistic details and allegorical typology.[9] The Bay's more immediate posterity considered it so trivial—or, given the colony's refusal ever to lift its ban on Williams,[10] so threatening—that in the only eighteenth-century reprinting of extracts from the *Key*, in 1794 and 1798, the Massachusetts Historical Society omitted all the poems and also severely edited those observations that were critical of the Puritan settlers or openly admiring of the Native Americans. Only in 1827 was the text reprinted in its entirety, as the first volume of the *Collections* of the Rhode Island Historical Society. Thereafter, it was valued more as a source of anthropological information than as literature or polemic.

Our ability to read Williams's poetry depends, first, upon our understanding of the autobiographical context that motivated its composition and generates its strategic positioning of voice; and second, upon a careful analysis of the structure of the text and the positioning of poems within each chapter. Williams directed the *Key* expressly to those New England Puritans who had cast him out, yet with whom he felt racially aligned. Native culture is his subject matter, but ultimately he allegorizes and thus objectifies it. These contradictory impulses are clearly present in his actions. For example, he played a crucial role in the colonists' brutal extermination of the Pequots in 1636–37 (recorded in chapter 29 of the *Key*); and he facilitated, albeit unwillingly, the annihilation of the Narragansett, by urging them not to make alliances with other native tribes against the English in King Philip's War, 1675–76.[11] When asked by the Narragansett sachem why Philip and the settlers of Plymouth could not fight it out alone, he replied, in the voice of a loyal countryman and staunch imperialist, that it was "our duty and engagement, for one English man to stand to the death by each other, in all parts of the world" (Wroth, 28).[12] Ultimately, he could not betray his cultural allegiance to Europe; he was, as Lawrence Wroth sadly concludes, "unable to transcend the limitations of his race and creed" (29). Yet, the *Key* unerringly, perhaps unintentionally, demonstrates those racial and religious limitations in its blistering presentation of so-called civilized and Christian morality. Williams deftly exposes what Francis Jennings calls "the cant of conquest," the linguistic and discursive means by which imperialist domination operates, but he continually retreats from explicitly privileging the Native Americans or denouncing the actions of the settlers. These divided loyalties and qualified assertions account for the heterogeneous structure of the text and Williams's strategic handling of allegory, both of which reveal more about his opinions than he could consciously express to his audience, perhaps even to himself.

Williams's long and bitter attack upon the New England Way began almost as soon as he arrived in Boston in 1631. He was known to the founders of the colony from meetings held in England to discuss the prospects of emigration. Governor John Winthrop, a lifelong friend, described him on his arrival as "a godly minister" (*Winthrop's Journals*, 1:57), and the Boston Church invited him, only twenty-eight years old, to take over in John Wilson's absence. He shocked the community by refusing, and then, adding insult to injury, he told them that "he durst not officiate to an unseparated people" (Gura, 159). He went first to Plymouth, where he began his study of native language, and then to Salem, where he found a congregation more receptive to his separatist views. There, he ran afoul of the authorities for broadcasting his opinion that civil magistrates had no right to enforce religious doctrine and that the Bay's charter was invalid because the king had no right to grant possession of native lands. Williams was given several opportunities to "repent" and "reform" his positions, but never did, and in the winter of 1635 he fled to Plymouth only days before the order exiling him to England reached his home. Being informed by Governor Bradford that he was still within the jurisdiction of the Bay, Williams, with his small party of followers, pushed further east into Narragansett territory. There they were welcomed by the native inhabitants, and there Williams founded Providence Plantation, which became a haven for refugees fleeing the Bay's religious persecution.

Williams's version of this story forms an indelible background to the *Key*. I cite two important passages that are echoed throughout the text—the first from a letter written on 22 June 1670, and the second from a testimony given in 1682, the year before he died, "relative to his first coming into the Narragansett country":

> When I was unkindly and unchristianly, as I believe, driven from my house and land and wife and children, (in the midst of a New England winter, now about thirty-five years past,) at Salem, that ever honored Governor, Mr. Winthrop, privately wrote to me to steer my course to Narragansett Bay and Indians, for many high and heavenly and public ends, encouraging me, from the freeness of the place from any English claims or patents. I took his prudent motion as a hint and voice from God, and waving all other thoughts and motions, I steered my course from Salem (though in winter snow, which I feel yet) unto these parts, wherein I may say Peniel, that is, I have seen the face of God. (*CW*, 6:335)

> . . . I desire posterity to see the gracious hand of the Most High, (in whose hands are all hearts) that when the hearts of my countrymen and friends and brethren failed me, his infinite wisdom and merits stirred up the barbarous heart of Canonicus to love me as his son to his last gasp, by which means I had not only Miantonomo [his nephew and a great sachem] and all the lowest Sachems my friends, but Ousamaquin [a Wampanoag chief] also, who because of my great friendship with him at Plymouth, and the authority of Canonicus, consented freely, being also well gratified by me, to the Governor Winthrop and my enjoyment of Prudence [an island in Narragansett Bay], yea of Providence itself, and all the other lands I procured of Canonicus which were upon the point, and in effect whatsoever I desired of him; and I never denied him or Miantonomo whatever they desired of me as to goods or gifts or use of my boats or pinnace, and the travels of my own person, day and night, which, though men know not, nor care to know, yet the all-seeing Eye hath seen it, and his all-powerful hand hath helped me. (*CW*, 6:407–8)

In both of these accounts, written years after the events described, we find the allegorical features of displacement, suffering, and relocation typical of the conversion narrative with its requisite elements of forced exile, wandering in unchartered territory, and providential mercy. However, Williams invests his major players with the inverted values they will display in the *Key*. His Puritan brethren treat him "unchristianly," while Canonicus loves him like a son. He, in turn, shows tremendous respect for the old sachem and for his nephew, the powerful Miantonomo, later murdered by the "sanctified Commissioners" of the confederation of the United Colonies (P. Miller, *Roger Williams*, 51). The passages and poem from chapter 18 discussed above exploit a similar inversion: Europeans are apostate disciples, while the Narragansett are the angels of God. This technique—retaining the familiar story and its theological meaning, while shifting around the occupants of the various allegorical positions—is one key to Williams's *Key*.

Hounded out of England for his religious beliefs, Williams found no relief from persecution in the fledgling commonwealth. His enemies pursued him to the very margins of civilized territory and alternately harassed him—the formation of the United Colonies of New England precipitated his journey to England to seek a charter for Providence[13]—and required his apparently invaluable assistance in negotiating with the Native Americans during the various colonial wars. He shared with the New England ministers especially the privileges of calling, class, and education, but he rejected those privileges and fiercely denounced the softness, ambitions, and corruption of what he called in a vitriolic pamphlet "a hierling ministry." The wildness of the New World fertilized his millennial epistemology; he came to believe that the entire world was in a "wilderness" condition that called, not for the maintenance of the status quo, but for a ministry like Christ's, among the poor and unconverted.[14] More moderate New England leaders like Winthrop and Cotton took the reformation of the Church just so far, and then sought to consolidate and stabilize their delicately balanced theocracy; Williams, like Anne Hutchinson—another famous dissenter who was banished from Massachusetts for advocating a radical spiritual subjectivity and who took refuge in Providence—pushed the logic of Puritan doctrine to conclusions his brethren dared not entertain.[15] He found refuge with the native inhabitants whom his Christian brethren regarded typologically as devils and enemies of the Puritan errand. Williams was cast out, displaced, on the margins—literally, psychologically, and spiritually.

It is not surprising, then, that in the *Key*, which he composed during the summer of 1643 on a sea voyage to England, Williams locates himself neither in the Old World nor in the New. Rather, he strategically establishes what Edward Said calls a "flexible positional superiority"—a term Said uses to describe the placement of the narrative voice in Orientalist texts, "which puts the Westerner in a whole series of possible relationships with the Orient without ever losing him the relative upper hand" (*Orientalism*, 7).[16] Williams, as we might expect, adopts a flexible positional superiority with respect to the Narragansett on the grounds of his Christianity and their paganism. What is surprising is that he adopts a similar attitude with respect to members of his own culture by whom *he* has been forced into the position of "other"—an exile from the Bay, a "son" of Canonicus.

Strategic maneuverings for position appear in the explanatory letter that prefaces the *Key*, which opens: "I present you with a *Key*," a very unique key, Williams explains, because it "respects the *Native Language* of it, and happily may unlocke some *Rarities* concerning the *Natives* themselves, not yet discovered" (83). Playing upon his readers' curiosity and economic interests, he recommends "this *Key, pleasant* and *profitable* for *All*, but specially for my *friends* residing in those parts"—that is, New England. A key was a treatise purporting to unlock esoteric, obscure, or difficult subjects;[17] Williams plays upon the association of keys and hermeneutics when he intones cryptically: "A little *Key* may open a *Box*, where lies a *bunch* of *Keyes*." The expected treasure trove contains, ambiguously, only more keys. But, he assures his readers, "With this I have entred into the secrets of those *Countries*" for the purposes of trade and converse, "and by such converse it may please the *Father* of *Mercies* to spread *civilitie*, (and in his owne most holy season) *Christianitie*." The long paragraph ends with an allusion to Matthew 13:33, "and it may please *God* to blesse a *little Leaven* to season the *mightie Lump* of those *Peoples* and *Territories*" (83–84).

The text equivocates cleverly between literal and figurative meanings. Whether the "Rarities" and "secrets of those Countries" are literal wealth or spiritual riches, or both, remains unclear. Only in chapter 24 is commercialism displaced by a wholly spiritual notion of treasure: "The

Sonnes of men having lost their Maker, the true and onely Treasure, dig downe to the bowels of the earth for gold and silver; yea, to the botome of the Sea, for shells of fishes, to make up a Treasure, which can never truly inrich nor satisfie." The concluding poem for that chapter declares, *"nought's worth ought but Grace"* (214). This is how Williams attempts to attract and draw in an audience he intends shortly to accuse of moral decadence and religious impropriety. He acknowledges the Puritans' practical and commercial interests in the native tribes, yet he declares that the truly Christian mission is the spread of a civility that will allow for conversion. The unspoken question is whether civility is compatible with colonial commerce.

Williams assumes the authority to pose, even implicitly, such probing questions by exploiting the resonances of the word "key." According to the *OED*, "key" refers to its possessor's power of custody, control, admission, disclosure, or opportunity, and is often used as a symbol of office. In framing a "key" to something as important as "the language of America," Williams creates a powerful "unofficial" office for himself as its possessor. "Key" has an even more potent theological significance. The "power of the keys"—a phrase alluding to Matthew 16:19, in which Christ gives to Peter "the keys of the kingdom of heaven"—was understood by Protestants to refer to the spiritual power of priests as successors of the apostles. John Cotton, Williams's adversary in the bitter debate over freedom of conscience, used the same passage in Matthew as a proof-text for his defense of New England's ecclesiastical polity in a widely read tract entitled *The Keyes to the Kingdom of Heaven*, published in London in 1644. Cotton had been preaching on this topic for some time; it is more than likely that Williams would have been familiar with his argument, and with his use of parabolic rather than typological interpretation of Scripture, which, according to some scholars, was the bone of contention between Williams and Cotton in their subsequent debate.[18] My point is that the idea of "keys" as a symbol of divinely sanctioned power was part of the contemporary discourse that Williams could count on his audience to know. But while Cotton uses his key to unlock in Scripture a blueprint for clerical power bolstered by state enforcement, Williams has more subversive hermeneutic uses in mind. It is not difficult to imagine him punning on the line of thinking asserted in the title of Cotton's learned treatise: the bunch of keys of the kingdom of heaven is unlocked by the key to the language of America, which neither Cotton nor his fellow ministers possessed—without Roger Williams.

Arrogant as he was, Williams would never presume to possess such "keys," and it was precisely his overzealous millennialist principles that kept him from accomplishing the goal—the conversion of the Native Americans—that had brought the *Key* into being.[19] The key he does appropriate is Christ's power of parable. His reference to Matthew at the end of the long opening paragraph of his prefatory letter quoted above paraphrases the last in a series of Christ's parables describing the kingdom of heaven, the secrets of which he "opens" to his disciples. Williams's comparison of his *Key* to the "*little Leaven*" helping to raise "the *mightie Lump*" of the unconverted suggests that it will act like the parables to unlock or lock up spiritual secrets, an exercise of Christ's hermeneutic spiritual power.[20] To tell parables is to speak doubly, to tell one story while meaning another—to speak about oneself and one's experiences, only to take refuge in a larger, greater, impersonal meaning in which the concrete details of physical experience are infused with intense and paradigmatic spiritual significance. In taking on this ambiguous power as the possessor of the key to an indigenous, originary American language, Williams can speak of himself and yet lose himself in spiritual allegories: worldly and heavenly meanings exist simultaneously.

Retelling Christ's parables is also a way of controlling meaning and establishing the positional superiority that Williams seeks with respect to his Puritan audience. To reinforce this position scripturally, the *Key* takes up Christ's jeremiad on the function of parable. Christ explains to his disciples that he speaks to the people in parables to fulfill the prophecy of Isaiah that warns: "this people's heart has grown dull, and their ears are heavy of hearing, and their eyes they have closed, lest they should perceive with their eyes, and hear with their ears, and understand with their heart, and turn for me to heal them" (Matt. 13:15). From Williams's point of view, the likeliest object of this prophecy is the Narragansett, whom Williams believes are spiritually "lost." But his descriptions all through the *Key* belie this attitude with references to the natives' "*quicke* faculties" (113), "quick apprehensions" (130; see also 128, 149), and eagerness to hear the Gospel. In one long anecdote, Williams recounts a particular occasion on which he preached so fervently to a group of natives "that at parting many burst forth, *Oh when will you come againe, to bring us some more newes of this God?*" (108). The dullards are not his native companions, but his fellow Europeans, converted nationally and worshipping in unseparated churches "drawn after *Romes pattern*"; Williams judges them unsparingly, never questioning that they are anything but "unconverted and *unchristian Christians*, . . . not yet knowing what it is to come by true Regeneration within" (*Christenings*, in *CW*, 7:35).[21] Thus, in the process of allegorizing his own experiences in the *Key*, Williams transforms his marginality into the ultimate *imitatio Christi*.

The strategic positioning of the narrative voice in the *Key* is both complemented and challenged by its curious structure. The text contains thirty-two chapters, each describing an aspect of native life and culture, and each chapter is divided into three interrelated parts: vocabulary, observations, and a short poem. In the "Directions for the use of the Language," appended to his prefatory letter, Williams explains that he deliberately avoided structuring the *Key* as either a "Dictionary *or* Grammer" and took "*no small paines*" to frame "*every Chapter and the matter of it, as I may call it an Implicite Dialogue*" (90). This "implicit dialogue" emerges most clearly in the vocabulary sections but is not, I think, confined to them; in fact, it provides a powerful metaphor for the entire text as a dialogue between two cultures and two different cultural constructions of subjectivity. Thus, on one level, the text's structural procedure makes an extraordinary recommendation for colonial contact: that it proceed by, and achieve, intersubjectivity.[22]

In the first part, as Williams explains, "*The* English *for every* Indian *word or phrase stands in a straight line directly against the* Indian" (90), presenting, visually, a text of parallel columns with the Narragansett terms on the left and their English equivalents on the right. By italicizing the English words, Williams suggests that they constitute a response, so that read horizontally the vocabulary sections represent an interchange between Narragansett and English speakers. This impression of exchange is reinforced by the vertical columns of words. Sometimes these are lists of single words, or conventional phrases, such as the following exchange from the beginning of the first chapter:

Asco wequássin, Asco wequassunnúmmis.   *Good morrow.*
Askuttaaquompsìn?   *How doe you?*
Asnpaumpmaûntam.   *I am very well.*

Taubot paumpmaúntaman.	*I am glad you are well.*
Cowaúnckamish.	*My service to you.* (94)

Usually, and we can see this happening even in the above example, the columns can be read vertically as a series of questions and responses or as the skeleton narrative of moments of contact between Williams and the Narragansett told in both tongues at the same time, as in this example from later in the same chapter:

Cowâwtam tawhitche nippeeyaûmen?	*Doe you know why I come?*
Cowannántam?	*Have you forgotten?*
Awanagusàntowosh.	*Speake English.*
Eenàntowash.	*Speake Indian.*
Cutehanshishaùmo?	*How many were you in Company?*
Kúnnishishem?	*Are you alone?*
Nníshishem.	*I am alone.* (98)

Sometimes the juxtaposition of phrases is exploited to produce an arresting effect:

Cowàmmaunsh.	*I love you.*
Cowammaûnuck.	*He loves you.*
Cowámmaus.	*You are loving.*
Cowâutam?	*Understand you?*
Nowaûtam.	*I understand.* (98)

Here, a grammatical lesson on verb conjugation invites us to ponder the association of "understanding" another's language and "loving" in interracial relations.

The second part of each chapter consists of two kinds of "observations," both in the narrative voice, but serving different functions. The first kind precedes or follows the dialogues as explanatory or anecdotal comments, such as this observation from chapter 1: "They are exceedingly delighted with Salutations in their own Language" (93). Based upon Williams's experience and expertise, these observations spotlight the white narrator who speaks in a kind of stage whisper or aside to the implied audience of white readers.

The second kind of observation, called "generall," concludes the first two parts of the chapter by drawing out a moral or spiritual truth from the thematic presentation of native life, which is then read allegorically. An example, again from chapter 1, reads: "From these courteous *Salutations* Observe in generall: There is a savour of *civility* and *courtesie* even amongst these wild *Americans*, both amongst *themselves* and towards *strangers*" (99). The narrator addresses his audience with the imperative, "observe," almost as if he expects them to be surprised and unwilling to concede his point.[23] But this is a relatively benign comment. In Williams's own experiences with the "tame" Americans, as he calls the English settlers, he found them highly uncivil and extremely discourteous to the natives inhabiting the land they coveted, yet he does not disturb his readers' preconceptions. He only points to the "savour" of civilized virtues in those Americans who he somewhat cagily agrees are "wild." However, he is treading close to contradiction. If the natives behave in a civilized manner, can they rightly be called "wild"? Furthermore, their treatment of each other and of strangers stands in stark contrast to his brethren's "unchristian" treatment of him—an allusion to the autobiographical context of the *Key*, which always hovers just beneath the surface. In later chapters, the general observations open up the allegorical significance of many of the narrator's reflections, the largest group of which inevitably turns on a comparison and contrast of native and English. In these comments, the tempered voice of the veteran trader segues into the higher-toned pronouncements of the critic and witness and serves as a bridge to the third and final part of each chapter, the short, didactic poem.

All but five of the thirty-two poems consist of three stanzas of ballad measure—an alternating line of tetrameter and trimeter, rhyming *a b c b*. The anomalies occur in chapters 4, 7, 8, 30, and 32: the first two have two stanzas of ballad measure; the next is one six-line stanza of pentameter couplets; the next has three stanzas of iambic pentameter; and the last poem has four stanzas of ballad measure. The poems are always introduced with the heading "More particular," indicating that the poetic form particularizes the general sentiment of the final observation. Frequently, the poems restate in simple language and sharp images the spiritual truths of the general observations, as in this example from chapter 1:

> *The Courteous* Pagan *shall condemne*
> Uncourteous Englishmen,
> *Who live like Foxes, Beares and Wolves,*
> *Or Lyon in his Den.*

Let none sing blessings *to their soules,*
For that they Courteous are:
The wild Barbarians *with no more*
Then Nature, goe so farre:

If Natures Sons both wild *and* tame,
Humane and Courteous be:
How ill becomes it Sonnes of God
To want Humanity?

(99)

If we think of the chapter's tripartite structure in terms of conventional Puritan sermon form, then the poem constitutes the last part, or "application," of the scriptural textual explication. Its purpose, like the sermon's application, is to drive home with great force to each listener the charges of hypocrisy, arrogance, materialism, exploitation, moral turpitude, and spiritual deadness that Williams's "sermon" on the "text" of Narragansett culture levels at his fellow English. Here, the comparison between the "*Courteous* Pagan" and the "Uncourteous Englishmen," which is only implied in the general conclusion, condemns the latter, thus setting the satirical tone of the entire text. The poems, then, refocus the vocabulary lesson of each chapter by moving the reader's gaze from a fascination with an alien culture to the eternal verities affecting his own soul.

There are literary historical precedents for the structural elements in the *Key*, but their combination and interrelation defy generic classification.[24] For the combination of poetry and observation, Williams may have taken his cue from William Wood's *New England's Prospects* (1634), a promotional account of the natural advantages of New England; the second part of this work, a description of the native inhabitants, includes five short poems interspersed among the chapters, and a brief glossary of native words. Wood, however, treats the natives as comical exotics, and his tone is uniformly procolonialist. Williams might have found a scathingly anticolonialist tone in the work of another casualty of the Bay oligarchy, Thomas Morton. Arrested in 1630 for selling liquor and guns to the Native Americans and thus disrupting Plymouth's fur trade, Morton was immortalized by Nathaniel Hawthorne for the purportedly "licentious" activities that occurred at his plantation, known as Merrymount. After his release, he returned to England and published *New English Canaan; or, New Canaan . . .* (1632). An Anglican loyal to the church and crown, he tried to garner support for revoking the Bay's charter not only by bad-mouthing the nonconformist settlers of New England, but by accusing them of concealing the beauty and richness of the land. He returned there after Archbishop Laud's downfall and took brief refuge in Providence in 1643. An authentic critique of the duplicitous Puritan attitudes toward the Native Americans, religion, and trade emerges from his propaganda, and in passages like the following he seems to have anticipated some of the sentiments, and even some of the phraseology, of the *Key*: "And this as an article of the new creede of Canaan, would they have received of every new commer there to inhabit; that the Salvages are a dangerous people, subtill, secreat, and mischeivous [*sic*], and that it is dangerous to live separated, but rather together, and so be under their Lee, that none might trade for Beaver, but [at] their pleasure . . . but I have found the Massachussets [*sic*] Indian more full of humanity, then the Christians, and have had much better quarter with them" (quoted in Jennings, 37).[25]

These possible sources lack Williams's extensive linguistic focus, which ran counter to the current beliefs concerning native languages. Stephen Greenblatt argues that "powerful cultural presuppositions asserted themselves almost irresistibly" upon explorers recounting their experiences in America to confirm the generally held belief, despite evidence to the contrary, that native speech was close to gibberish (565). The need of Europeans to divest native populations of a fully significant language—and thus of a fully human reality, which might interfere with divinely sanctioned conquest—persisted, he contends, "at least into the seventeenth century" (564). Advertised explicitly as an aid to trade and travel—that is, economic conquest—the *Key* was a remarkably thorough and accurate inventory of the Narragansett tongue for its time. What is most remarkable about it, however, is its orientation. According to Gordon Brotherston, most contemporary dictionaries and grammars of New World languages were compiled with reference to European norms, and conversions, when they were attempted, generally employed the language of the colonizer and converter. By contrast, the *Key* acknowledges the richness and the poetry of Narragansett speech, often giving several native terms for one English word, or emphasizing and explaining the figurative nature of native words and phrases.[26] Believing that religious conversion and the repentance upon which it depended were largely discursive affairs conducted through language, and best pursued in the language of the unconverted, Williams was forced to grapple not just with native beliefs, but with all aspects of the culture.[27] Like Caliban, Shakespeare's native "other" inhabiting the "brave new world" of *The Tempest*, Williams's natives are presented as living in a world of inescapable "opacity"—Greenblatt's phrase for "the rich, irreducible concreteness" of Caliban's world as evoked in Shakespeare's verse; this opacity compels us to "acknowledge the independence and integrity of [his] construction of reality" (575), to regard the native not as the other/object, but as a subject different from ourselves.

We sense the presence of real people behind the unnamed voices in the *Key*'s dialogic vocabulary lessons, most of which sound like transcripts of actual conversations between Williams and his native hosts. Williams's canon indicates that, like Bradstreet, he was drawn to dialogue not just as a rhetorical strategy, but as a thematic principle. Most of his published works are explicitly framed as letters or responses. For example, he initiated the debate with John Cotton with a tract entitled *Mr. Cotton's Letter Examined and Answered*; his spiritual guide, *Experiments of Spirituall Life and Health*, was written to his wife; and his famous defense of liberty of conscience in the third part of *The Bloudy Tenent of Persecution* takes the form of a dramatic dialogue between Truth and Peace, the personifications most popular with the busy pamphleteers of his day (Chupack, 87). His last extensive work, *George Fox Digg'd Out of His Burrowes*, written at the end of his life, grew out of a grueling and sometimes comical four-day-long debate with three Quaker adversaries. Henry Chupack contends that it was Williams's emotional commitment to his idea of liberty of conscience that did not allow him to "think about its defense in the form of a logical treatise," and so he resorted to the "device of a dramatic colloquy" (87). What Williams was defending, however, was not a particular truth, but an individual's freedom to follow his or her own lights. It is more helpful to think of Williams's use of dialogue as characteristic of his notion of fallen epistemology: until further divine revelation, truth is merely provisional, in this world engaged in a continuous dialogue with peace. Thus, the principle of dialogue can be seen as a structural effect of Williams's belief in the freedom of conscience, a freedom he extended to his Narragansett hosts.

Most of the chapters launch immediately into an interracial exchange, thereby immersing the reader in a dialogue that is not simply between the red race and the white race, or between heathen and Christian, savage and civilized, enemy and friend, but between the Other and the Self, the whole, vast, unknown wilderness and all that is familiar, dear to the Puritan reader, and known. The centrality of dialogue to the *Key* is reinforced thematically by the very topic of the first chapter, "Of *Salutation*," which introduces various modes of greetings and address. As if setting the tone for interchange, the first vocabulary word is "Netompaûog/*Friends*" (93); the entire text, then, assumes that the encounter between unknowns will be friendly. The lesson teaches courteous ways of initiating contact and ends by indicating that the visit has been mutually enjoyable:

Kukkowêtous.	*I will lodge with you.*
Yò Cówish.	*Do, lodge here.*
Hawúnshech.	*Farewell.*
Chénock wonck cuppeeyeâumen?	*When will you be here againe?*
Nétop tattà.	*My friend I can not tell.* (99)

An interesting reversal takes place here. Williams opens chapter 1 with the following observation: "*What cheare* Nétop? *is the generall salutation of all English toward them* [the natives]," a greeting which, he says, "the English generally begin, out of desire to Civilize them" (93). But this desire to civilize and the implied courtesy of "*all*" English run counter to the conclusions drawn in the poem for this chapter, and to the historical facts. Williams won the charter for Providence Plantation despite the shrewd and fierce lobbying (which included the acquisition of a fraudulent Narragansett patent) of the Bay's agent, Thomas Weld. The parliamentary commissioners on colonial affairs who made the grant specifically commended Williams's "great industry and travail in his printed Indian labours" (Chupack, 70), putting the Bay to shame for its lackadaisical efforts. Williams may be representing at the outset how he would like his readers to act, or, better, how they would like to imagine themselves acting. But in Williams's experience, probably his most crucial—he would say providential—contact with the Native Americans was initiated by them. The story goes that in his search for a settlement outside the jurisdiction of the Bay where he could reside unmolested, he sailed down the Seekonk River in a canoe and was greeted from a rocky point, later named Slate Rock, by a band of Narragansett with the friendly salutation

"What cheer, Netop." The field beyond the rock Williams called What-cheer Field; he founded Providence Plantation at the site of a freshwater spring not far away (M. E. Hall, 55–57).

Even in chapters, such as this one, that open with an observation (chaps. 1, 9, 24, 27, 28, 30), the parallel columns of words and phrases are the most prominent visual element. They disrupt the unity of the narrator's voice, thus preventing the text from resting within the single perspective of the European scientific essay, or the mere travel report that enforces the dominant culture's unitary view. Another perspective is incorporated into the text, which provides a submerged narrative that is told through dialogue, gaps, and juxtapositions, and which reinforces the cultural, social, and theological reality implied by the lists of native words. The horizontal dialogue between speakers of different cultures, between difference itself, remains a constant feature of the text. The identity of the speakers in the vertical dialogues, however, is not always clear; this ambiguity, which Williams exploits, minimizes the importance of the individual speaker and maximizes the significance of interchange. One of the most startling effects of the "implicite dialogue" is the representational equality of the races and all the opposed elements they imply. Williams derives this basic assumption from the teaching of Jesus and buttresses it with Scripture, as in the theme of chapter 7 summarized in "The generall Observation from the parts of the bodie": "Nature knowes no difference between *Europe* and *Americans* in blood, birth, bodies, &c. God having of one blood made all mankind, *Acts* 17. [v. 26] and all by nature being children of wrath, *Ephes.* 2. [v. 3]" (133).[28] The first stanza of the poem that follows chastises fellow whites and warns that their attitudes are racist and have no place in soteriological concerns:

Boast not proud English, *of thy birth & blood,*
Thy brother Indian *is by birth as Good.*
Of one blood God made Him, and Thee & All,
As wise, as faire, as strong, as personall.

(133)

Williams's verse confirms that the English did indeed believe in and "boast" about their racial superiority. The phrase "*birth & blood*" rings with the kind of class snobbery and obsession with genealogy and blood

ties that is associated with the English system and is expressly con-
travened in Christ's teaching, though conveniently overlooked by many
orthodox Puritans.

The theoretical and structural equality between the races that is built
into the interracial dialogues does not go unchallenged; it is seriously
modified by the monologic observations and the allegorical tendencies of
the concluding poems. Whereas the modern editors of the *Key* sense no
conflict in the structure of the chapters, finding instead an "organicism"
that is peculiarly "American," I sense a pervasive, irreconcilable yet pro-
ductive tension—even, perhaps, a purposeful incongruence—among the
various parts of the text and the very different ways they implicate the
reader, the author/narrator, and the subject matter.[29]

Consider, for example, some possible effects of the observations. Although they provide necessary clarification and interesting anthropological and autobiographical commentary, they are, in their turn, a disruption
of the vocabulary sections. Always and unmistakably in the narrator's
voice, they interrupt the narrative and structurally reassert Williams's
positional superiority over his native hosts as well as his spiritual superiority over his Puritan readers. Spoken with an air of expertise, and commanding the very specific point of view of the (seemingly) dominant
culture, these brief prose passages rest upon the authority of Williams's
experience. He reassures his readers with the frequently repeated phrases
"I have seen" or "I have heard" or "I have known them [the natives]
to. . . ." Interposing his "I," a white gaze and voice and understanding,
almost literally between the dialogues, these passages also provide a running commentary in the knowledgeable voice of the narrator who serves as
guide to his white readers, appearing to anchor them in a similar positional superiority with respect to the Native Americans. In her cogent analysis
of the function of representation in pornography, Susanne Kappeler argues that the pornographer performs similar roles in the communicative
act and that these roles have been culturally and historically gendered: not
only does the pornographer objectify the woman/victim, thus reinforcing
his own status as agent and subject, but he communicates with a viewer or
reader whom he provides with a "locus of identification" that installs his
agency and subjectivity as well (52, 58).[30] Through Williams's structural
reassertions of his experience with and perceptions of the Narragansett,
his readers can temporarily forget the linguistic opacity—that is, the

subjectivity—of the natives, who become the voiceless objects of the narrator's quasi-scientific observations and, ultimately, the vehicles of his allegorical manipulations. Brotherston points out that the progression of chapter topics enacts a similar defamiliarization, the last twelve topics being "grammatically distinguished and disowned as Indian by the pronoun 'their' ('Of their nakednesse,' 'religion,' etc.)" (86).[31] Although much historically valuable information about Narragansett culture is imparted in these short prose observations, the emphasis falls upon the observer's acuity, the range of his exposure to native life and customs, and, most importantly, his *interpretation* of what is, essentially, a foreign culture. Dialogic intersubjectivity is at odds with the "I/eye" of European consciousness and Puritan patriarchy where subjectivity is achieved through dominance over an Other.

Yet, strange things happen to this dominant perspective when it is particularized in the poetry. Anthropological explanation gives way to humanist moralizing and finally to prophetic allegory—a perfectly acceptable progression for Puritan readers, who were accustomed to and had come to expect the "spiritualizing" of ordinary occurrences to reveal divine providence. The same readers were probably also accustomed to exhortations, sermonizing, even attacks from the pulpit and in pietistic handbooks on their spiritual hypocrisy, laxity, and sinfulness, although the really thunderous jeremiads would not begin for another twenty years or so. They did not, however, expect their righteousness to be assailed in a phrase book purporting to aid trade, travel, and converse with native inhabitants. Furthermore, Williams's moralizing has an uncomfortable edge to it. In chapter 1, for example, where the steady and recognizable voice of the white guide into unknown native territory sums up the theme by finding a surprising quality of "civilitie" and "courtesie" among the wild Americans, the poem goes on to compare the "*Courteous* Pagan," many testimonials to which have been given in the preceding dialogues and observations, with the "Uncourteous Englishmen," whose existence is a function of Williams's say-so. In the comparison the former "condemns" the latter, whose unconscionable "*want* [of] *Humanity*" calls their Christianity into question altogether. It is important to note that Williams's point here depends upon the earlier demonstration in the dialogues and the assertions in the observations of native courtesy and civility. It also depends upon the ironic reversal of the meaning of key

words. Although the paragons of courtesy are redundantly called "*wild*
Barbarians*" (l. 7), it is the "Uncourteous Englishmen, / *Who live like
Foxes, Beares and Wolves, / Or Lyon in his Den*" (ll. 2–4), who behave in the
predatory manner of the wild animals they take the natives to be. This is a
serious charge. The critique is indirect, however, for, ending on a rhetorical question, the poem asks the reader to draw his own conclusions.

In chapter 2, "Of *Eating* and *Entertainment*," dialogue and chatty asides
about Narragansett fare and hospitality give way in the general observation to more pointed language and an unsettling revelation: "It is a strange
truth, that a man shall generally finde more free entertainment and refreshing amongst these *Barbarians*, then amongst thousands that call
themselves *Christians*" (104). Such a conclusion does not call Williams's
allegiance completely into question, but it does make it difficult for the
English reader to identify comfortably with his voice or with the positions
it takes, because that means identifying against oneself. The climax of the
chapter comes in the poem, where the speaking subject and the position
denominated by the labels "English," or "European," or "civilized"—and
most significantly, "Christian"—completely diverge:

> *Course* bread *and* water's *most their fare,*
> *O* Englands *diet fine;*
> *Thy* cup *runs ore with plenteous store*
> *Of wholesome* beare *and* wine.
>
> *Sometimes* God *gives them* Fish *or* Flesh,
> *Yet they're* content *without;*
> *And what comes in, they* part *to* friends
> *And* strangers *round about.*
>
> *Gods* providence *is rich to his,*
> *Let none* distrustfull *be;*
> *In* wildernesse, *in great* distresse,
> *These* Ravens *have fed me.*
>
> (104–5)

We expect the comparison in the first two stanzas, but the personal testimony in the last stanza is an unexpected twist; from it, the condemnation
emerges indirectly, strengthened by its resonant personal allegorical dimension.

The final "me" of the poem is a composite of earlier voices in the chapter's dialogues, which hint of near starvation, as in this series:

Assámme.	*Give me to eate.*
Ncàttup.	*I am hungrie.*
Wúnna ncáttup.	*I am very hungry.*
Nippaskanaûntum.	*I am almost starved.* (101)

—and of the voice of the observer, who says in the last observation: "many a time, and at all times of the night (as I have fallen in travell upon their houses) when nothing hath been ready, have themselves and their wives, risen to prepare me some refreshing" (104). But neither of these instances captures the density of the final poetic line. Calling the natives "ravens" suggests dark, wild, scavenger birds that feed on flesh—"ravenous," as the English settlers imagined them, for white blood. Here, as in all of Williams's allegorical readings of experience, the Narragansett become the instruments of God's providence. The biblical allusion is to 1 Kings 17:1–6, in which God is preparing the prophet Elijah to face the evil king Ahab and orders him to retire to a brook where he is fed meat and bread by ravens; later on in the story the prophets of Israel, hidden from Ahab in caves, are fed bread and water, the standard native fare (18:4). Williams reads his own miraculous preservation by the Narragansett as divine intervention and as a providential sign confirming his prophetic role as witness, like Elijah, to a degenerate Israel.

This poem, like all of Williams's poems, turns upon the doubly faceted meaning of key words. Take, for instance, the word "rich," whose connotations we have already begun to explore. The material richness and abundance of English fare is a gift from God, which the English abuse by not appreciating or sharing it. The well-fed Christian who thinks his good fortune signifies favor in God's eyes mistakes means for ends. Williams, a victim of English inhospitality, has been truly thrown upon God's mercy. Ironically, he finds more generosity among the supposed savages, who are depicted as completely dependent upon God for all their provisions, yet who share gladly the little they have with friends as well as strangers. They, not the so-called saints, are models of Christian generosity, and the little they offer makes the speaker "rich" spiritually. This reversal is reiterated by the miracle of being saved by birds that normally attack and eat flesh. In fact, their very offer, which revives and sustains the speaker, is part of the scriptural experience that confirms his redeemed identity. The lesson is as much what Williams learned by his experiences—faith means total trust in God's plan—as what he wants to show the English by comparing their decadence to native asceticism: just as God provides materially for the natives and the wild birds, so he will provide spiritually for "his," the persecuted and truly righteous. The internal rhyme in line 11, "*In* wildernesse, *in great* distresse," heightens the implication developed throughout the *Key* of a moral and spiritual as well as a physical wilderness.[32] Though not coterminous, the two realms overlap: when sheer survival is at issue, giving and getting nourishment are crucial; when the context is a biblical experience, the same gestures take on a sacramental quality.

Starting with chapter 2, the poems explicitly target for criticism not just "Englishmen" but, more specifically, "Christians"—a focus that in later poems is sharpened to "*Gods Saints*" (241), and "*Gods children, and / Members of Christ to be*" (239). Nor are the attacks as subtle or indirect. For example, in chapter 22, in a discussion of tribal justice, Williams observes:

> I could never discerne that excesse of scandalous sins amongst them, which *Europe* aboundeth with. Drunkennesse and gluttony, generally they know not what sinnes they be; and although they have not so much to restraine them (both in respect of knowledge of God and Lawes of men) as the *English* have, yet a man shall never heare of such crimes amongst them of robberies, murthers, adulteries, &c. as amongst the *English*: I conceive that the glorious Sunne of so much truth as shines in *England*, hardens our *English* hearts; for what the Sunne softeneth not, it hardens. (203)

The "glorious Sunne of so much truth" is, of course, Christ the son of God, and hearts hardened against grace are a pietistic commonplace; but the action of softening by exposure to the sun refers to the native method of tanning hides, which Williams observed in his sojourns with the Narragansett. The harshness of this attack is, perhaps, mitigated by his use of the pronoun "our," by which he includes himself, at least rhetorically, as one of the jaded English. Williams includes himself in references to the English in several other places in the text, but they are all moments of denunciation and, like his allegorical applications, leave the European reader no comfortable point of identity. In the above example, for instance, the reader has several options: to identify with the persecuted prophet, which is also to identify with Williams, and thus radically misread the poem; to accept the implication of the Native Americans as instruments of God, a meaning that the Puritans' treatment of them contradicts; or to identify with the materialistic hypocrite/persecuting tyrant of Israel—the position that Williams clearly means, yet one containing a self-accusation hard to acknowledge.[33] Other options are to refuse all identifications and ignore the poem's allegorical dimensions, or, as the Massachusetts Historical Society did, to simply ignore the poem.

In the ensemble of each chapter the poem is the site of the most disturbance and the most revelation, the place where the narrative comes to terms with its two "Others"—its Puritan persecutors, and its native instruments. We need to investigate the effects of the poems before we can evaluate the ironic reversals that Williams orchestrates in the *Key* in his attempts to discern and reinforce his own redeemed identity.

Although sites of disturbance, the poems return the European reader to a familiar, particularly English, even Protestant rhythm—the common or ballad measure. This was the form in which the committee of Puritan divines cast their overly scrupulous translation of the Psalms for the ever-popular *Bay Psalm Book*, first published in 1640. No English reader, and certainly no New Englander, would have been unfamiliar with the form. Barbara Lewalski makes a well-researched case for the influence of biblical Psalms on Protestant lyric poetry; it is a tempting thread to follow. But the polemic and allegorical tenor of these lyrics tugs in another direction. They do not explore the intense personal psychological interiority of the English lyrics, or the meditative introspection of the New England tradition. Williams's allegorical sense is antihistorical and Bunyanesque; it is not about *applying* typology to experience, but about recognizing that one's experience *is* biblical. The "I" of the poems reads the experiences of the twice-persecuted separatist and wily veteran trader in the service of spiritual truths, wrapping up each chapter's topic with a characteristically Puritan literary form that balances and competes with the alternating rhythm of the dialogues, the exoticism of the Narragansett tongue, and the prose observations. Because the poems' allegories "open" up events, images, and sentiments expressed earlier in the chapters, we are encouraged to read the chapters backwards—not, as John Teunissen and Evelyn Hinz suggest, as a progression from the empirical and specific to the general moral to the poetic explication, but in the light of the revelation of the spiritual dimension that exists in all human encounters and endeavors.[34]

Historically, the ballad measure has been the art form of the common people, a communal form that acts as the repository of folk wisdom and history. Ballads often use this form, as do nursery rhymes and children's songs. Williams's poems fit squarely into this didactic mode, which also hints at the measure's political possibilities. For example, medieval English ballads have been read in terms of the social relations of feudalism, idealizing the bond between the different classes while simultaneously presenting the point of view of the peasantry (Easthope, 83). The ballad measure and other popular forms, such as fourteeners and poulter's measure, were consciously taken up by the strong biblical poetry movement that gained momentum during the reign of Edward VI. In what John N. King terms "a major shift in mimetic theory," these fiercely Protestant poets rejected the courtly forms of the sonnet and *ottava rima* and embraced the native, populist forms as fit vehicles for their biblical subjects (16, 210).

A cogent example of popular literary forms in the service of radical sectarian politics in the seventeenth century is the case of Anna Trapnel. On 7 January 1654, while accompanying Vavasor Powell, an ardent and outspoken Fifth Monarchist preacher, to his examination for sedition by the Council of State sitting at Whitehall, Trapnel fell into a trance that lasted for twelve days. Removed to a bed in the Ordinary in Whitehall, and visited by several notables who brought her to the attention of the public and of Oliver Cromwell himself, she uttered a continuous series of visions and revelations of the imminence of the heavenly kingdom, interlaced with fervent and politically astute denunciations of the materialism and corruption of Cromwell and his army, the churches, the ministry, and the universities. All of "those blessed songs," as she styled them (*Cry of a Stone*, 16), that were transcribed and preserved, are in common measure. They reflect the diction and imagery of the Psalms and Revelation, and their meter, like Williams's, echoes contemporary hymnody, but they have become the vehicle of a divinely inspired jeremiad against a theocratic state that has fallen short of its revolutionary promise. Williams was in London in 1654 and would at the very least have heard of Trapnel's notorious performance.[35]

Williams also adroitly exploits the theological associations of the form. The composers of the *Bay Psalm Book* chose this meter so that their translations of David's Psalms would fit the familiar hymn melodies and thus be easily sung as a part of the worship service. But like the verse of Emily Dickinson, another New Englander of heretical disposition, Williams's poems are not explicitly celebrations of faith or private *cries du coeur*. Dickinson rejected the content of Puritanism but retained its characteristic form, transforming the hymn's usual expressions of faith into ironic, intensely compressed parables of the self's Christic suffering and desolation. From her Puritan forebears she inherited the habit of reading her own life in terms of biblical topoi, calling herself the "Empress of Calvary" (no. 1072), claiming her confirmation "by the Right of the White Election" (no. 528), and occasionally wearing her "Thorns" (no. 1737). She also shared Williams's metaphor of the soul's trial and temptation in the moral—for her, existential—wilderness (see no. 458, "Like Eyes That Looked on Wastes"). Her use of the hymn form— familiar, humble, constraining, at times childlike—was also an ironic comment on the subject matter and style to which respectable lady-poets in the mid-nineteenth century were confined. Like Anna Trapnel, she found an effective though costly way around these proscriptions. Dickinson spoke profoundly about doubt, using the forms of faith.[36] Williams's ironic use of the form celebrates a faith that strengthened him to witness against the faithlessness of his own brethren and to acknowledge the exemplary "natural" virtue of those they regarded as heathen.

Though the comforting rhythm of the hymn at the conclusion of each chapter in the *Key* brings the readers back to a familiar structure for the expression of faith and fellowship (hymns are usually sung in groups), the content reprimands rather than includes them. What was familiar now seems strange. The overall effect of the chapters, taken structurally, is to pry apart the shifting positions of speaker and reader until they are completely severed and inverted. The once-dislocated exile who acts as narrator and guide finds a permanent and unassailable location as a witness and Christic parabolist of his own culture's hypocrisy. His readers, formerly "worthy" gentlemen who passed judgment on their "unworthy country-man," suffer the fate predicted by Jesus in his Sermon on the Mount, which Williams alludes to in the first chapter of the *Key*: "For with the judgment you pronounce you will be judged, and the measure you give will be the measure you get" (Matt. 7:2).[37] The effect of the text, then, is not to confirm or solace its readers with a comfortable, stable, and superior point of view with which to identify, but to discomfit and dislocate them—a prelude to repentance, which, as Williams repeats over and over in the *Key*, is requisite for true conversion. The poems offer the reader reorienting perspectives—alternative models of redeemed subjectivity—but an orthodox "visible saint" would find the points of identity they supply disconcerting, to say the least.

Structurally, the poems employ a dialectical system rather than the one-on-one interchange of the dialogues. Because the few one- and two-stanza poems occur early in the text, it seems plausible to conclude that Williams considered doing more variations, but fell back upon the three-stanza form as that most fitted to his didactic purposes. The dialectic depends upon the rhetorical equation of a "natural" morality with the "*wild* Barbarians" who do not know the Gospel, and a cultural immorality with the civilized English who pervert it. Both positions are finally contrasted to the spiritual standard set up by Scripture and modeled by Christ for the "Sonnes of God" or the truly converted, the place of redeemed subjectivity that Williams redefines, and which he seeks to occupy. The thematic contrast between the "*Courteous* Pagan" and the "Uncourteous Englishmen," to use the example from chapter 1 cited earlier, is then allegorized as the difference between "*Natures Sons both wild* [the natives] *and* tame [the English]" and the "*Sonnes of God* [the elect]."

The association of Native Americans with "nature" and "natural virtue" is troubling for the postmodern reader because it smacks of reductive essentialism. By employing such an association Williams appears to fall into self-contradiction, because he clearly grants the Narragansett an efficient and complex culture, aspects of which greatly influence his ideas on communalism, land use rather than ownership, and religious toleration. Looking more closely at the opposition of "natural" and "civilized" (not properly "cultural"), as Williams saw these terms, reveals that the opposition is misleading. He makes it clear in the poem from chapter 1 that he regards both the natives and the English as "*Natures Sons*" with respect to grace. Being in a natural condition is the antithesis of being in a spiritual state of grace. At issue is precisely the difference between the fallen self and the regenerate self. The Narragansett may be "wild" and

the English "tame," but neither race, nor nationality, nor cultural achievement, nor material riches is a guarantee of true Christianity. As Williams
says in the poem concluding chapter 5, "*The* Pagans *wild*" prove themselves superior to the civilized man in terms of "*Natures distinctions*, and
Natures affections." The person who lacks "*Naturall* affections . . . *is sure /
Far from* Christianity"—but, the punning on the word "nature" continues,

> *Best nature's vaine, he's blest that's made*
> *A new and rich partaker*
> *Of divine Nature of his God,*
> *And blest eternall* Maker.

(116)

Even the "best nature" of the noblest natural man is "vaine" in spiritual
terms. To be the redeemed subject, according to Williams's perfectly
Christian view, is to be "made" a "*partaker / Of divine Nature*," to have
one's fallen self made over, made "*new*" and "*rich*" by participating in
God's nature through the gift of grace. The "*Best nature*" is neither English nor Indian, is not human at all, but is "*divine Nature.*"

Yet the "wildness" of the Native Americans and their environs has
rhetorical advantages, associating them with the prelapsarian Garden of
Eden and its unfallen inhabitants. Williams makes this connection explicit
in his model bilingual catechism in chapter 21, "*Of Religion, the soule, &c.*"
It is the closest we come to seeing Williams's missionizing in action. In his
version of the story of Genesis, which he tailored specifically to the
Narragansetts' particular "Estate," he refers four times to the creation of
"Adam" from "red Earth" (196), drawing on the etymological origins of
the name "Adam" to suggest the Adamic nature of the "red" man. In so
doing he also hints at his theory of the direct descent of the Native
Americans from the Hebrews of biblical times, which he explained in his
introductory letter (85–86; and see 42–43). Their inherent nobility, physical grace, and natural sense of morality make them superior to civilized
men, and Williams confesses, "I must acknowledge I have received in my
converse with them many Confirmations of those two great points, *Heb.*
11.6. *viz*: 1. That God is. 2. That hee is a rewarder of all them that
diligently seek him" (189). These two points are, according to Paul, the
foundations of faith. And though Williams finds "A strong Conviction
naturall" in their souls (191)—that is, everything one would need in order

to come to a very radical conclusion about the Native Americans—he cannot draw the conclusion obvious from his own observations, insisting instead that their natural faith in no way mitigates "their lost *wandring Conditions*" (87) spiritually. Still, he uses the example of the "heathen" natives to whip civilized believers and, echoing Paul's words to the Ephesians, warns the English that they are no better off spiritually than their "*brother* Indian": "*By nature wrath's his portion, thine no more / Till Grace his soule and thine in Christ restore*" (133).

In *Christenings make Not Christians* Williams states definitively his opinion on the spiritual status of the Native Americans: "If we respect their sins, they are far short of *European* sinners: They neither abuse such corporall mercies for they have them not; nor sin they against the Gospell light, (which shines not amongst them) as the men of *Europe* do: And yet if they were greater sinners then they are, or greater sinners then the *Europeans*, they are not the further from the great *Ocean* of mercy in that respect" (*CW*, 7:35). This assertion of the potential spiritual equality of natives with Europeans is fairly daring for the time, but more shocking is the question left suggestively open: Are they closer? And if they are closer, can they possibly offer hints toward the reformation of redeemed subjectivity?

Through the use of puns and emblems, the manipulation of positions in allegories, and especially through ironic reversals, Williams directs our attention, inviting us to answer that question with the view of Native Americans that his text presents, but that he always shrinks from endorsing. Directed seeing in the form of observations is a principal structural element of each chapter, and several poems clustered around the chapters on the Narragansetts' natural environment develop the motif of sight. As Williams compares seeing naturally with seeing spiritually, he puns on two pervasive pairs of homonyms—eye/I, and sun/son—thus commenting on the larger comparison of nature with spirit, and of the natural with the redeemed self. This cluster begins with chapter 9, "Of *the time of the Day.*" Having no "*artificiall helps*" such as clocks or watches, the Native Americans "overprize" the sun by making it into a God; "*We,*" on the other hand, having the benefit of mechanical aids, "*unthankfully despise*" God's creatures. Williams addresses the question of which attitude is worse by implying in the final stanza that the Native Americans err only in having the metaphor backwards: "God *is a* Sunne," but neither natives nor English *"see"* the spiritual "Light" of this metaphor (143). The comments in chapter 10, "Of *the season of the Yeere*," draw the conclusion that is implicit in the previous chapter. Williams asserts that the heavenly bodies and the seasons "doe preach a *God* to all the sonnes of men, that they which know no letters, doe yet read an *eternall Power* and *God-head* in these" (145–46), and then he asks in the accompanying poem:

> *If so, what doome is theirs that see,*
> *Not onely* Natures *light;*
> *But* Sun *of* Righteousnesse, *yet chose*
> *To live in darkest* Night?
>
> (146)

In chapter 13, "Of *the Weather*," Williams bluntly states that God's judgment "will fall most justly upon those *Natives*, and all men who are wise in Naturall things, but willingly blind in spirituall" (158). The emphasis here falls upon "willingly," for to know the Gospel and ignore it, one must exercise free will and is, thus, liable for the choice. The highly charged regenerated vision that Williams identifies as spiritual sight is, as the poem beginning *"They see Gods wonders that are call'd"* (179) makes clear, a function of one's spiritual vocation, being "called" or tested by God in difficult and extreme conditions. Earlier in the *Key*, Williams glosses a description of *"God's call,"* which will set both English and native *"to worke for God"* (129), with a reference to Matthew 20:7, the parable of the householder hiring laborers. Its moral is "the first shall be last and the last first" (Matt. 19:30)—the spiritual principle of irony that inverts worldly hierarchies.

Williams makes extensive use of this principle to invert roles and thus subvert Puritan readers' expectations and assumptions about their superiority. Ironic inversions occur throughout the *Key*, but are nowhere more striking or pervasive than in chapter 11, "Of *Travell*." The theme of travel resonates richly for Puritans, who spiritualized the pilgrimage tradition they inherited from medieval Christianity. "For the first generation of New England Puritans," Charles Hambrick-Stowe writes, "actual travel, and especially the ocean passage, provided a context for understanding spiritual progress" (71). As in Williams's unorthodox allegorical representation of the ocean passage discussed earlier, chapter 11 also calls into question the exclusively Puritan identity of the pilgrims and the nature of their progress. The topic of travel is included in the cluster of chapters on the natural environment because, as Williams comments, "[the Narragansett] are so exquisitely skilled in all the body and bowels of the Countrey (by reason of their huntings.)" This intimacy with the landscape serves the white trader well; he affirms, "I have often been guided twentie, thirtie, sometimes fortie miles through the woods, a streight course, out of any path" (149). Skillful pathfinding notwithstanding, Williams uses imagery associated with travel in a wilderness—"lost," "wandering"—to describe the soul's spiritual condition.

Chapter 11 begins:

Máyi.	*A way.*
Mayúo?	*Is there a way?*
Mat mayanúnno.	*There is no way.*
Peemáyagat.	*A little way.*
Mishimmáyagat.	*A great path.*
Machípscat.	*A stone path.*

Obs. It is admirable to see, what paths their naked hardned feet have made in the wildernesse in most stony and rockie places.

Nnatotemúckaun.	*I will aske the way.*
Kunnatótemous.	*I will inquire of you.*
Kunnatotemì?	*Doe you aske me?*
Tou nishin méyi?	*Where lies the way?*
Kokotemíinnea méyi.	*Shew me the way.*
Yo áinshick méyi.	*There the way lies.*
Kukkakótemous.	*I will shew you.*
Yo cummittamáyon.	*There is the way you must goe.*
Yo chippachâusin.	*There the way divides.*
Maúchatea.	*A guide.*
Máuchase.	*Be my guide.* (147)

The observation following the final request explains, "it is a mercy, that for a hire a man shall never want guides" to navigate him through the vast wilderness.

These exchanges seem perfectly straightforward in the context of the *Key* as an aid to trade and travel in the New World. However, we do not need a familiarity with Bunyan's classic Puritan allegory, *Pilgrim's Progress,* to read these dialogues allegorically. Williams himself suggests as much in the following exchange from his native catechism in chapter 21, where he even takes his cue from a principle of Narragansett speech patterns:

Tasuóg Maníttowock?	*How many Gods bee there?*
Maunaúog Mishaúnawock.	*Many, great many.*
Nétop machàge.	*Friend, not so.*
Paúsuck naúnt manìt.	*There is onely one God.*
Cuppíssittone.	*You are mistaken.*
Cowauwaúnemun.	*You are out of the way.*

A phrase which much pleaseth them, being proper for their wandring in the woods, and similitudes greatly please them. (195)

The "pleasing" nature of this comment becomes ironic when we realize that it is the Narragansett response to Williams's assertion of monotheism. In their minds, he is mistaken, or "out of the way"—when, of course, he expects his Christian reader to perceive how far the natives are "out of the way" spiritually. The metaphorical origin of the phrase harks back to Williams's depiction of the Native Americans' frequent "wandering in the woods." This image implies an aimlessness that native hunting expeditions, mobility, and seasonal removal to different locations never had, in reality. The image of "wandering," however, is a charged figure, because it associates the natives with the Jews and their forty years of wandering in the wilderness, and thus it becomes Williams's metaphor for their spiritual condition: "I believe they are *lost*" (emphasis his), he tells his readers, "and yet hope (in the Lords holy season) some of the wildest of them shall be found to share in the blood of the Son of God" (87). He later sums up his account of their religious practices with the general observation, "The wandring Generations of *Adams* lost posteritie, having lost the true and living God their Maker, have created out of the nothing of their owne inventions many false and fained Gods and Creators" (200). Here the natives are doubly lost: first, because their descent from Adam has been obscured, and second, because they have forgotten the one true God. By contrast, but using the same metaphor, Williams specifies his understanding of "Gods way [as] first to turne a soule from it's Idolls, both of heart, worship, and conversation, before it is capable of worship, to the true and living God, according to I *Thes.* 1. 9." (199).

Thus, when Williams begins chapter 11 with "Máyi / *A way*" (147) it is difficult not to read both literally and allegorically. However, one of the many ironies in this chapter is that here the English ask the natives for guidance in finding the "way." Furthermore, because the speakers in the vertical dialogue are sometimes unclear from the context, it is possible, indeed the text invites us, to read both the white and the red men as lost and in need of guides. If we assume that the white man asks the first question, "*Is there a way?*" then the chapter demonstrates his dependence upon the "exquisite skill" of the Native American to guide him through a wilderness that is moral as well as physical. Williams reinforces this reading with the observation, "I have heard of many *English* lost, and have oft been lost my selfe, and my selfe and others have often been found, and succoured by the *Indians*" (148). The autobiographical allusions are extremely prominent in this passage, which resembles Williams's comments on sea voyages in chapter 18, but it is also possible to read the passage as an indictment of the spiritual degeneration of the English professors of Christianity, a predominant theme of previous chapters. Williams even captures the English arrogance (for which he explicitly admonishes them in two other poems[38]) in the interchange that directly follows the above observation: "Pitchcowáwwon. / *You will lose your way.* / Meshnowáwwon. / *I lost my way*" (148).

The chapter continues with many interesting details concerning the pace of travel, traveling by horseback, dangerous circumstances in which women and children take refuge in thick woods and swamps,[39] and the Narragansetts' joy in meeting other travelers and stopping to converse; but it climaxes in the following exchanges and observation:

Mesh Kunnockqus kauatímmin?	*Did you meet? &c.*
Yò Kuttauntapímmin.	*Let us rest here.*
Kussackquêtuck.	*Let us sit downe.*
Yo appíttuck.	*Let us sit here.*
Nissówanis, Nissowànishkaûmen.	*I am weary.*
Nickqússaqus.	*I am lame.*
Ntouagonnausinnúmmin.	*We are distrest undone*, or *in misery.*

Obs. They use this word properly in wandring toward Winter night, in which case I have been many a night with them, and many times also alone, yet alwayes mercifully preserved.

Teâno wonck nippéeam.	*I will be here by and by againe.*
Mat Kunníckansh.	*I will not leave you.*
Aquie Kunnickatshash.	*Doe not leave me.*
Tawhítch nickatshiêan?	*Why doe you forsake me?*
Wuttánho.	*A staffe.*
Yò íish Wuttánho.	*Use this staffe.* (151)

The joyful meeting during travel turns quickly into an admission, first, of weariness, then of lameness, and then of great misery. Williams's translation of the key word "Ntouagonnausinnúmmin" as *"We are distrest"* recalls his earlier identification with Elijah, *"in* wildernesse, *in great* distresse," fed by the ravens/natives. Specifying the season of winter dramatizes the privation and hardships of native life while also evoking Williams's description of his own flight from Salem, quoted earlier in full: "When I was unkindly and unchristianly, as I believe, driven from my house and land and wife and children, . . . (though in winter snow, which I feel yet) unto these parts, wherein I may say Peniel, that is, I have seen the face of God" (*CW*, 6:335). The reference to "wandring towards Winter night" and the rest of the explanation remind us that the Narragansett, too, are lost, miserable, and undone from a spiritual perspective, a meaning reinforced by the transition from *"I"* to *"We"* in the dialogue. In this extreme instance the natives are no longer the explicit instruments of Williams's rescue, but fellow wanderers, for both with them and alone he has been "always mercifully preserved" by God.

This sense of a constant presence, of a guide and support, emerges in the dialogue following the observation, in which the personal pronouns are completely ambiguous and open to multiple interpretations. But read vertically, the dialogue hints at a crisis of faith in the allusion to the utmost *imitatio Christi*—what Emily Dickinson, using the same topos, calls her "newer—nearer Crucifixion" (no. 553), in which she utters the same "Prayer . . . / That Scalding One—Sabachthani— / Recited fluent here—" (no. 313).[40] The first two exchanges promise a return visit and then, in response to some urgent request or desperate situation that is undisclosed, give unambiguous assurance against abandonment. The plea not to be deserted follows these assurances, as if the speaker does not believe his interlocutor, and it is followed in turn by an intensified version, the paraphrase of Christ's prayer on the cross, "'Eli, Eli, lama sabachthani?' that is, 'My God, my God, why hast thou forsaken me?'"

(Matt. 27:46). Read autobiographically, this sequence and the use of the voice of Christ capture the extremity of Williams's suffering during the flight of his exile, and they also suggest his miraculous "resurrection" in the place he named Providence to mark God's intervention on his behalf. In the letter quoted earlier, he gives the biblical parallel of this event in the words Jacob spoke to commemorate the spot where he wrestled with the angel and won God's blessing, his life preserved even though he saw God "face to face"—the meaning of "Peniel" (Gen. 32:24–30).

An answer to the Christic sufferer's despairing prayer comes, in the dialogue, in the form of a concrete aid, "Wuttánho / *A staffe.*" Given the intensity of the intertextual context, this seems strangely disjunctive, especially when it is followed by the superfluous observation that "a Staffe is a rare sight in the hand of the eldest, their Constitution is so strong," until we remember the words of Psalm 23, which must have resonated deeply for Williams: "Yea, though I walk through the valley of the shadow of death, I will fear no evil: for thou art with me; thy rod and thy staff they comfort me" (Ps. 23:4). Both the physical aid of a staff upon which to lean and its metaphorical significance as the consolation of God's presence reinforce the theme of travel, literally and allegorically.

Chapter 11 ends as suggestively as it began, with an example of Narragansett courage in the face of overwhelming enemy numbers; potential robberies and murders; an explanation of intertribal justice; and a final dialogue that begins

Cutchachewussímmin.	*You are almost there.*
Kiskecuppeeyáumen.	*You are a little short.*
Cuppeeyáumen.	*Now you are there.*

and ends with a cathartic sense of release:

Pónewhush.	*Lay downe your burthen.* (152–53)

Again, the situation and the players are not specified; the final invitation to relieve oneself of one's load could be addressed to Williams by his Narragansett friends as he arrives in their town to trade, or by him to the natives, soliciting their belief in the Christian Gospel. It could be the voice of God. In any case, it has allegorical significance as the termination of an experience of travel that has taken on the character of a pilgrimage of the spirit as well as the body.

As if recognizing that he blurs the question of who is guiding whom and through what, Williams specifies in the "*Generall Observations of their Travell*" that "As the same Sun shines on the Wildernesse that doth on a Garden! so the same faithfull and all sufficient God, can comfort, feede and safely guide even through a desolate howling Wildernesse" (153). God shines equally upon the redeemed and the lost and is the only truly dependable guide, as the poem concluding the chapter explains:

God makes a Path, provides a Guide,
And feeds in Wildernesse!
His glorious Name while breath remaines,
O that I may confesse.

Lost many a time, I have had no Guide,
No House, but hollow Tree!
In stormy Winter night no Fire,
No Food, no Company:

In him I have found a House, a Bed,
A Table, Company:
No Cup so bitter, but's made sweet,
When God shall Sweet'ning be.

(153–54)

This poem is as close as Williams comes in the *Key* to the conventional Puritan poetic celebration of faith; thus, more than any other poem it maps out a subjective space in which a very personal "I" appears. Dispensing with the usual comparison of English and native morals, Williams expands on the allegorical interpretation of "travel" given in the general observation and, picking up on the reference to Psalm 23 in "Wuttánho / A staffe," composes a variation on the popular psalm. Like Edward Taylor and every other Protestant lyric poet who took the Psalmist as a scriptural model, he understands his religious poetic as a joyous responsibility to "*confesse*" (Taylor calls it "praise") God's "*glorious Name while breath re-maines*" (l. 3). The word "*breath*" refers to life, but it also suggests the lyric nature of the religious task: to speak or sing, to raise one's voice, to expend one's breath or spirit, in God's service. The invocation in the fourth line reinforces the pun in a device that occurs again in chapter 3 in reference to native worship: "*'Fore day they invocate their Gods, / Though*

Many, False and New: / O how should that God worshipt be, / Who is but One and True?" (109).

The subjective and discontinuous dimension that Northrop Frye finds constitutive of lyric is here more insistent than in Williams's more polemical poems. In a sense, the speaker puts his burden down and stops to praise God. Even the trusty Narragansett drop away as the instruments of divine providence. The autobiographical elements of survival in uncharted territory are filtered through the familiar imagery of Psalm 23: the Lord who is David's shepherd, who restores his soul and leads him "in the paths of righteousness for his name's sake" (Ps. 23:3), appears to Williams as the consummate pathfinder, guide, and sustainer not merely through the New World wilderness that he traverses in his travel, trade, and missionizing, but also through the wilderness condition of the world before the second coming. In this complete dependence upon God, Williams's customary positions are again disrupted, as the speaker takes up the position usually assigned to the Native Americans. In stanza 2 he represents himself as "*Lost many a time*" and as having "*no Guide*" and "*No House*" but the empty trunk of a hollow tree. This description fits the Native Americans whom he believes to be spiritually lost and in need of a guide, yet who trust completely in God's bounty and live closely and harmoniously with nature. What differentiates him from the natives huddled around a sparse fire on a bitterly cold winter night is how he represents that experience—which is synonymous with how he experiences it: in his lostness he finds a God whose comforting presence is "*a House, a Bed, / A Table, Company.*" The bare necessities of physical survival in the wilderness become the spiritual emblems of his abiding faith.

It is a faith he struggles to maintain in the face of persecution and privation. Part of King David's comfort is that the Lord "preparest a table before me in the presence of mine enemies: thou anointest my head with oil; my cup runneth over" (Ps. 23:5); God chooses David, prefers him above all others, and fulfills him. In his hymn Williams blunts the idea of ascendance over "enemies" connected to the image of the "table," but substitutes Christ's cup of suffering for David's overflowing one. The "cup *run*[ning] *ore with plenteous store*" in Williams's allegorical universe is filled with the "*wholesome* beare *and* wine" of the rich English diet that he contrasts with the simple fare of the Narragansett, in the poem from chapter 2. There he rejects the richness of the English table for the providential nourishment he takes at the hands of the natives. Here, in stripping away that detail from his literal experience, he strips away all worldly mediations, declaring himself, like Christ, prepared to drink the sacramental cup of suffering if it be sweetened by assurances of God's presence.

Such suffering constitutes *him* a fitter "guide" to lead his wayward Puritan brethren through the wilderness experience, both literally and allegorically—the millennialist form of his *imitatio Christi* as well as an allegorical identification with the exquisitely skillful native guides. Yet, for all of Williams's positional superiority in relation to his native friends, he is quick to embrace their Edenic harmony with nature and the morality and simplicity of their lifestyle as analogues of the saint's spiritual reliance upon God's will. In the above poem, Williams takes this even further: he uses his reliance upon native guides who are so "exquisitely skilled in all the body and bowels of the Countrey" (149) to figure his reliance upon God, who "can comfort, feede and safely guide even through a desolate howling Wildernesse" (153). Although the Native Americans are sub-sumed in this analogy, some traces of divinity, so to speak, cling to them in their own natural sphere and in their interaction with the narrator. His allegories use the Native Americans in similar ways, representing them in terms of extremes: as ravens, biblical emblems of Godly instruments; and, indirectly, as angels, messengers of God's consolation. The one constant in both of these images is that the instrument is either less or more than human—that is, it is dehumanized, and objectified, while the allegorist retains his humanity and authority. This is an effect of Williams's ra-cialized gynesis. Yet, in contrast to the Puritan gynesis we have seen in previous chapters, the Narragansett gain a moral and even a spiritual authority, not just by what Williams imagines they represent, but by what he represents them as saying.

In several poems in the last third of the *Key*, Williams represents the Narragansett speaking directly and indirectly—sometimes to him, and sometimes overheard by him. Such representation is not the same as "assum[ing] the Indians' point of view" (Johnston, 16) because Williams's own point of view, while sometimes similar, remains distinct. As polemic, having the supposedly savage natives direct moral criticism at the sup-posedly civilized English accomplishes two goals: it intensifies that crit-icism, and it calls into question the moral values conventionally attached to the position each group occupies. On the rhetorical level, it invites us to regard the native speakers as subjects in their own right, as agents of moral deliberation, as speakers given credibility and authority by the narrator—the white guide—who represents them. Williams prepares his readers for such a ploy in the conclusion to the *Key*'s introductory letter, where he confirms his "hopes" for native conversions not just with the story but with the dying words of Wequash, "the *Pequt Captaine*." Several years before Wequash's fatal illness, Williams had "acquainted him with the *Condition* of *all mankind*, & his *Own* in particular." Now, on his deathbed, Wequash confesses to his old friend, "*your words were never out of my heart to this present*; and said hee *me much pray to Jesus Christ*: I told him so did many *English*, *French*, and *Dutch*, who had never turned to *God*, nor loved Him: He replyed in broken English: *Me so big naughty Heart, me heart all one stone!*" (88). Williams sets off this final, repentant cry in broken English to great effect against the empty prayers and (what he conceives to be) the false repentance of the Europeans. Later, in the poem for chapter 13, "Of *the Weather*," he even borrows this pious language, addressing recalcitrant Native Americans as well as English with Wequash's highly scriptural self-image: "*O hearts of stone that thinke and dreame, / Th'everlasting stormes t'out-face*." These tempest-tossed dreamers founder because they do not anchor themselves upon "*That* Rocke [Christ] *that changeth not*" (159). Compare Wequash's "*Savory expressions . . . from compunct and broken Hearts*" (88) with the fearful cry of Williams's fellow passengers aboard the European ship. It is supremely ironic, though not surprising, that in a text that defers native conversions, a Native American provides the model of true repentance.

Native speech in the poems is not pious but morally outraged. The poem for chapter 22, "Of *their Government* and *Justice*," begins with the narrator's observation that the "*Wild* Indians *punish*" the crimes of "*Adulteries, Murthers, Robberies, Thefts*" (204)—crimes Williams estimates to occur much less frequently in wild America than in civilized Europe (203). But instead of the customary spiritualizing of this theme, the poem concludes with the "barbarians" airing their opinions:

When Indians *heare the horrid filths*,
Of Irish, English *Men*,
The horrid Oaths and Murthers late,
Thus say these Indians *then*:

We weare no Cloaths, have many Gods,
And yet our sinnes are lesse:
You are Barbarians, Pagans wild,
Your Land's the Wildernesse.

(204)

In this unsparing, though stylized, speech, the Narragansett speaker makes explicit what Williams has only been able to utter indirectly: from a moral perspective, the positions of English and native are completely reversed. Even his yoking of "Irish, English *Men*" in the preceding stanza is an oblique way of attributing to the English the paganism and barbarism they attribute to the Catholic Irish, whom they colonized and disdained in a manner that anticipated their treatment of Native Americans.[41]

By allowing the native speaker to condemn the supposedly civilized English, Williams gives the Native Americans the moral high ground and ascribes to them a large degree of self-consciousness. They realize that their lack of clothing and practice of polytheism appear barbarous to Europeans who, Williams contends, are intolerant of cultural differences. The poem for chapter 20, "Of *their nakednesse* and *clothing*," for example, mockingly asks:

O what a Tyrant's Custome long,
How doe men make a tush,
At what's in use, though ne're so fowle:
Without once shame or blush?

Many thousand proper Men and Women,
I have seen met in one place:
Almost all naked, yet not one,
Thought want of clothes disgrace.

The pun on the theologically sensitive word "disgrace" is sharp, for Williams concludes this scolding by drawing the spiritual lesson that

Israell was naked, wearing cloathes!
The best clad English-man,
Not cloth'd with Christ, more naked is:
Then naked Indian.

(188)

By contrast, he observes in the Narragansett "a modest Religious perswasion not to disturb any man, either themselves *English, Dutch,* or any in their Conscience, and worship" (193)—the principle of freedom of conscience that he embraces and enshrines at the heart of his most famous tract, *The Bloudy Tenent of Persecution.* These are important lessons, which his Narragansett friends seem to have learned without the benefit of "civilization," and which fuel their indignation at the immorality of civilized men. Their final point is perhaps the most subtle and telling. The term "wilderness," as Williams has hinted all along, is also a function of cultural relativism, denoting not a mere physical condition, but a moral, ethical, and spiritual one. The native speaker implies that just as Milton's Satan carries Hell within his own vengeful bosom, civilized men who act barbarously carry the wilderness within them and spread it about wherever they reside.

Williams may be willing on occasion to cede his privileged place as speaking subject to his Narragansett friends, especially when it advances his own critique, but there are occasions when his representation of their reality runs absolutely counter to his overarching spiritual ends. This conflict produces self-contradiction and disjunctive reasoning best illustrated in the poetic conclusion to chapter 25, "*Of buying and selling.*" The poem begins by emphasizing how frequently Williams has heard the Narragansett voice their well-founded mistrust of the colonists:

Oft have I heard these Indians *say,*
These English *will deceive us.*
Of all that's ours, our lands and lives,
In th'end they will bereave us.

(220)

Tragically, these apprehensions were confirmed: the English settlers deceived the Narragansett over and over and finally destroyed them, an eventuality not hard to predict, given the portrait of the English painted in the *Key.* Yet the poem trivializes these fears in stanza 2 by ascribing them to the natives' "shyness" of strangers and their (perfectly reasonable) dislike of being cheated in even the smallest trade. The final stanza of the poem draws the most conventional of spiritual lessons:

Indians *and* English *feare deceits,*
Yet willing both to be

Deceiv'd and couzen'd of precious soule,
Of heaven, Eternitie.

(220)

As the *Key* moves to its apocalyptic conclusion, more of this kind of
parallelism appears, admonishing both English and native of the consequences of spiritual ignorance. What is particularly heartless in this instance is the deafness of the narrative voice to its own words. The poem
makes space for the expression of a native perspective, only to "clothe" it
with a spiritual "truth" that ignores—and, by implication, condones—the
very real and finally devastating economic exploitation of the Narragansett. The spiritualization permits the narrator to avert his gaze from the
economic greed of his Puritan brethren, whose immorality he has cen-
sured all along.

The final poem of the last chapter concerning "their Death *and* Buri-
all" also places Native American and English on equal footing—but the
ground they stand on is familiar to the former, and the latter get taken
down a peg. Though they are unsaved, the natives' untutored belief in the
immortality of the soul shames those supposedly civilized men, like John
Milton, who, according to Teunissen and Hinz (*Key*, 314), supported the
Mortalist heresy. The final stanzas appropriately call up a vision of the
Last Judgment, where

Two Worlds of men shall rise and stand
'Fore Christs most dreadfull barre;
Indians, *and* English *naked too,*
That now most gallant are.

True Christ most Glorious then shall make
New Earth, *and Heavens New;*
False Christs, false Christians then shall quake,
O blessed then the True.

(249–50)

Williams has delineated the "two worlds of men" in earlier poems: the
natives who are ignorant of the Gospel yet live virtuously according to
natural lights, and the Europeans who know the Gospel but ignore or
pervert it. All through the *Key* he implies that because of their active
disregard of religion, their hypocrisy, and their immorality, the English are

the greater sinners. That implication is intensified rhetorically by describing the English at the bar of judgment as "naked too"—that is, naked and natural like the uncivilized natives and thus on a par with them; naked and thus stripped of their formerly "gallant" garb, which they thought made them superior to the natives; and naked, or not "clothed with Christ," and thus spiritually vulnerable, unconverted, *"false Christians."* At that ultimate test, only the "True" will be safe, saved, and blessed. The natives' nakedness, conventionally a mark of their wild condition, comes to look like the unadorned plainness urged upon saints in various spheres by Puritan divines. Williams makes this rather shocking equation in the most philosophic and difficult poem in the *Key*, which appears in chapter 30, *"Of their paintings,"* and concerns the sinful incongruence of surface and depths, appearance and reality—the self-representation of the saint. In lofty tones augmented by the unusual use of pentameter throughout, Williams parallels the beautiful nakedness of the natives with the spiritual beauty of the elect:

> *Truth is a Native, naked Beauty; but*
> *Lying Inventions are but Indian Paints;*
> *Dissembling hearts their Beautie's but a Lye.*
> *Truth is the proper Beauty of Gods Saints.*
>
> (241)

Despite this extraordinary comparison, Williams ends the *Key* by reverting to conventional representations of native and Puritan. In the final untitled paragraph, he invokes a divine transcendental perspective with which he aligns his own speaking voice and thanks "the most High and most Holy, Immortall, Invisible, and onely Wise God" for assistance in framing "this poore KEY, which may, (through His Blessing in His owne holy season) open a Doore; yea, Doors of unknowne Mercies to Us and Them" (250). Through his use of pronouns, Williams replaces the natives squarely in the position of the dehumanized Other, and reidentifies himself with his Puritan audience. Though neither position ascribes agency to its occupants, both groups being the objects of God's "Mercies," the discourse of "us-them" as the last word creates a sense of racial separation and opposition.

It is futile to attempt to reconcile what Williams invites us to conclude from his ironic reversals, provocative ambiguities, and juxtapositions, with what he is willing and able publicly to endorse. His refusal to assert unequivocally the truth of his position, like his vehement rejection of the Puritans' hegemonic subjectivity, is reflected structurally in his habit of ending the general observations and poems with rhetorical questions. This technique gives his text an exclamatory tone, and also protects him from having to state explicitly troubling or subversive or totalizing conclusions. Nevertheless, he devises a structure that calls into question the Puritans' cherished moral righteousness. By embedding the first-person speaker in several other modes of discourse, Williams ensures that his story cannot be read apart from the interracial exchanges and the allegorical figurations that are a complicating but necessary part of it. The dialogues do not merely illustrate a linguistic exchange but offer a model of subjectivity through intersubjectivity. They unhook speakers from set identities, emphasizing communication, context, and contact.

The allegories serve a complementary function, deferring Williams's critical responsibility in an ingenious and convenient way. In each case, he invites us to recognize the allegorical story by a deliberate biblical allusion: a staff, a storm at sea, ravens that nourish, angelic words. Like righteous Puritans we gather the story's significance, which is clear and unchanging, "biblically sound." But then Williams invites, sometimes forces, us to swap around the positions in the application: imagine that the Native American is showing "the way"; imagine that the English are apostate—out of the way, lost; even imagine that the natives are more "Christian" than the Christians! Williams never relinquishes Christianity—that is, Christ—as his standard of measure; he only questions the appropriateness of those who historically have claimed to fit and guard that standard. By using familiar Bible stories as a way of seeing and mediating his own unorthodox experiences, he is able to guarantee an acceptable interpretation for these experiences even as they often indict the English and ennoble Native Americans. And by allowing key positions in the parables to shift back and forth, he is able to invite subversive readings while pretending no more than an application of sound biblical hermeneutics. Every emblematic story packs a double punch: reinforcing his own Christic identity, and indicting the Puritans on their own terms. In the process Williams's own story emerges, not as a straightforward, first-person narrative, but in an appropriately fragmentary form, inserted into, and indelibly marked by, his encounters with a linguistically sophisticated Otherness he has difficulty finding inferior on any level.

It is true that the ultimate goal of the *Key*, and of Williams's efforts to obtain proficiency in the Narragansett dialect, is the suspiciously coupled incentives to trade and to evangelize—a tangle of worldly and other-worldly desires for profit that we can never untangle. It is also true, as Mary Poovey says in another context, that "signifying practices always produce meanings in excess of what seems to be the text's explicit design" (16). Texts produce multiple effects that both participate in their culture's values and challenge those values. For example, by narrowing the available positions with which its white readers can identify, the *Key* forces their gaze back upon themselves.[42] But in order to do so, the text attempts to subordinate the literal reality of the native world—which is also, after all, the world Williams enters, observes, and to a large extent shares—to the atemporal spiritual reality of scriptural allegory. The Narragansett become instrumental, mediating between Williams and God, Williams and his foes. Yet, his reductive efforts are not wholly successful. The form presenting the rich, "exceeding copious," and finally "irreducible" word-mass of the Narragansett tongue does not subdue it.[43] Instead, the structure of the text allows the two contradictory worlds implied by their linguistic representations to exist fruitfully side by side.[44] The world of the Narragansett, replete with an undeniable opacity, provides Williams with a reference against which to measure and test his own society, and to reenvision the Puritan ideology of redeemed subjectivity.

This study began by peering over the shoulder of a fictional "son" of New England Puritanism, the sensitive and tragic Arthur Dimmesdale. In my examination of representative colonial lyric, I have continued to peer over the shoulders and into the psyches of Puritan "sons" who embraced, transmitted, and resisted the paradoxical rule of New England's theocratic fathers. John Fiske was a loyal son mourning the loss of fathers; Edward Taylor was a son determined to maintain the outmoded rule of the fathers; Anne Bradstreet was a daughter imitating sons and used by the fathers; and Roger Williams was a troublesome son forced to expose the hypocrisy of the fathers' rule. Lyric, with the subjectivity it implies and displays, is the cultural site in which I chose to explore the contested activity of self-representation, the discursive work of the Protestant ethic. While gender was, and to a large extent still is, our culture's most convenient metaphor for the difference that constitutes subjectivity, other factors such as race, class, and familial position (in androcentric culture, especially filial and Oedipal roles) have emerged in this study as historically specific figures for displacement.

In closing, I want to offer some further speculations on the construction of masculine identity—which over the centuries has been nearly synonymous with cultural identity—by musing on the story of a "real" son. Daniel Paul Schreber was an eminently respectable and professionally successful man who lived in Germany in the latter half of the nineteenth century and the early twentieth century. He held important positions in his community: first as the presiding judge of an inferior court in Leipzig, then as *Senatspräsident*, or presiding judge, of the Dresden Court of Appeals. In 1884 he suffered the first of two extended, debilitating mental breakdowns for which he was institutionalized. Beset by apocalyptic visions of the end of the world, Schreber came to believe that only he could save it, and only by being miraculously transformed into a woman.

Schreber perceived a complex cosmology at the center of which was a wrathful and arbitrary, though limited, God whose exacting demands could be satisfied only by strict obedience. In an account of his extraordinary experiences, *Memoirs of My Nervous Illness*, published in 1903, he explained that "in order to maintain the species, one single human being was spared—perhaps the relatively most moral—called by the voices that talk to me the *Eternal Jew*"; after thorough purification, he continued, "the Eternal Jew (in the sense described) had to be unmanned (transformed into a woman) to be able to bear children," and thus renew the human race. According to Schreber, this process of "unmanning" or being transformed into a woman occurs with the attainment of "the State of Blessedness" upon returning to God after death, and it "is felt, if not exclusively as, at least accompanied by, a greatly increased feeling of voluptuousness; on the other hand it is connected with the basic plan on which the Order of the World seems to rest . . ." (72–73). After much suffering, Schreber became convinced that God demanded emasculation from him for divine satisfaction and as evidence of his "God-fearing" (Freud, 131, 128). Only at a very late stage in the evolution of this intricate system did Schreber assert his identity with Christ as the redeemer destined to save the world (Freud, 125).

Schreber's case was so fascinating that it induced Sigmund Freud to write an extensive essay theorizing the disorder of paranoia, which has become a classic in its field. Summing up Schreber's system, he said that "the two principal elements of his delusion (his transformation into a woman and his favoured relation to God) are united in his assumption of a female attitude toward God" (132). The task of interpretation was to show the "essential *genetic* relation" between the two elements. Freud diagnosed Schreber as suffering from a "father complex" and attributed his obsessional thoughts to his repressed homosexual desires for his father. He theorized that Schreber experienced his father's interference with the satisfactions of his infantile autoeroticism as persecution. His own desires could become acceptable only if he imagined them consonant with God's imperious demands for a constant state of "voluptuousness." Such a state was only possible and acceptable, Schreber reasoned, in females, who are "naturally" passive in the sexual act and with respect to sexual pleasure. "The male state of Blessedness," he asserted, is "superior to the female state; the latter seems to [consist] mainly in an uninterrupted feeling of voluptuousness" (Schreber, 52). Freud argued that Schreber "believed that emasculation was to be effected for the purpose of sexual abuse and not so as to serve some higher design." He emphasized repeatedly that the idea of emasculation "was the primary delusion" and explained that "a sexual delusion of persecution was later on converted, in the patient's mind, into a religious delusion of grandeur" (114).

On the basis of his exhaustive reading of the *Memoirs*, Freud considered Schreber "psychotic." His delusional system, however, at least in the basic outlines sketched here, recapitulates some of the major elements and psychological features of the Puritan paradigm of conversion as I have presented it. Schreber carefully distinguished his cosmology from Christianity, certain that a comparison would prove the superiority of his own system (Chabot, 15). Nevertheless, both center upon an inexplicable and powerful, essentially masculine and patriarchal, God. Both share an apocalyptic vision that lends urgency to its believers' undertakings; both figure believers as wandering and persecuted Jews. Most important, both systems radically distinguish between males and females in their capacities and their relation to the divine. Schreber, as C. Barry Chabot comments, does not consider the much simpler solution to the destruction of humankind—the saving of a female (15). Only a feminized man can serve that sacrosanct function, positioned by God as a woman in relation to God-as-man. In both systems, feminization is synonymous with persecution and is required to make men eligible for their reward—a privileged status in relation to the persecuting God/father; in both, female bodily functions are rhetorically appropriated by men and applied to male spiritual aspirations.

The crucial difference between these two conceptions is one of degree, not kind. Schreber's discourse of "voluptuousness" and his claim to have briefly possessed female genitals point up the Puritans' unwillingness to literalize the figures that pervade their religious rhetoric. Edward Taylor, often considered an extreme example, merely imagines himself as the Spouse of Christ, wooed, kissed, and embraced. Schreber, with his modern sensibility, literalizes these figures in his own body, imagining himself not only as God's betrothed, but as God's wife impregnated by his seed.[1] What in the seventeenth century pressed up against the limits of the figural, in the twentieth century crosses that boundary and unveils a hystericized male body.

Mainstream Puritans were careful not to cross the boundary between the figurative and the literal, and they severely punished those of the radical sectarian fringe who, in the middle of the seventeenth century, leaped over it in droves.[2] The ideology of redeemed subjectivity was meant to contain such heretical trespasses; but its strict imposition suggests the extent to which sectarian leanings existed in the colonies and presented a threat to the established theocracy. Given the resemblance between Schreber's hysteria and Puritan figural self-representation, New Englanders were certainly equipped to comprehend the way Schreber responded to his feelings of persecution by embracing and occupying the feminine position explicitly as a man transformed into a woman; in that role he, like them, imagined the cultural debasement of femininity transmuted into importance and its silence metamorphosed into prophecy. Alice Jardine cites Schreber's case as "not only a classical example of male paranoia, but . . . a perfect representation of the crisis of knowledge intrinsic to modernity": a man denying sexual difference by imagining himself as both woman (matter) and spirit (Christ), in order to confront the violent and oppressive Father at the heart of phallocentric culture (98–99). This darkened heart is precisely what Puritan culture could not confront.

And with good reason, if the story of the "real" son is any measure. Schreber was not paranoid in the terms theorized by Freud, because the terrorizing paternal power he attributed to God proved to be not merely the delusions of a son suffering for his real or imagined inadequacies in the eyes of an exacting father. In his extensive case study, Freud notes that Schreber's father was the eminent Dr. Daniel Gottlieb Moritz Schreber, a physician and promoter of "the harmonious upbringing of the young." As "founder of therapeutic gymnastics in Germany," Freud continues, the elder Schreber was a public figure "whose memory is kept green to this day by the numerous Schreber Associations which flourish especially in Saxony," and whose "activities exerted a lasting influence upon his contemporaries"; such a man was "by no means unsuitable for transfiguration into a God in the affectionate memory of the son from whom he had been so early separated by death," he concludes, viewing the idiosyncratic deity of Schreber's imaginary world as a displaced father figure (151).[3] Yet Schreber's father was possessed by his conviction of the divine soundness of his ideas about the world and human nature, which reinforced his own dominating and oppressive centrality. Studies have revealed that the eminent Dr. Schreber imposed a cruel regimen of unspeakable practices upon his infant son in the name of his philosophy of child-rearing and discipline. Furthermore, scholars have demonstrated that the imagery of Schreber's ravings corresponds eerily with his father's detailed descriptions of the physical ordeals to which he recommended that parents begin subjecting their children from the age of six months, in order to break their will and exact "*unconditional obedience*" to paternal authority (*Kallipädie*, 135; quoted in Schatzman, 23).[4]

The elder Schreber believed that fathers should reign supreme in the home and were mainly responsible for the upbringing of children (Schatzman, 17). Encouraging fathers to impose what he called the "law of habitation" on infants as a means of "developing and consolidating moral will power and character," he advised:

> *Suppress everything* in the child, keep everything away from him that he should not make his own, and guide him perseveringly towards everything to which he should habituate himself.
>
> If we habituate the child to the Good and Right we prepare him to do the Good and the Right later with consciousness and out of free will. . . . The habit is only a necessary precondition to make possible and facilitate the proper aim of *self-determination* of free will. . . . The thought should never even occur to the child that his will could be in control, rather should the habit of subordinating his will to the will of his parents or teachers be immutably implanted in him. . . . There is then joined to the feeling of law a feeling of impossibility of struggling against the law; a child's obedience, the basic condition for all further education, is thus solidly founded for the time to come. (*Kallipädie*, 60, 66; quoted in Schatzman, 20–22)

According to a perverse logic, Schreber sought to foster in children a "self-determination" and a "free will" that are no more than the internalization of the paternal will, and that can only be achieved by complete submission.[5] How far is this from the "freely" chosen subjection of Christian liberty that John Winthrop recommended to the enfranchised men of the Massachusetts Bay commonwealth?

Not only do the principles of Schreber's program resemble the pietistic regimen of Puritan conversion, but they uncannily echo seventeenth-century child-rearing practices recommended in order to prepare saints for the rigors of religious training. Compare Dr. Schreber's preaching of "household totalitarianism" (Schatzman, 170) with the following advice on child-rearing offered by Puritan pastor John Robinson to his congregation:

> . . . surely there is in all children, though not alike, a stubbornness, and stoutness of mind arising from natural pride, which must, in the first place, be broken and beaten down; that so the foundation of their education being laid in humility and tractableness, other virtues may, in their time, be built thereon. . . . For the beating and keeping down of this stubbornness parents must provide carefully . . . that the children's wills and willfulness be restrained and repressed, and that, in time; lest sooner than they imagine, the tender sprigs grow to that stiffness, that they will rather break than bow. Children should not know, if it could be kept from them, that they have a will in their own, but in their parents' keeping; neither should these words be heard from them, save by way of consent, "I will" or "I will not." (*Works*, 1:246–47; quoted in Greven, 37)[6]

Ultimately, Schreber urged the state to regulate child-rearing, using his methods to produce citizens who would constitute "an ever better realisation of the divine plan of human creation, as this plan is revealed both by philosophy and the spirit of universal history as well as by the spirit of Christianity" (*Concerning the Education of the Nation*, 4; quoted in Schatzman, 169). These ideas have been linked to Nazism, not just philosophically, but in a more direct way. Psychoanalyst Morton Schatzman points out that members of Adolf Hitler's generation were products of the Schreberian system (170).

Dr. Schreber tortured his children, especially his sons—driving one to madness and the other, Daniel Paul's older brother, to suicide. That much is clear. Though his sadistic ideas about children were fueled by a personal pathology and virulent nationalism, they were not unusual. William Neiderland explains that "the authoritarian regimentation of children with its emphasis on coercive disciplinary measures was probably typical of the country and the era in which Dr. Schreber lived, [although] it is a matter of record that the straps, belts, and other forms of mechanical restraint were his personal inventions" (57).[7] However, in a series of

moving expositions on the prevailing attitudes toward children, psychoanalyst Alice Miller goes much further.[8] Haunted by a need to explain the
atrocities committed by men like Adolf Hitler and the millions who followed him, Miller traces the roots of violence back to the hidden cruelties
of child-rearing practices. She begins her demonstration of the "poisonous pedagogy" of child-rearing with the sensational example of Dr.
Schreber (*For Your Own Good*, 4–6), but her study is prefaced with epi-
graphs of similar philosophical persuasion from Robert Cleaver and John
Dod's widely read seventeenth-century domestic manual, *A Godly Form of
Household Government* (1621), and a passage from John Eliot's *Harmony of
the Gospels* (1678) (*For Your Own Good*, xviii).

Miller argues that parents have been exhorted to persecute their
children with the same coercive discipline imposed upon them—a crucial
part of which is intimidation from an early age, so that parental cruelty
posing as love can go undetected. The early internalization of parental
right allows children to "forget" what has been done to them and explains
the phenomena of self-regimentation that we observed at the basis of the
Puritan ideology of redeemed subjectivity. Accepting another's will as
one's own allows people to perpetrate horrors without feeling personally
responsible—and the license is unlimited when that other is God. Submission to a higher power allows people to accept without question or
resistance a morphology of conversion that demands humiliation, abjection, and complete self-abasement. Such early training also explains why
Freud thought Dr. Schreber eminently suitable to be the deific figure in
his son's tortured universe, and why he dismissed his female patients'
claims of sexual abuse as pure fantasy or wish fulfillment in the construction of his Seduction theory.[9]

Patriarchal culture, with its roots in Puritan ideologies of redeemed
subjectivity, and its gender and racial hierarchies, is committed to protecting and preserving the fathers' rule and the sons' obedience. And as long
as "woman," portrayed as the figure of man's interiority and difference,
prevents the emergence and self-representation of all those classed as
"other," this patrimony remains ours.

Chapter 1

1. For a recent reading of Hester in this tradition see Bercovitch's pair of essays, "A-Politics of Ambiguity" and "Hawthorne's A-Morality of Compromise." Readers of Hawthorne's time preferred the author's ambiguous confessions to Hester's struggles. In her astute contextual reading of Hawthorne's tales and romances, Tompkins finds it was "the custom house essay and not Hester's story that drew the most unstinting praise from contemporary reviewers of *The Scarlet Letter*" (34).

2. In H. L. Mencken's famous definition, Puritanism was "the haunting fear that someone, somewhere, may be happy" (see Stewart, 4).

3. See especially Ong's essay, "The Lady and the Issue," where he argues that Protestantism's suppression of Mary as a presence in the Godhead indicates a dread of the feminine—that is, the material, fleshly, passive, and sinful elements of our human existence—and an unwillingness to bring "this feminine, passive polarization of reality into the terms which fix one's relationship with God." The suppression of the feminine principle, he argues, leads to the rejection of the Mother Church, human sexuality, and a crucial sense of the mystery in the world, and "is *the* obsession which has constituted separatism" (*Human Grain*, 193). Leverenz (*Language*, 113, 297) cites several other critiques of Puritanism as a predominantly masculine religion: namely, Warner, *The Living and the Dead*; Pfister, *Christianity and Fear*; and Faber, *Psychology of Religion*.

According to the logic of his own statements, however, the effect of Ong's Catholic celebration of woman in the form of a virgin mother is not strikingly different from the effect of Puritanism's repression of the feminine. If the presence of the feminine principle in Catholicism insures a "sexed" or balanced economy, then woman is always a marker of gender difference, while the masculine is normative, homogeneous, and unmarked. How is this different from "the religious economy of the Puritans," where "[w]oman and sex [are] surrogates for one another" (Ong, 195)? Leaving aside Ong's wholly unsupported assertions about the "naturalness" of motherhood ("Woman is deeply committed to the lowliness of matter. . . . Nothing higher than a human being can be a mother. Nothing higher than a woman can be. Motherhood, woman's greatest glory . . ." [197–98]), his basic equation of woman and flesh reaffirms the assumptions behind the Cartesian derogation of nature and matter as inert, feminine, and

Other. In this scheme, woman, like nature, exists for man's use, whether that use be spiritual or material; she is the object of his desires and manipulations, coming to life only with an infusion of his spirit or mind, not a subject or agent in her own right.

4. P. Miller's condescending comment comes in a discussion of how covenant theology negotiated a middle road between the passivity of antinomianism and the preparationism of Arminianism, and it reinforces the clearly masculine (and positive) nature of the middle way: "It ought to have been easy for poor Mistress Hutchinson to understand the true basis for assurance; it was not an immediate revelation, an inward ecstasy or some ineffable prompting of the soul, it was a hard and mathematically calculable test. He who fulfilled the condition of the Covenant could gain assurance, and the condition was belief followed by a conscious effort toward sanctification" (*Mind*, 1:389). The other woman whose existence he acknowledges is Anne Bradstreet.

5. Phyllis Jones argues that the subject heard most frequently from pulpits during the first generation was the scriptural account of the soul's progress in faith; that Paul was the favored example of the emotions a saint should exhibit; and that among the most common analogies for conversion, taken from Paul, were love and family relationships, including marriage, betrothal, divorce, adultery, parent-child obligations, and the nurturing of babies (see especially 250–53).

6. My thinking about subjectivity and its social and historical construction has been most fruitfully influenced by recent work in semiology, materialist feminism, and British cultural studies. The essay by Fiske, cited below, provides a good introduction to the terms and methods used in cultural studies. Other contributions to this growing field that I have found helpful are Coward and Ellis, *Language and Materialism*; Kaja Silverman, *The Subject of Semiotics*; Easthope, *Poetry as Discourse*; P. Smith, *Discerning the Subject*; and de Lauretis, *Feminist Studies/Critical Studies*.

7. The clergy's association of Hutchinson with the devil and illicit sexuality is explicit in the following portion of the trial transcripts in response to her declaration that the Lord revealed himself to her directly: "Mr. Nowell: I think it is a devilish delusion. . . . Deputy gov. Dudley: . . . I am fully persuaded that Mrs. Hutchinson is deluded by the devil, because the spirit of God speaks truth in all his servants. . . . Mr. Brown: . . . this is the foundation of all mischief and of all bastardly things" (quoted in Erikson, 99).

8. I summarize here from Judith Gardiner, presenting the arguments made by Nancy Chodorow, *Reproduction of Mothering*, which are sociological rather than biological. Several influential accounts of colonial Puritan history also employ "identity" theory in their descriptions of the conversion process and the generational conflict, but their choice of models accounts for the basically masculine focus of their work. The two I have most in mind are Rutman's *American Puritanism* (1970) and Elliott's *Power and the Pulpit in Puritan New England* (1975). Both depend upon the ideas of the American psychoanalyst Erik Erikson, author of

Childhood and Society (1950) and *Identity, Youth, and Crisis* (1968), who applied his notions specifically to Protestantism in a celebrated psychobiography of Martin Luther, *Young Man Luther: A Study in Psychoanalysis and History* (1959). Erikson popularized the idea of an "identity crisis" through which youth passes on its way to maturity. Gardiner points out, however, that though "Erikson believes that both sexes pass through the same stages on their way to maturity, he also believes in basic biological and psychosocial differences between the sexes. In his theory, the paradigmatic individual achieving a mature identity is male, whereas the female has a specialized role as childbearer. Her biological structure, her unique 'inner space,' is congruent with this role, and she seeks to fill and to protect this inner space rather than forge into outward accomplishment. Therefore a young woman spends adolescence looking for the man through whom she will fulfill herself, and the maturational stages of identity and intimacy are conflated for her" (180).

9. For an analysis of "the negations on which the assumptions of a singular, fixed, and essential self is based," still very much operative in United States culture and the basis of sexism and racism, see B. Martin and Mohanty, 196–97.

10. The terms of the argument between these two traditions on the subject of "the subject" were set in the fifties in a well-known debate between Jean-Paul Sartre and Claude Lévi-Strauss. For a summary of these positions and a brief history of this period in critical thought, see Donato, "Two Languages of Criticism." Jardine (97) and de Lauretis (*Alice Doesn't*, 160) explore its implications for feminist thought.

P. Smith takes up the critique of postmodern theories of subjectivity in a systematic way, looking at the major varieties in turn and finding that "the contemporary intellectual abstraction of the 'subject' from the real conditions of its existence continues—and is perfectly consonant with—a western philosophical heritage in which the 'subject' is construed as the unified and coherent bearer of consciousness" (xxx). Thus, privileged or decentered, the subject is abstracted, a status that tends "to foreclose upon the possibility of resistance" (xxxi).

Feminists have long debated the effects of postmodernism's dismantling of a notion of subjectivity, seeing it as the flip-side of humanism's exaltation of the Self. Huyssen wonders: "Isn't the 'death of the subject/author' position tied by mere reversal to the very ideology that invariably glorifies the artist as genius . . . doesn't poststructuralism, where it simply denies the subject altogether, jettison the chance of challenging the *ideology of the subject* (as male, white, and middle-class) by developing alternative and different notions of subjectivity?" (44). N. Miller stops wondering and argues that "the postmodernist decision that the Author is dead, and subjective agency along with him, does not necessarily work for women and prematurely forecloses the question of identity for them. . . . [It] has not so much made room for a revision of the concept of authorship as it has, through a variety of rhetorical moves, repressed and inhibited discussion of any writing identity in favor of the (new) monolith of anonymous textuality, or 'transcendental anonymity,' in Michel Foucault's phrase" ("Changing the Subject," 106, 104).

11. Jardine discusses at length how postmodernism's "valorization of a neuter-in-language-without-subject" is parallel with the "regenderization" of the space of alterity, which "always already must connote the female." She points out Julia Kristeva's claim that the Other is always the "other sex," that "The difference between 'I' and 'you' turns out to be coextensive with the *sexual difference*" (*La révolution du langage poétique*, 326; cited in Jardine, 114). The best articulation of feminism's response to the modern and postmodern conceptions of subjectivity, the conception of "identity," is de Lauretis's introduction, "Issues, Terms, and Contexts."

12. Feminists have insisted upon the distinction between "Woman," a kind of essential femaleness; "woman," a category of gender; and "women," the group of historical subjects—though women of color and third-world women have been insisting for a long time, with little effect until recently, upon the crucial differences among women which make all these labels, invaluable as a rallying cry for political and social change, oppressive. See, for example, Riley, *"Am I That Name?"*

13. Pudaloff makes a similar argument for the significance of the antinomian controversy using Foucauldian terms, but his position on gender is less clear.

14. Joyce Irwin brings together some essential documents containing the most common arguments mounted by Protestant clergy on the issue of women's status in the church; see especially chap. 4, "Women in the Church," 157–99. See also Dempsey Douglass, *Women, Freedom, and Calvin*, which contextualizes the question for Calvin of women in the church, and concludes that while he "understood the theological possibility of giving freedom to women," he "decided not to make any practical attempt to do so" and "can be held perhaps more accountable than other Reformation theologians for Protestant women's continued subordination to men in the church" (10). On the Puritans' treatment of Africans and Native Americans as potential converts, see Ruchames; Segal and Stineback; and Vaughan. See also Barker-Benfield, 70, 85.

15. Rosemary Keller also reviews the historical sources for the Puritan view of woman's nature in medieval, Reformation, and English thought. Puritan rejection of the Anglican church hierarchy placed increasing importance on the laity and the family, which in turn enhanced the role of women, but required the creation of a "new conception of 'woman' . . . one that simultaneously denied her special proclivity for evil and enjoined 'voluntary subjection . . . for conscience sake'" (137; Keller is quoting from Karlsen, 165).

16. Maples Dunn has perhaps the most nuanced analysis of the role played by gender in the formation of the Puritan religious settlement. She argues that the ministerial response to the antinomian controversy was to resist "*all* claims to lay prophetic power" since it threatened the ministers' status, with the result that by 1660 "lay contribution to the making of the church in New England was re-

duced," and church membership had become a socially feminized role. Men retained their social and political dominance, so that "only for women did religion and social goals maintain a close correlation" (37–39).

17. The consequences of such skewing have been enormously damaging, and are at the heart of much feminist critical revision. Rich, in an important essay, asserts: "In denying the validity of women's experience, in pretending to stand for 'the human,' masculine subjectivity tries to force us to name our truths in an alien language" (207). Building on this idea, Fetterley coined the notion of women as "resisting readers" to combat "the consequence of the patriarchal predication that to be human is to be male" (ix). For a discussion of the paradoxes plaguing feminist efforts to unseat the assumption of masculinity in the universal, see de Lauretis, *Alice Doesn't*, 161.

18. Leverenz himself cites the different paths to gender identity that girls and boys were encouraged to take in the seventeenth century (*Language*, 102). For a description of women's training in humility, see Hull.

19. Leverenz suspects that the Puritan rhetoric of "woman" in both its positive and negative aspects had a profoundly different effect on each sex. But because the psychoanalytic tools he uses do not give him a handle on gender difference or a means of insight into the relation of discourse and subjectivity, he has only this comment on the possible effect on women of pervasive ministerial images of "the whore" as spiritual evil: "Despite the obvious sexism of fantasizing that the father is in charge of all the mother's virtues, first-generation American Puritanism perhaps unwittingly fostered assertive energies in women's behavior as well as dependent female fantasies in men. Anne Bradstreet's poetry, Anne Hutchinson's heresies, Mary Dyer's Quaker attraction to the Puritan flame, the later incidence of witches, and especially the great variety of ordinary women mastering homes, farms, Indians, and the wilderness all reflect a rich spectrum of practical as well as religious female purposefulness. Though several women do seem to have been driven mad by their circumstances, the Puritan rhetoric of whoredom does not appear to have been nearly as incapacitating to women as we might suppose" (*Language*, 140).

20. See, for example, Freud's late essay, "Femininity," in which he opens with a discussion of the "unhesitating certainty" with which anatomical science distinguishes male and female, yet concludes that "what constitutes masculinity or femininity is an unknown characteristic which anatomy cannot lay hold of" (Strouse, 75).

21. See Freud's essay, "Some Psychical Consequences of the Anatomical Distinction Between the Sexes," and Juliet Mitchell's commentary on it, "On Freud and the Distinction Between the Sexes," in Strouse, 17–36. Mitchell concludes, "where the boy's resolution and abandonment of his Oedipus complex is his entry into his cultural heritage, the girl, on the contrary, finds her cultural place in patriarchal society when she finally manages to achieve her Oedipal love for her father" (35). Compare this with Leverenz's description of conversion as bringing

"sinful selves to a female receptivity, purified of all feelings except desire for the Father and his Son" (*Language*, 103).

22. For example, the antinomian argument that the Holy Spirit dwells within a justified person implies that justified saints—male or female—are above moral law, without need of church ordinances or the guidance of ministers, and in a position to judge the justification of others. Gura argues that it was the *social* implications of the Hutchinsonian position on justification that forced John Cotton to abandon it (171).

23. This accounts, as W. Martin points out, for the Puritans' suspicion of the unbridled—that is, self-determining—imagination (65). Bordo explains the age's negative attitude toward subjectivity. In exploring the emergence of "inwardness" in the sixteenth and seventeenth centuries, she finds that it is first described as "an untrustworthy 'inner space,'" not as a mirror that reflects the world "as it is," "but as *subjectivity*—the capacity of the knower to bestow false inner projections on the outer world of things" (51). She traces the "interiorization" of Renaissance culture (54), making stops at Hamlet and Montaigne, and finds in Descartes "the first real 'phenomenology' of the mind," the central disclosure of which is "the deep epistemological alienation that attends the sense of mental interiority," which only God can bridge (55). Interiority and individualism brought with them the fear that all beliefs were *merely* subjective responses—a state of "epistemological *fallenness*" (43). Descartes's solution, what Bordo calls "the flight to objectivity"—"a compensatory turning toward the *paternal* for legitimation through external regulation, transcendent values, and the authority of law," and away from "the *maternal*—the immanent realms of earth, nature, the authority of the body" (58)—was meant to assuage the anxiety, skepticism, and doubt spawned by epistemological fallenness. Protestantism's paradigm of salvation shares some, but by no means all, aspects of Cartesianism, such as: the exorcism and subjugation of the feminine and transcendence of the flesh; the idea that nature is a book of God's will, fallen for the Puritans, barren for Descartes; God, the father, a paternal principle, takes over generativity, which, in the religious sphere, becomes a spiritual regenerativity; the spiritual rebirth out of fleshly man to spiritual man resembles the rebirth into objectivity; and finally, the Puritan metaphor of the spiritual marriage offers not rape or coercion, but the legal restraint of females, and insures male dominance.

24. See, for example, John Cotton, *The Way of Life* (London, 1641), 277; quoted in Kibbey, 53.

25. For a harrowing account of the evangelical Puritan's seemingly unrelieved self-loathing, see Greven's collection of passages from private writings in his section "'That Monster, Self'" (74–86).

26. Calvin spells out this relationship in terms of the marriage metaphor in his discussion of the first two commandments (see 2.8:16, 18).

27. Greven gives a striking example from Jonathan Edwards of how Puritan ministers, as late as the mid-eighteenth century, used the metaphor of the spiritual

marriage, advising all saints to follow its implications, and yet in the same breath articulating common assumptions about the "natural" roles that men and women played in marriage, which made it unnatural for men to be other than dominant, assertive, protecting—that is, it was unnatural for them not to occupy the godlike position (127–29).

28. The terms are Thickstun's, from "The Pauline Precedent for the Puritan View of Women," the introduction to her study on Puritan doctrine and representations of women. Thickstun's overview is helpful in pointing out how the contradictions in Paul's pronouncements shape Puritan thinking about women and establish in English narrative "a recurrent pattern in which male protagonists displace female characters from their traditional roles as Brides of Christ and representatives of chastity" (x). I would add that the dynamics of Puritan conversion, in which men took up feminized positions, materially influenced that displacement.

29. Moran, in his study of Puritan "Sisters in Christ," found that it was easier for submissive wives to identify with marriage and humiliation to Christ in the process of regeneration than for husbands to switch roles (61). Both Greven and Masson acknowledge this conflict in roles; it is enlightening to see what they make of it. Greven argues that Puritan men experienced "profound discomfort . . . with regard to sexuality," "unresolved doubts about their own identity as males," and even "latent homosexuality"—all associated with identifying with, and feeling intense hostility toward, women, and their own mothers in particular (132). In Greven's analysis, "The power of unconscious oedipal conflicts as a factor in shaping the 'feminization' of young males" (133) has nothing to do with fathers or father figures. Masson suggests that "the projection of the female role onto the congregation in its relation to Christ . . . suggests that the norms of spouses could be separated from gender . . . [and] was also an effective reminder that in the hierarchy of the church (as in the state) man could be subordinate as well as dominant" (310). She retreats from the social and political implications of her findings, however, when she concludes that ministers minimized "the idea of innate, sex-related personality traits" in order to "diminish the potential role conflict in men" and attract them to the church (315).

30. In *The Language of Puritan Feeling*, Leverenz reviews the recent arguments derived from research into Puritan family tracts; see his chap. 3, "Mixed Expectations: Tender Mothers and Grave Governors," especially p. 72. He concludes that they do not emphasize the loving aspect of mothering that occurred in the seventeenth century, which had to be counteracted by "the father's more distant governance" to "slowly bring the child to God's authority" (72). Whereas the majority of scholars argue that Puritan modes of child-rearing, especially among evangelical families, produced rigid, anxious, and overly controlled personalities, Leverenz argues that ambivalence, not repressed rage, was the dominant Puritan characteristic (101).

31. The suppression or negation of woman is a theme running through several

cultural critiques of very different theoretical orientations. It is, as we saw above, the critique that Ong levels at Protestant separatism. Jean-Joseph Goux, one of Jardine's touchstones among current French thinkers "emphasizing the neurotic borders of 'Western thinking'" and exploring postmodern alternatives, constructs what he calls "a history of symbolization," in which he finds "*the* founding fantasy" of Western culture to be "the active negation of the Mother"; characteristics of this cultural idealism are "a certain relationship to death and desire, a fear of fusion, prohibitions of incest with the Mother, the horror of 'nothing to see' (castration), the anxiety of presence and absence, the separation of form and content, spirit and matter, value and exchange" (Jardine, 32). Bordo builds upon the recent spate of studies of modern science and epistemology that discover in Baconian empiricism and Cartesian mechanism a "masculine" aggression and impulse to dominate and control nature, the body, and the phenomenal world, which have brought modern culture to the brink of breakdown and disaster (see, specifically, Berman; Merchant; and Easlea). Bordo finds in Descartes's *Meditations* a "masculinization of thought" that is "one intellectual 'moment' of an acute historical flight from the feminine, from the memory of union with the maternal world, and a rejection of all values associated with it" (9).

32. This settlement was not static. Both Masson and Dunn argue that ministerial use of the metaphor of the spiritual marriage increased in the second and especially the third generations in New England. Masson claims that this increase, as well as the attention paid to women, coincided with a rise in male admissions after 1675 (315). Dunn places the increased rhetoric at the turn of the century and sees it as a validation of the "symbolic reduction of a Christian congregation to a company of women" (38), that is, the triumph of clerical power over lay participation and the beginnings of the privatization, feminization, and domestication of religion (39).

33. Fiske explains that cultural theorists do not use the term "hegemony" as Antonio Gramsci originally formulated it; currently, it is used to describe "the process by which a dominant class wins the willing consent of the subordinate classes to the system that ensures their subordination," and, like Althusser's theory of ideology, discussed below, it "is not a static power relationship, but a constant process of struggle . . . in which victory is not necessarily total" (259). For a more thorough explanation, see Raymond Williams, chap. 6, "Hegemony."

34. Wendy Martin offers an explanation of the gendered nature of these perennial Puritan heresies. The spiritism of Anne Hutchinson appealed to women and other persons on the margins of society's power structure because "preparationism was derived from the male paradigm of combat with Satan and emphasized the necessity of a continual battle, a battle that was waged more effectively by those with sufficient aggressive energy and confidence that it could be won." Thus, traditional female qualities made it harder for women to imagine themselves defeating Satan, "a powerful demonic male," and male aggression, though spiritually effaced, familiarized men with prolonged effort and battle experience (62).

The historian Barker-Benfield also frames what P. Miller labeled "covenant theology" in the context of gender. His analysis of male Puritan reactions to Anne Hutchinson, though flawed, contains extraordinary insights and anticipates some of my arguments in this "Introduction," as well as the findings of other scholars of the period. Predicating the "ambivalence" of Puritanism on its use of the metaphor of the Bride for the passive, dependent side of saints' relation to God, he speculates that "covenant theology was constructed to soften the unmitigated tension of living under God's unknowable omnipotence" and that "males exclusively handled the softening operation" because they monopolized the control of admission to church membership. Male clergy found Calvinism's absolute dependence upon God's will too feminizing, and minimized it through covenant theology's commitment to sanctification and preparation, which "in effect helped make men gods to themselves and to their families." Women, Barker-Benfield suggests, "perceived the dice of predestination loaded against them because of their physiology," just as blacks and Native Americans suffered from assumptions based on racial stereotypes. The burden of his argument is that Anne Hutchinson "invalidated the divines' contract with God" by advocating a total dependence upon the will of God and threatening to destroy their control over the soul's union with Christ (69–72).

35. The phrase "almost irresistible," whose echo of Puritan doctrine I could not resist pointing out, is Fiske's (259). He levels it as a (recurring) critique of Althusser's theorizing the ubiquity of ideology and the immunity of the subject, after interpellation, to experience (all experience becomes ideology), the unconscious, or any form of agency that would make ideological struggle possible. Gramsci's notion of hegemony modifies the functionalism of Althusser's somewhat more static system (Fiske, 259–60). For an excellent critique of Althusser's theory of the subject, which argues that it maintains the unified Cartesian subject, the basis of which is now not certitude but misrecognition, and which sets this theory in the context of Raymond Williams' literary Marxism, see John Higgins, "Raymond Williams and the Problem of Ideology." Paul Smith also mounts a thoughtful critique of Althusser's theory, and decides that despite its problems, "interpellation . . . is an indispensable tool" for any discussion of ideology and subjectivity (21). He is particularly good on Althusser's use of Lacan and what Lacanian psychoanalysis can add to this theory; see especially 14–23.

36. The term "displacement" has a specific technical meaning in Derrida's philosophical vocabulary. "Derridean deconstruction proceeds by way of displacement, first reversing the terms of a philosophical opposition, that is, reversing a hierarchy or structure of domination, and then displacing or dislodging the system" (Krupnick, 1). Because feminists argue that the primary form of domination is male oppression of females, the gendering of displacement seems logical and inevitable. For an introduction to this concept and its impact on literary studies see the collection of essays, *Displacement: Derrida and After*, edited by Krupnick.

37. I am borrowing heavily from Jardine's concluding remarks on the differences between contemporary Anglo-American and French instances of gynesis.

She anchors her speculations in the different symbolic economies constructed by a Protestant democracy and a Catholic monarchy (I apply this distinction more thoroughly in Chapter 4 in my discussion of Berryman's poem, *Homage to Mistress Bradstreet*). The important point Jardine makes is that, in her opinion, Anglo-American gynesis is not radical but reactionary; see 231–36.

38. See Jardine's discussion of this disturbing development: "The women theorists in France whose work has had or is beginning to have a major impact on *theories of writing and reading*, and who at one level or another are writing about women, at the very least do not call themselves feminists either privately or in their writing, and, at the most, posit themselves and their work as hostile to, or 'beyond,' feminism as a concept. These are the names we hear in the United States: Hélène Cixous, Sarah Kofman, Julia Kristeva, Eugénie Lemoine-Luccioni, Michèle Montrelay, among others" (19–22). The "anti- and/or post-feminism" that Jardine sees as characteristic of the "major new directions in French theory over the past two decades—those articulated by both men and women" is "exemplary of modernity" [her term for postmodernism] and a phenomenon important for feminism to address (19–22).

39. The phrase is Caldwell's. She goes on, in her fine examination of colonial Puritan conversion narratives, to assert that "the first faint murmurings of a truly American voice" spoken "from the first moment the Puritans alighted on the hopeful, holy land of America" can be heard there (41). I have trouble with making conversion narratives our first "original" literary products, and with the entire effort of locating original and specifically "American" voices; "America" is not an idea or a construct reserved exclusively for United States culture. However, the paradigm of conversion and how it was used by the theocracy *is* specific to New England. Morgan argues that the use of the conversion narrative as a test of visible sainthood evolved in the colonies and was then exported to England (*Visible Saints*, 66). I think we can say that it represents an ideology intimately attached to New England and its errand, which has greatly influenced subsequent ideological development in the later colonial period and United States history.

40. The purpose of overreading, N. Miller explains, is "to unsettle the interpretive model" that we, women readers, have developed from what we have already read, and to read texts as if they have never been read before ("Arachnologies," 274). Another goal is to read texts that have not been read before, especially texts by women, for the "female signature": "to put one's finger—figuratively—on the place of production that marks" the author's or subject's attachment to her text (287–88)—and thereby to counteract postmodernism's tendency to view self-representation as dependent upon the unraveling of identity.

Chapter 2

1. For a discussion of the genre of elegy and the types of New England funeral elegy, see Scheick, "Tombless Virtue," 286–87.

2. See Draper for an account of the establishment of the Puritan elegy. Analyses of the development and function of the New England funeral elegy are found in Silverman, 127–31, and Scheick, "Tombless Virtue," 287–89.

3. In his study of the development of the elegy from 1660 to 1750, Elliott finds a "notable increase in the number of elegies on women and children" during the first two decades of the eighteenth century ("Development," 153), an observation that only calls attention to the fact that few were written about them earlier. He goes to great lengths to point out that the "writers of these verses do not appear to have been especially conscious of making distinctions between the sexes. Elegies about women use the same language and imagery to describe the virtues of their subjects as those about men" (154). As I pointed out in the previous chapter, in a religious regime where salvation is signified by one's adoption by God as a son, all saints held up as models are spiritually masculine. By the same logic, the woman saint is an "honorary man."

4. I recognize that in resisting the current critical trends concerning New England elegies, Scheick also rejects Henson's claim that "the primary influence upon the genre originates from the funeral sermon, particularly from the portrait-exhortation technique of the application sections of these sermons" ("Tombless Virtue," 298). "This approach," he argues, "not only denies the genre any integrity as a form in itself, but it also fails to take account of precedent English elegies and the development of the funeral sermon in England and New England" (288). Neither of these objections seems strong enough to dismiss what is an obvious structural influence upon many New England elegies written by ministers.

5. A useful introduction to postmodern criticism and theory of lyric is the volume *Lyric Poetry: Beyond New Criticism*, edited by Hošek and Parker. For a discussion of recent critical thinking on the issues of voice, identity, subjectivity, and authority, see especially P. Parker, 11–28.

6. All citations for this text come from *Seventeenth-Century American Poetry*, edited by Harrison Meserole (187–90); line numbers in parentheses follow citations. The complete text of the elegy appears at the end of this chapter. Although I use this version of the text, I am attracted to Astrid Schmitt–von Mühlenfels's "revised transcription" of Fiske's elegy, reprinted in her essay, "John Fiske's Funeral Elegy on John Cotton." She omits lines 25–32 of Meserole's version, arguing that these lines appear in the margin of the manuscript and were not, therefore, intended as part of the original text. It is true, as she claims, that without these eight lines of trimeter, "the intricate poetic form at which Fiske arrived and for which he has been justly praised becomes the more apparent" (50); nevertheless, her version introduces variant readings that produce garbled lines for which she offers no explanation (see especially lines 12 and 77 in her version).

7. Biographical information on Fiske can be found in Meserole's headnote (185–86) and in Pope, vii–xxxix.

8. Elliot details how in the 1670s Samuel Willard began broadening this standard imagery for the second generation; using the term previously reserved for

ministers and the first generation, he started calling every Christian a "gap-man" protecting the wall around New England (*Power*, 110–13).

9. Elliott does a particularly insightful analysis of the generational conflict between first- and second-generation men, concentrating on its psychological dynamics and the "myth of the decline"; see *Power*, chaps. 2 and 3.

10. See, respectively, Murphey; Reed; and Leverenz, *Language*. For a general comparison of Puritan theology and psychoanalysis, see Feinstein. Cohen considers all of these approaches, but he rejects the analogy of conversion to the resolution of the Oedipus complex because he accepts the latter's gender specificity and rejects the idea of gender specificity in the process of conversion (17, 222–23). He also rejects the Bakhtinian analysis of J. O. King (*Iron of Melancholy*). Cohen embraces a Geertzian ethnographic approach for understanding the conversion psychology of "letting the natives speak" (20). In doing so, however, he assumes that "their language reveals real personal experience, not merely a tradition of speech" (19), even though he recognizes that "ministers . . . articulated models of the new birth, forecasting believers' thoughts and directing them what to feel" (21). As far as I can tell, Cohen's analysis never addresses or resolves this problem of the "personal reality" versus the cultural construction of experience.

11. Someone named Mary Fage took this advice seriously. According to White, Anne Bradstreet's biographer, "in 1637 there appeared a work of remarkable ingenuity, *Fame's Roule: or, the Names of K. Charles, Q. Mary and his Posterity; together with the Names of the Dukes, Marquesses, &c. of England, Scotland, and Ireland; anagrammatiz'd and expressed by acrosticke Lines on their Names. By Mistris Mary Fage.* Four hundred examples are here set forth of the popular anagram, each one followed by a poetic tribute developing the anagram's theme, and with the initial letters of each line forming the subject's name" (282).

12. Puttenham's anagrams, formed from the Latin title *Elissabet Anglorum Regina* (whose orthography he defends by saying the *zeta* of the Hebrews and Greeks is a double *ss*), are *Multa regnabis ense gloria*, "By the sword shalt thou raigne in great renowne," and *Multa regnabis sene gloria*, "Aged and in much glorie shall ye raigne." About them he says, with an air of genuine surprise: "Both which resultes falling out upon the very first marshalling of the letters, without darknesse or difficultie, and so sensibly and well appropriat to her Maiesties person and estate, and finally so effectually to mine own wish (which is a matter of much moment in such cases), I took them both for a good boding, and very fatallitie to her Maiestie appointed by Gods prouidence for all our comfortes" (114). Waller calls into question the representative nature of this esteemed poetic commentator when he points out that lyric, the Renaissance genre that has most excited readers over the last century and that is considered most characteristic of the age, was denigrated by Puttenham as the "meanest sort" to be "used for recreation only" (Waller, 72); an explanation of this may be that Puttenham and others had to defend poetry against Puritan deriders, but most of the lyricists of the Renaissance were themselves pious Protestants (95).

13. Discussion of the status of anagrams in Puritan poetics has often led readers to dismiss them as aesthetically unpleasing and anachronistic. For example, Daly concludes that "the poems resulting from [anagram] are nearly all terrible, judged by modern standards for poetry. Though they undoubtedly pleased some Puritans, they say nothing to the modern reader" (149). Waggoner calls the form "displeasing," "arbitrary," and "peculiarly inappropriate—death the occasion for a display of ingenuity and wit?" he asks, and goes on to say: "The error here is not so much logical as cultural, aesthetic, and rational in the existential sense. The epistemology is all wrong: verbal ingenuity seems to be placed on a par with reason, insight and intuition as a method of discovering truth" (13–14). The ahistoricism of these comments is blatant. Pearce recognizes anagram as a central if outmoded strategy, but he regards it as a crutch when he commends Edward Taylor and elevates him above the common run of Puritan poets precisely because "he did not have to fall back on anagrammatic invention as an excuse (or an occasion) to write poems" (42). On the other hand, Schmitt–von Mühlenfels finds Fiske's employment of the anagram innovative and aesthetically important (50), while Jantz calls Fiske's elegy derived from anagram "sternly perfect," with a structure as intricately worked out as the "Baroque tension" in the contrapuntal music of J. S. Bach (30–31).

14. Mather goes on to cite "even the *temurah*, or *mutation*, with which the Jews do criticise upon the oracles of the Old Testament: 'There,' they say, 'you'll find the anagram of our *first father's* name *Haadam* to express *Adamah*, the name of the *earth*, whence he had his original.' An anagram of *good* signification, they'll show you [Gen. vi. 8,] and of a *bad* one [Gen. xxxviii. 7,] in those glorious oracles; and they will endeavour to perswade you, that *Maleachi* in Exodus is anagrammatically expounded *Michael*, in Daniel" (*Magnalia Christi Americana*, 1:318). His skepticism did not, however, stop him from liberally engaging in "such *grammatical curiosities*."

15. See Jantz, 279–81, for a list of Wilson's anagrammatic elegies—especially the series on Thomas Shepard, which yielded four anagrams, and the series on John Norton, which yielded three. Besides the anagram of the elegy under consideration, Fiske found three more in Cotton's name: two in English, which headed consolatory verses to his widow, and one in Latin. The first two contain the pun that immediately comes to the postmodern mind, "knott" as "not": "Tho onc', I not" and "I onc', tho not." For the texts, see Jantz, 121–22.

16. Scheick uses this anagram to frame his discussion of the role of anagram as the New England Puritans' "mode of elegiac-emphasis on the collective self, modelled on their concept of the individual self and designed to bring that self into conformity with the ideal" in the nonconsoling elegy ("Tombless Virtue," 297–98).

17. Friedman and Friedman, who style themselves "professional cryptologists," insist on a strict standard of "perfection" for "authentic anagrams"—that is, no changing, adding, or substituting letters. "Some of indisputable authenticity are

those made by Galileo, Huygens, and Roger Bacon, all of whom wished to make a record of priority of scientific discovery and did so by anagramming the letters describing their discoveries, and later when disposed to reveal their discoveries, reconstituted the transposed letters. Only they themselves could attest to the authenticity of the anagrammatic solution" (6–7). Friedman and Friedman also disparage "this sport," opining that anagrams "occupy far greater space in literary history than is justified by their value" (6), but they are unable to explain why.

18. "But," Meserole continues, placing himself in the camp with Pearce on the prophetic value of anagram, "it would be a mistake to think it mere verbal virtuosity. It had as its basis the Puritan belief that nothing in this world, including nomenclature, was haphazard" (xxx).

19. See, for example, Clark's discussion of "the Puritans' adamant refusal to accord to man more than a dim reflection of Christ's signifying power," where he cites John Cotton ("we are forbidden to add ought to the Word written") and Samuel Mather ("God did not forbid his own Institution of signs, but only our own inventions") ("Honeyed Knot," 77–78). Grabo discusses the doctrinal bases for Puritan strictures against the creation of images, and suggests how the meditative tradition offered Puritan poets a solution; see "Puritan Devotion." Haims reviews the evidence of colonial Puritan iconophobia, at the same time noting a contending desire, as she describes it, "to see God's face." She also reviews the critical debate, mainly between Daly and Clark, and concludes that "Puritans exhibited an ambivalence toward images. They both needed them and needed to deny them. They apologized for their poetry and explained that their images were sanctioned or dictated by the Holy Ghost, and considered their poets merely translators of God's types spelled out in earthly things. Then they wrote poetry" (21).

20. Fish comes to a similar conclusion in his consideration of George Herbert's shape poems. He asks, "If the thrust of Herbert's art is in the direction of its own self-consumption (and therefore in the direction of the consuming of the self) what are we to make of 'Altar,' 'Easter Wings,' 'Deniall,' and other poems which ostentatiously declare the wit and ingenuity of their author? I would answer this question with another—who *is* their author?—and assert further that the two questions are intimately related; for it is characteristic of these poems that at precisely those points where we are most aware of them as formal structures, we are aware of them as formal structures that have been mended or completed or given meaning by God. The moment of highest artfulness always coincides with the identification of the true source of that art; the wit and ingenuity are referred to that source rather than to the poet, who in losing title to his poem also loses (happily) the presumption of its invention, and is known for what he always was, a discoverer, one who copies out" (203).

21. But the two hermeneutic systems use anagrams for very different aims, according to my colleague Lynn Higgins, who ably explores the "poetics of ana-

gram" in the avant-garde novels of Jean Ricardou, and to whom I am indebted for many insights into this literary trope. Current French novelists and theorists (whose work on anagrams I take up later in this chapter) are working against spirituality, God, and the notion of a "transcendent signified." Yet, there is an interesting parallel between these two opposed systems of thought and representation, of which the common use of anagrams is an indication.

22. Kenneth Silverman finds "knott" to be "a recurrent term in Puritan verse"; John Danforth elegized John Eliot with the anagram "HONY . . . TOILE," which he considers a version of the honi knot (126–27).

23. Kibbey, in examining John Cotton's use of puns, ties their rhetorical function to the paradoxical nature of redeemed subjectivity. She points out that puns assert "that two contradictory concepts of proper meaning can be acknowledged simultaneously," thus replicating "the way in which spiritual and ordinary propriety collide in the polarized 'self' of the Puritan convert" who must live in contradictory social and spiritual worlds at the same time (33).

24. Clark defines the "gurdeon knot" as "a small lump of crystalline brown sugar" ("Honeyed Knot," 79).

25. See Bray for a more extensive discussion of "arboreal" imagery in Fiske and Taylor on which he bases his claim for a connection between the two poets, and for a summary of other critical studies of the imagistic pattern.

26. One school of thought fed by P. Miller's seminal study, *The New England Mind*, finds Ramist logic and its companion rhetorical method adopted from Ramus's associate, Talon, essentially damaging to Puritan poetics (1:146–50). See also Feidelson, 90–94; Pearce, 31–34; and Ong, *Ramus*. The other school of thought follows from Tuve's study in the late 1940s, *Elizabethan and Metaphysical Imagery*, which claims a positive influence for Ramism on Anglican and Metaphysical poetry. See also Daly, 50–56, and Blake. For a discussion of the application of Ramism to elegy, and to Fiske's elegy in particular, see Schmitt–von Mühlenfels, 55; Pearce, 28; and Bray, 28.

27. Henson cites how Cotton Mather adjusts and justifies Norton's portrait (20); he discusses the elegy's presentation of zeal and love extensively, but he does not focus on its paradoxical quality (14–22).

28. "Nonsense from a Lisping Child" is Scheick's description of Edward Taylor's spiritual/rhetorical stance in relation to God, in his essay that takes its title from the poet's phrase. He also says about Shepard as elegized by Oakes that "his language mirrored the internal harmony between his reason (wisdom) and will (love)," and that "to some extent Oakes's complaint of verbal deficiency in himself dramatizes th[e] communal loss of internal harmony" occasioned by the death of the influential minister ("Standing in the Gap," 304).

29. Fiske's emphasis on tenses is imitated by Oakes, who laments, "He was (ah woful word! to say he was) / Our wrestling *Israel* . . ." (Meserole, 212).

30. Elliott points out that second-generation ministers made the image of the

wall and garden "one of the most vivid symbols of the intimacy between inner corruption and exterior events" (*Power*, 106). Benjamin Woodbridge's elegy on John Cotton names his successor and hails this as the mourner's consolation:

> But let this Mourning Flock be comforted,
> Though *Moses* be, yet *Joshua* is not dead:
> I mean Renowned NORTON; worthy hee
> Successor to our MOSES is to be,
> O happy *Israel* in AMERICA,
> In such a MOSES such a JOSHUA.
>   (ll. 61–66; in Meserole, 411)

31. A similar sentiment, and one related also to mourning, is found in Job: "Naked came I out of my mother's womb, and naked shall I return thither: the Lord gave, and the Lord hath taken away; blessed be the name of the Lord" (1:21)

32. Schmitt–von Mühlenfels, who like all the other readers of Fiske's elegy seems not to notice the apostrophic quality of the anagram or the elegy itself, argues that "during these shifts of perspective Fiske avoids the impression of disconnected parts by returning throughout to the same imagery" (57). Culler offers an explanation for these omissions in his essay on "Apostrophe," which opens with a discussion of "the minor embarrassment" caused by apostrophe, speculating that this "may be taken as a sign of a larger and more interesting embarrassment which leads literary critics to turn aside from apostrophes they encounter in poetry: to repress them or rather to transform apostrophe into description. Whether this is because writing, in some innate hostility to voice, always seeks to deny or evade the vocative, it is a fact that one can read vast amounts of criticism without learning that poetry uses apostrophe repeatedly and intensely. . . . The fact that it is systematically repressed or excluded by critics suggests that it represents that which critical discourse cannot comfortably assimilate" (*Pursuit*, 135–37).

33. Fiske comments more directly on the instrumentality of ministers in bringing souls to God in this stanza from his elegy on Nathaniel Rogers, whose anagram was "He in a large Rest. / No.":

> He sought this rest, whilest heere, exemplarly,
> He instrumentally many thereto
> hath brought by His incessant labours heere
> and therefore He in Rest himselfe also.
>   (Jantz, 128)

34. L. Higgins cites the following comments by Saussure: "Actually one understands the superstitious idea that could have suggested that in order for a prayer to be effective, it was necessary for the syllables themselves of the divine name to be indissolubly mixed in it; the God was, as it were, riveted to the text, or else, if one introduced at the same time the name of the devotee and the name of the God,

one created a tie between them that the divinity was not, so to speak, free to ignore" (485; from "On the Anagrams [Letter to Antoine Meillet]," in *Semiotexte* I. 2 [Fall 1974], 70).

35. Starobinski is quick to point out that the "emanatist conception" of the function of the hypograms, which sounds suspiciously close to Puritan aesthetic theory, runs counter to the idea of literary production, neither of which was hypothesized by Saussure; see 43–46.

36. However, Clark argues that the "literal hermeneutic" characteristic of Puritan poetry produces anagrams. He uses as his example the anagram of the elegy on Thomas Dudley possibly composed by Fiske (mentioned above), where "the semantic differences between 'Thomas Dudley' and 'ah! old, must dye' fade away," and the "truth conveyed by this poem is . . . derived within a domain developed by the movement of the letters as they pass from one word to another" ("Honeyed Knot," 72).

37. In an earlier essay on Taylor's semiotics of representation, I trace the progress of this imagistic transformation in detail; see "Semiotics of the Sacrament and Edward Taylor's *Preparatory Meditations.*"

38. In another elegy Fiske exhorts his audience, "Mourne over your selves, your Losse looke to make up / In Him who full supplies hath yet in store" (Jantz, 128).

39. Scriptural use of this charged term is often also reversible. For example, "Thou hast taken away all thy wrath: thou hast turned *thyself* from the fierceness of thine anger. / Turn us, O God of our salvation, and cause thine anger toward us to cease" (Ps. 85:3–4); and "O Lord, why hast thou made us to err from thy ways, *and* hardened our heart from thy fear? Return for thy servants' sake, the tribes of thine inheritance" (Isa. 63:17).

40. This meaning of "turn" is clear in Cotton Mather's comment on John Wilson, the notorious anagrammatizer: "I believe there never was a man who made so *many*, or so *nimbly*, as our Mr. Wilson; who, together with his *quick turns*, upon the names of his friends, would ordinarily *fetch*, and rather than *lose*, would even *force* devout instructions out of his anagrams" (*Magnalia*, 1:318; emphases in the original).

41. Lang ably traces how various Puritan histories generalize the figure of Anne Hutchinson into "'Woman' . . . taken to embody the danger of lawlessness inherent in the repudiation of visible signs" and recount her story as "the victory of human (that is, male) reason and order over unreason, embodied as fecund woman" (105, 68–69).

Chapter 3

1. All citations of Taylor's poetry are from *Poems* edited by Stanford, unless otherwise indicated. Citations from *Preparatory Meditations* will be followed by the series number, the number of the Meditation, and the line numbers; in the case of unnumbered Meditations, a page number will be added.

2. All citations of Herbert's poems are from *Works*, edited by Hutchinson.

3. Not the gender, but the maturity of Taylor's persona is the question most commonly at issue. In Meditation 1.34, Taylor deprecates his poetic prattling as "Non-Sense" which still "very Pleasant is / To Parents, flowing from the Lisping Child" (1.34:7–8), a posture before God that Scheick dubs "characteristic" for Taylor (*Will*, 110). Meditating upon a ritual in which he ingests signifiers of Christ's body and blood, Taylor finds an injunction to imitate the life of Christ specifically in his role as the perfectly compliant son (*Christographia*, 34). But the child persona is not pervasive in the *Meditations*, nor does it fully capture the eroticism, subjection, violent displacement, and irreducible difference from God that characterize many of Taylor's self-representations.

4. All citations of Donne's poems are from *Poems* edited by Grierson.

5. Grabo's recent revision of his celebrated 1961 study of Taylor reinforces my sense of the importance of "difference" for Taylor's poetry. Buttressing his earlier claims for Taylor's participation in "a mystical literary tradition without himself being a mystic," Grabo finds himself persuaded that Taylor's overriding theme was "the failure to attain mystical assurance" of his grace and salvation (*Edward Taylor*, xi).

6. Taylor's emphasis on the importance of sacramental worship was part of a larger movement. In 1690, eight years after Taylor began composing the *Preparatory Meditations*, Cotton Mather published *A Companion for Communicants*, the first sacramental handbook to be printed in New England. Soon, a flood of sacramental manuals poured into the colonies, bringing with the renewed interest in sacramental piety a new receptivity to the symbolic in Puritan culture. For an account of this renewed sacramental piety in New England, and an estimation of Taylor's place in it, see Holifield, 197–224.

7. Rowe comments: "The church militant in New England seems less substantial, more ephemeral to Taylor's introspective imagination than the church triumphant, wherein each saint as a Bride would be wed to Christ the Bridegroom for eternity—a nuptial that his final meditations (1713–25) on Canticles joyfully celebrate" (*Saint and Singer*, xii).

8. In a discussion of Taylor's concerns with sin and purity in relation to the sacrament, Rowe points out how he harps on the Old Testament trial of an alleged adulteress who must "drinke the bitter Water" to prove herself a harlot. Taylor interprets this bitter water as a type of the sacramental elements; thus, "Depending upon his inward pollution or holiness, the gospel partaker of the Lord's Supper, comparable to the lewd woman, will be either refreshed or cursed, subject to 'Eternal Salvation, or Damnation' (*Upon the Types of the Old Testament* [by Edward Taylor], p. 632)" (*Saint and Singer*, 142–43).

9. Although the majority of scholars concur on the conservatively orthodox nature of Taylor's theology, David Parker argues that in relation to preparation understood in its wider context, Taylor was "actually more liberal than Stoddard" (259).

10. Grabo, as mentioned above, feels perfectly comfortable with claims of Taylor's mysticism (see n. 5 above). Rowe summarizes the debate over Taylor's orthodoxy that stems from a view of the *Meditations* on Canticles as themselves outside the pale of Puritan poetics, and she demonstrates convincingly that Taylor's interpretation of Canticles falls well within the mainstream tradition of Puritan exegesis; see "Sacred or Profane?"

11. The most thorough list of treatments of Taylor's use of Canticles is Rowe, *Saint and Singer*, 328–29, n. 18. I have consulted the discussions in Rowe, "Sacred or Profane?"; Lowance, 91–96; Lewalski, 416–25; Hammond; and Watters, 167–87. Lewalski gives a good deal of space to Taylor's Canticles *Meditations*, but she often resists the implications of her readings. Her treatment of the late poems is cramped by an overriding concern to defend Taylor against the charge of mysticism.

12. Gelpi finally argues that "Taylor's poems represent his attempt to pitch himself beyond the paradoxes and divisions of our natural experience, epitomized in the sexual polarity, into a transpolar, transsexual, androgynous wholeness of mind and heart and soul posited in the images of God husbanding human nature and manhood brided to Godhead" (42)—a position quoted approvingly by Rowe (*Saint and Singer*, 258). I wholly disagree with this conclusion, but I find Gelpi's exploration of Taylor's "strategies" extremely helpful.

13. See also Corum's perceptive analysis of the "gender structure" of Puritan heaven before and after Satan's rebellion in *Paradise Lost* (127–33).

14. According to Grabo, Taylor knew Bernard's sermons on the "Cantica Canticorum" (*Edward Taylor*, 49).

15. Hammond points out the parallel, but takes the relationship between the Song and the sacrament no further. It is important to emphasize the interdependence of the two discourses, especially in the light of Brumm's claim that in the last fifty Meditations on Canticles "the word of the Bible has now become entirely symbolical, and topics specifically connected with the Lord's Supper have disappeared" (*American Thought*, 62). Meditations 2.157A and 2.157B, which meditate on the verse, "He brought me into the Banqueting house and his banner over me was Love" (Cant. 2:4), are specifically concerned with discovering sacramental imagery in the drama of Canticles. Rowe, who argues persuasively for the interrelation of the two discourses on the basis of shared typological imagery, provides a more detailed discussion of these two Meditations (*Saint and Singer*, 257–61). However, her assertion of the connection between the two discourses finally does not illuminate Taylor's self-representational strategies. In tracing the typological manifestations of Taylor's "wedden garment" in the sacramentalism of his sermons and meditations, Rowe confines it to Taylor's final years with the comment that "the twin notions of a wedding feast and wedding robes momentarily enter in Meditation II.71, not at all in Sermon II.71, and then prominently only among the later meditations on the sacraments and Canticles" (211). In the final chapter, she asserts that "Taylor's Christocentric typology leads almost inevitably to his final

poetic epithalamium" (258), while a few pages later she parallels Taylor's use of types, or "Christomimetic imitations," with "the allegorical roles of Canticles" as means of "seeking to insert himself in a nearer relationship with Christ" (263). By omitting any consideration of gender, Rowe presents Taylor's strategies for self-representation as if they were unproblematic. In a treatment of the Lord's Supper as a figure for the "celestial wedding feast," she points out that Taylor "envisions himself under several aspects: a ministerial disciple, comparable to Christ's apostles, who must preach the Word and administer the Sacrament; an elect saint who like all other 'Subjects' and 'Guests' must come to the Supper 'drest / In Spirituall apparell whitend white'; and a betrothed saint who anticipates the heavenly nuptials for which all earthly meditations and robings in the 'Wedden garment' are mere preliminaries" (227); but she does not note any conflicts or tension among these positions. The same is true of her discussion of Taylor's identification with the Bride of Canticles, which she treats as merely "the most effective scriptural text through which to express both his desire and satisfaction" (257–58).

16. Taylor expands upon his notion of the correct sacramental "frame" of mind in his *Treatise*. The effect of discerning grace and one's worthiness to attend the Supper brought communicants to "an eucharistic frame . . . of spiritual thanksgiving and praise to God" (*Treatise*, 159), the "frame" of mind, heart, and soul suitable for humans experiencing the "mystical union" with God through communion with Christ. He advised his congregation:

> See that you get, and mentain a festival frame of spirit spiritually. . . . Whet thy appetite unto the provision. Hunger and thirst after this table; eat and drink liberally at it. Christ saith, "Eat, O friends. Drink, yea, drink abundantly, O beloved!" Keep a right spiritually festival frame of spirit, in respect unto God that invites, and Christ that weds thee, and the Spirit that adorns thee, and this is a spirit of love, self-denial, humility, joy, thankfulness, reverence, honor, and obedience. And in respect unto the guests, and this consists in love, meekness, sympathy, condescention, affability, honor, pleasantness, delightfulness, holy conference and the like. And in respect unto the provision, and this lies in a right appetite unto it, esteeming of it, hungering and thirsting after it, relishing, eating, and digesting of it. (199–200)

The hungering and thirsting heart is a common description of what the Puritans thought of as "directed desire," the "natural" longing of the mind that could be turned to a transcendently good object—here, the spiritual provisions of the Supper—by the disciplining of reason, will, and imagination (Clark, "'Crucified Phrase,'" 284–85). The arousal of "directed desire" through meditation was necessary to a correct sacramental frame.

17. Unfortunately, Karl Keller's notion of gender is unhistoricized and he assumes essentialized definitions of masculine and feminine. For example, pointing out how "election takes on the imagery of seduction, almost a rape of the will"

(an idea Taylor would have, at least consciously, rejected), he comments: "At first he is feeble (therefore feminine), but after the divine rape he takes on a more active, masculine role, in imitation of Christ the Lover" as he is manifested in the Lord's Supper (214).

18. Fish's discussion of the progressive stages in "the dialectic of the self" in the poetry of George Herbert is relevant here and sheds light on the gendered nature of representations of desire. In the poet's determination to "let go" and "do" nothing, he also lets go of conventionally significant distinctions; the examples Fish offers are between "loved and loving man, between the heart as agent and Christ as agent, between letting in and forcing entry." Such distinctions, Fish argues, "are no longer operative. In a world where Christ occupies every position and initiates every action, ambiguity—of place, of person, of agency—is the true literalism. His word is all" (173). These distinctions have a peculiarly sexual cast, summed up in the difference between voluntary and coerced sex.

For a discussion of desire in its role in Puritan faculty psychology and semiology, see Clark, "'Crucified Phrase.'" Puritans theorized what Clark calls "a *directed desire*," which had to be moved by reason, will, and a directed imagination, working together, to lead desire to the transcendent good (284–85). Taylor explores the subject in Meditation 2.42, where his worldly desires overtake his desire for God and so he asks for "one Sparke of heavenly fire" to "burn my trash up" and produce "refin'de desire" (ll. 7–9). His detachment from the "insurrections" against the free movement of Christ's "good Spirit" is frightening; one senses the enormous effort required to achieve passivity in such a system when, in the final prayer, Taylor cries, "I thee implore to make / Me, what thou, and thy Father ever love. / Empt me of Sin: Fill mee with Grace" (ll. 43–45).

19. But, Leverenz contends, Taylor's playing at being female, which he wittily calls "spiritual cross-dressing," springs more from the "framework of patriarchal manhood" than from Puritan doctrine. It is not clear, however, to what extent masculinity as a class-based ideology is separable from the spiritual/social values disseminated by Puritan theological doctrine. (Leverenz's comments were made at the 1987 MLA Early American Division meeting in San Francisco and are extrapolated from my notes.) Leverenz refers specifically to Taylor's typological and personal minor poems, which he sees having a "gender frame." He historicizes the class-based ideology of masculinity for nineteenth-century U.S. culture in his new book, *Manhood and the American Renaissance*.

20. For an emblem that answers this description very closely, see Lewalski, fig. 11, and her discussion of Taylor and the emblem tradition (209–12).

21. In his discussion of the saint's consent, Scheick introduces the same stanza, saying, "The imagery of the following passages suggests this intimate and inseparable union between the two wills" (*Will*, 72). Omitted is any discussion of the extreme price at which saints experienced such intimacy and union.

22. Hammond, reading this Meditation, suggests that by focusing on Canticles,

"the Bible's most intense view of celestial joy, [Taylor] left himself ample room to fail, because the promised fulfillment of the Canticles vision in heaven decreased the need to achieve it fully in this world" (201).

23. In an earlier close reading of Meditation 1.6 in the light of Taylor's sacramental semiology, I demonstrated how the effacement of the saint's active self requires his transformation from writer to reader; see "Semiotics of the Sacrament."

24. See Luxon, "Puritan Allegory," 87–105, and "Pilgrim's Passive Progress," 91–96.

25. For accounts of contemporary influences on Taylor's interpretation of Canticles and how he uses them, see Rowe, "Sacred or Profane?" and Hammond. This dialogue can be seen at work in Meditation 2.138, where Taylor considers several readings of Canticles 6:6, which describes the Spouse's teeth as "a flock of Sheep that come Up from Washing whereof every one bears twins," and discards them in favor of his own reading, which encompasses the sacrament of the Supper. For Taylor, the Spouse's teeth are Faith and Meditation, the two elements necessary for "Chewing Spiritually the Cud" of the sacramental "Meat and food," fitting it "for the Stomach there to sooke / In its Concoction" to produce "Choice Spirituall Cheer" (2.138:44–58). Eating becomes the primarily hermeneutic act. For a more detailed analysis of this poem, see Rowe, "Sacred or Profane?" 135–36.

26. Watters points out that Puritan gravestone carvers of the period represented the face of the Spouse as the face of resurrected saints, part of the eschatological system that Taylor shared (185).

27. Rowe, who employs this Meditation as one of her test-cases to disprove critical claims of Taylor's un-Puritan sensuality, demonstrates that his allegory of pregnancy is "an appropriate analogy for the Church's new covenant state of redemption" and would have been accepted by his colleagues "as an appropriate spiritual explication of Canticles 7:2" ("Sacred or Profane?" 133–34). He used it in an earlier Meditation, 2.80, to explore John 6:53: "Except you eate the flesh of the Son of Man, etc. ye have no Life in you," and imagined his own soul as a womb impregnated by Christ, the "Spermodote" (l. 31); "When of this Life my soule with Child doth spring," he concluded, "The Babe of Life swath'de up in Grace shall sing" (ll. 47–48). Rowe confirms that other Puritan readers (male) develop the metaphor of pregnancy to describe the formation and nourishment of new converts ("Sacred or Profane?" 134).

Chapter 4

1. Recorded in *Transcript of the Registers of the Worshipful Company of Stationers for 1640–1708*, 1:346. For an account of the publishing history of this volume, its contents, and its significance, with which I often disagree, see White's critical

biography, *Anne Bradstreet: "The Tenth Muse,"* chap. 8. White's unironic use of the 1650 title as the subtitle of her biography implies that she regards it as a compliment, not a put-down. She argues that putting Bradstreet in the context of her female poetic predecessors and contemporaries shows that *"The Tenth Muse* was the first printed work of poetry by an English woman that was not liable to be viewed as something of a curiosity, because of either the exalted position of the author or the very limited nature of the subject" (256).

2. All citations from Bradstreet's poetry, unless otherwise specified, are from *The Works of Anne Bradstreet*, edited by Hensley. Line numbers follow the citation. On the stress colonial Puritans placed upon the education of children for the purposes of promoting spiritual growth, see Morgan, *Puritan Family*, 87–108. He makes no distinction between the sexes, though all the children he refers to are male. Ulrich does not discuss colonial women's education, except to say in an aside that "formal book-learning . . . was denied to women" (132). Morison asserts that female literacy was very low in the colonies, and that, while girls attended primary schools, they learned only to read, not to write (83–85). See also C. Walker, 3–4.

3. The role of women in Renaissance and seventeenth-century culture, and attitudes toward their education and visibility, have been much discussed in recent years. See especially Kelly-Gadol's ground-breaking essay, "Did Women Have a Renaissance?"; the collection of primary documents in Henderson and McManus, *Half Humankind*; and Hannay, *Silent But for the Word*, especially Hannay's introduction and Lamb's essay, "The Cooke Sisters." On the connection between woman's fame and ungovernable bodies, see A. R. Jones. W. Martin argues for the existence of a New England "Puritan bias against intellectual women" and cites the fate of Anne Yale Hopkins (mentioned above) (58). For the Puritan bias against women's visibility, she cites the case of Anne Hutchinson, and this frank opinion by Thomas Parker, who condemned his sister in a public letter for publishing a book in London: "Your printing of a Book beyond the Custom of your Sex, doth rankly smell" (W. Martin, 58). The extent to which women internalized the censorship of their public voices is recorded in this ambivalent comment made by Dorothy Osborne in a letter to her fiancé, Sir William Temple, in 1653, referring to the well-published and well-publicized writer Margaret Cavendish: "let me ask you if you have seen a book of poems newly come out, made by my Lady Newcastle? For God's sake if you meet with it send it to me; they say 'tis ten times more extravagant than her dress. Sure, the poor woman is a little distracted, she could never be so ridiculous else as to venture at writing books, and in verse too. If I should not sleep this fortnight I should not come to that" (Osborne, 103).

4. In an earlier essay, "Anne Bradstreet Wrestles with the Renaissance," I did a detailed analysis of Bradstreet's complicated bid for poetic voice and authority in the androcentric Elizabethan poetic tradition. It is not surprising that in her early public poetry, she positions herself as a "son" wishing to inherit the mantle of

several awe-inspiring fathers; yet she ultimately finds solace in the figure of Queen Elizabeth, a woman who, by virtue of her many self-representations, evades gynesis. My focus on how and why Bradstreet's self-representations became cultural objects of value and exchange finds support in Susanne Kappeler's explanation of the function of representation, which she applies to pornography. She argues that "representations are not just a matter of mirrors, reflections, keyholes. Somebody is making them, and somebody is looking at them, through a complex array of means and conventions. . . . they have a continued existence in reality as objects of exchange; they have a genesis in material production. They are more 'real' than the reality they are said to represent or reflect" (3). The first move in her feminist critique of pornography is shifting the ground from a focus on content to an analysis of representation itself, and especially the "crucial factors" of authors and perceivers—roles taken up by social beings in a context that is simultaneously political, cultural, and economic. In other words, Kappeler takes "representation" out of the rarefied atmosphere of the "aesthetic." I refocus in a similar way by shifting the emphasis from Bradstreet's "art" to a context for that art and an examination of how her authorship, her agency, has been appropriated by her family, who reauthor and authorize her for a cultural consumption that benefits them.

5. White calls this poem "a by-product" of "The Four Monarchies" and says that "it undoubtedly accompanied the manuscript of her long verse-history when that was finally put into the hands of her father and her circle of close friends" (238). Clearly, then, Bradstreet felt disapproval before she was published, but her family and friends approved of her poetry, which is perhaps why she persevered. McElrath and Robb, who argue that Bradstreet's poetic activity "may indicate that her society was less repressive in its attitude toward women than we imagine" (Bradstreet, Complete Works, xii), read "The Prologue" as "raillery" in which male readers must be "willing to have their male noses playfully tweaked by a worthy antagonist" (xiii). Given this attitude, one wonders what kind of generalizations they would draw from the Bay Colony's treatment of Anne Hutchinson.

6. Koehler points out that the three other works by women out of the 911 published in New England in the seventeenth century were Mary Rowlandson's Indian captivity narrative (1682), M. Hooper's Lamentations for her Sons, Poisoned by Eating Mushrooms, August 1, 1693 (1694), and Valedictory and Monitory-Writing (1682), a private journal kept by Sarah Goodhue of Ipswich (54).

7. The narrator of The Scarlet Letter is contradictory on Hester's art as a signifier of her love of beauty and "voluptuous nature" or of her need for expression. Needlework, he says, "was the art—then, as now, almost the only one within a woman's grasp. . . . She had in her nature a rich, voluptuous, Oriental characteristic,—a taste for the gorgeously beautiful, which, save in the exquisite productions of her needle, found nothing else, in all the possibilities of her life, to exercise itself upon. Women derive a pleasure, incomprehensible to the other sex, from the delicate toil of the needle. To Hester Prynne it might have been a mode

of expressing, and therefore soothing, the passion of her life. Like all other joys, she rejected it as sin" (61, 63). The logic here is insidious. Men limit women to the art of embroidery, and then observe that they derive an incomprehensible amount of pleasure from it, and might even use it as a means to express their frustration at being limited to a decorative form of darning not particularly valued by society except insofar as it indicates that women are, indeed, in their places. The narrator of *The Marble Faun* attempts to redeem the dichotomy of women as either artists or seamstresses in a long meditation on Miriam, a painter, "busied with the feminine task of mending a pair of gloves." He concludes, however, that sewing is somehow synonymous with femaleness: "Methinks it is a token of healthy and gentle characteristics when women of high thoughts and accomplishments love to sew; especially as they are never more at home with their own hearts than while so occupied" (36). For a contemporary attempt to undo the bias against needlework as a devalued women's art, see Judy Chicago, *Embroidering Our Heritage*, an account of her feminist art work, *The Dinner Party*.

8. The whole issue of an authoritative text remains problematic for Bradstreet studies, since her published poems first appear under an ambiguous—and, given Woodbridge's manipulations, a deliberately ambiguous—authority. Her authorial oversight is proleptically coopted from the first public appearance by men anxious about the precedent it would set. The persisting ambiguity over just what is Bradstreet's own work, and what is not, is potent testimony to the success of Woodbridge's strategy of subtle deauthorization of the very work he pretends to celebrate in public. It is on the basis of this indeterminacy that McElrath and Robb decided to use the text of the 1650 edition of *The Tenth Muse* as their authoritative text for Bradstreet's published poems, rather than the second edition, *Several Poems*. In my mind, this represents a conservative choice that prefers versions of Bradstreet's early poetry, which we know to have been published without her supervision, over versions of poems that we have some evidence to indicate she revised to some extent. The McElrath and Robb edition serves, appropriately, as a convenient record of Bradstreet's poetry as it was authorized for publication by a male relative who usurped her authority.

9. The term "muse," according to the *OED*, was used occasionally in the seventeenth century to mean "poet," "one under the guidance of a Muse"; see also Milton's *Lycidas*, ll. 19–22. But the inflexible gender roles of Muse and poet would stem any confusion in the metonymy. For evidence of Bradstreet's uncomfortable relationship with the Muses of classical tradition, see "Elegy upon . . . Philip Sidney," ll. 70–85.

10. DeShazer surveys the literary history of the Muse of male poets as well as, more recently, female poets; see her chap. 1, "'A Whole New Psychic Geography': Women Poets and Creative Identity" (1–44).

11. The poem was first published in *Partisan Review* in 1953, and then in book form here in 1956, and in London in 1959. All citations are from the 1956 version, with stanza and line numbers following in parenthesis.

12. Carol Johnson dwells on this at length. Comparing Berryman's approach to that of Ford Madox Ford in *The Good Soldier*, she declares: "the whole narrative responsibility rests with a speaker who, in seeing and telling all, perceives less than the reader must through her agency comprehend. She must represent a good deal more than she relates and she must elicit a sympathy larger than the sum of her virtues, her writings, or her suffrances requires. She must, in short, assume the dimensions of a person in order to become an acceptable archetype. And for this it is positively preferable that she should have been, like her unfortunate models Du Bartas and Quarles, an undistinguished versifier. (In fact she is far more in the American vein by being the first with the most: the first woman to write English verse in America, 7,000 lines of it.) The stature which her own art cannot confer accrues in another century through her subjection to superior praise" (392–93). In a funny way, the last part of this comment unconsciously redeems Bradstreet's reputation. Johnson obliquely acknowledges the amazing fact of her poetic achievement and recognizes that Berryman's praise constitutes a "subjection."

13. I am thinking particularly of Louise Bogan, who in 1935 wrote to her editor, John Wheelock, that "Malcolm Cowley, a month or so ago asked me to edit an anthology of female verse, to be used in the pages of the New Republic. They have, as you know, already published groups of Middle-Western verse, and what-not. They are now about to divide mankind horizontally rather than vertically, sexually rather than geographically.—As you might have expected, I turned this pretty job down; the thought of corresponding with a lot of female songbirds made me acutely ill. It is hard enough to bear with my own lyric side" (Bogan, 86). Robert Lowell put the ultimate negative spin on the term when he began his introduction to the posthumously published *Ariel*, with the sensational assertion that in these poems "Sylvia Plath becomes herself, becomes something imaginary, newly, wildly and subtly created—hardly a person at all, or a woman, certainly not another 'poetess,' but one of those super-real, hypnotic, great classical heroines" (vii).

14. See, for example, Holder's essay, which catalogues the discrepancies between the poem's historical claims and Berryman's major source for Bradstreet's life and circumstances, the already semifictional biography by Helen Campbell, *Anne Bradstreet and Her Time* (1891). Holder argues that because Berryman's approach in the poem is "Yeatsian," he was drawn to a figure like Bradstreet who had an interesting life [really, one that would serve his purposes], but was a dull poet (16). He, as other critics, seems to miss the point that nothing would have been known about Bradstreet if it were not for her poetry.

As for critical suspicion of Berryman's procedures in casting the character of "Anne Bradstreet," Provost has a purchase on his motivations, yet she joins the (mostly male) chorus in calling Bradstreet "Anne." The finale of "Homage," Provost says, eerily echoing John Winthrop's attitudes toward Anne Hopkins, "restores the woman to her proper place . . . serv[ing] to further, rather than hinder, the poet's work" (73), and she adds this disturbing disclaimer: "It might be appropriate to note here that I do not intend a feminist bias. The pain of feeling powerless and the attempt to regain power happen here to be male, but could as easily be found in the works of Rich, Piercy, et al." (79 n. 13). Perhaps—but powerlessness for women has different roots, psychologically and historically, and is not necessarily addressed by dominating others. Yet even Rich, in her foreword to Hensley's edition of Bradstreet's *Works*, called "Homage" "a great poem" (xx n. 7), though ten years later she decided that she had been writing from an androcentric perspective. In a passing comment, Watts calls the poem "macho" ("'The posy unity,'" 34 n. 4). Feminist criticism has allowed readers a more critical perspective. Ostriker sees the poem's opening gambit as "good seducer's tactics," and, noting how he slights Bradstreet's poetry, concludes that "Berryman created, out of his own yearning, a lover-anima-muse figure who would never be seen as a colleague, collaborator, or equal" (26–27). Gilbert and Gubar find, similarly, that despite Berryman's ostensible reverence for Bradstreet, he, like fellow poets Roethke and Lowell, who celebrate female contemporaries, has "made a critical gesture that suggests some measure of hostility toward literary women" (158).

15. Gilbert and Gubar point out that Berryman does go on to fantasize about sex with Dickinson and other female poets in the following passage from *The Dream Songs*, no. 187 (1969):

> Them lady poets must not marry, pal.
> Miss Dickinson—fancy in Amherst bedding her.
> Fancy a lark with Sappho,
> a tumble in the bushes with Miss Moore,
> a spoon with Emily, while Charlotte glare.
> Miss Bishop's too noble-O.
>   (206; in Gilbert and Gubar, 159)

16. Other critics have come to similar conclusions without focusing on the biographical context of the poem. Mazzaro extends Holder's speculation that Berryman's interest in Bradstreet is "Yeatsian," and he suggests that "Bradstreet is herself an antithetical self for the poet" (125), making her both subject and object. Haffenden enlarges upon other critical hints about Bradstreet as a "mask" for Berryman and declares that "Berryman is in fact treating his own guilt feelings by shedding them in the person of Anne Bradstreet. . . . She is substantiated in order that Berryman may introduce himself almost as a projection of her fantasy" (10–11).

17. Compare Milton's description of Eve in relation to Adam: "Thy likeness, thy fit help, thy other self, / Thy wish exactly to thy heart's desire" (*Paradise Lost*, 8.450–51).

18. No one has pointed out that Berryman finds this startling image in Bradstreet's poetry and prose. In her letter to her children, she recounts: "when I have been in sickness and pain, I have thought if the Lord would but lift up the

light of His countenance upon me, although He ground me to powder, it would be but light to me" (*Works*, 243). The image is treated emblematically in Meditation 19 of her "Meditations Divine and Moral": "Corn, till it have past through the mill and been ground to powder, is not fit for bread. God so deals with his servants: he grinds them with grief and pain til they turn to dust, and then are they fit manchet for his mansion" (*Works*, 275). In "As Weary Pilgrim," she describes the "grinding pains" that afflicted her frail body (l. 28).

19. Berryman insisted that *Homage* was a historical poem, and he liked to quote Robert Lowell's pronouncement that it was "the most resourceful historical poem in our literature" ("Changes," 101). In a later interview, however, he admitted knowing that Bradstreet loved her husband "with a passion that can hardly be described, through their whole life together, from the age of sixteen on. I decided to tempt her. I could only do this in a fantasy; the problem was to make the fantasy believable" (Stitt, 196).

20. Between the *Sonnets* to Lise and *Homage*, Berryman worked on a series of poems concerning victims of the Holocaust entitled *The Black Book*, which he abandoned because the topic was too painful. During this period he also had recurring dreams in which he killed women (Provost, 70, 78; Haffenden, 19).

21. Berryman describes the voices' dialogue as "a sort of extended witch-seductress and demon-lover bit" ("Changes," 101).

22. Berryman's wife at the time, Eileen Simpson, records in her memoir that when Berryman finished the passage on Bradstreet's delivery, he threw himself down and said, "Well, I'm exhausted. I've been going through the couvade. The little monster nearly killed *me*" (226). Provost points out that accounts of Berryman's creative process repeatedly compare it to birth-throes; she argues that the "children" he wanted were his poems, birthed just as women birth children, but at their expense (76). Stanford Friedman insists that "Men's use of the metaphor [of childbirth] begins in distance from and attraction to the Other" and appears to be a "tribute to woman's special generative powers," but is ultimately "an appropriation of women's (pro)creativity [because it] subtly helps to perpetuate the confinement of women to procreation" (84).

23. See, for example, Milton's famous invocations in *Paradise Lost*, a text highly relevant to *Homage*. Book 1 begins, "Of man's first disobedience, [etc.] . . . / Sing heavenly Muse . . ." (ll. 1–6).

24. Jardine ends her study of gynesis with a discussion of some of the differences between gynesis in Anglo-American cultures, particularly the United States, and in France. One major factor is the divergent symbolic traditions of the French Catholic monarchy, with its emphasis on an authoritative father figure and the Virgin Mother as "sacred object," both conspicuously absent in the Protestant democracy of the United States. She argues that whereas French male gynesis is an internal process of erotic merging with and excavation of the feminine, Anglo-American gynesis tends to be external and representational, an evacuation of the feminine, "an avoidance strategy mediated by technique," "a technical mastery

protecting the self from the dangerous power of the signifier" (233–34). Berryman's poem exhibits this protective deployment of technical mastery. *Homage* has been lauded for its technical innovations, but critics have also been struck by the "peculiar energy of the language," which draws attention away from Bradstreet to itself and its creator, and which comes into being at her expense. The language that male critics use to describe this, records obliquely the violence (to woman, language, style—all feminine) that they perceive but do not name. Stanley Kunitz holds that "the poem as a whole lacks inherent imaginative grandeur; whatever effect of magnitude it achieves has been beaten into it"; for John Ciardi, Berryman's linguistic "essence . . . is the compression of the language to squeeze out all but the most essential syntax," and he questions "whether the passion is as truly love as he asserts, or more nearly a thing literary and made"; James Dickey complains that "Berryman is a poet so preoccupied with poetic effects as to be totally in their thrall" (all quoted in Mazzaro, 125–26). The general critical opinion has been that Berryman's "dense verbal thicket" (Dickey) helps him evade the problems of "self."

25. Mather's discussion of poetry occurs in his *Manuductio ad Ministerium* (1726), reprinted in Miller and Johnson, *The Puritans*, 684–89. Addressing fledgling ministers, he recommends that they "make a little recreation of poetry in the midst of your painful studies," but he warns them, "Withhold thy throat from thirst" and "especially preserve the chastity of your soul from the dangers you may incur, by a conversation with muses that are no better than harlots" (686). Clearly, poetry had its dangers.

26. I am summarizing Henderson and McManus, 16–19; their entire first chapter is an excellent introduction to the history of the debates in England (3–46). For an account of the early continental history of this "querelle" and its effect on feminist discourse, see Kelly.

27. W. Martin lays out the issues in the Hutchinson affair (59–65) and concludes: "Surely the lesson of Anne Hutchinson was not lost on Anne Bradstreet" (64). For an extensive comparison/contrast of the two Puritan women, see Anne King.

28. I recount the major outlines of Sarah Dudley's life as told by White in *Anne Bradstreet*. Martin, in *American Triptych*, puts the story into the context of the Bay's treatment of other rebellious women. However, details that came to light in the course of research conducted by a student of mine cast suspicion on the character of Sarah's first husband. According to Augustine Jones, Thomas Dudley's biographer, Benjamin Keayne abandoned his wife and went to England, leaving her and his father in charge of an estate in Lynn, Massachusetts. Jones asserts that "it seems quite possible that Keayne went to England to avoid his American creditors" (469–70). Keayne's father, Robert, was charged on several occasions with swindling his associates and with drunkenness (Bailyn, 577). Sarah Keayne followed her husband to England and arrived penniless, having met with disaster on the rough seas (Jones, 470). Jones suggests that this misfortune caused Keayne to

repudiate his wife. In order to do so, however, he claimed in three letters—written to John Cotton, Mr. Wilson, and Thomas Dudley—that she had committed adultery as well as sacrilege and had infected him with venereal disease. In these letters, Keayne writes that Sarah "has vnwived her selfe": "she had ruined her selfe & would doe mee, if shee longer continued here; & hazarded my bodie by infection received from her self," and that "[this] vnsatiable desire & lust of a wife that in requitall impoysoned my body wth such a running of the reines that would, if not (through mercie) cured, haue turned vnto the french Pox & so indangered my life, & this I tould her selfe must needs come from her I haueing never knowne any woman but herselfe" (*Suffolk Deeds*, 1:84). The only mention of Sarah's daughter comes in a financial connection: in his will, Robert Keayne specified that "Sarah Dudley, now Sarah Pacye, may haue no part of my property, that I have bestowed upon her daughter" (Keayne, 48). Jones speculates that Benjamin Keayne's accusatory letters were false. It is interesting, however, that he, like John Winthrop, associates wayward sexual desire, venereal disease, and female visibility and volubility, and thus connects Sarah Dudley's "sins" with Anne Hutchinson's "heresies." I am indebted for this information to Shelley Bennett, a student in my course "Visions and Re-visions of Puritan New England" in Spring 1990.

29. Barker-Benfield analyzes several passages and recurring images in Winthrop's account that detail women's "seduction" of men's minds with their tongues. "The metaphor," he concludes, "is one of woman raping men" (78–79).

30. Kappeler's explanation of the function of representation, which she applies to pornography, fits Bradstreet's situation as I am presenting it. For a summary of her argument, see note 4 above.

31. Swetnam's comment echoes Henry Smith's advice in *A Preparative to Marriage* (58) and thus must have been fairly commonplace for the age.

32. I do not quote this merely to be polemical. A phrase in the longer passage in *The Simple Cobler* from which this scurrilous, though no doubt humorously exaggerated, opinion appears, is echoed in line 11 of Ward's poetic tribute to Bradstreet (quoted above) and connects them: "To speak moderately, I truly confesse it is beyond the ken of my understanding to conceive, how those women should have any true grace, or valuable vertue, that have so little wit, as to disfigure themselves with such exotick garbes, as not only dismantles their native lovely lustre, but transclouts them into gantbar-geese, ill-shapen-shotten-shell-fish, Egyptian Hyeroglyphicks, or at the best into French flurts of the pastery, which a proper English woman should scorne with her heels: *it is no marvell* that they weare drailes on the hinder part of their heads, having nothing as it seems in the fore-part, but a few Squirrils brains to help them frisk from one ill-favour'd fashion to another" (Ward, 26; emphasis added).

33. White cites an essay by Hans Galinsky, who concludes that Bradstreet "transplants and transforms" the style and structures of Du Bartas (65). Rich gives a detailed account of their stylistic differences (xii–xiii).

34. For an account and critique of women's activity and visibility during this period, see Mack, "Women Prophets during the English Civil War," and Thomas, "Women and the Civil War Sects."

35. See, for example, W. Martin, 43–48, and Eberwein.

36. Watts gives as her source for Mercy Woodbridge's poem Samuel Kettell, ed., *Specimens of American Poetry*, 3 vols. (Boston: S. G. Goodrich, 1829), 1:xxvii–xxviii.

37. Stanford Friedman provides an interesting example of a male writer excusing his brainchild's flaws on account of its premature birth. James Smith, in his "Epistle Dedicatory, to the Reader" (1658), claims: "Curteous Reader, I had not gone my full time when by a sudden fright, occasioned by the Beare and Wheelbarrow on the Bank-side, I fell in travaile, and therefore cannot call this a timely issue, but a Mischance, which I must put out to the world to nurse; hoping it will be fostered with the greater care, because of its own innocency" (97 n. 34). The difference between Smith's and Bradstreet's "premature" births is that Smith's was accidental, Bradstreet's forced.

38. This critical attitude is summed up by Requa, who says: "The public voice is imitative, the private voice original" (4). See C. Walker, who disagrees (156 n. 12). Like Walker, I cannot imagine poems more "personal" than Bradstreet's three early elegies.

39. Shakespeare treated this paradox in "The Phoenix and the Turtle" (1601):

So they loved as love in twain
Had the essence but in one;
Two distincts, division none;
Number there in love was slain.
(ll. 25–28)

Donne examined the circumstances of lovers' separation in "A Valediction: Forbidding Mourning" (1633):

Our two soules therefore, which are one,
    Though I must goe, endure not yet
A breach, but an expansion,
    Like gold to ayery thinnesse beat.
(ll. 21–24)

See also Sonnets 88 to 100 in Sidney's *Astrophel and Stella*, where Astrophel mourns Stella's absence.

Chapter 5

1. This phrase appears on the monument given to the city of Providence by the heirs of Governor James Fenner and erected in 1906 at the foot of Williams

Street, in Roger Williams Square. The dedication reads: "To the memory of
Roger Williams, the Apostle of Soul Liberty. . . . Below this spot, then at the
water's edge, stood the rock on which, according to tradition, Roger Williams, an
exile for his devotion to freedom of conscience, landed 1636." A bronze bas-relief
depicts the landing (M. E. Hall, 56).

2. J. L. Davis argues that an "intimate acquaintance with Narragansett culture
provided the catalyst for both his powerful attack upon New England theocracy
and his conception of an ideal commonwealth with which to supplant it" (603).
Perry Miller put it succinctly when he said of Williams's central ideas, "They are
all present, at least by implication, in the *Key*" (*Roger Williams*, 77). For example,
Williams vigorously opposed the Puritan orthodoxy's monopoly upon the truth
and its ministers' unwillingness to relinquish an absolutist conception of power,
which they located in a theocratic state. In his best-known tract, *The Bloudy Tenent
of Persecution*, published only ten months after the *Key*, Williams refuted John
Cotton's defense of state persecution of religious dissent, arguing that Christ did
not preach a new spiritual dispensation to be enforced by state power. The only
true conversion, he reasoned, proceeded from a conscience free and uncoerced;
all others were merely "formal," and were thus worse than having no religion at
all. "I desire all men and these worthy *Authors* of this Modell," Williams concluded, addressing in particular the New England clergy who in 1635 drew up a
"Model of Church and Civil Power," "to lay their hands upon their heart, and to
consider whether this *compulsion* of men to heare the *Word*, (as they say) whether it
carries men, to wit, to be of no *Religion* all their dayes, worse then the very Indians,
who dare not live without *Religion* according as they are perswaded" (*Bloudy
Tenent*, in *Complete Writings*, 3:290).

3. All citations are from Williams, *A Key into the Language of America*, edited by
Teunissen and Hinz. Page numbers in parenthesis follow citations. All other
references to Williams's work, unless specified, are from *The Complete Writings of
Roger Williams*, hereafter designated by *CW*.

4. Henson points out that in the discourse of the funeral elegy's portraiture,
"One of the most revered forms of zeal, unfortunately not available to native-born
Puritans, was emigration" (18). Bercovitch describes how Cotton Mather, in the
Magnalia, "speaks of the emigrants' flight from the Old World as an evangelical
call, and of their ocean-crossing as a spiritual rebirth" (*Puritan Origins*, 115), and
he concludes that "for many of New England's founders, the embarkation was a
literal one. Figurally and structurally, the migration to America displaces conversion as the crucial event"; he gives as an example Thomas Shepard, whose
"equation of new life with New World, and of baptism with the Atlantic as a
greater Red Sea, became a staple of early colonial autobiography" (118). Caldwell
also finds in first-generation conversion narratives that "migration . . . afforded a
test of that very inner heart that it was so vitally important to get to know" (128),
and that displacement "is meant to mark some kind of spiritual pivot"—but, in her
reading, the results of the test for first-generation Puritans are not positive (133).

5. It is important to note that "race" here refers somewhat inaccurately to indigenous peoples and not specifically to Africans, the meaning it takes on almost exclusively in the modern United States, and that colonists' attitudes to the native peoples of the New World differ substantially from modern attitudes toward specific racial groups. For a limited theoretical discussion of European attitudes toward the "otherness" or "alterity" of New World natives, see Todorov, *Conquest*; for its epistemological implications for Renaissance literature, see Greenblatt. Hulme explores the attitudes of Europeans growing out of their contact with Caribbean natives in *Colonial Encounters*. I have found Said's methodology in *Orientalism* extremely helpful. There were important differences in attitudes and approaches between Spanish/French (Catholic) and English/Dutch (Protestant) colonizers and missionaries, some of which are treated by Axtell. Cotton Mather's writings provide the best illustrations of the colonial Puritan attitude toward the Native Americans; see, for example, Bercovitch, *Puritan Origins*, 115; and Vaughan and Clark, 21. Hambrick-Stowe speculates that the emergence of violent imagery toward the end of the seventeenth century has more to do with the fact that the ocean-crossing as experience was no longer available to native-born, second-generation Puritans, and was replaced in the popular imagination by Indian captivity narratives (256–58). Kibbey, however, argues that the first generation "believed they had discovered apocalyptic enemies in the present, proper objects for violence who became the means for enacting the sacred figures of the Puritan imagination" (99), and that the Pequots "had become for the Puritans the living images of opposition to the New England Puritan living images of grace" (102). Jennings, whose radical ethnographic approach to the history of colonialism in the New World has profoundly influenced my views of European-Native contact, argues most persuasively that "a basic rule was that any given Englishman at any given time formed his views in accordance with his purposes. Those who came for quick plunder saw plots and malignancy on every side; in a mirror image of their own intent, their savages were sinister and treacherous. . . . When Indians were regarded as partners in profitable trade, they appeared less threatening, and their vices were excused. When they resisted eviction from lands wanted by the colonizers, they acquired demonic dimensions. When they were wanted as soldiers for war against the French, the martial abilities of these demons were appreciated rather than decried" (59). The last two cases particularly apply to the contact between the Massachusetts Bay Colony and surrounding tribes. If image mirrors intent, then Williams saw the natives as a mixture of wily survivors and potential saints.

6. Teunissen and Hinz do an insightful analysis of Williams's identification with Paul, from which I have liberally borrowed in the above passage. They find some internal evidence for seeing the Narragansett as "the American counterpart of the Athenian; Roger Williams, in bringing to them the Pauline 'Glad tidings,' is the seventeenth-century Apostle to the Gentiles" (43). The passage they cite to reinforce Williams's identification with Paul reiterates his condemnation of his own

kind: "In journeyings often, in perils of waters, in perils of robbers, in perils by mine own countrymen, in perils by the heathen, in perils in the city, in perils in the wilderness, in perils in the sea, in perils among false brethren . . . (2 Cor. 11: 26–27)" (44). See their introduction to the *Key*, pp. 43–44, and "Roger Williams, St. Paul, and American Primitivism."

7. For example, the following verses were supposedly found in the pocket of Thomas Dudley (father of Anne Bradstreet), former governor and lieutenant governor of the colony and prominent hard-liner, at his death:

> Let men of God, in courts and churches, watch
> O'er such as do a *toleration* hatch
> Lest that ill egg bring forth a cockatrice
> To poison all with heresie and vice
> If men be left, and otherwise combine,
> My *Epitaph*'s, I DY'D NO LIBERTINE.
>
> (Mather, *Magnalia*, 1:134)

So threatening was toleration to the New England Puritan elite that Dudley pledged to go to his grave defending the God-appointed experiment in state-enforced spiritual purity. He warns that men left on their own without strong watchdog and disciplinary powers of state and church will combine in what the Puritans called "promiscuous" ways, like the cock and the serpent that hatched the fabulous and pernicious cockatrice. "Cockatrice" also means "prostitute," and in the seventeenth century it was a term of reproach for a woman (*OED*).

8. This is not to say that gender is not an operative term in Williams's religious discourse. In fact, he used metaphors of the feminine fairly conventionally, returning over and over to the image of the Church like the Bride awaiting union with Christ, her lover, in order to describe his millennialist vision of paradise restored (Garrett, 8, 50), and using "whore" in an extended metaphor to describe the defiled members of the Church of England (Morgan, *Roger Williams*, 35–36).

Kappeler explains the association of gender and racial difference as part of the "sexualization of the political": "Sexual politics lends the most powerful metaphor to politics: a sexual difference (in the superficial anatomy) grounded in nature—male/female. Genderize political difference, the disequilibrium of power, . . . and naturalize it as masculine/feminine. The places are given, their gender established: henceforth the roles can be taken by anyone: man, woman, libertine, prostitute, black, white, Aryan, Jew or Palestinian." She also points out how this displacement blurs certain important categories and power relations (153–54).

9. That is, when it is included at all. Miller and Johnson do not include any of Williams's poetry in their anthology, *The Puritans*; nor does *The Norton Anthology of American Literature*, newly edited in 1985, which reprints the *Key*'s introductory letter, "Directions for use," and extracts from chap. 21 on Narragansett religion, but excludes the final poem of the chapter and any mention of poetry in the headnote. Jantz calls Williams "the finest poet among the heretics," mentions the

Key and the "true beauty of its lyrics," and laments the strange fate of the poems among literary historians (22–23). Meserole prints seventeen of the thirty-two poems, slighting their context but recognizing Williams's unusual "ability to evoke the quality of an image, both apart from and in complement to the moral meaning he assigns it, [which] sets him apart from many early New England verse writers" (177). But most critics and biographers dismiss the poetry as unimportant or artless. Perry Miller opines that Williams "was too turgid a writer to submit to the discipline of poetry, and his rhymes are not memorable art" (*Roger Williams*, 55). M. E. Hall says, "At the close of each chapter are a few lines of simple, crude verse that sounds for all the world like the pointed sermons with which good old-fashioned stories used to end" (83); and Garrett states flatly, "Each chapter closes with a few stanzas of sententious doggerel verse. Whatever virtues Williams had, he was no poet" (127). The only full-scale study of the poetry that I have been able to find appears as the first part of the unpublished 1968 dissertation of Thomas E. Johnston, Jr.

10. Williams's bitterness about his banishment and John Cotton's role in it can be heard in the following letter of 1670, where he recounts that after his service to Massachusetts in the Pequot war Governor Winthrop "and some other of the Council motioned and it was debated, whether or no I had not merited, not only to be recalled from banishment, but also to be honored with some remark of favor. It is known who hindered, who never promoted the liberty of other men's consciences" (*CW*, 6:339).

11. Williams's role in this "second Puritan conquest" is ambiguous. His letters to the Bay leaders are irritatingly deferential. Leach attributes to Williams the sincerest motives: to keep peace between his native friends and his countrymen (41); while Jennings argues that the English never intended to settle any of the natives' land disputes peacefully, were only concerned with gaining more territory, and aimed at subjugating the Narragansett (302–12). At the conclusion of the war, the Narragansett were crushed, many colonists were dead, and Providence alone had had more than one hundred of its original one hundred and twenty-three houses destroyed by fire (Chupack, 60).

12. Wroth's is the most even-handed, thorough, and eloquent evaluation of Williams's relations with the Native Americans; see especially pp. 20–29.

13. Williams's suit for a royal charter for Providence is only one of the many contradictions in his career. He, among few other Europeans, recognized that America was inhabited and disputed the right of foreign monarchs to grant sovereignty over occupied lands. He was willing to stand up for and act upon this belief, having written a treatise, now lost, against the Massachusetts patent and intending to apprise the king of his opinion in a letter. Yet he spent considerable energy securing a charter for his own plantation as protection against the depredations of the Bay.

14. Garrett is particularly good at tracing the winding path of Williams's eventual rejection of his class and calling. See especially chap. 4, "Pathway to Power:

Education," and chap. 5, "Personal Crisis: The Gentry." In chap. 6, "Outside the Camp: Mission," he details how Williams modeled his mission after Christ's. Gilpin explores Williams's millennialism to explain his piety and illuminates many crucial theological issues.

15. Hutchinson did not settle permanently in Providence, but moved into the Dutch settlements north of Manhattan where she and her family perished at the hands of the Native Americans in 1643. She and Williams also shared a significant relationship to John Cotton, Hutchinson's beloved minister in old and New England, who, to save his own position, withdrew his support for her during her trial, and who became Williams's major adversary in their famous pamphlet war.

16. Williams's self-references in the *Key* are characteristically unstable. At times he refers to himself as an Englishman, happy to be able "to bring some short *Observations* and *Applications* home to *Europe* from *America*" (87), and uses "we" when referring to the English. At one point in the text he refers to "our *New-English* parts" (220), as if he considered himself an inhabitant of New England. Johnston argues that this voice "*vacillating as it does between Old World and New World, is precisely the voice of the American Puritan*" (17; emphasis in the original)— but that is to conceive of the category of "American Puritan" much too monolithically.

17. "Keys," especially to Holy Scripture, flourished in the seventeenth century. For example, Williams's father-in-law, Richard Bernard, wrote a *Key of Knowledge for the Opening of the Secret Mysteries of St. Johns Mysticall Revelation*, published in 1617 (see Garrett, 154–55). Other examples are Robert Francis, *Clavis Bibliorvm. The key of the Bible, unlocking the richest treasury of the Holy Scriptures . . .* , first published in London in 1648 and in a fourth edition by 1675; *The Key of Revelation, searched and demonstrated out of the naturall and proper characters of the visions. . . . Translated into English by Richard Moore . . . with a preface written by Dr. Twisse now prolocutor in the present Assembly of divines* (London, 1643); Thomas Harby, *The Key of Sacred Scripture, and leading to it. . . . Wherein many mistakes, by which most professors wound themselves, . . . are clearly discovered . . .* (London, 1679); Benjamin Keach, *Tropologia: A Key to Open Scripture-Metaphors . . .* (London, 1681); and, in a slightly different vein, Richard Baxter, *A Key for Catholicks, to open the jugling of the Jesuits, and satisfie all that are but truly willing to understand, whether the cause of the Roman or reformed churches be of God; and to leave the reader utterly unexcusable that after this will be a papist. Containing some arguments by which the meanest may see the vanity of popery. . . . With some proposals for a (hopeless) peace* (London, 1659; second ed. in 1674). More familiar is the nineteenth-century parody of misguided erudition, Mr. Casaubon in George Eliot's *Middlemarch*, who is writing the impossible "Key to all Mythologies."

18. Bercovitch sees the crucial difference between Williams and Cotton as their allegiance to opposing forms of typology; see his "Typology in Puritan New England." He argues that Williams practiced an Augustinian or allegorical typol-

ogy, which strictly separated the literal and spiritual spheres and where events of the Old Testament signify atemporal states of the soul, while Cotton practiced a Eusebian or historical typology, which stresses the literal-spiritual continuity between Old and New Testament events and the colonial settlement in the New World (175–76). Kibbey disagrees with this, claiming that Williams was the typologist. Typology, she argues, was important to Cotton only as a minor exegetical tool, which is why he resisted Williams's attempt to make it the ground of their argument; he relied, rather, upon the "opening" of biblical symbol and parable (183–84). For Kibbey's analysis of *The Keyes of the Kingdom*, and how Cotton "shifted the focus of his hermeneutics away from typology and greatly increased the importance of imagistic figurative language," see pp. 72–73. Garrett, who does an extensive comparison of Williams and Cotton, concludes that "abstract analysis of toleration was foreign to their controversy" (158), as were debates over biblical hermeneutics; both acknowledged that the New Testament provided them with a "typological principle of interpretation. . . . They had simply to decide how to use it" (43); finally, "Cotton found Williams's openness maddening; Williams found Cotton's certainties stifling" (158–59).

19. The text, while it vividly demonstrates the possibility of sincere native conversions, brackets—and adroitly displaces—the timely issue. In the prefatory letter, Williams addresses "that great Point of their *Conversion* so much to bee longed for," and though he finds "no small *preparation* in the hearts of Multitudes of them," he confesses that "I know not with how little *Knowledge* and *Grace* of Christ, the Lord may save, and therefore neither will *despaire*, nor *report* much" (87). It seems that around 1639 Williams experienced a "theological reorientation" on the question of the Apostolic succession, which persuaded him to halt his active pursuit of native conversions. In a tract entitled *Christenings Make Not Christians*, written at the same time as the *Key* and mentioned twice in its pages (89, 251), but not published until 1645, he explains that the apostasy of the medieval Church obliterated the original form and spiritual authority of the Christian community; thus, the spiritually effective ordinances of conversion and the priestly authority to convert were in doubt and would be until after the millennial restoration (Gilpin, 121).

20. The *OED* indicates that a specifically seventeenth-century meaning of "key" is an explanatory scheme of the interpretation of a cipher, an allegorical statement, or any other composition of hidden or veiled meaning.

21. The "unchristian Christians" in Williams's personal allegory are clearly his Puritan persecutors. It is difficult to judge to what extent his critique is driven by personal pique. Even his millennialist vision affords him a positional superiority that looks like a fantasy of revenge. For example, in the observation preceding the poem for chap. 17, "*Of Beasts, &c.*," he finds in natural predation an emblem for the persecution of God's saints by "greedie and furious men," a thinly veiled allusion to his own treatment by the Bay. But he is consoled with the idea that

For though Gods children lose their lives,
They shall not loose an haire;
But shall arise, and judge all those,
That now their Judges are.

(175)

22. By contrast, in Brotherston's strictly Marxist reading of the *Key* the scope of interchange is narrower and not metaphoric: "In the circumstances he [Williams] creates, this dialogue exists between not just Algonkin (Narragansett) and English but two economies and their respective law and philosophy" (87).

23. Teunissen and Hinz claim that Williams's attitude was unique in its respect for the Native Americans and criticism of Europeans (but see the comment of Thomas Morton cited below); his contemporaries, such as John Smith and William Wood, tended to view the natives "as part of the exploitable potential of the country" and as figures of mirth and low comedy (*Key*, 31). These differences also emerge in the way writers recorded native speech; see *Key*, 33.

24. Piercy differentiates the structure of the *Key* from "the usual procedure of the 'pamphlet of newes'" (73) so popular in accounts of the New World (8–9) and places it in the category of "the scientific essay." Though scientific essays often turned to moralizing and were thus "metamorphosed into didactic 'essays'" (76–77), she recognizes the disjuncture in the *Key*: "There is a curious mixture of the informative and the creative writing, as if the scientist were struggling with the creative artist" (73; see also 76).

25. Morton spent a full winter in jail in Massachusetts, after which he was exiled to Maine, where he died in 1647. Franklin, in a brilliant analysis of "American narrative art, [which] has been a deeply political endeavor from the beginning, and has used language to enforce a given settlement over others" (181), modifies the centrality of writers like Bradford and Winthrop with the marginality of writers like Morton and Williams; see his revealing comparison of Morton and Williams, 184–86.

26. While Brotherston acknowledges that "the *Key* go[es] unrivalled among linguistic studies of the time" (86), his strict Marxist analysis condemns its scriptural allegorizing as "the masking ideology for Puritan capitalism Williams never failed to revere in common with the Bay, whatever their sectarian differences" (92). I have already discussed how Williams's use of allegory diverges sharply from the typologizing of the Bay theocracy, but I want to point out that it was Williams's religious mission, his thirsting after native "souls," that allowed him to take the native soul seriously. Despite their charter's declaration that "the propagation of the Gospel is the thing we do profess above all to be our aim in settling this Plantation" (Chupack, 63), the Bay Puritans were not interested in native souls and thus could simply annihilate them as impediments to their sacred errand.

27. Williams denounced the Spanish, Portuguese, and French "successes" at missionizing: "what monstrous and most inhumane conversions have they made;

baptizing thousands, yea ten thousands of the poore Natives, sometimes by wiles and subtle devices, sometimes by force compelling them to submit to that which they understood not, neither before nor after their monstrous Christning of them" (*Christenings*, in *CW*, 7:36). By contrast, for him a "true Conversion" involved the total transformation of the person, "as if an old man became a new Babe *Joh.* 3. yea, as amounts to Gods new creation in the soule, *Ephes*, 2. 10," and depended upon rational understanding "so farre as man's Judgement can reach which is fallible" (7:39). Thus missionaries needed a "propriety of speech to open matters of salvation to them." The greatest facility in native tongues was required because "in matters of Earth men will helpe to spell out each other, but in the matters of Heaven (to which the soule is naturally so averse) how far are the Eares of man hedged up from listening to all improper Language?" (7:40). When he speaks, however, of having "such a *Key* of *Language*, and such a dore of *opportunity*, in the knowledge of the Country and the inhabitants" (7:39–40), he alludes to Revelation 3:7 and thus places the work of native conversion outside ordinary human time and within the new dispensation of the millennia.

28. Williams frequently reiterated this sentiment in discussions of what makes a true Christian. See, for example, *The Examiner Defended* (1652), a concise recapitulation of the two *Tenents*: ". . . in *Christianity* the greatest respect is not given to greatness of *Place, Birth, Wealth, Authority, Braverie*, &c. but to the greatness of *Humility* and *Grace* of *Christ*, according to that of the *Lord Jesus* (Matth. 18). *Whosoever shall humble himself as this little child, the same is the greatest in the Kingdom of Heaven*" (*CW*, 7:225).

29. Teunissen and Hinz accept the text's own account of itself, explaining that "each chapter, in short, presents a three-part movement from the empirical and specific to the spiritual and general to the poetic and particular. The structure of each unit is an organic representation of the controlling thematic perspective— the metaphoric nature of the material world, an informing point of view which we later encounter in Jonathan Edwards and Ralph Waldo Emerson" (*Key*, 61). Certainly in the case of Edwards, and perhaps also for Emerson, one would have difficulty asserting that the material world is metaphoric, and not allegorical or typological. For Williams, allegory, and not metaphor, is the dominant figurative mode.

30. I am indebted to Dana Nelson Salvino, who referred me to Kappeler's book, and who wondered, astutely, whether by specifying Williams's "use" of the Native Americans, I imply a "balance of power that somehow inevitably links Williams to the colonizing impulse" (personal communication).

31. Compare Said's comment: "The Orient was . . . not Europe's interlocutor, but its silent Other" ("Orientalism Reconsidered," 215).

32. This idea gets treated explicitly in two analogous chapters: chap. 17, "Of *Beasts, &c.*," and chap. 27, "Of *their Hunting*, &c." For example, the general observation for chap. 17 develops the idea that "the Wildernesse is a cleere resemblance of the world, where greedie and furious men persecute and devoure

the harmlesse and innocent as the wilde beasts pursue and devoure the Hinds and Roes" (175). This is referred to in chap. 27, where the ironic reversal is made even more explicit. The "poore Deere" is named as "a right Embleme of Gods persecuted, that is, hunted people." Williams follows this with a long anecdote in which the deer is killed by a wolf, who is in turn assaulted and driven off by "two *English* Swine, big with Pig," who "devoured so much of that poore Deere, as they both surfeted and dyed that night." Williams explains, "The Wolfe is an Embleme of a fierce bloodsucking persecutor. The Swine of a covetous rooting worldling, both make a prey of the Lord Jesus in his poore servants" (225–26). The "greedie and furious men," later the wolf and swine, are the "wild" beasts. The natives also devour the deer (175, ll. 1–2), "whom they conceive have a Divine power in them" (225). The last stanza of the poem for chap. 17 completes the ironic reversal: "New-England's *wilde beasts are not fierce / As other wild beasts are: / Some men are not so fierce, and yet / From mildnesse are they farre*" (175).

33. The poem for chap. 30 makes this allegorical application explicit. Condemning the Native Americans' custom of face and body painting, but recognizing similar customs in the civilized society of England, Williams uses biblical allusions and typology to make his point:

> *Fowle are the* Indians *Haire and painted Faces,*
> *More foule such Haire, such Face in* Israel.
> England *so calls her selfe, yet there's*
> Absoloms *foule Haire and Face of* Jesabell.
>
> (241)

34. Besides being "the structural conclusions and thematic climaxes of each chapter," the poems, continue Teunissen and Hinz, are related to the chapters in a more "traditional way," as "emblematic, following a favorite seventeenth-century mode, and thus rely in part upon the didactic conventions popularized in England by Francis Quarles" (*Key*, 61). This is how they account for the tripartite structure of the chapters, the vocabulary/dialogue taking the place of the symbolic engraving, the general observations replacing the moral motto or epigram drawn from the Bible or classics, and the particularizing poem serving the same function as the traditional poetic explication. Williams himself suggests specifically emblematic readings of incidents, as in chap. 27, "Of *their Hunting*, &c," where he turns a description of the trapping of deer into a parable of his own persecution. There is, however, no conventional association of the ballad measure with the emblem tradition. Nor does this tradition account for the critical themes, the ironic and satiric tone, or, most importantly, the shifting positions of the speaker, reader, and subject in Williams's poems.

35. My information on Anna Trapnel comes mainly from Greaves and Zaller, 3:250–51, and *Cry of a Stone*. Gender plays an important role here, for only by entering into a trance and putting aside her body could she put aside her "self" and become the instrument and mouthpiece of God. For a feminist reading of

Trapnel's "prophetic delirium" in the context of interregnum sectarianism, see Berg and Berry.

36. For further discussion of Dickinson's use of the hymn form, see Porter.

37. The reference occurs in the next-to-last observation in chap. 1, and it is odd because Williams usually does not draw spiritual parallels until the general observation. The passage reads: "I have acknowledged amongst them an heart sensible of kindnesses, and have reaped kindnesse again from many, seaven yeares after, when I my selfe had forgotten, &c. hence the Lord Jesus exhorts his followers to doe good for evill; for otherwise, sinners will do good for good, kindnesse for kindnesse, &c" (97–98). The editors cite Matthew 5:44 and say, "The point being that the natural virtue of the Indian is very close—Williams does not say exactly *how* close—to the Christian virtues which Jesus defines in the Sermon on the Mount" (*Key*, 287–88).

38. They are his poem warning the English about their racism, "*Boast not proud English, of thy birth & blood*" (133), quoted earlier, and his poem accusing them of ruthlessness in war: "*But now that English Men, / (That boast themselves Gods Children, and / Members of Christ to be,) / That they should thus break out in flames, / Sure 'tis a Mystery!*" (238–39).

39. This description alludes to the Pequot massacre at Mystic, for which Williams provided crucial information, and it uncannily foreshadows the genocide of the Narragansett during the Great Swamp Fight in King Philip's War thirty years later. The nine strategic observations that Williams "gathered" from his conferences with various Narragansett and recommended to Governor Winthrop, in what Jennings calls "the first Puritan conquest," included as *their* contributions the description of "a marvellous great and secure swamp," and the cold-blooded suggestions that "the assault would be in the night, when they are commonly more secure and at home, by which advantage the English, being armed, may enter the houses and do what execution they please," and that "before the assault be given, an ambush be laid behind them, between them and the swamp, to prevent their flight, &c." Less frequently cited is the eighth point, "That it would be pleasing to all natives, that women and children be spared, &c" (*CW*, 6:18–19)—a humane request that was blatantly ignored by the presiding militia officers in the name of "the ALMIGHTY." See Kibbey's analysis (97–98), and Jennings's account, which points out that Captain Mason of Massachusetts had prior intent to massacre and plunder (220–27).

40. The same prayer, but to different ends, as the rest of Dickinson's extraordinary poem attests:

Earth would have been too much—I see—
And Heaven—not enough for me—
I should have had the Joy
Without the Fear—to justify—
The Palm—without the Calvary—

So Savior—Crucify—
Defeat—whets Victory—they say—
The Reefs—in old Gethsemane—
Endear the Coast—beyond!
'Tis Beggars—Banquets—can define—
'Tis Parching—vitalizes Wine—
"Faith" bleats—to understand!
(Complete Poems, 147–48)

41. The association of the Irish with the criminal element of the English is even stranger in light of an earlier and likelier association in the *Key* of the Irish and Native Americans: "These thick Woods and Swamps (like the Boggs to the *Irish*) are the Refuges for Women and children in Warre, whil'st the men fight" (150). English imperialists waged genocidal wars against both native populations.

42. This effect of the text bears out what Said discovers to be his "real argument . . . that Orientalism is—and does not simply represent—a considerable dimension of modern political-intellectual culture, and as such has less to do with the Orient than it does with 'our' world" (*Orientalism*, 12).

43. The first description is Williams's, who several times in the *Key* remarks upon the richness of the Narragansett tongue where "they have five or six words sometimes for one thing" (91). The second description is Brotherston's, who argues that "the chapter divisions serve to control an otherwise irreducible word-mass or potentially subversive native syntax" by "insulat[ing] each chapter topic in itself, with an appropriate touch of Christian or scriptural piety" (86). Despite Williams's orthodox Calvinism, I have tried to show the subversive uses to which he put it.

44. Franklin senses the importance of exiled writers like Williams defining "their stance by engrossing native American life, in varying degrees, into their own viewpoints. . . . Hence what they fight is not some archetypally New World opponent, but rather an 'alien' figure from the heart of European design. For it is often by such a paradoxical inversion of orthodox rhetoric, some alliance between a disaffected white and a stereotypic other, that the solitary Euro-American signifies his or her alienation. Nor does this alliance always remain rhetorical or stereotyped, difficult as true 'contact' surely is. The exclusion of one white from the center of white order converts the marginal fate of nonwhites into the source of a newly envisioned community, a congregation of the dispersed and lost" (186–87). Would that it were possible to constitute such a community!

Epilogue

1. Schreber's descriptions of this are very clear and very literal: "Something occurred in my own body similar to the conception of Jesus Christ in an immaculate virgin, that is, in a woman who had never had intercourse with a man. On two separate occasions (both while I was in Professor Flechsig's sanatorium) I have

possessed female genitals, though somewhat imperfectly developed ones, and have felt a stirring in my body, such as would arise from the quickening of a human embryo. Nerves of God corresponding to male semen had, by a divine miracle, been projected into my body, and impregnation had thus taken place" (quoted in Freud, 129 n. 25).

2. Many Quakers were persecuted for their literalizing of Puritan figural language. Most notable among the sectarians who unsettled an already unsettled English Puritan state were James Nayler, who rode into Bristol on an ass, claiming to be Jesus; and William Franklin and Mary Gadbury, who claimed to be Jesus and his bride (Ellis). For a further account and cogent analysis of the dialectic of literal and figurative in Puritan discourse, see Luxon, "'Not I but Christ.'"

3. How "affectionate" this memory was is debatable. Neiderland points out that chap. 3 of the *Memoirs*, in which Schreber detailed his early family life and relationships, was censored and deleted as "unfit for publication" (49). Freud's attitude exemplifies his uninspected protection of fathers.

4. For detailed accounts of the elder Schreber's techniques and philosophy of child-rearing, and their impact on his son's illness and imagery, see Neiderland, *Schreber Case*; and Schatzman, *Soul Murder*. Schreber's social influence was not totally baneful. He began what was known as the "Schreber movement," which inspired the development of the Schreber gardens (small allotments of ground in which city dwellers could garden) as well as the "Schreber Vereine," groups that encouraged outdoor activities, athletics, and sports for both sexes (Neiderland, 3).

5. On Dr. Schreber's motivations, Neiderland comments: "To the analytically trained observer, it is obvious that Dr. Schreber's energetic crusade was really directed against masturbation and other 'dangerous, hidden aberrations,' which in his thinking led to physical and mental 'softness' in children"; this, he adds, "was the accepted medical view during the Victorian era" (57 and n. 4).

6. Robinson's attitudes were prevalent among certain groups of Puritans in the seventeenth and eighteenth centuries, as Greven's study shows, but they may have been gender specific. For example, in her "Meditations Divine and Moral," Anne Bradstreet several times articulates a quite different, more relativistic approach to child-rearing; Meditation 10 counsels: "Diverse children have their different natures: some are like flesh which nothing but salt will keep from putrefaction, some again like tender fruits that are best preserved with sugar. Those parents are wise that can fit their nurture according to their nature" (*Works*, 273–74). See also Meditations 20, 23, and 61.

7. A study that puts Schreber's theory of child-rearing into a historical context is Dally, *Inventing Motherhood*.

8. Alice Miller's books on this topic are *Prisoners of Childhood* (reissued in paperback as *The Drama of the Gifted Child*); *For Your Own Good*; *Thou Shalt Not Be Aware*; and, most recently, *The Untouched Key*.

9. Miller rejects both this theory and Freud's theory of drives "solely on the basis of my psychoanalytic experiences" (*For Your Own Good*, 61n). She expands this insight in her third book, *Thou Shalt Not be Aware*.

WORKS CITED

Althusser, Louis. *Lenin and Philosophy and Other Essays.* Translated by Ben Brewster. New York: Monthly Review Press, 1971.

Axtell, James. *The Invasion Within: The Contest of Cultures in Colonial North America.* New York: Oxford University Press, 1985.

Bailyn, Bernard. "The Apologia of Robert Keayne." *The William and Mary Quarterly* 7 (1950): 568–87.

Bakhtin, Mikhail. *Marxism and the Philosophy of Language.* Translated by L. Matejka and I. R. Titunik. New York: Seminar Press, 1973.

Barker-Benfield, Ben. "Anne Hutchinson and the Puritan Attitude toward Women." *Feminist Studies* 1 (1972): 65–96.

Beauvoir, Simone de. *The Second Sex.* Translated by H. M. Parshley. New York: Vintage Books, 1974.

Bercovitch, Sacvan. "The A-Politics of Ambiguity in *The Scarlet Letter.*" *New Literary History* 19 (Spring 1988): 629–54.

———. "Hawthorne's A-Morality of Compromise." *Representations* 24 (Fall 1988): 1–27.

———. *The Puritan Origins of the American Self.* New Haven: Yale University Press, 1975.

———. "Typology in Puritan New England: The Williams-Cotton Controversy Reassessed." *American Quarterly* 19 (1967): 166–91.

Berg, Christine, and Philippa Berry. "'Spiritual Whoredom': An Essay on Female Prophets in the Seventeenth Century." In *1642: Literature and Power in the Seventeenth Century* [Proceedings of the Essex Conference on the Sociology of Literature, July 1980], edited by Francis Barker et al., 37–54. Essex: University of Essex, 1981.

Berman, Morris. *The Re-enchantment of the World.* Ithaca: Cornell University Press, 1981.

Bernard of Clairvaux. *On the Song of Songs I: The Works of Bernard of Clairvaux.* Vol. 2. Kalamazoo: Cistercian Publications, 1976.

Berryman, John. "Changes." In *Poets on Poetry,* edited by Howard Nemerov, 94–103. New York: Basic Books, 1966.

———. *Homage to Mistress Bradstreet.* New York: Farrar, Straus and Cudahy, 1956.

Blake, Kathleen. "Edward Taylor's Protestant Poetic: Non-transubstantiating Metaphor." *American Literature* 43 (1971): 1–24.

Bloom, Harold. *The Anxiety of Influence: A Theory of Poetry.* London and New York: Oxford University Press, 1973.

Bogan, Louise. *What the Woman Lived: Selected Letters of Louise Bogan, 1920–1970.* Edited by Ruth Limmer. New York: Harcourt Brace Jovanovich, 1973.

Bordo, Susan R. *The Flight to Objectivity: Essays on Cartesianism and Culture.* Albany: State University of New York Press, 1987.

Bradstreet, Anne. *The Complete Works of Anne Bradstreet.* Edited by Joseph R. McElrath, Jr., and Allan P. Robb. Boston: Twayne Publishers, 1981.

———. *The Works of Anne Bradstreet.* Edited by Jeannine Hensley. Cambridge: Harvard University Press, 1967.

Bray, James. "John Fiske: Puritan Precursor of Edward Taylor." *Early American Literature* 9 (1974): 27–38.

Brotherston, Gordon. "A Controversial Guide to the Language of America, 1643." In *1642: Literature and Power in the Seventeenth Century* [Proceedings of the Essex Conference on the Sociology of Literature, July 1980], edited by Francis Barker et al., 84–100. Essex: University of Essex, 1981.

Brumm, Ursula. *American Thought and Religious Typology.* New Brunswick, N.J.: Rutgers University Press, 1970.

———. "The Tree of Life in Edward Taylor's Meditations." *Early American Literature* 3 (1968): 72–87.

Burke, Kenneth. *The Rhetoric of Religion: Studies in Logology.* Berkeley: University of California Press, 1961.

Calamy, Edmund. *The Monster of Sinful Self-Seeking, Anatomized.* London: N.p., 1655.

Caldwell, Patricia. *The Puritan Conversion Narrative: The Beginnings of American Expression.* Cambridge: Cambridge University Press, 1983.

Calvin, John. *Institutes of the Christian Religion.* 2 vols. Translated by Henry Beveridge. Grand Rapids, Mich.: William B. Eerdmans, 1983.

Campbell, Helen. *Anne Bradstreet and Her Time.* Boston: D. Lothrop, 1891.

Chabot, C. Barry. *Freud on Schreber: Psychoanalytic Theory and the Critical Act.* Amherst: University of Massachusetts Press, 1982.

Chicago, Judy. *Embroidering Our Heritage: The Dinner Party Needlework.* New York: Anchor Books, 1980.

Chodorow, Nancy. *The Reproduction of Mothering.* Berkeley: University of California Press, 1978.

Chupack, Henry. *Roger Williams.* New York: Twayne Publishers, 1969.

Clark, Michael. "'The Crucified Phrase': Sign and Desire in Puritan Semiology." *Early American Literature* 13 (1978/79): 278–93.

———. "The Honeyed Knot of Puritan Aesthetics." In *Puritan Poets and Poetics: Seventeenth-Century American Poetry in Theory and Practice,* edited by Peter White, 67–83. University Park: Pennsylvania State University Press, 1985.

Cohen, Charles Lloyd. *God's Caress: The Psychology of Puritan Religious Experience.* New York: Oxford University Press, 1986.

Corum, Richard. "In White Ink: *Paradise Lost* and Milton's Ideas of Women."

In *Milton and the Idea of Woman*, edited by Julia M. Walker, 120–47. Urbana and Chicago: University of Illinois Press, 1988.

Coward, Rosalind, and John Ellis. *Language and Materialism: Developments in Semiology and the Theory of the Subject*. London and New York: Routledge and Kegan Paul, 1977.

The Cry of a Stone; or a Relation of Something Spoken in Whitehall by Anna Trapnel. . . . London: N.p., 1654.

Culler, Jonathan. *The Pursuit of Signs: Semiotics, Literature, Deconstruction.* Ithaca: Cornell University Press, 1981.

———. *Structuralist Poetics: Structuralism, Linguistics, and the Study of Literature.* Ithaca: Cornell University Press, 1975.

Dally, Ann. *Inventing Motherhood: The Consequences of an Ideal.* New York: Schocken Books, 1983.

Daly, Robert. *God's Altar: The World and the Flesh in Puritan Poetry.* Berkeley: University of California Press, 1978.

Davis, Jack L. "Roger Williams among the Narragansett Indians." *New England Quarterly* 43 (1970): 593–604.

Davis, Thomas M. Introduction to *Edward Taylor's Minor Poetry*, vol. 3 of *The Unpublished Writings of Edward Taylor*, edited by Thomas M. Davis and Virginia L. Davis, xi–xxiv. Boston: G. K. Hall, 1981.

de Lauretis, Teresa. *Alice Doesn't: Feminism, Semiotics, Cinema.* Bloomington: Indiana University Press, 1984.

———. "Issues, Terms, and Contexts." In *Feminist Studies/Critical Studies*, edited by Teresa de Lauretis, 1–19. Bloomington: Indiana University Press, 1986.

de Man, Paul. "Autobiography as De-facement." *Modern Language Notes* 94 (1979): 919–30.

DeShazer, Mary K. *Inspiring Women: Reimagining the Muse.* New York: Pergamon Press, 1986.

Dickinson, Emily. *The Complete Poems of Emily Dickinson.* Edited by Thomas H. Johnson. Boston: Little, Brown, 1960.

Donato, Eugenio. "The Two Languages of Criticism." In *The Structuralist Controversy: The Languages of Criticism and the Sciences of Man*, edited by Richard Macksey and Eugenio Donato, 89–97. Baltimore: Johns Hopkins University Press, 1972.

Donne, John. *The Poems of John Donne.* Edited by Herbert Grierson. 2 vols. London: Oxford University Press, 1912.

Douglas, Mary. *Purity and Danger: An Analysis of Concepts of Pollution and Taboo.* New York: Praeger, 1966.

Douglass, Jane Dempsey. *Women, Freedom, and Calvin.* Philadelphia: Westminster Press, 1985.

Draper, John W. *The Funeral Elegy and the Rise of English Romanticism.* New York: New York University Press, 1929.

Dunn, Mary Maples. "Saints and Sisters: Congregational and Quaker Women in the Early Colonial Period." In *Women in American Religion*, edited by Janet Wilson James, 27–47. Philadelphia: University of Pennsylvania Press, 1980.

Easlea, Brian. *Witch-hunting, Magic, and the New Philosophy*. Atlantic Highlands, N.J.: Humanities Press, 1980.

Easthope, Anthony. *Poetry as Discourse*. London and New York: Methuen, 1983.

Eberwein, Jane Donahue. "'The Unrefined Ore' of Anne Bradstreet's *Quaternions*." *Early American Literature* 9 (1974): 19–26.

Edwards, Jonathan. *Images or Shadows of Divine Things*. Edited by Perry Miller. New Haven: Yale University Press, 1948.

Elliott, Emory. "The Development of the Puritan Funeral Sermon and Elegy: 1660–1750." *Early American Literature* 15 (1980): 151–64.

———. *Power and the Pulpit in Puritan New England*. Princeton: Princeton University Press, 1974.

Ellis, Humphrey. *Pseudochristus*. London: N.p., 1650.

Erikson, Kai T. *Wayward Puritans: A Study in the Sociology of Deviance*. New York: John Wiley and Sons, 1966.

Faber, Heije. *Psychology of Religion*. Translated by Margaret Kohl. London: Westminster Press, 1976.

Feidelson, Charles. *Symbolism in American Literature*. Chicago: University of Chicago Press, 1953.

Feinstein, Howard M. "The Prepared Heart: A Comparative Study of Puritan Theology and Psychoanalysis." *American Quarterly* 22 (1970): 166–76.

Fetterley, Judith. *The Resisting Reader: A Feminist Approach to American Fiction*. Bloomington: Indiana University Press, 1978.

Fish, Stanley. *Self-Consuming Artifacts: The Experience of Seventeenth-Century Literature*. Berkeley: University of California Press, 1972.

Fiske, John. "British Cultural Studies and Television." In *Channels of Discourse: Television and Contemporary Criticism*, edited by Robert C. Allen, 254–89. Chapel Hill: University of North Carolina Press, 1987.

Franklin, Wayne. *Discoverers, Explorers, Settlers: The Diligent Writers of Early America*. Chicago and London: University of Chicago Press, 1979.

Freud, Sigmund. *Three Case Histories*. Edited by Philip Rieff. New York: Macmillan, 1963.

Friedman, Susan Stanford. "Creativity and the Childbirth Metaphor." In *Speaking of Gender*, edited by Elaine Showalter, 73–100. New York: Routledge, 1989.

Friedman, William F., and Elizabeth S. Friedman. "Acrostics, Anagrams, and Chaucer." *Philological Quarterly* 38 (January 1959): 1–20.

Frye, Northrop. *Anatomy of Criticism: Four Essays*. Princeton: Princeton University Press, 1967.

———. "Approaching the Lyric." In *Lyric Poetry: Beyond New Criticism*, edited by Chaviva Hošek and Patricia Parker, 31–37. Ithaca: Cornell University Press, 1985.

Gardiner, Judith Kegan. "On Female Identity and Writing by Women." In *Writing and Sexual Difference*, edited by Elizabeth Abel, 177–91. Chicago: University of Chicago Press, 1982.

Garret, John. *Roger Williams: Witness beyond Christendom, 1603–1683*. London: Macmillan, 1970.

Gelpi, Albert. *The Tenth Muse: The Psyche of the American Poet*. Cambridge: Harvard University Press, 1975.

Gilbert, Sandra M., and Susan Gubar. *The War of the Words*. Vol. 1, *No Man's Land: The Place of the Woman Writer in the Twentieth Century*. New Haven: Yale University Press, 1988.

Gilpin, W. Clark. *The Millenarian Piety of Roger Williams*. Chicago and London: University of Chicago Press, 1979.

Grabo, Norman S. *Edward Taylor*. Revised ed. Boston: Twayne Publishers, 1988.

———. "Puritan Devotion and American Literary History." In *Themes and Directions in American Literature*, edited by Ray B. Browne, 6–23. Lafayette, Ind.: Purdue University Studies, 1969.

———. "The Veiled Vision: The Role of Aesthetics in Early American Intellectual History." In *The American Puritan Imagination: Essays in Revaluation*, edited by Sacvan Bercovitch, 19–33. London: Cambridge University Press, 1974.

Greaves, Richard L., and Robert Zaller, eds. *Biographical Dictionary of British Radicals in the Seventeenth Century*. Brighton, Sussex: Harvester Press, 1984.

Greenblatt, Stephen J. "Learning to Curse: Aspects of Linguistic Colonialism in the Sixteenth Century." In *First Images of America*, edited by Fredi Chiappelli, 2:561–80. Berkeley, Los Angeles, London: University of California Press, 1976.

Greven, Philip. *The Protestant Temperament: Patterns of Child-Rearing, Religious Experience, and the Self in Early America*. New York: Alfred A. Knopf, 1977.

Grossman, Michael. "Servile/ Sterile/ Style: Milton and the Question of Woman." In *Milton and the Idea of Woman*, edited by Julia M. Walker, 148–68. Urbana and Chicago: University of Illinois Press, 1988.

Gura, Philip. *A Glimpse of Sion's Glory: Puritan Radicalism in New England 1620–1660*. Middletown, Conn.: Wesleyan University Press, 1984.

Haffenden, John. *John Berryman: A Critical Commentary*. New York: New York University Press, 1980.

Haims, Lynn. "The Face of God: Puritan Iconography in Early American Poetry, Sermons, and Tombstone Carving." *Early American Literature* 14 (1979): 15–47.

Halbert, Cecelia L. "Tree of Life Imagery in the Poetry of Edward Taylor." *American Literature* 38 (1966): 22–34.

Hall, David, ed. *The Antinomian Controversy, 1636–1638: A Documentary History*. Middletown, Conn.: Wesleyan University Press, 1968.

Hall, May Emery. *Roger Williams*. Boston: Pilgrim Press, 1917.

Hambrick-Stowe, Charles E. *The Practice of Piety: Puritan Devotional Disciplines in Seventeenth-Century New England*. Chapel Hill: University of North Carolina Press, 1982.

Hammond, Jeffrey A. "A Puritan Ars Moriendi: Edward Taylor's Late Meditations on the Song of Songs." *Early American Literature* 17 (1982/83): 191–214.

Hannay, Margaret P. Introduction to *Silent But for the Word: Tudor Women as Patrons, Translators, and Writers of Religious Works*, edited by Margaret P. Hannay, 1–20. Kent, Ohio: Kent State University Press, 1985.

Hawthorne, Nathaniel. *The Marble Faun*. New York: Signet, 1961.

———. *The Scarlet Letter*. Edited by Sculley Bradley et al. New York: Norton, 1962.

Henderson, Katherine Usher, and Barbara F. McManus, eds. *Half Humankind: Contexts and Texts of the Controversy about Women in England, 1540–1640*. Urbana: University of Illinois Press, 1985.

Henson, Robert. "Form and Content of the Puritan Elegy." *American Literature* 31 (1960): 11–27.

Herbert, George. *The Works of George Herbert*. Edited by F. E. Hutchinson. London: Oxford University Press, 1941.

Higgins, John. "Raymond Williams and the Problem of Ideology." In *Postmodernism and Politics*, edited by Jonathan Arac, 112–22. Minneapolis: University of Minnesota Press, 1986.

Higgins, Lynn. "Literature 'À La Lettre': Ricardou and the Poetics of Anagram." *Romantic Review* 72 (4 November 1982): 473–88.

Holder, Alan. "Anne Bradstreet Resurrected." *Concerning Poetry* 2 (1969): 11–18.

Holifield, E. Brooks. *The Covenant Sealed: The Development of Puritan Sacramental Theory in Old and New England, 1570–1720*. New Haven: Yale University Press, 1974.

Hošek, Chaviva, and Patricia Parker, eds. *Lyric Poetry: Beyond New Criticism*. Ithaca: Cornell University Press, 1985.

Hughes, Walter. "'Meat Out of the Eater': Panic and Desire in American Puritan Poetry." In *Engendering Men: The Question of Male Feminist Criticism*, edited by Joseph A. Boone and Michael Cadden, 102–21. New York and London: Routledge, Chapman and Hall, 1990.

Hull, Suzanne. *Chaste, Silent, and Obedient: English Books for Women 1475–1640*. San Marino, Calif.: Huntington Library, 1982.

Hulme, Peter. *Colonial Encounters: Europe and the Native Caribbean, 1492–1797*. London and New York: Methuen, 1986.

Huyssen, Andreas. "Mapping the Postmodern." *New German Critique* 33 (1984): 5–52.

Irigaray, Luce. "The Power of Discourse and the Subordination of the Feminine." In *This Sex Which Is Not One*, translated by Catherine Porter, 68–85. Ithaca: Cornell University Press, 1985.

Irwin, Joyce L. *Womanhood in Radical Protestantism, 1525–1675*. New York: Edwin Mellen Press, 1979.

Jantz, Harold S. *The First Century of New England Verse*. New York: Russell and Russell, 1962.

Jardine, Alice. *Gynesis: Configurations of Woman and Modernity*. Ithaca: Cornell University Press, 1985.

Jennings, Francis. *The Invasion of America: Indians, Colonialism, and the Cant of Conquest*. Chapel Hill: University of North Carolina Press, 1975.

Johnson, Carol. "John Berryman and Mistress Bradstreet: A Relation of Reason." *Essays in Criticism* 14 (1964): 388–96.

Johnson, Parker. "Poetry and Praise in Edward Taylor's Preparatory Meditations." *American Literature* 52 (1980): 84–96.

Johnston, Thomas E., Jr. "American Puritan Poetic Voices: Essays on Anne Bradstreet, Edward Taylor, Roger Williams, and Philip Pain." Ph.D. dissertation, Ohio University, 1968.

Jones, Ann Rosalind. "Surprising Fame: Renaissance Gender Ideologies and Women's Lyric." In *The Poetics of Gender*, edited by Nancy K. Miller, 74–95. New York: Columbia University Press, 1986.

Jones, Augustine. *The Life and Work of Thomas Dudley*. Boston: Houghton Mifflin, 1899.

Jones, Ernest. *Essays in Applied Psycho-analysis*. Vol. 2 of *Essays in Folklore, Anthropology, and Religion*. London: Hogarth Press, 1951.

Jones, Phyllis. "Biblical Rhetoric and the Pulpit Literature of Early New England." *Early American Literature* 11 (1976/77): 245–58.

Josselyn, John. *John Josselyn, Colonial Traveler: A Critical Edition of "Two Voyages to New-England."* Edited by Paul J. Lindholdt. Hanover, N.H., and London: University Press of New England, 1988.

Kappeler, Susanne. *The Pornography of Representation*. Minneapolis: University of Minnesota Press, 1986.

Karlsen, Carol F. *The Devil in the Shape of a Woman: Witchcraft in Colonial New England*. New York: W. W. Norton, 1987.

Keayne, Robert. "The Last Will and Testament of me, Robert Keayne all of it Written with my owne hands and begun by me, Mo: 6: I: 1653, Comonly calle August." In *Boston Record Commissioners Report*, 10:1–54. Boston, 1886.

Keller, Karl. *The Example of Edward Taylor*. Amherst: University of Massachusetts Press, 1975.

Keller, Rosemary Skinner. "New England Women: Ideology and Experience in First-Generation Puritanism (1630–1650)." In *Women and Religion in America: The Colonial and Revolutionary Periods*, edited by Rosemary Radford Reuther and Rosemary Skinner Keller, 132–92. San Francisco: Harper and Row, 1983.

Kelly, Joan. "Early Feminist Theory and the Querelle des Femmes, 1400–1789." *Signs: Journal of Women in Culture and Society* 8 (1982): 4–28.

Kelly-Gadol, Joan. "Did Women Have a Renaissance?" In *Becoming Visible: Women in European History*, edited by Renate Bridenthal and Claudia Koonz, 132–92. Boston: Houghton Mifflin, 1970.

Kibbey, Ann. *The Interpretation of Material Shapes in Puritanism: A Study of Rhetoric, Prejudice, and Violence*. New York: Cambridge University Press, 1986.

King, Anne. "Anne Hutchinson and Anne Bradstreet: Literature and Experience, Faith and Works in Massachusetts Bay Colony." *International Journal of Women's Studies* 1 (1978): 445–67.

King, John N. *English Reformation Literature: The Tudor Origins of the Protestant Tradition*. Princeton: Princeton University Press, 1982.

King, John Owen III. *The Iron of Melancholy: Structures of Spiritual Conversion from the Puritan Conscience to Victorian Neurosis*. Middletown, Conn.: Wesleyan University Press, 1983.

Koehler, Lyle. *A Search for Power: The "Weaker Sex" in Seventeenth-Century New England*. Urbana: University of Illinois Press, 1980.

Kristeva, Julia. *Semiotiké: Recherches pour une semanalyse*. Paris: Seuil, 1969.

Krupnick, Mark, ed. *Displacement: Derrida and After*. Bloomington: Indiana University Press, 1983.

Lamb, Mary Ellen. "The Cooke Sisters: Attitudes towards Learned Women in the Renaissance." In *Silent But for the Word: Tudor Women as Patrons, Translators, and Writers of Religious Works*, edited by Margaret P. Hannay, 107–25. Kent, Ohio: Kent State University Press, 1985.

Lang, Amy Schrager. *Prophetic Woman: Anne Hutchinson and the Problem of Dissent in the Literature of New England*. Berkeley: University of California Press, 1987.

Leach, Douglas Edward. *Flintlock and Tomahawk: New England in King Philip's War*. New York: Macmillan, 1958.

Leverenz, David. *The Language of Puritan Feeling: An Exploration in Literature, Psychology, and Social History*. New Brunswick, N.J.: Rutgers University Press, 1980.

———. *Manhood and the American Renaissance*. Ithaca: Cornell University Press, 1989.

Lewalski, Barbara Kiefer. *Protestant Poetics and the Seventeenth-Century Religious Lyric*. Princeton: Princeton University Press, 1979.

Lowance, Mason I. *The Language of Canaan: Metaphor and Symbol in New England from the Puritans to the Transcendentalists*. Cambridge: Harvard University Press, 1980.

Lowell, Robert. Foreword to *Ariel*, by Sylvia Plath, vii–ix. New York: Harper and Row, 1961.

Luxon, Thomas H. "'Not I But Christ': Self and Body in English Puritan

Spirituality." Paper delivered at Dartmouth College, Hanover, N.H., February 1987.

――――. "The Pilgrim's Passive Progress: Luther and Bunyan on Talking and Doing, Word and Way." *English Literary History* 53 (1986): 73–98.

――――. "Puritan Allegory and The Pilgrim's Progress." Ph.D. dissertation, University of Chicago, 1984.

Mack, Phyllis. "Women Prophets during the English Civil War." *Feminist Studies* 8 (1982): 19–45.

Martin, Biddy, and Chandra Talpade Mohanty. "Feminist Politics: What's Home Got to Do with It?" In *Feminist Studies/Critical Studies*, edited by Teresa de Lauretis, 191–212. Bloomington: Indiana University Press, 1986.

Martin, Wendy. *An American Triptych: Anne Bradstreet, Emily Dickinson, Adrienne Rich*. Chapel Hill: University of North Carolina Press, 1984.

Masson, Margaret W. "The Typology of the Female as a Model for the Regenerate: Puritan Preaching, 1690–1730." *Signs: Journal of Women in Culture and Society* 2 (1976): 304–15.

Mather, Cotton. *Magnalia Christi Americana*. 2 vols. New York: Russell and Russell, 1967.

Mazzaro, Jerome. *Postmodern American Poetry*. Urbana: University of Illinois Press, 1980.

Merchant, Carolyn. *The Death of Nature*. San Francisco: Harper and Row, 1980.

Meserole, Harrison T., ed. *Seventeenth-Century American Poetry*. New York: W. W. Norton, 1968.

Mignon, Charles. "Edward Taylor's Preparatory Meditations: A Decorum of Imperfection." *Publications of the Modern Language Association* 83 (1968): 1423–28.

Miller, Alice. *For Your Own Good: Hidden Cruelty in Child-Rearing and the Roots of Violence*. Translated by Hildegarde and Hunter Hannum. New York: Farrar, Straus and Giroux, 1983.

――――. *Prisoners of Childhood* [reissued in paperback as *The Drama of the Gifted Child*]. Translated by Ruth Ward. New York: Basic Books, 1981.

――――. *Thou Shalt Not Be Aware: Society's Betrayal of the Child*. Translated by Hildegarde and Hunter Hannum. New York: Meridian Books, 1986.

――――. *The Untouched Key: Tracing Childhood Trauma in Creativity and Destructiveness*. Translated by Hildegarde and Hunter Hannum. New York: Doubleday, 1990.

Miller, Nancy K. "Arachnologies: The Woman, the Text, and the Critic." In *The Poetics of Gender*, ed. Nancy K. Miller, 270–95. New York: Columbia University Press, 1986.

――――. "Changing the Subject: Authorship, Writing, and the Reader." In *Feminist Studies/Critical Studies*, edited by Teresa de Lauretis, 102–20. Bloomington: Indiana University Press, 1986.

Miller, Perry. *The New England Mind.* 2 vols. New York: Macmillan, 1939.

———. *Roger Williams: His Contribution to the American Tradition.* Indianapolis: Bobbs-Merrill, 1953.

Miller, Perry, and Thomas H. Johnson, eds. *The Puritans.* Revised ed. 2 vols. New York: Harper, 1963.

Milton, John. *Paradise Lost.* Edited by Alastair Fowler. London: Longman, 1971.

Moran, Gerald F. "'Sisters in Christ.'" In *Women in American Religion*, edited by Janet Wilson James, 47–66. Philadelphia: University of Pennsylvania Press, 1978.

Morgan, Edmund S. *The Puritan Dilemma: The Story of John Winthrop.* Boston: Little, Brown, 1958.

———. *The Puritan Family: Religion and Domestic Relations in Seventeenth-Century New England.* New York: Harper and Row, 1965.

———. *Roger Williams: The Church and State.* New York: Harcourt, Brace and World, 1967.

———. *Visible Saints: The History of a Puritan Idea.* New York: New York University Press, 1963.

Morison, Samuel Eliot. *The Puritan Pronaos: Studies in the Intellectual Life of New England in the Seventeenth Century.* New York: New York University Press, 1965.

Murdock, Kenneth, ed. *Handkerchiefs from Paul.* Cambridge: Harvard University Press, 1927.

Murphy, Murray G. "The Psychodynamics of Puritan Conversion." *American Quarterly* 31 (1979): 135–47.

Neiderland, William G. *The Schreber Case: Psychoanalytic Profile of a Paranoid Personality.* New York: Quadrangle/New York Times Book Company, 1974.

North, Michael. "Edward Taylor's Metaphors of Promise." *American Literature* 51 (1979): 1–16.

Nyquist, Mary. "Gynesis, Genesis, Exegesis, and Milton's Eve." In *Cannibals, Witches, and Divorce: Estranging the Renaissance*, edited by Marjorie Garber, 147–208. Baltimore: Johns Hopkins University Press, 1987.

Ong, Walter J. *In the Human Grain: Further Explorations of Contemporary Culture.* New York: Macmillan, 1967.

———. *Ramus: Method, and the Decay of Dialogue.* Cambridge: Cambridge University Press, 1958.

Osborne, Dorothy. *The Love Letters of Dorothy Osborne to Sir William Temple.* Edited by Edward Abbot Parry. New York: Dodd, Mead, 1901.

Ostriker, Alicia Suskin. *Stealing the Language: The Emergence of Women's Poetry in America.* Boston: Beacon Press, 1986.

Parker, David L. "Edward Taylor's Preparationism: A New Perspective on the Taylor-Stoddard Controversy." *Early American Literature* 11 (1976/77): 259–78.

Parker, Patricia. Introduction to *Lyric Poetry: Beyond New Criticism*, edited by
Patricia Parker, 11–28. Ithaca: Cornell University Press, 1985.

Pearce, Roy Harvey. *The Continuity of American Poetry*. Princeton: Princeton
University Press, 1961.

Pettit, Norman. *The Heart Prepared: Grace and Conversion in Puritan Spiritual
Life*. New Haven: Yale University Press, 1966.

Pfister, Oscar. *Christianity and Fear: A Study in History and in the Psychology and
Hygiene of Religion*. Translated by W. H. Johnston. London: Allen & Unwin,
1948.

Piercy, Josephine K. *Studies in Literary Types in Seventeenth-Century America
(1607–1710)*. New Haven: Yale University Press, 1939.

Pierpont, Philip E. "'Oh! Angells, Stand Agastard at My Song': Edward Taylor's Meditations on Canticles." Ph.D. dissertation, Southern Illinois University, 1972.

Poovey, Mary. *Uneven Developments: The Ideological Work of Gender in Mid-
Victorian England*. Chicago: University of Chicago Press, 1988.

Pope, Robert G. Introduction to *The Notebook of the Reverend John Fiske, 1644–
1675*, ed. Robert G. Pope, vii–xxxix, vol. 47. Boston: Colonial Society of
Massachusetts, 1974.

Porter, David. *Dickinson: The Modern Idiom*. Cambridge: Harvard University
Press, 1981.

Provost, Sarah. "Erato's Fool and Bitter Sister: Two Aspects of John Berryman." *Twentieth Century Literature* 30 (1984): 69–79.

Pudaloff, Ross J. "Sign and Subject: Antinomianism in Massachusetts Bay."
Semiotica 54 1/2 (1985): 147–63.

Puttenham, George. *The Arte of English Poesie* [1589]. Edited by Edward Arber.
London: Richard Field, 1869.

Reed, Michael D. "Early American Puritanism: The Language of Its Religion."
American Imago 37 (1980): 278–333.

Requa, Kenneth. "Anne Bradstreet's Poetic Voices." *Early American Literature* 9
(1974): 3–18.

Rich, Adrienne. *On Lies, Secrets, and Silence*. New York: W. W. Norton, 1979.

Riley, Denise. *"Am I That Name?" Feminism and the Category of "Women" in History*. Minneapolis: University of Minneapolis Press, 1988.

Rowe, Karen E. "Sacred or Profane?: Edward Taylor's Meditations on Canticles." *Modern Philology* 72 (1974): 123–38.

———. *Saint and Singer: Edward Taylor's Typology and the Poetics of Meditation*.
Cambridge: Cambridge University Press, 1986.

Ruchames, Louis. *Racial Thought in America: From the Puritans to Abraham Lincoln*. Vol. 1. Amherst: University of Massachusetts Press, 1969.

Rutman, Darrett B. *American Puritanism: Faith and Practice*. Philadelphia: J. B.
Lippincott, 1970.

Sacks, Peter. *The English Elegy: Studies in the Genre from Spenser to Yeats*. Baltimore: Johns Hopkins University Press, 1985.

Said, Edward. *Orientalism*. New York: Pantheon Books, 1978.

———. "Orientalism Reconsidered." In *Literature, Politics & Theory: Papers from the Essex Conference, 1976–84*, edited by Francis Barker, Peter Hulme, Margaret Iversen, and Diana Loxley, 210–19. London and New York: Methuen, 1986.

Schatzman, Morton. *Soul Murder: Persecution in the Family*. New York: Random House, 1973.

Scheick, William J. "Standing in the Gap: Urian Oakes's Elegy on Thomas Shepard." *Early American Literature* 9 (1975): 301–6.

———. "Tombless Virtue and Hidden Text: New England Puritan Funeral Elegies." In *Puritan Poets and Poetics: Seventeenth-Century American Poetry in Theory and Practice*, edited by Peter White, 286–302. University Park: Pennsylvania State University Press, 1985.

———. *The Will and the Word: The Poetry of Edward Taylor*. Athens: University of Georgia Press, 1974.

Schindler, Walter. *Voice and Crisis: Invocation in Milton's Poetry*. Hamden, Conn.: Archon Press, 1984.

Schmitt–von Mühlenfels, Astrid. "John Fiske's Funeral Elegy on John Cotton." *Early American Literature* 12 (1977): 49–62.

Schreber, Daniel Paul. *Memoirs of My Nervous Illness*. Translated by Ida Macalpine and Richard A. Hunter. London: Dawson, 1955.

Schweitzer, Ivy. "Anne Bradstreet Wrestles with the Renaissance." *Early American Literature* 23 (1988): 291–312.

———. "Semiotics of the Sacrament in Edward Taylor's *Preparatory Meditations*." In *Praise Disjoined: Changing Patterns of Salvation in Seventeenth-Century English Literature*, edited by William P. Shaw, 237–57. New York: Peter Lang, Seventeenth-Century Text and Studies, 1991.

Segal, Charles M., and David C. Stineback. *Puritans, Indians, and Manifest Destiny*. New York: Putnam, 1977.

Shepard, Thomas. *The Parable of the Ten Virgins Unfolded*. Vol. 2 of *The Works of Thomas Shepard*. Boston: Doctrinal Tract and Book Society, 1853.

Silverman, Kaja. *The Subject of Semiotics*. New York: Oxford University Press, 1983.

Silverman, Kenneth, ed. *Colonial American Poetry*. New York: Hafner, 1968.

Simpson, Eileen. *Poets in Their Youth*. New York: Random House, 1982.

Smith, Henry. *A Preparative to Marriage*. London: N.p., 1591.

Smith, Paul. *Discerning the Subject*. Minneapolis: University of Minnesota Press, 1988.

Spivak, Gayatri Chakravorty. "Displacement and the Discourse of Woman." In *Displacement: Derrida and After*, edited by Mark Krupnick, 169–96. Bloomington: Indiana University Press, 1983.

Stanford, Donald E., ed. *The Poems of Edward Taylor* [abridged]. New Haven: Yale University Press, 1963.

Starobinski, Jean. *Words upon Words: The Anagrams of Ferdinand de Saussure.* Translated by Olivia Emmet. New Haven: Yale University Press, 1979.

Stewart, Randall. *American Literature and Christian Doctrine.* Baton Rouge: Louisiana State University Press, 1958.

Stitt, Peter A. "The Art of Poetry XVI." *Paris Review* 53 (1972): 177–207.

Stone, Lawrence. *The Family, Sex, and Marriage in England 1500–1800.* New York: Harper and Row, 1979.

Strouse, Jean, ed. *Women and Analysis: Dialogues on Psychoanalytic Views of Femininity.* Boston: G. K. Hall, 1985.

Suffolk Deeds. Boston: Rockwell and Churchill, 1880.

Sweet, Timothy. "Gender, Genre, and Subjectivity in Anne Bradstreet's Early Elegies." *Early American Literature* 23 (1988): 152–74.

Taylor, Edward. *The Christographia.* Edited by Norman S. Grabo. New Haven: Yale University Press, 1962.

———. *Edward Taylor's Minor Poetry.* Vol. 3 of *The Unpublished Writing of Edward Taylor,* edited by Thomas M. and Virginia L. Davis. Boston: G. K. Hall, 1981.

———. *The Poems of Edward Taylor.* Edited by Donald S. Stanford. New Haven: Yale University Press, 1960.

———. *Treatise Concerning the Lord's Supper.* Edited by Norman S. Grabo. East Lansing: Michigan State University Press, 1966.

Teunissen, John J., and Evelyn J. Hinz. Introduction to *A Key into the Language of America* by Roger Williams, edited by Teunissen and Hinz, 13–69. Detroit: Wayne State University Press, 1973.

———. "Roger Williams, St. Paul, and American Primitivism." *The Canadian Review of American Studies* 4, no. 2 (1973): 121–36.

Thickstun, Margaret Olofson. *Fictions of the Feminine: Puritan Doctrine and the Representation of Women.* Ithaca: Cornell University Press, 1988.

Thomas, Keith. "Women and the Civil War Sects." *Past and Present* 13 (1958): 42–62.

Todorov, Tzvetan. *The Conquest of America: The Question of the Other.* Translated by Richard Howard. New York: Harper and Row, 1984.

———. *Mikhail Bakhtin: The Dialogical Principle.* Translated by Wlad Godzich. Minneapolis: University of Minnesota Press, 1984.

Tompkins, Jane. *Sensational Designs: The Cultural Work of American Fiction, 1790–1860.* New York: Oxford University Press, 1985.

Transcript of the Registers of the Worshipful Company of Stationers for 1640–1708. Edited by G. E. Briscoe Eyre and H. R. Plomer. 3 vols. London: Roxburghe Club, 1913–14.

Tuve, Rosemond. *Elizabethan and Metaphysical Imagery: Renaissance Poetic and Twentieth-Century Critics.* Chicago: University of Chicago Press, 1947.

Ulrich, Laurel Thatcher. *Goodwives: Image and Reality in the Lives of Women in Northern New England: 1650–1750.* New York: Oxford University Press, 1980.

Vaughan, Alden T. *New England Frontier: Puritans and Indians, 1620–1675.* New York: W. W. Norton, 1979.

Vaughan, Alden T., and Edward W. Clark, eds. *Puritans among the Indians: Accounts of Captivity and Redemption, 1674–1724.* Cambridge: Belknap Press of Harvard University Press, 1981.

Waggoner, Hyatt. *American Poets from the Puritans to the Present.* Boston: Houghton Mifflin, 1968.

Walker, Cheryl. *The Nightingale's Burden: Women Poets and American Culture before 1900.* Bloomington: Indiana University Press, 1982.

Walker, Jeffrey. "Anagrams and Acrostics: Puritan Poetic Wit." In *Puritan Poets and Poetics: Seventeenth-Century American Poetry in Theory and Practice*, edited by Peter White, 247–57. University Park: Pennsylvania State University Press, 1985.

Waller, Gary. *English Poetry of the Sixteenth Century.* London and New York: Longman, 1986.

Ward, Nathaniel. *The Simple Cobler of Aggawam in America.* Edited by P. M. Zall. Lincoln: University of Nebraska Press, 1969.

Warner, W. Lloyd. *The Living and the Dead: A Study of the Symbolic Lives of Americans.* New Haven: Yale University Press, 1959.

Watters, David H. *"With Bodilie Eyes": Eschatological Themes in Puritan Literature and Gravestone Art.* Ann Arbor: UMI Research Press, 1981.

Watts, Emily Stipes. *The Poetry of American Women from 1632 to 1945.* Austin: University of Texas Press, 1977.

———. "'The posy UNITY': Anne Bradstreet's Search for Order." In *Puritan Influences in American Literature*, edited by Emory Elliott, 23–37. Urbana: University of Illinois Press, 1979.

Wheatley, Phillis. *The Poems of Phillis Wheatley.* Edited by Julian D. Mason, Jr. Chapel Hill: University of North Carolina Press, 1966.

White, Elizabeth Wade. *Anne Bradstreet: "The Tenth Muse."* New York: Oxford University Press, 1971.

Willard, Samuel. *A Compleat Body of Divinity.* Boston: N.p., 1726.

Williams, Raymond. *Marxism and Literature.* New York: Oxford University Press, 1977.

Williams, Roger. *The Complete Writings of Roger Williams.* 7 Vols. New York: Russell and Russell, 1963.

———. *A Key into the Language of America* [1643]. Edited by John J. Teunissen and Evelyn J. Hinz. Detroit: Wayne State University Press, 1973.

Winthrop, John. *Life and Letters of John Winthrop: Governor of the Massachusetts-Bay Company at their emigration to New England* [1630]. Edited by Robert C. Winthrop. Boston: Little, Brown, 1869.

———. *A Short Story of the Rise, reign, and ruine of the Antinomians, Familists and Libertines* [1644]. In *The Antinomian Controversy, 1636–1638: A Documentary History*, edited by David D. Hall, 199–310. Middletown, Conn.: Wesleyan University Press, 1968.

————. *Winthrop Papers*. 5 vols. Boston: Massachusetts Historical Society, 1931.

————. *Winthrop's Journal: "History of New England" 1630–1649*. Edited by James Kendall Hosmer. 2 vols. New York: Charles Scribner's Sons, 1908.

Wroth, Lawrence. *Roger Williams*. Brown University Papers 14. Providence: Brown University, 1937.

Ziff, Larzer. *The Career of John Cotton*. Princeton: Princeton University Press, 1962.

————. *Puritanism in America: New Culture in a New World*. New York: Viking Press, 1973.

Adam, 29, 93, 97, 98, 106, 117, 176, 177, 211, 215
Alexander the Great, 56
Allegory, 39, 106, 107, 109, 185, 202, 203, 215, 228. *See also* Bunyan, John
Allen, John, 91
Alterity, 11, 34, 111; revalorization of, 33
Althusser, Louis, 30–32, 244 (n. 33). *See also* Interpellation
Anagram, 37, 49, 68, 164–65; history of, 49–50; role in Puritan poetics, 50–52, 249 (n. 13); Baroque quality of, 55
Antinomian controversy (antinomianism), 9, 30, 47, 57, 138, 152; and female sexuality, 13. *See also* Hutchinson, Anne
Apollo, 156, 157, 162, 166
Apostrophe, 37, 49, 52, 53, 54, 63, 73; as spiritual vocation, 53, 72. *See also* Invocation
Arminianism, 30, 164
Augustine, Saint, 8

Ballad measure, 196, 207, 208
Baxter, Richard, 8
Bay Psalm Book, 207, 209
Bean, Joseph, 26
Beauvoir, Simone de, 11–12
Begley, Walter, 49
Bercovitch, Sacvan, 6, 8, 22, 72
Bernard of Clairvaux, 98

Berryman, John, 38, 132, 155, 160; relationship to Bradstreet, 132–36; and the Muse, 135; aggression toward women, 139, 142; and couvade, 144, 264 (n. 22) —Works: *Berryman's Sonnets*, 135; *The Dream Songs*, 263 (n. 15). See also *Homage to Mistress Bradstreet*
Blake, Kathleen, 86, 87
Bradford, William, 188
Bradstreet, Anne, 3, 38, 39, 48, 54, 125, 136, 143, 154, 155, 186, 199, 229; cultural construction of, 127–29, 161, 165; and response to cultural construction, 128, 169; and family, 128–29, 148, 149, 152–53, 162, 166; deauthorization of (robbed of voice), 129, 131, 134, 145, 157; and self-representation, 129, 170, 171, 172, 178; and gynesis, 129, 180; and Muse/Muses, 130, 131, 159, 167, 171; as model woman, 130, 160; and feminine "place" (subordination), 131, 147–48, 157, 173, 177–78; male readers of, 145, 148, 166, 168, 171; and male authentication of women, 148; acceptance of roles (of dominant ideology), 154, 168, 173; gynocentric vision of, 167; patriarchal voice of, 167–68; awareness of gender politics, 169, 176–77; revalorization of female roles, 171; and later poems, 172, 173,

178; and redeemed subjectivity,
174, 175; compared to Edward
Taylor, 174–75, 176–77, 178, 180;
and interpellation, 175, 179
—Works: "Another," 178; "As Weary
Pilgrim," 142, 178–79, 264 (n. 18);
"In My Solitary Hours," 177;
Meditation 71, 177; "Meditations
Divine and Moral," 60, 264 (n.
18), 279 (n. 6). See also *Tenth
Muse, The*
Bray, James, 57–58
Brewster, Martha, 148
Brotherston, Gordon, 198, 203
Bulkeley, Peter, 4
Bunyan, John (Bunyanesque), 207,
214. *See also* Allegory

Calamy, Edmund, 29
Calvin, John, 8, 23, 24, 28
Calvinism, 22, 86, 108
Campbell, Helen, 145, 146
Cartesianism (Descartes), 11, 33, 35,
237–38 (n. 3), 242 (n. 23)
Chabot, C. Barry, 231
Christ, 55, 70, 108, 115, 119, 230; as
bridegroom, 4, 16, 23, 93, 113,
121; as willing castrate, 19, 29,
102; as womb substitute, 29; as
model of Christian obedience, 29,
98; as model of redeemed subjec-
tivity, 55; and cross-gendering, 98;
and reading, 114. *See also* Taylor,
Edward: relation to Christ
Chupack, Henry, 199
Clap, Roger, 3
Clark, Michael, 59, 72, 85
Cleaver, Robert: and John Dod,
235
Cohen, Charles L., 14
Colonial Puritanism (Puritans), 3, 53,
232; effect on sons, 1, 25, 48, 235;
as predominantly masculine, 2–3;
and Canticles (Song of Songs), 4–

6, 95, 100, 107, 109; cultural consensus about, 6; and regimentation
of selfhood, 6–7, 8, 30, 43, 227;
and radical sectarians, 9, 38; and
"otherness," 10, 11, 20; and gender, 10, 20, 98; and Native Americans, 10, 39, 184, 190–91, 192,
197, 198, 274 (n. 26); defined
through deviancy, 10–11, 38; compared to contemporary cultural attitudes, 14–15, 17; and myth of
declension, 18, 48; and psychoanalysis, 18–19; and Pauline metaphysics of gender, 24, 29; child-
rearing practices of, 25, 233, 234,
235, 259 (n. 2); appropriation of
maternal roles and female imagery,
27, 28, 121; patrimony (legacy) of,
29, 235; and ideology, 31; notion of
covenant in, 31, 107, 150; and
postmodernism, 33, 34; and dilemma of poet, 36, 37, 45, 51–52, 69,
79, 106, 250 (n. 19); and practical
conformity, 37, 60, 61, 91, 104;
and redeemed subjectivity, 38, 98,
102, 181, 186, 187, 232, 235; androcentrism of, 39, 111, 125; and
gap imagery, 47, 63–64; and generational conflict, 48–49; aesthetics
of, 59, 70, 72, 85, 87, 131; and
semiology, 72; and sacrament, 85,
86, 88, 254 (n. 6); gynesis in, 87,
110, 112, 121, 129, 221; and desire, 102, 257 (n. 18); and ocean
crossing, 182, 184, 213, 268 (n. 4).
See also Conversion—paradigm of;
Puritan men; Puritan spirituality;
Puritan women
Conversion, 4, 19, 53, 112; narratives, 9, 45, 190
—paradigm of, 8, 21, 35, 66, 231; as
social control of visible sainthood,
8–9; and subjectivity, 9, 22, 29,
31–32, 43; feminization of saint in,

18–19, 23, 28, 49, 87, 96, 104; as narrative of gendered subjectivity, 20, 36; and violence, 22, 23, 96, 103; and paradox, 22, 25, 100; and humiliation, 22, 49, 235; gendered metaphors for, 23; and mystical bride (Spouse of Christ), 25, 104; and adoption, 27; and remasculinization, 27, 28; ideological workings of, 31–32, 146; outlined in Romans, 44; morphology of, 44, 235; and gynesis, 45; and lyric, 45, 72, 73, 80; as mourning, 49; nonspecificity of female in, 49; psychoanalytic investigations of, 49; and return, 71, 73; compared to Schreber, 231, 233; compared to Cartesianism, 242 (n. 23). *See also* Paul; Puritan spirituality

Cotton, John, 4, 27, 43, 45, 62, 68, 70, 87, 164, 190; *A Brief Exposition of Canticles*, 4, 57; role in antinomian controversy, 47, 57; and Roger Williams, 47, 192, 199, 268 (n. 2), 272, (n. 15); and Anne Hutchinson, 57, 138, 272 (n. 15); *See also* "Elegy" on John Cotton

Cromwell, Oliver, 208

Culler, Jonathan, 52, 63

Daly, Robert, 50

Davis, Thomas, 91, 95

De Lauretis, Teresa, 34, 35

De Man, Paul, 53, 54

Derrida, Jacques, 33, 245 (n. 36)

Dickinson, Emily, 135–36, 209, 217, 277–78 (n. 40)

Dimmesdale, Arthur, 1–2, 229

Donne, John, 23, 80, 83, 94, 96, 267 (n. 39); "Holy Sonnet XIV," 81

Draper, John W., 42

Du Bartas, Guillaume, 131, 146, 156, 157, 165, 166

Dudley, Dorothy, 127

Dudley, Thomas, 48, 49, 50, 151, 152–53, 164, 166, 170, 270 (n. 7)

Dunn, Mary Maples, 9, 17–18

Duplicity, 170

Durham, James, 109

Dyer, Mary, 153–54

Edwards, Jonathan, 50, 275 (n. 29)

Elegy. *See* Funeral elegy

"Elegy" on John Cotton (John Fiske), 37, 45, 47, 51, 52, 53, 54–77; as representative, 45–46; and redeemed subjectivity, 53, 55; convention of modesty in, 54; Cotton likened to Christ, 55, 56, 58, 59; major imagery of, 55–62, 66, 67; tree of life imagery in, 57–58, 59; and stages in salvation, 58, 66, 71; Ramist logic (dichotomy) in, 58–61; Baroque aesthetics of, 59; and *imitatio Christi*, 62, 68; positionality in, 65; self-representation in, 65, 66, 70, 71–72; Muse in, 66. *See also* Anagram; Apostrophe; Fiske, John (poet)

Eliot, John, 235

Elizabeth I (queen of England), 12, 50, 146, 158, 167, 260 (n. 4)

Elliott, Emory, 48

Endecott, John, 150

Epicene, 165, 166

Erikson, Kai T., 10

Eve, 97, 98, 99, 106, 111, 176, 177

Feminine, the. *See* "Woman"

Feminism, 34, 173

Fetterley, Judith, 167

Fish, Stanley, 81, 82

Fiske, John (poet), 46–47, 51, 80, 109, 186, 229; and self-representation, 37, 48, 72; and Edward Taylor, 46, 57, 66–67, 79; and defacement, 53, 68

—Works: *The Notebook of John Fiske*,

46; elegy for Thomas Dudley, 48, 253 (n. 36); elegy for Nathaniel Rogers, 56, 252 (n. 33); elegy on Samuel Sharpe, 65. *See also* "Elegy" on John Cotton

Fiske, John (theorist), 7

Friedman, Susan Stanford, 171, 172

Freud, Sigmund, 19, 230–31, 235

Frye, Northrop, 59, 73, 220

Funeral elegy, 36–37, 41, 68; and redeemed subjectivity, 41, 43, 44, 45; English Puritan elegy, 41–42; didacticism of (nonconsoling type), 42, 43, 44; New England Puritan elegy, 42, 44–46; structure of, 44–45; as communal expression, 47–48; and psychoanalytic paradigm, 49; anagrammatic, 51. *See also* Fiske, John (poet)

Gelpi, Albert, 95, 96, 101

Gender, 10, 12, 13, 16, 17, 20, 98, 136, 229; and grace, 14; and the universal, 14, 15, 17, 34; and sex, 19, 87; Pauline metaphysics of, 24, 29. *See also* Masculinity; "Woman"

Greenblatt, Stephen, 198, 199

Greven, Philip, 25, 243 (n. 29)

Grossman, Marshall, 97

Gura, Philip, 9

Gynesis, 32, 33, 34, 45, 112, 121, 129, 133, 145, 264–65 (n. 24); of race, 186–87, 221. *See also* Jardine, Alice

Halbert, Cecelia, 98–99

Hall, David D., 14

Hambrick-Stowe, Charles, 3–4, 5, 14, 95, 179–80, 213

Hammond, Jeffrey, 100

Hawthorne, Nathaniel, 1–2, 197

Henson, Robert, 41, 42, 44

Herbert, George, 70, 79, 96, 257 (n. 18)

—Works: "The Church-porch," 80; "The Collar," 81; "Jordan II," 70; "The Temper" (I), 80, 81, 82, 106; *The Temple*, 80

Holifield, E. Brooks, 88

Homage to Mistress Bradstreet, 38, 132, 135, 136–44, 265 (n. 24); courtly discourse in, 133–34; sexual politics of, 134, 136–37; treatment of Anne Bradstreet, 137–38, 139–40, 145, 173; birth imagery in, 141, 142. *See also* Berryman, John

Hooker, Thomas, 8, 22, 42

Hopkins, Anne Yale, 128, 150, 153

Hopkins, Gerard Manley, 73

Hutchinson, Anne, 3, 47, 151, 152, 174, 190, 238 (nn. 4, 7), 244–45 (n. 34), 253 (n. 41); like Native Americans, 10, 13; and libertinism, 27, 87; and John Cotton, 57, 138, 272 (n. 15); in *Homage to Mistress Bradstreet*, 138–39; and John Winthrop, 150, 151, 152, 160; and Anne Bradstreet, 150, 153, 170, 265 (n. 27); and covenant of works, 164, 175. *See also* Antinomian controversy

Interpellation, 31–32; in Edward Taylor, 99, 100, 101, 122; in Anne Bradstreet, 175, 179. *See also* Althusser, Louis

Intersubjectivity, 11, 12, 39, 194

Invocation, 52, 71; as spiritual vocation, 52–53, 72. *See also* Apostrophe; Puritan spirituality: and calling

Jantz, Harold, 49, 56, 59

Jardine, Alice, 32, 112, 232. *See also* Gynesis

Jennings, Francis, 188

Johnson, Carol, 132

Jones, Ernest, 19–20

Jonson, Ben, 147, 165

Kappeler, Susanne, 202, 259–60 (n. 4)

Karlsen, Carol, 27

Keats, John, 139

Keayne, Benjamin, 150, 265–66 (n. 28)

Keayne, Sarah Dudley, 150–51, 152, 169, 265–66 (n. 28)

Keller, Karl, 95, 101

Key to the Language of America, A, 38, 146, 181, 187; divine providence in, 182, 185, 205, 220; representation of New England Puritans in, 182–83, 206, 225–26; instrumentality of Native Americans in, 183, 184, 205, 220, 221, 228; representation of Native Americans in, 184, 185, 190, 203, 204, 210, 221, 224–25, 226; allegory in, 184–85, 190, 193, 196, 207, 210, 213, 216, 218, 219, 227, 228; comparison of English and Native Americans in, 185, 193–94, 196, 197, 203–4, 205–6, 220–21; autobiographical context of, 187, 189–90, 196, 216, 218; positionality in, 187, 191, 194, 202, 204, 209, 227; poetry in, 187, 196–97, 203, 207, 210, 270–71 (n. 9); key imagery in, 191, 192–93; intersubjectivity in, 194, 203, 227; dialogism in, 194–95, 199–200, 201, 202; structure of, 194–97, 187, 202, 209, 227, 228; representation of Native American speech in, 198, 221–24; ironic reversals in, 205–6, 212, 213, 227, 275–76 (n. 32); image of wilderness in, 206, 220, 224, 275–76 (n. 32); Native Americans associated with Jews in, 211, 215; motif of sight in, 212–13; theme of travel in, 213, 214, 218, 219; and Psalm 23, 218, 219, 220. *See also* Williams, Roger
—poems in: chapter 1, 196–97, 203–4, 210; "Course bread and water's" (chapter 2), 204–5, 220; chapter 3, 219–20; chapter 5, 211; chapter 7, 201–2, 212, 277 (n. 38); chapter 9, 212–13; chapter 10, 213; "God makes a path" (chapter 11), 219, 220, 221; chapter 13, 222; chapter 17, 273–74 (n. 21), 277 (n. 38); "They see Gods wonders" (chapter 18), 181–83, 185, 190, 213; chapter 20, 223–24; chapter 22, 222–23; chapter 24, 192; chapter 25, 224–25; chapter 29, 206, 277 (n. 38); chapter 30, 206, 226, 276 (n. 33); chapter 32, 225–26

Kibbey, Anne, 13, 25

King, John N., 208

Lang, Amy, 27

Leverenz, David, 18, 19, 20, 25–26, 102, 241

Lewalski, Barbara, 95, 207

Lyric poetry, 36, 72, 207, 220, 229; and postmodern theory, 52; tension between narrative and, 72–73; as vertical mode, 73; as blazon, 113. *See also* Funeral elegy

Makin, Bathsua, 169

Marvell, Andrew, 142

Mary (Virgin), 3, 49, 111, 237 (n. 3)

Masculinity: as masculine identity, 10, 112, 229; as normative, 12, 13, 14, 237 (n. 3), female usurpation of, 12, 151, 160; and gendered universal, 14, 15, 17, 34; as purgation of sexual difference, 29; privileges of, 29, 158; and recuperation of the feminine, 34, 133; crisis in, 35; Puritan construction of, 45; and writing, 167–68; in Western thought, 244 (n. 31)

Masson, Margaret W., 23, 243 (n. 29)

Mather, Cotton, 43, 50, 146, 168, 249 (n. 14), 269 (n. 5)

Meserole, Harrison, 47, 51, 55, 70

Mignon, Charles, 92

Miller, Alice, 235

Miller, Nancy, 35

Miller, Perry, 3, 238 (n. 4)

Milton, John, 53, 97, 131, 157, 176, 177, 224, 225

Mitchell, Jonathan, 147

Morgan, Edmund S., 4, 8, 164

Morton, Thomas, 197–98, 274 (n. 25)

Moses, 31, 114, 115

Muse/Muses, 66, 96, 130, 131, 135, 144, 156, 261 (n. 9). *See also* Berryman, John; Bradstreet, Anne

Narragansett Indians, 184, 185, 187, 197, 200, 206, 210, 228; dialect of, 38, 181, 198, 207, 228; subjectivity of, 39, 184, 222; relations with English, 224, 225, 271 (n. 11). See also *Key to the Language of America, A*; Williams, Roger

Native Americans, 12, 14, 15, 185, 190, 211, 212, 227; and colonial Puritans, 10, 39, 184, 190–91, 197, 198, 274 (n. 26); allegorical representations of, 221. *See also* Narragansett Indians; Pequot Indians

Neiderland, William, 234

Norton, John, 61, 147

Oakes, Urian, 47–48; "An Elegy upon the Death of the Reverend Mr. Thomas Shepard" (II), 56

Oliver, Mistress, 150, 151–52

Ong, Walter J., 3, 237 (n. 3)

Ostriker, Alicia, 170

Otherness (difference), 10, 11, 13, 35, 38, 89, 136, 228; as feminized, 32, 34, 186, 187; the Other, 32, 96, 97, 98, 101, 111, 199, 200, 202, 207, 226, 235; and salvation, 68. *See also* Alterity; Race; "Woman"

Paul (apostle), 7–8, 22, 185, 212, 238 (n. 5); and doctrine of spiritual equality, 14; and six stages of regeneration, 21; and metaphysics of gender, 24, 29. *See also* Conversion—paradigm of

Pearce, R. H., 50

Pennington, Isaac, 26

Pequot Indians, 10, 187, 269 (n. 5); Pequot War, 13, 46. *See also* Native Americans

Perkins, William, 21–22

Philips, Katharine, 148

Poovey, Mary, 228

Pope, Robert, 46

Positionality, 12, 35, 36; positional superiority in Roger Williams, 186, 191, 193, 221, 273–74 (n. 21); for Puritan females and males, 24; in Edward Taylor, 98, 99, 100. *See also* Puritan men; Puritan women

Postmodernism, 33, 38, 145; androcentric bias of, 11; decentered subject of, 11, 239; and colonial Puritanism, 33, 34; masculine recuperation of the feminine in, 34. *See also* Colonial Puritanism: and postmodernism

Powell, Vavasor, 208

Preparatory Meditations, 71, 87, 95, 100, 103, 110, 130; and musical allusions, 37, 84, 107, 122; violence in, 37, 102, 103, 104; vessel imagery, 37, 118, 119; "Prologue," 79–80, 81, 82, 84, 92, 109; strategies of self-representation in, 80, 92; "The Experience," 83, 96–97,

98, 177; and sacramental imagery
("wedden robe"), 85, 89, 92–93,
99, 101, 105, 113, 125, 258 (n.
25); and gendering, 93; theme of
spiritual marriage, 95, 104; "The
Reflexion," 98; "The Return," 102.
See also Taylor, Edward
—numbered meditations: Meditation
1.1, 93–94, 95, 96, 107; Meditation 1.3, 102–3; Meditation 1.8,
93; Meditation 1.16, 102; Meditation 1.23, 101, 175; Meditation
1.25, 102; Meditation 1.29, 28;
Meditation 1.35, 109; Meditation
1.37, 105, 106, 107; Meditation
1.39, 104; Meditation 2.4, 102;
Meditation 2.9, 115; Meditation
2.13, 121; Meditation 2.51, 111;
Meditation 2.53, 103–4; Meditation 2.69, 108; Meditation 2.79,
108; Meditation 2.92, 115; Meditation 2.95, 93; Meditation 2.96,
107; Meditation 2.97, 86, 106;
Meditation 2.106, 88; Meditation
2.111, 93; Meditation 2.119, 115,
116; Meditation 2.123B, 114;
Meditation 2.125, 114; Meditation
2.126, 119; Meditation 2.128, 115;
Meditation 2.129, 111; Meditation
2.132, 115; Meditation 2.133, 110,
115; Meditation 2.134, 119; Meditation 2.135, 119; Meditation
2.136, 110; Meditation 2.137, 120;
Meditation 2.139, 120; Meditation
2.140, 120; Meditation 2.143, 117,
118, 120; Meditation 2.147, 118;
Meditation 2.149, 120; Meditation
2.150, 121; Meditation 2.151, 110,
116, 121; Meditation 2.152, 121;
Meditation 2.153, 121–22; Meditation 2.156, 122; Meditation
2.158, 122; Meditation 2.161A,
106; Meditation 2.161B, 123;

Meditation 2.163, 123, 124; Meditation 2.164, 123
Provost, Sarah, 135, 136
Prynne, Hester, 1–2, 130, 260–61 (n.
7)
Psychoanalysis, 18, 19, 34, 49. *See
also* Colonial Puritanism; Freud,
Sigmund
Punning, 52, 55, 64, 251 (n. 23)
Puritanism. *See* Colonial Puritanism
Puritan men, 19, 27, 87, 95: and
feminine role, 4–5, 18; God-like
position of, 24–25; emasculation
of, 25; private writings of, 25, 26;
and homoeroticism, 26, 243 (n.
29). *See also* Conversion—paradigm
of: feminization of saint in;
Masculinity
Puritan spirituality, 3, 26; and *imitatio
Christi*, 7, 29, 98; self-effacement
in, 8, 235; conversion narratives, 9,
45; religious discourse of, 14, 15;
and phallologocentrism, 28; and
rebirth, 29; as subjectivity deferred,
29; and calling (interpellation), 31;
iconophobia in, 39; and psychoanalysis, 49; role of narrative in,
72–73; self-regimentation in, 72–
73; role of lyric in, 73. *See also*
Conversion—paradigm of
Puritan women, 14, 18–19, 24, 34,
38, 148; silenced in church, 9, 14;
male attitudes toward, 13, 18–19;
invisibility in religious discourse
and modern scholarship, 17, 18;
virgin-whore conception of, 19, 20;
subjection to husband, 19, 24, 32,
102, 176; equation with body and
flesh, 24; self-effacement of, 27;
double displacement of, 29, 34; in
their place, 103, 146, 157, 173,
177–78; in public sphere, 127,
128, 151, 152; education of, 127,

259 (n. 2); and poetry, 129–30, 132, 145, 146; debate over ("querelle des femmes"), 149, 154, 159, 162; defiance of male hegemony, 150, 151

Puttenham, George, 50, 51

Race, 12–13, 14, 15, 38, 186, 188, 200, 201, 202, 211, 226, 229, 245 (n. 34), 269 (n. 5)

Redeemed subjectivity. *See* Subjectivity

Reformation, 6, 14, 53, 176

Rich, Adrienne, 167, 172, 173

Robinson, John, 234

Rogers, John, 26, 130, 147

Rowe, Karen, 109

Rutman, Darrett B., 7, 30

Sacks, Peter, 49

Said, Edward, 191

Sartre, Jean-Paul, 11

Saussure, Ferdinand de, 68–69

Schatzman, Morton, 234

Scheick, William, 42–43, 102

Schindler, Walter, 53

Schmitt-von Mühlenfels, Astrid, 41

Schreber, Daniel Gottlieb Moritz, 232–33, 234, 279 (n. 4); child-rearing practices of compared to those of Puritans, 233–34

Schreber, Daniel Paul, 229–31, 232, 278–79 (n. 1); compared to New England Puritans, 231

Self-representation, 37, 38, 125, 129, 185, 229, 232, 235. *See also* Bradstreet, Anne; Fiske, John (poet); Taylor, Edward; Williams, Roger

Several Poems. See *Tenth Muse, The*

Sewall, Samuel, 3, 5–6

Shakespeare, William, 147, 199, 267 (n. 39)

Shepard, Thomas, I, 3, 15–17, 18, 23, 47

Shepard, Thomas, II, 47

Sherlock, Dr. William (sherlosism), 108

Sidney, Sir Philip, 146, 157, 267 (n. 39)

Silverman, Kenneth, 60, 65

Spenser, Edmund, 170, 171

Spiritual marriage, 4, 18, 23, 95, 111, 242 (n. 23); discourse of, 5, 6; Psalm 45 as source of, 6; Song of Songs as source of, 6, 18. *See also* Christ; Spouse of Christ; Taylor, Edward

Spivak, Gayatri, 33, 34

Spouse of Christ, 23, 37, 175, 178, 231. *See also* Conversion—paradigm of; Puritan spirituality; Taylor, Edward

Starobinski, Jean, 69–70

Stoddard, Solomon, 90

Stone, Lawrence, 17

Subjectivity, 29, 35, 36, 202, 203, 227, 240 (n. 11); as construction of selfhood, 7; redeemed, 7, 21, 22, 25, 30, 34, 37, 41, 45, 92, 98, 112, 175, 210; and conversion, 20, 22, 36, 68; and gender, 12, 20, 34, 35; and ideology, 30; historicization of, 35, 242 (n. 23); orthodox conception of, 38; of Native Americans, 39, 184, 203; and male gaze, 116–17;. *See also* Althusser, Louis; Colonial Puritanism: and redeemed subjectivity; Narragansett Indians: subjectivity of

Sweet, Timothy, 168, 172–73

Swetnam, Joseph, 153

Talbye, Dorothy, 150, 151

Taylor, Edward, 4, 37, 39, 70, 90–91, 123, 130, 180, 186, 219, 229, 231; relation to Christ, 28, 38, 84, 92–

93, 99, 100, 116; and dialectic of difference, 37, 85, 89, 92, 96, 98, 108, 110, 125; and sacramental theology, 37, 85, 90, 94, 108–9; and gynesis, 37, 112, 121; and Spouse of Christ, 37–38, 89, 95, 98–121 passim; and Canticles (Song of Solomon), 38, 86, 95, 100, 102, 105, 108, 112–23 passim; tree of life imagery in, 57, 99, 105–6; and dilemma of Puritan poet, 80; compared to Donne, 80, 81; compared to Herbert, 80, 81–82, 83–84; self-representation in, 80, 86, 93, 109, 124–25, 255–56 (n. 15); compared to John Fiske, 80, 109; desire in, 81, 82, 94, 96, 101, 102, 103, 107, 110; and gender, 81, 86, 87, 96, 125; and semiology, 83, 85; and sacrament of communion, 83, 88, 89, 99, 256 (n. 16); and spiritual marriage, 85, 86–87, 89, 94, 100; and redeemed subjectivity, 87, 92, 110; and positionality, 87, 96, 98, 99–100, 110, 115; and language, 88; and orthodoxy, 90–91, 255 (n. 10); and interpellation, 99, 100, 101, 122; and "woman," 100, 104, 110, 116, 125; and reading, 109, 112, 114, 116–17; and mirror/sight imagery, 114–15, 118, 119, 120; and Moses, 114–15, 119; male gaze in, 116–17, 118; compared to Anne Bradstreet, 174, 175, 176, 178
—Works: *Christographia*, 111–12, 113–14; *God's Determinations*, 89, 92; *Minor Poetry*, 91; *Treatise Concerning the Lord's Supper*, 83, 85–86, 88–89, 90, 99, 109, 256 (n. 16); "Upon Wedlock, and Death of Children," 67. See also *Preparatory Meditations*

Tenth Muse, The, 38, 130, 145, 165; "On My Dear Grandchild Simon Bradstreet," 54; "An Epitaph on my Dear and Ever-Honoured Mother," 127; publishing history of, 127, 130, 145, 261 (n. 8); "The Prologue," 129, 135, 154–57, 166, 168; second edition (*Several Poems*), 130, 147, 169; "The Author to Her Book," 130, 154, 169, 172; prefatory material, 131, 145–48, 153–65 passim; The Quaternions, 133, 166–67, 172; "Contemplations," 140; "Elegy upon . . . Philip Sidney," 140, 155, 159, 167; "To My Dear and Loving Husband," 144, 176; "Of the vanity of all worldly creatures," 146; metaphor of childbirth in, 154, 160, 161, 169, 170; gender competition in, 155–56, 157, 163; "In Honour of Du Bartas," 157, 163, 171–72; "To Her Most Honoured Father," 157, 166, 167; "The Four Monarchies," 166, 167, 172; praise of, 157, 168–69; "Of the Four Ages of Man," 167; "Of the Four Humours," 167, 168; "David's Lamentation for Saul and Jonathan," 167–68; gender transformation in, 168; and maternal imagery, 171, 173; "In Honour of Queen Elizabeth," 172; and Spouse of Christ, 175, 178, 179, 180; "A Letter to Her Husband," 176–77. See also Bradstreet, Anne

Teunissen, John: and Evelyn Hinz, 207, 225

Todorov, Tzvetan, 12

Trapnel, Anna, 208

Typology, 69, 184, 190; of regenerate subjectivity, 27; and natural world, 50; Roger Williams compared to

John Cotton on, 192, 274 (n. 26); Roger Williams's view of, 207

Waggoner, Hyatt, 51, 134
Walker, Cheryl, 167, 168, 172
Ward, Nathaniel, 147, 155, 158, 163, 164–65
Weber, Max, 30
Weld, Thomas, 154, 200
Wheatley, Phillis, 148
Wheelwright, John, 164
White, Elizabeth Wade, 134, 149, 162, 172
Willard, Samuel, 27, 53, 58, 85
Williams, Roger, 38–39, 47, 159, 181, 186, 188–89, 190, 199–200, 227–28, 229; attitudes toward Native Americans (conversion of), 39, 188, 192, 193, 212, 274 (n. 26), 274–75 (n. 27); and redeemed subjectivity, 181, 185, 207, 210, 211, 228; conception of faith, 182; and self-representation, 182–83, 184, 185, 219, 272 (n. 16); use of parable/allegory, 184, 187, 188, 193, 194, 207; parallel with Christ (*imitatio*), 185, 194, 217, 221, 227; and Paul (apostle), 185, 269–70 (n. 6); positional superiority of, 186, 191, 193, 221, 273–74 (n. 21); and gynesis of race, 186–87, 221; relations with Native Americans, 187, 190, 198–99, 206, 228; attacks on New England Way, 188, 268 (n. 2); millennial epistemology of, 190; and wilderness, 190
—Works: *The Bloudy Tenent of Persecution*, 199, 224, 268 (n. 2);

Christenings Make Not Christians, 194, 212, 273 (n. 19), 274–75 (n. 27); *Experiments of Spirituall Life and Health*, 199; *George Fox Digg'd Out of His Burrowes*, 199; *Mr. Cotton's Letter Examined and Answered*, 199. See also *Key to the Language of America, A*
Wilson, John, 2, 50, 147, 164, 188, 253 (n. 40)
Winthrop, John, 10, 164, 182, 190; and feminine role, 5, 32, 102, 147, 173; and liberty, 32, 233; and Puritan women, 127–28, 150, 151, 154; and Anne Hutchinson, 150–53, 160; and Roger Williams, 188
"Woman" (the feminine), 11, 13, 29, 34, 174, 175, 235; dread/suppression of, 3, 237 (n. 3) as Other/difference, 12, 237 (n. 3) as symbolic category, 13, 16; as rhetorical position of subordination, 20; displacement of, 29, 33; discursive deployment of, 38; in Edward Taylor, 100, 104, 110, 116, 125; as Spouse of Christ, 110–11, flight from, 243–44 (n. 31). *See also* Gynesis
Wood, William, 197
Woodbridge, Benjamin, 61, 147, 162, 163, 252 (n. 30)
Woodbridge, John, 130, 131, 147–62 passim, 167, 169, 261 (n. 8)
Woodbridge, Mercy, 169
Wroth, Lawrence, 188

Ziff, Larzer, 10